Lachlan McGillivray, Indian Trader

EDWARD J. CASHIN

Lachlan McGillivray, Indian Trader

The Shaping of the Southern Colonial Frontier

THE UNIVERSITY OF GEORGIA PRESS

Athens and London

Paperback edition, 2012
© 1992 by the University of Georgia Press
Athens, Georgia 30602
www.ugapress.org
Designed by Sandra Strother Hudson
Set in 10.5 on 14 Janson Text by Tseng Information Systems, Inc.

Printed digitally in the United States of America

The Library of Congress has cataloged the hardcover edition
of this book as follows:

Cashin, Edward J., 1927–
Lachlan McGillivray, Indian trader : the shaping of the southern
colonial frontier / Edward J. Cashin.
x, 405 p. : maps ; 24 cm.
ISBN 0-8203-1368-8 (alk. paper)
Includes bibliographical references (p. 373–389) and index.
1. McGillivray, Lachlan. 2. Pioneers—Georgia—Biography.
3. Indians of North America—Georgia—History—Colonial period,
ca. 1600–1775. 4. Georgia—History—Colonial period,
ca. 1600–1775. I. Title.
F289.M43 C37   1992
975.8'02'092—dc20   91-12479
[B]

Paperback ISBN-13: 978-0-8203-4093-7
ISBN-10: 0-8203-4093-6

British Library Cataloging-in-Publication Data available

Dedicated to the memory of Heard Robertson,
for whom the colonial period was the best part of our history.

Contents

Contents

Acknowledgments

One of the most rewarding ways to begin research on a historical character is to visit his native country and walk by the same streams and gaze at the same hills that he saw in his lifetime. I am indebted to Loraine McLean of Dochgarroch, a fine historian and an excellent guide, who drove us from Inverness to the lovely valley of the Nairn River, once the stronghold of Clan Chattan and home of Lachlan McGillivray. The rock cairns of Clava, which were ancient when McGillivray was there, lent an air of timelessness. We walked silently over the treeless Culloden moor and read the inscriptions on the stones which memorialize the clans that fought for Prince Charles on that snowy day in April 1746. We paused at the Well of the Dead, where Alexander McGillivray, chief of the McGillivrays and on that day commander of the Clan Chattan, breathed his last. It was easy to imagine how Lachlan McGillivray must have felt as he visited the same site.

I am grateful for the assistance of the staff at Farraline Park Library in Inverness and for the professionals at the various depositories listed in the bibliography, especially to John Dann and Rob Cox at the William L. Clements Library, at the University of Michigan. I am particularly indebted to those colleagues who read the manuscript and made useful suggestions: Professors George Rogers of the University of South Carolina, William Coker of the University of West Florida, Russell Snapp of Davidson College, and my friend Heard Robertson of Augusta. Linda Jones scrutinized the text for errors and Kaye Keel's typing chores were only slightly eased by the technological advances of a word processor. To both I am grateful. Bob Davis, a resource for all Georgia historians, contributed several items of information. Lynn Thompson of Stockton, Alabama, who is writing about William Weatherford, corresponded about the confusing details of Lachlan's Indian relations and sent John McGillivray's will to me. Dr. W. W. Wallace, a direct descendant of Lachlan, mailed a copy of Lachlan's first will to Professor William Coker, who forwarded it to me.

Financial assistance for the research was provided by the American Association for State and Local History, the Porter Fleming Foundation, and the Augusta College Faculty Research Fund.

I wish to acknowledge the encouragement and support of my wife, Mary Ann, who cheerfully finds other things to do when I disappear into foreign record offices. As a librarian at Augusta College's Reese Library, she and Elise Little arrange for a necessary supply of interlibrary loans. When all else is done, she does the tedious but essential task of indexing.

Finally, it was a signal honor to have the manuscript read by George B. Macgillivray, commander of Clan Macgillivray and coauthor of his clan's history. As satisfying as walking among the hills of Strathnairn is the realization that clans, too, are timeless.

Prologue

The colonial frontier in Georgia, as in the remainder of eastern North America, was a duality. It was the frontier of those who were advancing (often, but not always the Europeans), and simultaneously the frontier of those who were being advanced upon (often, but not always the Indians). The frontier should be viewed as a dynamic zone of interaction between inventive and energetic Europeans and equally capable Indians.

LOUIS DEVORSEY, JR.
"Indian Boundaries in Colonial Georgia," 1970

In the case of the long conflict between the whites and woodland Indians, one may view the whole story as part of a process that transformed provincial America into the modern American nation of today.

WILBUR R. JACOBS
Dispossessing the American Indian, 1972

The frontier experience, I believe, was the most important factor in the creation of the South. The frontier gave meaning to the basic facts of southern history; after two and a half centuries of intimate contact, cultural exchange, competition, and warfare with aborigines, Frenchmen and Spaniards, the British plantation system prevailed in the Southeast.

ALAN GALLAY
The Formation of a Planter Elite, 1989

The three quotations in the epigraph are eloquent explanations of the meaning of *frontier* for the purposes of this study. The southern colo-

I

nial frontier was not the edge of European civilization, beyond which lay a wilderness waiting to be subdued. Rather, it was a zone between people of viable cultures. When James Edward Oglethorpe sailed for Georgia in the waning days of the year 1732, neither he nor his contemporaries could predict the future shape of the southern frontier. The area between the mountains and the sea, between the Savannah and the Mississippi rivers, was a rich prize for which there were several contenders. A French map made in 1718 showed Louisiana extending eastward even beyond the Savannah River into Carolina.[1] Spain considered much of the region to be part of La Florida. The loose confederation of Muskhoge people, whom the English called Creeks, claimed a huge portion of the interior and regarded the Europeans as intruders. The Cherokees hunted along the upper reaches of the rivers that ran into the Atlantic and the Gulf. The Choctaws occupied the region between the Mississippi and the Alabama and contended with their traditional enemies to the north, the Chickasaws.

The European intrusion had begun with the explorations of Hernando DeSoto, Tristan De Luna, and Angel de Villafañe of the sixteenth century followed by the missionary activity of the Spanish Franciscans in Apalache in the seventeenth century. The contest for supremacy was signaled by Henry Woodward's opening of the Creek country to the Carolina trade and the almost simultaneous descent of René Cavalier, Sieur de LaSalle, down the Mississippi under the banner of Louis XIV, the Sun King of France. The French staked a claim to the region by settlements at Biloxi in 1698 and Mobile in 1701. The Carolinians won an advantage as the result of James Moore's brutal raids along the Florida coast in 1702 and into the Apalache country in 1704.

Because Indians were accustomed to trading among themselves, even over long distances, they adjusted readily to the trading practices of the Europeans. The pattern of accommodation noted by James H. Merrell among the Catawbas was also true of the Creeks.[2] The first whites to enter the Indian country had to do business on the terms set by the Indians; trade was essentially an exchange of gifts. Guns and liquor changed the relationship, however. The Carolina traders took advantage of their clients' eagerness for those items and raised their prices ruthlessly. The bloody war waged by the Yamassee against the Carolinians in 1715 was a necessary lesson in the wisdom of fair trading practices and a becoming humility. The French took advantage of the distraction of the English to improve their position by building a fort in the heart of the Upper Creek country and supplying the Indians with trade goods.

The process of retrieving the lost trade involved rebuilding trust. For at least a decade, the Carolina traders managed to behave themselves in their conduct of the trade. Their most effective innovation after 1720 was the practice of taking Indian wives and fathering children of mixed blood, living links between the two cultures.[3] By settling among the Indians, building houses, learning the language, and respecting the traditions, the Carolinians borrowed tactics long practiced by the French.

The impact of the trade was profound. European diseases introduced by the traders took a dreadful toll among most North American tribes. The Creek Nation, however, continued to grow in numbers during most of the eighteenth century.[4] The goods supplied by the traders resulted in an enhanced quality of life and an improvement in their ability to defend themselves against intruders. By the year 1733, when Oglethorpe climbed Yamacraw Bluff and surveyed the site of Savannah, the Indians were accustomed to the presence of white men among them. They depended upon the traders for their guns, powder, and balls, for their tools, saddles, and coats, for the paint with which they decorated themselves, and for the brightly colored, thick-woven stroud cloth used by their women.

If, after climbing up Yamacraw Bluff, Oglethorpe gazed upon the vast frontier before him with the "wild surmise" the poet Keats attributed to the discoverer of the Pacific, he might have wondered what the future held. Would the interior belong to the French, Spanish, or English? What destiny awaited the native Americans? What kind of society would evolve in this latest colony?

The course of history depended on the decisions made and the actions taken by the men and women of that generation. Like architects whose names are fastened on the buildings they designed, the great governors left their mark on the history of the southern frontier. Other than Oglethorpe himself, there were the Frenchmen Bienville, Vaudreuil, and Kerlérec. Their counterparts and competitors were Glen and Lyttelton of Carolina, Ellis and Wright of Georgia. The Spanish governors of Florida were too weak to engage in this game of empire, and the English governors of the Floridas entered the contest too late to play a decisive role.

The course of events was influenced by the superintendents of the Southern Department, the able but officious Edmond Atkin, the diplomatic John Stuart, and the energetic Thomas Brown. Although the generals were more interested in the northern theater, Amherst and Gage managed to give some helpful advice from time to time. The king's ministers were enormously influential when they chose to be. Walpole and Newcastle did not so choose, but the great Pitt planned to invade the Louisiana strongholds. The imperial secretaries, Egremont, Shelburne, and Hillsborough, influenced Indian policy, not always wisely.

On the other side of the frontier the great chiefs were major actors in the drama. The Emperor Brims adhered to a cautious neutrality, a policy followed by his son Malatchi. The Mortar viewed the English as the more threatening and consorted with the French. By contrast, Emistisiguo was a loyal friend of the English even at the cost of his life.

Only rarely did the European leaders meet face-to-face with the Indian chiefs. Oglethorpe visited Coweta in the Lower Creek country, but none of the governors went beyond Augusta. Edmond Atkin made much of his one expedition into the Creek country but probably did more harm than good. John Stuart was satisfied with hosting conferences on the perimeter, at Augusta, Mobile, and Pensacola.

The mediators between the governors and the chiefs were the traders. The governors were dependent on the traders for the intelligence on which their policy was based, unless they were willing to resort to the costly expedient of sending out special agents. The Indians, who were remarkably well informed about what was going on in the interior, used the traders as messengers. The traders were an economic, political, and social connection between the native Americans and Europeans. Lachlan McGillivray was a worthy representative of the men of the trade. His American career coincided almost exactly with Georgia's colonial period. He was involved in the major events of the four decades from 1736 to 1776. The changes in his life paralleled the changes in the frontier. By following McGillivray through the complexities and confusion of the last half-century of the colonial period it is possible to understand at least one aspect of that formative epoch of American history.

McGillivray's story begins in the Highlands of Scotland, in the valley of the Nairn, not far from Inverness.

CHAPTER ONE

Strathnairn in Invernesshire

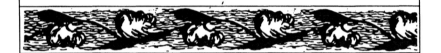

Lachlan McGillivray was sixteen when Captain George Dunbar arrived at Inverness in the summer of 1735 as the agent of James Oglethorpe of Georgia. Tall in stature, red-haired, cheerful of disposition, Lachlan was ready for anything, and Dunbar brought an invitation to adventure. A Highlander himself, Dunbar was a companion of General Oglethorpe in the highly publicized Georgia project, an effort to convert the hardworking, honest poor of Britain into soldier-settlers on the southern frontier. With Dunbar was Hugh Mackay, son of the commander of the garrison of Castle Ruthven, now also in the service of the Trustees of His Majesty's latest colony. The two were on a mission that would have a major effect on the history of Georgia and would change the life of Lachlan McGillivray in a manner beyond his imagining.[1]

Lachlan had lived in the mansion house of Dunmaglass in the strath, or valley, of the river Nairn since his birth. His grandfather Farquhar McGillivray was chief of the Clan McGillivray and the builder of the great house in which Lachlan lived with his parents, William and Janet, his sister, Jean, and his younger brother, Alexander. In the year 1685 Farquhar had been rewarded for his loyalty to the Stuarts by a government position, that of commissioner of supply. Grandfather Farquhar died in 1714, before his loyalty could be tested by the rising in 1715 on behalf of James Stuart, the Pretender. His sons were ardent Jacobites, and they responded to the call of the bagpipes when the Earl of Mar rallied the clans in support of the Stuarts; the oldest, Farquhar, the seventh chief, served as captain; the second son, William, who was to be Lachlan's father, was a lieutenant. The McGillivrays, like most Highlanders, fought with a wild impetuosity and an almost complete lack of discipline. They depended on their first fierce charge and bloodcurdling screams to overwhelm an enemy. This tactic worked well enough at Sheriffmuir but not at all at Preston in northern England, where their army was besieged. The inept commander, Thomas Forster, chose to surrender rather than fight. Sixteen McGillivrays were among the prisoners. Thirteen were deported to South Carolina, where they constituted a new colony of the clan. Among these Highlanders of the diaspora were some who left their mark on the history of Carolina, such as Archibald, John, and an older Lachlan. Others disappeared from public records.[2]

Though a small clan, really a sept within the larger Clan Chattan, the McGillivrays made a name for themselves in the fight for James Stuart in 1715 and for Charles Edward in 1745. The historian Thomas Macaulay would write that King George and his court were as alarmed at the invasion of 1745 as though "the wild Macgillivrays were even then plundering in the Strand."[3]

Farquhar the chief and his brother William escaped deportation and returned to Strathnairn with the enhanced reputation of men who had met the supreme test of battle. William was known thereafter as Captain Ban because of the whiteness of his hair. William, not Farquhar, made his home at Dunmaglass, the ancestral seat. The arrangement was made on the occasion of William's marriage to Janet McIntosh of Kyllachy on February 9, 1714. Farquhar bestowed "free and life rent" not only to William and Janet but also to their son and male heir.[4] Farquhar made his residence at Gask, at the northern extremity of Strathnairn, where the valley opened to form the boggy Culloden Moor.

Thus, even before his birth in 1719, Lachlan was assured of a home at Dunmaglass. Of all estates in the valley of the Nairn, Dunmaglass was the most honored and probably the most favored. It was the seat of the chiefs of the McGillivrays even before the written history of the clan began. It was the home of Gillivray, who in 1268 took protection for himself and his posterity of Farquhar Mackintosh, chief of the Mackintoshes. Since then other families, or septs, had affiliated themselves with the Mackintoshes, so that Strathnairn and the neighboring valleys were populated with MacBeans, Macphails, Macphersons, McQueens, Gows, and Shaws. All these and a few others who were separated from larger clans, such as some Frasers and MacTavishes, formed the Clan Chattan, the Clan of the Cat. Their emblem was a fighting cat with the inscription "Touch me not but a glove." The phrase makes sense when it is explained that the ancient meaning of "but" is "without." [5]

Dunmaglass was an estate of seventeen thousand acres situated on high ground near the headwaters of the northerly flowing Nairn, a clean, swift stream, rich in salmon and trout. The valley of the Nairn was twenty-three miles long and about seven wide. The long, bleak, and barren Monadliath range formed an eastern barrier. To the west the hills were broken by lochs, the largest of which were Ruthven and Duntelchaig. Fertile land was scarce; centuries of erosion had washed the soil from the hills to the narrow stretch of bottomland. Strathnairn was better endowed than most of the Highland valleys and supported about two thousand people during the years of Lachlan's youth. The best tracts were awarded to the best warriors, not necessarily the best farmers. When the best warriors were also closely related to the chief, they were doubly favored, as was William McGillivray of Dunmaglass and Farquhar's other brother, Donald of Dalcrombie. The feudal lord to whom the McGillivrays pledged fealty was the Earl of Moy. His lordship was prepared to turn out the tenants of the estate of Petty to make room for William McGillivray, but McGillivray preferred Dunmaglass. The earl's agent was opposed to the grant to McGillivray. "I must say I am already sick of too many gentlemen tenants in Pettie," he confessed.[6]

The number of occupations open to men like Lachlan's father was limited. If they were Jacobites, as the members of Clan Chattan were, the ranks of government were closed to them. There was little commerce and no industry in the Highlands. Supervision of tenant farmers

Clan Chattan Country
Invernesshire, Scotland

Moray Firth

Beauly Firth

Petty Church
Lonnie
Termit

INVERNESS

Culcabock

Culloden Moor

Military Road

Culclachy

Nairn

Knocknagael

Essich

Kinchyle

Daviot

River

Faillie

Midlairgs

Mains of Gask

Wester Lairgs

Moy Hall

Dores

Loch Ashie

Loch Ness

Dunlichity

Inverarnie
Farr

Loch Duntelchaig

Leiterchullin

Achnabat

Brin

Tullich

Dalcrombie

Elrig

Nairn

Dunchea

Loch Ruthven

Aberarder

River

River Farigaig

Clovendale

Garbole

Dunmaglass Lodge

Balnagaig

Farraline

Drawn from map in Robert McGillivary and George B. Macgillivary, *A History of the Clan McGillivary*.
Cartographic Services Laboratory, The University of Georgia.

was the usual occupation. The tenants were required to do more than pay rent for their patch of land. They could be called to repair the mill, cart peat for the landlord's fires, thatch his roof, manure, sow, and reap his fields. Their lands were divided into rigs, or ridges, according to the ancient open-field or "runrig" system. Only oats and barley were grown. Trees were considered a nuisance because they harbored birds, which might snatch up the scattered seed or peck at the young shoots. Weeds were accepted as a necessary fact of life along with the other distressing results of Adam's fall. If the tenant dared to improve his land by draining or fertilizing it, his rent might be raised. As a result, most tenant farmers eked out a bare subsistence for themselves and their livestock. Those of Strathnairn were perceptibly better off than the average. Cattle droving was considered an honorable profession, and many gentlemen, including Lachlan's father, dressed in their plaids, slashed waistcoats, targets, and broadswords to drive cattle to the Crief tryst. The drover had to be as sharp of mind as impressive of dress to get a good price from the shrewd Lowlanders at the great market. The Highland country was virtually inaccessible to wheeled vehicles because roads were little better than rocky cowpaths interspersed with treacherous bogs. When Lachlan was six years old, the Inverness folk witnessed the first chaise to appear in their town. The government of Robert Walpole concluded that Scotland could not be civilized unless roads were built through the Highlands. As a result, General George Wade began his famous network of roads in 1726, employing five hundred soldiers and constructing more than forty stone bridges in the process. The roads failed in comparison to those laid by the ancient Romans, but when a stranger remarked on their poor quality, the retort was that he should have seen what was there before. It was a source of great excitement to young Lachlan that one of the new highways lay just over the Dunmaglass hill, past his Aunt Fraser's estate at Farraline on Loch Mhor. Wade's roads would indeed open up the Highlands. Among others, the soldiers of the Duke of Cumberland would find them useful. And it was to guard the road to Inverness that Prince Charles would station his army on the unfriendly moors of Culloden instead of seeking a more defensible higher ground in April 1746.[7]

The daily routine at Dunmaglass was not unlike that of the households of other Highland gentlemen. The master would be up at an early hour and have his "morning," a glass of ale or brandy. Then he would inspect his stables and fields. Breakfast consisted of gruel and collops or mutton, washed down with ale. Wheat bread was a novelty; oatmeal cakes were standard fare. At one o'clock in the afternoon there was dinner of barley broth and salted meat with Captain William presiding in his high-backed chair and a hat on his head. At four o'clock, "the four hours," there was a pause for ale or wine. Like bread, tea was slow in penetrating the Highlands, although smugglers were working hard to make it cheaper. Ministers denounced tea as a corrupter of morals; medical men warned against it. In 1729 Brigadier Lachlan Mackintosh of Borlum, whose nephew would seek his fortune in Georgia, lamented the changing customs: "When I came to my friend's house of a morning, I used to be asked if I had my morning draught yet? I am now asked if I have had my tea." Supper came at seven or eight in the evening and featured salted meat (fresh meat was available only in the summer or fall), chicken (part of the tenants' rent), or grouse. There were few vegetables, apart from turnips and cabbage. Potatoes were new to the Highlands. There were no sweets and no desserts but plenty of ale and stronger spirits. After the evening meal the boys would recite their lessons. In the McGillivray household, English was spoken, and Lachlan mastered the written language. They had no need to practice Gaelic; it was still the language of the people and the only way a laird might speak to his people. It was the custom among the gentry to board their sons with tutors in Inverness, and undoubtedly Lachlan and Alexander studied this way. It is a tribute to the tutors, many of them clerics sponsored by the Society for the Propagation of the Gospel, that the English spoken in Inverness today is without the glottal lowland burr.[8]

A description of the Highlands of Lachlan's youth would be incomplete without mention of the fairy folk. It was well known that fairies had golden locks and wore green mantles; they carried bows and a quiver of arrows. There were those who swore they could hear the hubbub of fairy voices on the first night of summer. A newborn had to be carefully watched lest the fairies carry off the babe and put a changeling in its place, and so family members and friends stayed round the clock at the cribside. Only after the christening was the little one safe.[9]

Lachlan's father, the tall, handsome Captain Ban, was the subject of a well-known fairy tale. The wife of one of the tenants of Dunmaglass was kidnapped by fairies and taken for a year. She was so bewitched by the fairy music that she danced the entire time. Fairies were suspected from the first. The brave Captain Ban volunteered to find her. John McQueen of Pollochaik, who was known to be on good terms with fairies, furnished the captain with a magic candle which guided him to the right hill. He found the lady dancing a reel and gallantly joined in. She was surprised that a year had passed; she had thought it only a day. When he saw his chance, Captain Ban bore the lady away. The fairies, now furious, promised revenge. The lady, restored to her husband, kept the candle to ward off future attacks by fairies, witches, brownies, and water kelpies. It was in her house when Lachlan was a boy, and it was still there when he returned to Dunmaglass as a man. As for the hero, the fairies exacted their price. On a dark night while riding alone, Captain Ban was attacked and beaten by unknown assailants, widely thought to be the irate fairies. Those who believed in strange creatures had no trouble accepting as a fact that the greatest kelpie of all swam in Loch Ness, just across Glenmor, and had inhabited the loch since the time of good Saint Columba.[10]

The summer of 1735 was an opportune time for Captain George Dunbar and Hugh Mackay to come to Inverness to recruit men for Georgia in America. A succession of poor crops had reduced gentlemen and tenants alike to poverty. The town council of Inverness thought so well of the idea of sending a hundred or so hungry men to Georgia that it made Georgia's founder, James Oglethorpe, an honorary burgess of the town. The authorities were even more pleased that the emigrants were Jacobites. Dunbar was wise to the ways of his native shire. He obtained the support of William Mackintosh, chief of Clan Chattan, for the venture. The chief was called Mackintosh of Mackintosh, and he lived at Moy Hall, where Bonnie Prince Charlie would one day be a guest. He borrowed money on his lands to assist the gentlemen who should go to Georgia. Most of them were chosen for their leadership qualities. Outstanding among them was John Mohr Mackintosh, who had gone off to fight in 1715 with his uncle Brigadier Lachlan Mackintosh of Borlum. According to the clan historian, he was called "Mohr" because of his great size.[11] Dunbar's tactic, as Oglethorpe explained it to his fellow Trustees of Georgia, was "to bring the enterprise into vogue with the chief gentlemen" so as to secure their tenants. He was fully aware that these gentlemen "were unused to labour," and therefore each had to bring a man capable of working.[12] John Mackintosh of Holme, aged twenty-four, with the chief's money and his own, paid for himself and sixteen-year-old Lachlan McGillivray. Lachlan's aunt Magdalen was married to William Mackintosh of Holme, brother to John. Seventeen gentlemen paid their own passage on Dunbar's ship the *Prince of Wales*, and the Georgia Trustees paid for 146 others.[13]

Among the emigrants was a confusion of Mackintoshes. Besides John Mohr Mackintosh of Borlum and John Mackintosh of Holme, there were John Mackintosh of Kingussie, John Mackintosh of Dornes, John Mackintosh Bain, and John Mackintosh Lynvilge. The McGillivrays were represented by Lachlan, his cousin Farquhar, aged thirty, and Archibald, aged fifteen.[14]

Why would the Mackintosh of Moy Hall pay to speed the departure of his clansmen? For one thing, his brother Aeneas Mackintosh was already in Georgia in the service of James Oglethorpe. In 1735 this Aeneas was stationed at a fort on the Carolina side of the Savannah River to protect the new German settlement at Ebenezer, forty-five miles above Savannah. The agricultural depression undoubtedly was a factor in the migration of so many from the same district. It has been suggested that Mackintosh would never have been able to enclose his lands for sheep raising if the likes of John Mohr Mackintosh still occupied the estates.[15]

In going to Georgia, Lachlan McGillivray was not running away from home, as has been suggested.[16] He was going with his clan to join others already in Georgia and Carolina. He must have felt a touch of nostalgia as the blue-green hills faded from view, but he must also have felt the quickening flush of adventure. Oliver Goldsmith caught something of the spirit of the enterprise when he wrote, "to distant climes, a dreary scene they go. Where wild Altama murmurs to their woe." [17]

The poet was also prophet; the future would hold sorrow enough. But the Highlanders knew only that they were needed to protect the vulnerable British frontier. The prospect of a noble fight for a worthy cause was incentive enough.

CHAPTER TWO

Forming a New Colony

The three-month voyage was uneventful. The *Prince of Wales* left Inverness on October 20, 1735, and arrived at Tybee Roads in January 1736. The single sign of civilization along the sandy strand was an unfinished lighthouse. Fifteen miles up the broad Savannah River the town of Savannah, laid out by Oglethorpe three years earlier in a unique pattern of squares, was struggling into existence. In 1736, it was impressive only in conception. Its two hundred or so inhabitants were demoralized by the long absence of its founder. Some of the paying passengers aboard the *Prince of Wales* decided to stay in Savannah, but most went with those indentured to the Georgia Trust to the new settlement on the Altamaha, Georgia's southern boundary.[1]

There were not enough boats to transport them all, and some of the Highlanders had to remain on board for a week. When they were warned by people from Carolina that they would have nothing to live in, whereas the Spanish had a strong fort, the Scots boasted that they would beat down the fort and live in the Spanish houses.[2]

Oglethorpe returned to Georgia on February 12, 1736, aboard the *Symonds*, only a few days after the last Highlanders had gone south. Captain George Dunbar greeted him with the news of his successful mission and told him that the Scots had named their town Darien to commemorate an earlier unsuccessful Scottish colonizing effort in

Panama. The district was called New Inverness. Oglethorpe was eager to meet these new Georgians, and Dunbar went along to introduce him and, in Oglethorpe's words, "to instruct me a little in their manners."[3]

On February 22, Oglethorpe arrived at Darien, so well coached by Dunbar that he wore a plaid. Kilts had not yet been introduced to the Highlands, and men wore a fourteen-foot-long swath of cloth gathered at the waist and falling freely to the knees, the loose ends pinned at the left shoulder to leave the right arm free to brandish a sword. Oglethorpe was as impressed with them as they were with him. He described to the Trustees what "a most manly appearance" they had, with their plaids, broadswords, targets (shields), and firearms.[4]

The Highlanders, under Hugh Mackay, commissioned captain by Oglethorpe, had been busy during their first three weeks. The site they selected was a clearing on a bluff three miles up the Altamaha River. The Carolinians had built Fort King George near the place in 1721 and abandoned it in 1729. Only the ruins of the fort and the graves of the soldiers who died there marked the site. The Scots mounted a battery consisting of four small cannon and built a guardhouse and a chapel and several huts for the women and children. While Oglethorpe was at Darien, Captain James McPherson and a company of rangers arrived overland from Savannah. Oglethorpe ordered a road laid out connecting the towns and hoped it would have the same beneficial effects in Georgia as General Wade's roads in Scotland.[5]

Captain Hugh Mackay had the nominal military command, but the real authority figure in Darien was John Mohr Mackintosh. Oglethorpe soon discovered that he could deal with the Gaelic-speaking indentured servants only through their leaders. Because they spoke no English, they could not be dispersed among the other settlements. John Mackintosh set them to work clearing fields and planting corn before he let them build houses. Lord Egmont, chairman of the Georgia Trustees in London, heartily approved the priority, remarking that the people of Savannah should have done the same thing.[6]

Although the Highlanders managed to raise enough corn that first year to supply themselves, farming was not their long suit. They were not good at it in Scotland, and they were less proficient in America, where they had more excuses for leaving off such disagreeable labor. They much preferred cutting down trees and sawing wood for their own houses and for their sister settlement, Frederica, on St. Simon Island. They must have wondered at the number and size of the tall sea pines and the girth and spread of the giant oaks. There were more trees in Darien than in all of Invernesshire in Scotland.

Another diversion from the tedious work of farming was the frequent visits of Indians. A party of curious Creek Indians went to see the Highlanders even before Oglethorpe arrived in Darien. The Indians and the Scots got along famously from the start. They discovered that they shared the same values. The clan system was not unlike the tribal divisions. Status was the product of kinship and prowess. The manly arts were esteemed in both cultures; both had their war songs, their traditional dances, their reciters of the great deeds of the past. The Gaels and the native Americans were born storytellers, given to flights of imagery and metaphor. The world of spirits was real to both cultures. The mutual respect led to friendly competition in an American version of the Highland games as Scots vied with Creeks in feats of swiftness, strength, and dexterity.[7]

William Mackintosh, a youthful companion of Lachlan, recalled in later life that a quick friendship developed between the visitors and the men of Darien. We can picture the Scottish lads engrossed in their effort to communicate with the young warriors, first in sign language and then in sound recognition. We can only guess at the wonder they felt as they were introduced to a culture as rich and proud as their own. Both William and Lachlan learned the language of the Creeks. William later became a planter on the Georgia coast, but Lachlan was intrigued by the glimpses into the world of the Creeks. He had relatives already engaged in the Indian trade. He would join them as soon as he had satisfied his obligations to his patron, John Mackintosh of Holme.

The Highlanders learned more about their situation from the Indians than they did from the busy Oglethorpe. They were aware of the threat from the Spanish in St. Augustine and from their Indian allies. Some of the Darien men accompanied Oglethorpe on his reconnaissance through the debatable land below the Altamaha River. Highlanders were posted on Amelia Island at the entrance to the St. Johns River. They called their fort St. Andrews and the island Highland and bid defiance to the dons. They knew that Oglethorpe was preparing Frederica as his garrison town for the inevitable war.[8]

From the Indians they learned that the French were an even greater danger. The French had built a fort where the Coosa and Tallapoosa rivers flowed together to form the Alabama River. Lachlan McGillivray would come to know a great deal about this fort called Toulouse. The elderly Chief Tomochichi had explained to Oglethorpe when they first met in 1733 that the Carolina traders were alienating the Creeks by the use of rum and by cheating in weights and measurements.[9] The Upper Creeks were already succumbing to the French influence. Oglethorpe decided that king and country would be best served if he secured control of the Indian trade. To that end he and his fellow Trustees pushed a bill through Parliament giving Georgia control of the Indian trade within the bounds of the colony. Since no one was quite sure where the boundaries were, Oglethorpe claimed jurisdiction over the entire territory between the Savannah and Mississippi rivers.

The Carolinians conducted their trade from a place called Savannah Town on the river of the same name, so called because the Savannah Indians had helped drive out the previous inhabitants a half-century before. Since 1716 the town had been protected by the guns and garrison of Fort Moore, built after the frightening Yamassee uprising of 1715. Lately the Carolina government attempted to induce settlement in the area by organizing the region under the title of the New Windsor district. Here the Carolina traders kept their warehouses and formed their caravans which transported goods to the Cherokees at the headwaters of the Savannah, to the Lower Creeks along the Chattahoochee, to the Upper Creeks on the Coosa and Tallapoosa, and to the Chickasaws beyond.[10]

A delegation of Indians visited Oglethorpe in June 1736 and asked him to establish a town on the Georgia side of the upper Savannah River. Oglethorpe had already made up his mind to do just that. On June 14, 1736, he instructed Noble Jones, the surveyor, to lay out a town with the same forty-lots pattern as Savannah at the head of navigation of the Savannah River. The town would be called Augusta in honor of the new bride of the Prince of Wales, whose own name was bestowed upon the town of Frederica. Roger Lacy, a planter who had fortified his farm at Thunderbolt near Savannah, was put in charge of building a proper fort at Augusta. Oglethorpe later installed a garrison, headed by Lacy, to police the Indian traders. First, Lacy had the difficult diplomatic task of going out into the Indian country and informing the Carolina traders that a new law required them to obtain a license in Georgia and a second law forbade the use of rum. Realizing that his message would be badly received, Lacy took along an escort of ten hardy frontiersmen who were promised five hundred acres of land in Augusta as a reward for their services. Lacy was instructed to go into the Cherokee country and "take and seize all and singular of the goods, wares, merchandises, slaves, furs, wax and skins" in the possession of persons not licensed by Georgia.[11] For good measure, he was to smash all the rum kegs he found. John Tanner, a young neighbor of Oglethorpe's from Surrey who had come over to Georgia "for his amusement," was dispatched on the same mission to the Creeks. Tanner needed an escort even more than Lacy because of his youth and inexperience; a Creek chief remarked scornfully that "he from Georgia was a child." At the end of the year, Tanner returned to England with Oglethorpe and reported to the Trustees that all the Indian traders had wives. There was a hint of amazement in his remark that they had fathered more than four hundred children.[12] Tanner's chance remark is evidence of the successful infiltration of the Carolina traders into the Creek country. The implications for the future were profound. These children of mixed blood would grow up to be what one historian has called "cultural brokers," influenced by the capitalistic values of their fathers and bound to their clans by the traditions of their mothers.[13]

The Carolina traders had been alerted to Oglethorpe's intentions as early as 1734, when Oglethorpe deputed Patrick Mackay, brother of Hugh, to spread the word that Georgia claimed jurisdiction over the Indian trade. Mackay executed his mission with such forthrightness that he infuriated the governor of South Carolina and offended the French and Spaniards. Oglethorpe appreciated his services, but the

Trustees in effect repudiated him. They failed to reimburse him for his considerable expenses because the Indian Act, which gave Georgia control of the trade, did not go into effect until July 1735, after Mackay had completed his work. Mackay moved to Carolina to recoup his losses.[14]

Because of Oglethorpe's intrusion into the Indian trade, relations between Georgia and Carolina were soured by the summer of 1736. Oglethorpe was convinced that a devious plan was afoot to take over Georgia; he thought Carolina would then oppress the English poor as well as the Indians.[15] William Stephens kept a journal of his trip to the Carolina rendezvous at Savannah Town in July 1736 and noted that the traders were uneasy about Oglethorpe's plans and admitted that "cause enough they have for this jealousie." He meant that they were right to be apprehensive; Oglethorpe intended to bar them from the trade unless they purchased a Georgia license. Stephens correctly predicted that the traders would simply move across the river to the new town of Augusta and that the river Savannah would become as noted as any in America for its commerce. He remarked that, in spite of the volume of water, the Savannah "glides Smoothly on as the River Thames at Putney."[16] Stephens's chatty account pleased the Trustees; they made him their secretary in Savannah and encouraged him to continue sending information about Georgia.

The contest between Georgia and Carolina for control of the Indian trade was of more than passing interest to young Lachlan McGillivray. The largest company trading to the Creeks happened to be headed by Archibald McGillivray, one of the kinsmen exiled after the rising of 1715. Another member of the clan, an older Lachlan McGillivray, who pioneered in the trade, died in 1735. One of the first settlers in Augusta was a John McGillivray. Thus the name McGillivray was already important in the Indian country, and Lachlan of Dunmaglass was certain of a warm welcome when the time came to enter the business of trade.[17]

During the first eventful summer of 1736, when the Darien settlers were learning about this strange and vast land, a party of Chickasaws appeared in Savannah to talk to James Oglethorpe. Their tribal lands were beyond even those of the Upper Creeks. They hunted along the great Mississippi. Their neighbors were the Natchez, a small tribe that had made the mistake of attacking a French post on the Mississippi. The unforgiving French were determined thenceforth to stamp the Natchez out of existence, and because the Chickasaws gave refuge to the Natchez, the French extended their animosity to the Chickasaws. The veteran governor of Louisiana, Jean Baptiste LeMoyne, Sieur de Bienville, enlisted the numerous Choctaws in the war against the Chickasaws. In 1736, Bienville's army invaded the Chickasaw country but was unable to dislodge the hard-fighting Chickasaws from their dugout forts. The invaders retired to plan a new strategy.[18]

Such was the gist of the history the Chickasaw chiefs told Oglethorpe in Savannah in July 1736. "We heard you were a Red Woman's Child . . . but now I have seen you I believe you have as white a body as any in Charles Town," said a chief. "I am a Red Man, an Indian, in my heart, that is I love them," answered Oglethorpe. The Chickasaws told Oglethorpe how the Carolina traders at Savannah Town tried to dissuade them from going to Georgia; they were told that they would be tied up and not permitted to return, "but we have seen you and are satisfied." [19]

In their second day's talk, the Indians got down to business. Seven hundred enemies came into their towns twice "but have not killed us all." The people of Carolina promised guns but never sent them. "We are so big," said the spokesman, making a circle with his fingers, "you English are so big," making a larger circle, "but the French are quite round us all," stretching out his arms, "and kill us like hogs or fowls." The French governor had sent for cannon, then he would come back and blast the Chickasaws out of their huts.[20]

Oglethorpe explained that grenades and mortars could do terrible damage in a confined space. "I was bred to war," he said, "and I know those things." He advised the Indians to keep to the open fields or fight from behind trees. The Chickasaws thanked him for his advice and hoped for something more tangible.[21]

Oglethorpe enlisted the Georgia Trustees as a powerful lobby to convince the Duke of Newcastle to send help to the Chickasaws. He warned that the French were constantly encroaching. They had constructed a new fort on the Tombigbee River to maintain their control of the Choctaws, and they rebuilt Fort Toulouse in the Upper Creek country. The French were strengthening their position in time of peace so that the English settlements would fall to them in time of war. The future shape of the frontier was at issue.[22]

The Darien settlers soon realized that they were caught up in this international struggle for control of the continent. To the south was the fortress town of St. Augustine, from which the Spanish governors supplied the Florida Indians, mainly the Apalachee and the Yamassee. To the west were the French settlements at Mobile, Biloxi, and New Orleans, and the two forts, Tombigbee and Toulouse. The Choctaws were under the French influence as were the Alabamas, whose villages dotted the river of that name. The Upper Creek towns leaned toward the French. The Lower Creeks maintained a neutral stance and accepted presents from all the rival powers. The practice of giving presents had its origin in the hospitable traditions of the Indians, who showered gifts upon visitors. The custom of giving token gifts to visitors would not seem strange to Scots like McGillivray because it was the custom in the Highlands, also. The European governors, French and British alike, took a more pragmatic view and regarded the presents as bribes.

Against this formidable array, the Darien outpost in 1736 seemed particularly vulnerable. Darien's twin town on St. Simon Island, Frederica, was a garrison post whose garrison did not arrive until 1738. Augusta was still a blueprint; its fort would not be built until 1737, although the Savannah Town traders had already begun to move across the river. Savannah, in its third year of existence, was wracked by dissent. Its inhabitants increasingly objected to the Trustees' prohibition of Negro slavery and the limitation to fifty acres of land imposed on all those sent over by the Trustees. More and more inhabitants ignored the prohibition on rum. The tiny settlements around Savannah, Joseph's Town, Hardwicke, and Abercorn, were hardly more than plantations. Ebenezer, a German community at the tidewater line above Savannah, was struggling for survival. The only military protection was Captain James McPherson's corps of rangers, Captain Aeneas Mackintosh's company at Fort Palachacola, and Captain Daniel Pepper's command at Fort Moore. The most important asset Georgia had was Oglethorpe's boldness.

The Georgia founder had established Darien in spite of the Trustees' instructions to defer planting any new settlements on the Altamaha. He went to England in 1736 to persuade Robert Walpole to give him a regiment or else abandon Carolina and Virginia to the ravages of the Spaniards. He succeeded in getting the Gibraltar regiment assigned to Georgia and returned with his new command to Frederica in 1738.[23]

The first reports from Darien were promising. More servants were needed, and Oglethorpe was prevailed upon to allow Archibald McBean to go to Scotland to recruit forty more Highlanders. He explained to the Trustees that McBean "has a very good interest among the common people of that country."[24] On the way to Scotland, McBean stopped by London to call on Lord Egmont, chairman of the Trustees, and present him with a live Georgia black bear. Egmont was a bit stuffy about it and noted in his journal that he refused to accept the bear. McBean's news was more welcome than his present. The people of Darien were said to be "extraordinary industrious" and would have enough corn for themselves and a surplus for sale. John McLeod, the Presbyterian minister from the Island of Skye, was "much beloved." McBean, aided by the reliable George Dunbar, accomplished his mission and returned with his recruits to Georgia on the ship *Two Brothers*, reaching Darien on January 14, 1738.[25]

The *Two Brothers* carried a consignment of saws for the use of the newly arrived servants, some of whom were distributed among the freeholders and some put under the charge of John Mohr Mackintosh. The crusty Thomas Causton, the Savannah storekeeper, was instructed to dispatch a number of guns to Mackintosh and was cautioned that on all occasions he was to show Mackintosh proper regard.[26]

The situation at Darien was not as pleasant as the Trustees were led to believe. Hugh Mackay and Mackintosh were frequently arbitrary in their punishments. Servants were bound and whipped for slight infractions. One freeholder was arrested for refusing to sing out the words "all is well" while on sentry duty. His reason was readily understandable: all was not well. Spanish-allied Indians had fired at the sentry when he called out the night before. Supplies ran so low in 1737 that the settlers went in a body to see Major William Horton at Frederica. If he did not furnish them with the goods they needed, they threatened to go to Savannah and break open the Trustees' store there. Horton postponed the crisis by supplying the Highlanders from his store.[27]

Unfortunately, the year 1738 was much worse for young Lachlan and his friends. A drought ruined the corn crop and discouraged the people from further planting. The freeholders decided to depute two of their number to go to Charlestown and apply for a grant of land in Carolina. The entire colony would then move to Carolina. John Mohr Mackintosh persuaded them to accept an alternative; he would ask Oglethorpe to set up a storehouse in Darien, and the settlers would then be secure against a repetition of the shortage of the previous year.[28]

William Stephens in Savannah was alarmed at the "universal defection" of the Highlanders, which he learned about in December 1738. He noted in his journal that a deputation visited Oglethorpe at Frederica and presented their grievances. Among these were a removal of restrictions on landholding and the establishment of a store from which they could obtain needed supplies. The petitioners were willing to pay for what they needed by cutting shingles and planking. Stephens observed that this arrangement would put an end to planting in Darien — and Georgia was supposed to be a colony of farmer-soldiers.[29]

The demands from Darien were made at a propitious time. The Savannah settlers had filed a petition of their own, requesting unrestricted title to their land grants and "the Use of Negroes." The statement was dated December 9, 1738, and signed with 117 names, an impressive number. Oglethorpe was furious when he read the document; he blamed "negro-merchants" in Carolina for seducing the Georgians.[30]

Historian Harvey H. Jackson has made the case that Oglethorpe arranged a deal with John Mohr Mackintosh.[31] If the Darien people would sign a counterpetition, Oglethorpe would see that they got a store, cattle, and a loan of money. The ever-present George Dunbar was summoned to write a statement refuting the Savannah petition. He did so, arguing that the proximity of the Spaniards would encourage slaves to run away; that white men could be "more usefully employed"; that the Darien people would have to go into debt to the "Negro Merchant" and therefore become slaves themselves; and that there would be as great a danger from the enemy within as from that without. After listing these pragmatic reasons, Dunbar rose to an impressive level of moral outrage: "It's shocking to human Nature, that any Race of Mankind, and their Posterity, should be sentenced to perpetual slavery . . . and as Freedom to them must be as dear as to us, what a Scene of Horror must it bring about!"[32] The statement was signed with eighteen names and dated January 3, 1739.

Reverend John McLeod later stated that Dunbar used his great influence to prevail upon the people to sign. One of the signers, Alexander Monroe, was more explicit about the pressure that was brought to bear. He was at his plantation two miles from Darien when he was told by William Mackintosh, John Mohr's son, that he was to come at once to a meeting. He was told that he would be ruined forever if he did not come. At 9 P.M. he reached the Mackintosh house. There he was told that Oglethorpe would give him cattle and servants if he would sign but that he would suffer if he did not, just as the people of Savannah would suffer. Monroe did not read the statement, but "with his Hopes on one Side and Fears on the other," he signed. He regretted doing so when he learned the contents and concluded he had harmed rather than helped the community.[33]

Lachlan McGillivray was not yet twenty when signatures were solicited for the loyalty petition, and it is impossible to know whether he would have signed it. It is significant that his cousin John Mackintosh of Holme did not sign. It is also interesting that an even stronger opposition statement delivered by Thomas Stephens to Parliament in 1742 was signed by at least a dozen Highlanders, including Farquhar McGillivray and "John M'Intosh." With so many John Mackintoshes, the undifferentiated name amounts to anonymity, but it could have been John Mackintosh of Holme. The protesters were characterized by the Trustees as "clamorous malcontents."[34]

That so many Darien Scots opted for the introduction of slave labor demonstrates the attraction the Carolina life-style exerted on Georgia. The Trustees' vision of Georgians as contented soldier-farmers producing silk cocoons and wine continued to fascinate the Trustees but appealed to fewer and fewer Georgians. The Darien inhabitants never seriously considered following the Trustees' ideal.

Oglethorpe kept his part of the bargain. Darien got its store and a loan of £200 to buy cattle. Unfortunately, the concession failed to bring peace to the troubled community. John Mohr Mackintosh was accused of managing the store in a dictatorial manner. It was said that he issued rotten corn to the people and kept the good corn for himself and his family and that he fed some of the good corn to his hogs. He was quoted as saying that he did not care what happened to his people, "they might go wander in the woods with the Indians."[35] The words sound like those of one who, if not a cruel chief, at least was disappointed with his subjects. It would not be long before some of the Darien people, Lachlan McGillivray among them, would go wandering in the woods with the Indians.

The conscience-stirring antislavery statement deserves a place among the documents that chronicle the progress of human rights. On the face of it, it is a credit to James Oglethorpe, George Dunbar, and John Mohr Mackintosh, but the credit is vitiated by the Darien leaders' disregard of the human rights of their own countrymen. In Darien, clan loyalty was breaking down. In September 1739, the people decided again to move en masse to Carolina and asked Benjamin McIntosh, first cousin of John Mohr, to represent them in negotiating with the authorities in Charlestown.[36] War intruded on the plans of the disaffected Highlanders. All able-bodied men, including freeholders and servants whose indentureship was over, were required to join the Independent Company of Foot for the invasion of Florida. John Mohr Mackintosh stated that love of king and country impelled the Scots to enlist. That was undoubtedly true, but there were other incentives as well. Alexander Monroe said that they were promised cattle, servants, and pay of £12 a month if they went.[37]

No one welcomed the news of the outbreak of war more than Oglethorpe, whose patience was badly frayed by the criticism from malcontents. He had returned from England in November 1738 with the regiment he wanted, the Forty-Second, formerly stationed in Gibraltar. During the course of the year, Frederica was converted into the strongest English bastion on the Atlantic coast.

The war began in the west. In July 1739 the English governor of New York alerted the governor of South Carolina that the Senecas, accompanied by a detachment of Canadian militia, were on the march to join Bienville's army in a two-pronged attack against the Chickasaws. That tribe, though badly outnumbered, was prepared for the invasion. English traders, notably Nicholas Chinnery and John Campbell, had supplied them with ammunition and had supervised the construction of a defense line of log posts on terraced hillsides. Behind these were three forts with dugout caves to provide shelter from mortar fire. Interspersed among the forts were the low-lying, strongly built huts with loopholes commanding every approach. An enemy Shawnee conceded that the Chickasaws were "real warriors who are fed in war and instructed by the English."[38]

The French offensive was delayed by the temporary defection of Red Shoes, a powerful Choctaw chief. Red Shoes led a delegation of Choctaws to Charlestown seeking guns and ammunition but received only presents. Disappointed, he returned to his country and joined in the preparation for invasion of the Chickasaw country.[39]

The Lower Creeks were alarmed at the warlike activity. Chigilly, chief of the Cowetas, invited Oglethorpe to a tribal gathering. Tomochichi urged him to go; it was the last advice the old chief gave. He died in November 1739 and was buried with honors in Savannah. On July 8, 1739, Oglethorpe left Frederica accompanied by Captain Aeneas Mackintosh, commander of Fort Palachacola; George Dunbar, now with the rank of captain lieutenant in the Forty-Second Regiment; Adjutant Hugh Mackay, Jr.; and about twenty others, many of them from Darien. From the Uchee town on the Savannah River the party cut across country to Coweta, on the Chattahoochee, which they reached on August 8, 1739. The Creeks delighted their visitors with their lavish hospitality. The reception was repeated at Cusseta. A treaty was drawn up reaffirming to the English the right to settle between the Savannah and Altamaha rivers as far as the tidewater, excepting three coastal islands and the plantation outside Savannah where Mary Musgrove Mathews lived.[40] She was a privileged person, the niece of Chigilly and the cousin of Malatchi, a great chief. In time, she would claim the coastal islands for herself.

Oglethorpe could not persuade the Creeks to join him in a war against the Spanish and French, but he was convinced that he had quieted their worries about the English intentions. He could promise also to regulate the activity of the traders from his post in Augusta. "If I had not gone up," he informed the Trustees, "the misunderstandings between them [the Creeks] and the Carolina traders would have brought on a war." By establishing Augusta, he could control the trade. Augusta, he said, was "the Key of the Indian Countrey." [41]

Oglethorpe, battling a fever, returned by way of the fall-line trading path, which led to Augusta, where he was welcomed by a salute of cannons from the handsome new fort. The general thoroughly approved of the conduct of young Lieutenant Richard Kent, successor to Roger Lacy, who had brought a semblance of order to this trading rendezvous and on the spot promoted him to captain and "Conservator or Justice of the Peace for Augusta and the Indian Nations within the colony of Georgia." Kent's jurisdiction was staggering. He was expected to police traders who traveled as far as the Mississippi River. Oglethorpe was pleased that the first settlers had harvested a bumper crop of corn. He was able to give fifteen hundred bushels to a visiting party of Cherokees, whose nation was afflicted with a smallpox epidemic.[42]

While at Augusta, Oglethorpe heard the news that he had been waiting for: England and Spain were at war. The settlement of Georgia and especially Oglethorpe's encroachments below the Altamaha were a major irritant to Spain and reason enough for war. A relatively minor incident provoked Robert Walpole's government. An English smuggler named Robert Jenkins was caught by the Spanish coast guard. As an object lesson to other smugglers, the authorities punished him by cutting off his ear. Jenkins preserved the dismembered part and dis-

played it to an outraged Parliament. So this war began as the War of
Jenkins' Ear.

On his way to Savannah, Oglethorpe heard the startling news of
a slave rebellion on the Stono River in Carolina. Armed blacks had
killed twenty-three people and attempted to escape to Spanish Florida.
The revolt was quickly suppressed by the Carolina militia. In spite
of the small scale of the uprising, South Carolina was "closer to the
edge of upheaval than historians have been willing to consider," according to Peter H. Wood.[43] Fort Palachacola on the lower Savannah
River controlled one of the fords in the river. Captain Aeneas Mackintosh assumed his former command of the post and patrolled the river,
watching for runaway slaves. The episode convinced the Trustees that
they were right in banning slavery in Georgia. Carolina's response was
to enact a more repressive slave code.

Because the Spanish in Florida were blamed for inciting slaves, Carolinians were receptive to Oglethorpe's appeal for troops to join him in
an attack on St. Augustine. Meanwhile, he mobilized the Highlanders
and the Forty-Second Regiment for the campaign.

While Oglethorpe was on his western circuit, Bienville's ponderous
invasion of the Chickasaws was carried out. Captain Richard Kent kept
Oglethorpe informed about the progress of the French expedition.[44]
Seneca Indians attacked the Chickasaws from the north. The Chickasaws should have been overwhelmed, but the enemy attack was badly
coordinated. By chance, the fields around the Chickasaw town were
so wet that the heavy cannon could not be brought into action. The
French withdrawal turned into a rout when the triumphant Indians
poured out of their forts and went after scalps. Bienville's army retired
the next day.

The Louisiana French and their Choctaw allies were only one prong
of the offensive. The valiant Chickasaws had to withstand the harass-
ment of Seneca Indians from New York and their Canadian leaders.
After inconclusive skirmishing, the exhausted Chickasaws reached a
compromise with their enemies. They would not give up the Natchez
refugees, but they would prevail upon them to leave the Chickasaw

villages. Actually, the Natchez had already begun to filter into the Cherokee country.[45]

Oglethorpe launched his Florida campaign before he knew the outcome of Bienville's strategy. His report to the Trustees on November 16, 1739, contained brave words: "The French have attacked the Carolina Indians and the Spaniards have invaded us. I wish it may not be resolved between them to root the English out of America. We here are resolved to die hard and will not lose one inch of ground without fighting."[46] The French government would not enter the war officially until 1744, but the struggle for America had begun.

Oglethorpe's first success was the capture of Fort San Francisco de Pupo on the west bank of the Saint Johns River directly west of the town of St. Augustine. Two volleys from Oglethorpe's cannon forced the defenders to surrender on January 7, 1740. Some of the Darien Highlanders were stationed there, dangerously exposed to a Spanish attack, while Oglethorpe returned to Frederica to plead with South Carolina to send assistance and to recruit Indian allies.[47]

The Creeks were too concerned about the French war against the Chickasaws to leave their nation. George Dunbar and Aeneas Mackintosh went to Augusta in November 1739 to solicit the help of the band of Chickasaws who lived on the Carolina side of the Savannah River opposite Augusta. Squirrel King, their chief, was a renowned fighter and gladly volunteered his warriors. William Gray, a veteran of the Chickasaw trade, was commissioned captain and placed in command of the Chickasaws.[48] More than a hundred Cherokees were escorted to Frederica by Oglethorpe's agent Thomas Holmes. A few Uchees and Yamacraws from the lower Savannah River joined the expedition.[49]

Most of the men of Darien served under John Mohr Mackintosh in the Highland Independent Company of Foot as distinguished from the mounted rangers at Fort Pupo under Captain Hugh Mackay, Jr. The Highlanders joined Oglethorpe at Frederica in May 1740. Nineteen-year-old Lachlan McGillivray was almost certainly one of the seventy Darien Scots who were enlisted by Mackintosh. They wore their colorful tartans and were armed with their traditional weapons, broadswords and dirks, with muskets that were notoriously unreliable, and targets or shields for defense in hand-to-hand fighting.[50]

When the Carolinians turned out under Colonel Alexander Vanderdussen in May, Oglethorpe began his delayed campaign. He commanded a force of about fifteen hundred men, including four hundred Carolinians and the same number of Indians. On June 2, 1740, Oglethorpe paraded before St. Augustine in an effort to draw the Spaniards out of their coquina stone fortress, the Castillo de San Marcos. Governor Manuel de Montiano refused to accept the challenge. Without cannon, Oglethorpe could not blast the Spaniards out of their stronghold. Oglethorpe then shifted his attention to the two points of land that guarded the entrance to St. Augustine harbor. The Carolinians occupied Point Quartell to the north, and Oglethorpe landed on Anastasia Island with the soldiers of the Forty-Second. His plan was to use the few mortars he had to clear the harbor of Spanish ships. He intended to return then to the land side for a final assault on the town.[51]

When the main body of the English army removed to the seaward side of St. Augustine, a "flying force" of just over a hundred men was left on the mainland to monitor the movements of the enemy. The Highland Independent Company of Foot and ten of the Highland Rangers were among the number. Some of the Highlanders were left behind at Fort Diego, the English base camp, where Captain George Dunbar commanded. It is not known whether Lachlan McGillivray remained at the base camp or marched out with the "flying party" that left Fort Diego on June 10. The party included about twenty Carolinians. There was an unfortunate division of command. Colonel John Palmer, a Carolina volunteer, was given operational control, but because he did not hold a regular military commission, Captain Hugh Mackay claimed the right of command. The Highlanders were inclined to take orders only from their chief, John Mohr Mackintosh.[52]

The flying party quickly became stationary, finding that the abandoned earthen fort called Mosa was a convenient place from which to observe St. Augustine. The Carolinians camped outside the fort, and the Highlanders moved inside. Their traditional disregard for military discipline was revealed in their failure to guard against surprise. On the night of June 14, three hundred men under Captain Antonio Salgado slipped quietly out of St. Augustine.[53]

At Fort Mosa, Colonel Palmer expected an attack and at 3 A.M. had his Carolinians awake and dressed. Palmer tried in vain to arouse the Highlanders inside the fort. The Spaniards were within a hundred yards of the fort before they were seen by a sentry. The Carolinians took up a position in the ditch in front of the fort but were quickly overwhelmed. Hand-to-hand fighting ensued within the fort, Spanish bayonets against Scots broadswords, but the Highlanders had left their shields behind at Fort Diego. Some of the defenders managed to scramble over the wall and escape. Sixty-three men of the British party were killed; twenty or so were captured, including John Mohr Mackintosh. Governor Montiano claimed that only ten of his men were killed in the battle.[54]

The Scots refused to believe that they were beaten by mere three-to-one odds. From a prison in Spain, John Mohr Mackintosh told a different story to a relative in Scotland; according to him, seven hundred Spaniards attacked, and "we were only eighty." Three hundred Spaniards were killed on the spot, he thought.[55]

The Fort Mosa battle was the turning point of Oglethorpe's invasion. The British navy failed to prevent enemy supply ships from reaching St. Augustine. On July 4, 1740, Oglethorpe ordered a withdrawal. Some men of the Forty-Second deserted on the way to Frederica. Oglethorpe himself was physically exhausted and sick with a fever. The Darien community had suffered a mortal blow. By May 1741 there were only sixteen men left of the seventy who had enlisted under John Mohr Mackintosh. Fifteen new recruits from Scotland enabled the unit to survive as an independent company.[56]

Oglethorpe's critics blamed him for deceiving the Highlanders, putting them into an exposed position, and causing the disaster "which has put a period to the settlement of Darien."[57] They were wrong in placing all the blame on Oglethorpe, but their assessment of the impact on Darien was right. Some who could not have been among the faction of "malcontents" confirmed the virtual demise of the original Highland community on the Altamaha. George Whitefield, the great evangelist and founder of the Bethesda Orphanage, wrote to the Trustees before the Florida invasion to say that he did not know which was the worst, Savannah, Frederica, or Darien. The Darien people worked at sawing, to the neglect of planting, and as a result, "I scarce saw a garden with anything in it through the whole town." [58] Thomas Eyre, who had accompanied Oglethorpe on his western tour, gave his opinion at the end of the year 1740 that only the pay of three shillings per week kept men at Darien: "I have been in that town and know most of the inhabitants and I assure you that the improvements of the whole are not able to afford a comfortable living to one family." [59]

Thomas Causton, the target of many of the criticisms of the malcontents and one who might be expected to put the best face on things, painted a dismal picture: "Most of them went to the siege of Saint Augustine, where the generality of them were either killed or taken prisoners. So that the town being almost depopulated of its first inhabitants, the remaining widows and broken families are a melancholy object." [60]

In fact, the prospect for the future of the entire colony of Georgia was bleak. A census of the colony, ordered by the Trustees, revealed that there were 86 persons at Darien; 14 were prisoners in Havana, Cuba, and 2 were held in Spain. Some of the 86 were newcomers from Scotland in 1740; in 1741 43 more were sent over. There were 163 persons at Frederica, not including Oglethorpe's reduced regiment. In Savannah, the population was reduced to 292, of whom 92 were German servants. The most industrious settlement was Ebenezer, with its 195 Salzburgers. There were small pockets of settlers at Village Bluff, St. Simon, Jekyll, Abercorn, Hampstead, and Highgate. In addition, there were 105 men, women, and children at the Reverend George Whitefield's orphan house. The total population of Georgia was 1,278, of whom 570 were non-British. Nearly 2,000 had been sent over to Georgia on charity. If those who paid their own way were added, it appears that about half the number of those who had migrated to Georgia were still there by June 1741. [61]

Of all the Georgia settlements, Augusta showed the most promise. William Stephens, the Trustees' diligent reporter, noted that six hundred men gathered there in 1740 for the spring rendezvous of the traders, and five large boats made regular runs to and from Charlestown. The Trustees' critics thought that Stephens counted too many traders, but they acknowledged that there were thirty or more resident storekeepers in the town. The old gathering place at Fort Moore was practically abandoned. Thomas Causton explained, "All the inhabitants which dwelt on the Carolina side of the river called New Windsor or Fort Moore are removed from thence and are become inhabitants of the town of Augusta." Carolina continued to maintain a garrison at Fort Moore, but the commanding officer admitted that there was little for them to do. He recorded only four residents in 1743.[62]

Many of the principal traders were men of standing and ability, but the lesser traders they employed and the packhorsemen were a rough lot. The Trustees were informed that in the year 1741 the traders were lawless runaways from Carolina who disputed Captain Richard Kent's authority on the grounds that his appointment came solely from Oglethorpe and not from the body of Trustees.[63]

Upon hearing this news, the Trustees officially ratified Kent's appointment as captain and magistrate. Kent's conduct gained more respect for him than any action of the Trustees. While Oglethorpe was besieging St. Augustine, some unlicensed traders among the Creeks attacked others holding Georgia licenses. Kent boldly led his Augusta garrison into the Indian country in search of the culprits. He arrested three of the troublemakers and brought them down to Savannah for trial. That decisive action impressed the traders and lessened what William Stephens called their continual "jangling." Kent's status was measurably bolstered when Oglethorpe increased his command from twelve to twenty in April 1741.[64]

It was of immediate relevance to the career of Lachlan McGillivray that the largest company trading to the Creek Nation was the one headed by Archibald McGillivray. Partners in the trade were Daniel Clark, a neighbor from Strathnairn in the old country, Jeremiah Knott, William Sludders, and George Cussings. The company employed about twenty packhorsemen and owned 123 horses. Eight more men and 60 horses were added in 1741 when Alexander Wood and Patrick Brown joined McGillivray and Company. A notice in the *South Carolina Gazette* made it clear that Archibald McGillivray was the sole manager and director of the company.[65]

The prominence of Archibald McGillivray and the presence of other kinsmen in Charlestown aided in the twenty-one-year-old Lachlan McGillivray's decision to seek his fortune in Charlestown. There were other reasons. Highlanders were loyal to their chiefs, and the Darien Scots had lost their leaders at Mosa. John Mohr Mackintosh was a prisoner in Spain; others were dead or in prison. The beloved minister John McLeod abandoned his declining flock and moved to Charlestown, telling all who would listen that there was no hope for Darien. The Trustees disliked discouraging news and put McLeod down as disloyal. Lachlan's cousin to whom he had been indentured for his passage, John Mackintosh of Holme, went to Charlestown. Mackintosh of Holme was important enough to rate notice in Lord Egmont's journal; under the date October 21, 1740, he noted that "John Holmes Mackintosh had quitted Darien to settle in Carolina."[66]

The most important member of Clan Chattan to leave Georgia in 1740 was Captain Aeneas Mackintosh, commander at Fort Palachacola. His reasons had nothing to do with the dissolution of the Darien community. His brother William, chief of the Clan of the Cat, died on September 24, 1740, and Aeneas succeeded to the title of Mackintosh of Mackintosh. Captain Aeneas had served James Oglethorpe faithfully and well, and Oglethorpe wrote a generous recommendation to Duncan Forbes, lord president of the Court of Sessions at Inverness. "His long absence from his Country is the only reason that makes it necessary for me to recommend him, for otherwise his birth, being the Laird of Mackintosh's Brother, is such as would have made recommendation entirely needless."[67] Soon after returning to the Highlands, on February 13, 1741, Aeneas married the beautiful and high-spirited Anne, daughter of John Farquharson of Invercauld. Aeneas joined the famous Black Watch Regiment and kept his rank, but Anne would be celebrated throughout the Highlands as "Colonel Anne" when she rallied Clan Chattan for Bonnie Prince Charlie.[68]

35

Lachlan McGillivray found ready acceptance in Charlestown. The community of Scots was well established. The St. Andrew's Society was organized in 1729; the Indian merchant John McGillivray, who later settled in Augusta, was a charter member. The "Scotch" Presbyterian church was founded in 1731. One historian of early Charlestown has written that the Scots tended to prefer the company of fellow Scots to association with other people. They were the envy of many inhabitants and sometimes the objects of ill will. When James Glen, another Scot, became governor of South Carolina in 1743, it was thought that he especially favored his countrymen.[69]

When McGillivray went there in 1740, Charlestown was recovering from a disastrous fire that had destroyed more than three hundred buildings. New regulations required the exteriors to be constructed of brick or stone. A more handsome town arose on the ashes of the old. The prevailing style was the single house, one room wide and two or three rooms deep. Those who could afford to do so used the adjacent lot as a garden and entry way and constructed porches or piazzas overlooking the yard. The buildings were eloquent testimony to the affluence of Charlestown. The Indian trade, the first enterprise of the colony, was supplemented by a profitable rice and indigo production. Increasing numbers of slaves were imported to work the scattered plantations. The Stono Revolt in 1739 indicated that white fears of slave uprisings were well founded. Charlestown society was based on commerce and bent on pleasure. The town had a racetrack, a theater, and a multiplicity of social clubs. There were dozens of opportunities for a young, ambitious man. Lachlan's brother Alexander, who seems to have come directly to Charlestown and not by way of Darien, began a career as a successful sea captain. Farquhar, Lachlan's cousin, was a carpenter and a Presbyterian minister.[70]

The Indian trade was to be Lachlan's destiny, not only because of his well-placed connections in that business but also, and perhaps mainly, because he had mastered the language of the Creeks by 1741. It is not known whether he accompanied one of Archibald McGillivray's caravans before June 1741, but it is likely that he did. When he launched his career on June 12, 1741, he was already recognized as a competent interpreter.

Although the South Carolina Assembly was concerned about the Spanish threat to the south and had sent Colonel Alexander Vanderdussen with four hundred men to assist Oglethorpe in his abortive campaign, the designs of the French in the west were a cause of greater anxiety. The Carolinians were convinced that Bienville's 1740 expedition was meant to open a path to the conquest of Carolina by way of the Tennessee River. The focal point of their concern was Fort Toulouse, the "Alabamas Fort." The French used the base to spread their propaganda throughout the Creek country. On infrequent crisis occasions, the South Carolina Assembly was willing to spend money on diplomatic missions to the Indians. In 1741, James Bullock was selected to visit the Creek towns and to confirm the friendship of the Indians by the time-tested method of distribution of presents. Bullock was a respected trader, a Scotsman, and a charter member of the St. Andrews Society. He knew the McGillivrays and was willing to do a favor for Archibald McGillivray's young kinsman. Lachlan McGillivray, aged twenty-two, was signed on to the Bullock expedition as an interpreter; he served from June 12 until October 13, 1741, and was paid £45 for his work.[71]

Bullock's mission stirred jealousies in Georgia. Richard Kent in Augusta notified Oglethorpe about Bullock's activities. William Stephens in Savannah was alarmed and Oglethorpe almost as annoyed as if Bullock were in the employ of the Spanish. Faithful Captain George Dunbar was dispatched into the backcountry to spy on the Carolinians. Stephens noted in his journal that Oglethorpe instructed Dunbar "to have a watchful eye upon what that agent was doing and how far he was breaking into the Rights of this Province." While Dunbar was about it, he was also "to learn how the French behaved."[72]

Dunbar was delayed by a severe illness he contracted in Augusta. In fact, the *South Carolina Gazette* reported that he was dead and wrote a succinct eulogy: "He was an experienced and brave officer, and an indefatigable friend to his country-men who were transported from

Scotland under his direction, anno 1735, settled at Darien, anno 1735–1736, and were destroyed at Mosa, anno 1740." The last clause was a slap at Oglethorpe, whom the Carolinians blamed for the failure of the Florida campaign.[73]

Dunbar recovered and carried out his assignment, a Georgia spy watching a Carolina spy, both of them Scots. If Dunbar encountered his young countryman McGillivray and his older countryman Bullock, he might have felt reassured about the integrity of the Carolinians. Bullock's report on his excursion into the Creek country is missing along with the other records of the Indian commissioners that made up the second volume of the Carolina "Indian Book." The French archives, however, reveal the main outlines of the events in the Indian country at that time. On February 18, 1742, Bienville wrote that the Lower Creeks at Coweta had refused the presents offered by the governor of Carolina. The Carolinians were said to have attempted to persuade the Cowetas to join the war against the Spanish. If true, this was information of importance to Oglethorpe. If Bullock's mission was to solicit help for Oglethorpe, it is passing strange that Oglethorpe had to send agents on a covert operation to find out about it.[74]

Whether Bullock was responsible for it or not, an important Upper Creek chief went to Savannah in June 1741 to see Oglethorpe. The chief was called "the Wolf" by the English; his village was Muccolossus on the Tallapoosa River, not far from Fort Toulouse. The Wolf had proven his loyalty the year before, when d'Erneville, the commandant at the French fort, had promised rum and goods to any Indian who would destroy John Spencer's trading house at Muccolossus. When eager warriors in war paint approached Spencer's house, they found the Wolf there, threatening to shoot the first man who came closer. There were no takers for d'Erneville's bribes.[75]

Richard Kent was pleased to escort the Wolf to Savannah, and William Stephens tried his skill at giving talks and considered his first try a success. He simply repeated over and over variations on the theme that the good king across the water would never desert his faithful friends, only, as he phrased it, "a little diversified in Expressions" each time. The Wolf went on to Frederica for his interview with Oglethorpe "in mighty good Humour."[76]

In July, Oglethorpe received a large delegation of Lower Creeks, headed by Chigilly, chief of the Cowetas, eight other headmen, twenty-five warriors, and fourteen attendants. They stayed a month to prove their friendship and promised to send a large number of men to fight against the Spaniards.[77]

Although the Upper and Lower Creeks were distracted by an outbreak of hostilities with the Cherokees, they managed to keep their pledge to Oglethorpe. A succession of war parties made the long march to Florida. From his stronghold in Frederica, the general reported to the Trustees that the Indians kept the Spaniards and their Indians shut up in St. Augustine. There was little else that Oglethorpe could boast about in 1741.[78]

That the Creeks helped the Georgians lends credence to the French report that the purpose of the Carolina mission was to persuade them to do so. Bullock's efforts were important because the Creek war parties prevented the Indian allies of Spain from harassing a grievously weakened Georgia. So Lachlan McGillivray served his apprenticeship in Indian diplomacy on a productive mission. In a remarkably short time he became one of the most skillful of the diplomats of the forest.

McGillivray must have learned a lesson in how not to behave from an episode that happened just before he joined Bullock. An English baronet, Sir Richard Everard, went on a curious mission. He was a guest of one of Augusta's earliest settlers, Kennedy O'Brien, when he decided to pay a visit to Coweta town. O'Brien's financial backing enabled Everard to make the journey in the style to which he was accustomed. He was greeted by Chigilly with the usual hospitality. Everard explained that he was a person of distinction, a beloved man of King George himself. The chief was impressed and summoned his "beloved men" to listen to the important guest. Everard was such a novice that he did not know that a good talk was expected. He was asked if he brought a talk from the king. "No," he replied. "What brought you here?" the Indians wanted to know. The dandy replied that he had come to lie with their women. Chigilly told Everard that when his daughters wanted a husband, he would send for him and abruptly terminated the meeting. Sir Richard was the laughingstock of Georgia for the rest of his short stay in the colony.[79]

CHAPTER THREE

The Clan Chattan Connection

In the first years of Lachlan McGillivray's apprenticeship in the trading business, the Clan Chattan connection linked far-flung and disparate events. Members of the clan engaged in a cold war against the French in the Upper Creek country, against the Spaniards along the Georgia-Florida frontier, and in Scotland they rallied to the banner of Prince Charles Edward Stuart and did battle against the English, who supported the Hanoverians. In America they served the king; in Britain they fought him.

It is difficult to reconcile the traditional version of Lachlan's introduction into the trade with his service as interpreter under Bullock. Albert J. Pickett is the authority for the story that the boy Lachlan was taken along on a caravan to the Chattahoochee by a trader who was so pleased with the young man's services that he gave him a jackknife. Lachlan swapped the knife for an Indian's deerskins, which he sold in Charlestown and thus began to lay the foundation for his fortune.[1] Pickett's source for much of what he knew about the McGillivrays was Lachlan's grandson, and so there must have been some basis for the tradition. One of Pickett's contemporaries, Thomas Woodward, drew upon his acquaintance with Lachlan's granddaughters, as well as his conversations with veteran traders, to reveal the names of Lachlan's first sponsors. According to him, they were Malcolm McPherson and

Daniel McDonald, both Scots. Both were Clan Chattan names. Woodward's statement that Oglethorpe had employed McPherson earlier as a courier to the Creeks might indicate that he and possibly McDonald were among the Darien settlers. Daniel McDonald later changed his name to McGillivray, perhaps to identify himself more closely with the clan. Very likely, both McPherson and McDonald were employees of Archibald McGillivray and Company.[2]

Archibald McGillivray intended to return to Scotland in 1740, according to notices he posted in the *South Carolina Gazette*.[3] He changed his mind and postponed his departure for four years. Was his wish to accommodate the Darien Scots a reason for the delay? Clan loyalty ran deep. Archibald would have done his duty for his kinsmen. He would have been especially solicitous for Lachlan, the nephew of the chief of the McGillivrays.

There are other tantalizing clues to a connection between Archibald and Lachlan. In 1759 a veteran observer of Indian affairs commented that Lachlan McGillivray's privileged position among the Upper Creeks had made him and his "family" wealthy for the previous thirty years. Lachlan's license to trade dated from 1744. Archibald McGillivray, or a member of his company, held the license before that. A final coincidence was that 1744, when Lachlan was awarded the coveted license by the legislature, was the year Archibald renewed his notice that he would depart the province.[4] A Charlestown merchant who had done business with McGillivray for some years noted his departure in a letter to a brother in London, adding that he was "a Good plain sort of a Man and always kept his Credit exceeding well here."[5] By his industry he had accumulated a small fortune. McGillivray reached Scotland in a fateful year for his relatives and for Clan Chattan. In August, Bonnie Prince Charlie raised his standard at Glenfinnan and the McGillivrays rallied to the martial squeal of the bagpipe.

If Archibald had left Scotland in his twenties after the 1715 affair, he would have been in his fifties for the second rising of the clans. There is no evidence that he took up the claymore for Prince Charles. Instead, he married Lucy McIntosh and purchased an estate in Strathnairn. The contract was drawn up in 1749 between Archibald, formerly of South Carolina, and Aeneas Mackintosh, "Captain of Clan Chattan" and former captain of Oglethorpe's rangers. Archibald obtained the town and lands of Daviot in the valley of the Nairn for the princely sum of £10,180. He and Lucy raised three sons, James, Alexander, and Lachlan, and one daughter, Janet. James and Lachlan, like their father, went to America to seek their fortunes.[6]

A convincing clue to a connection between Lachlan and Archibald is that Lachlan remembered his benefactor in a will he drew up in 1767. He also included a bequest of £500 to Lachlan McGillivray, son of Archibald of Daviot. We may assume that Lachlan considered this younger Lachlan his namesake.[7]

As an apprentice in the company headed by Archibald McGillivray, Lachlan learned not only the technique of trade but valuable lessons about the arcane world of international intrigue. McGillivray's men lived in the principal Creek towns and were in a position to observe and influence events. During the winter of 1742 English traders among the Upper Creeks prodded the Abeikas on the Coosa River into a war with the Choctaws to divert the Choctaws from their unrelenting campaign against the Chickasaws.[8] Then the English prepared for the inevitable retaliation by rebuilding a fort near Okfuskee town.

Such a fort was a long-held ambition of the Carolina traders. The French had taken advantage of the cessation of English trade during the 1716 Yamassee War to open a trade with the Alabamas. The French were diplomats enough to insist that they needed a post from which to distribute goods. The fort would be for the Indians' welfare; it would not serve as an instrument of oppression. Only a month after a French party had begun building the fort in 1717, an English peace mission headed by Theophilus Hastings reached the Upper Creek country with the intention of building a fort. "If I had arrived one month later . . . the English would have won the [Creek] Country," reported Lieutenant La Tour Vitral.[9] The place was well chosen, just below the hill country along the lower trading road which led eastward to Fort Moore on the Savannah River. To the west the path forked, one path leading northerly to the Chickasaws and the other to the Choctaws. Charlestown was twenty-seven days distant by packhorse. Mobile was only five days downstream by boat; however, the upriver voyage required twenty days of hard rowing. In the summer months the river was frequently too low for the large flatboats. When the naturalist William Bartram visited the site in 1776, he was impressed by the fertility of the soil and the potential of the place as a commercial center. Although the Tallapoosa was a comparatively short river, the Coosa drained out of the Appalachian Mountains and connected the Cherokee country to that of the Creeks. Bartram noted that "this is perhaps one of the most eligible situations for a city in the world, a level plain between the conflux of two majestic rivers." [10] The gentle Quaker was nearly right in his prediction; the modern city of Montgomery grew up just below the confluence of the two rivers. In 1989 a historical park featuring a replica of Fort Toulouse occupied the site. The narrow neck between the two rivers is only five hundred yards wide at this point. The original fort overlooked a high bluff on the Coosa River side just above the point where the Tallapoosa joined the Coosa.

The Charlestown traders regarded the construction of the fort as an intrusion that deprived them of a major share of their business. In answering a query posed by the Lords Commissioners of Trade in 1719, they stated that because of Fort Toulouse, "we lost the Trade of the Chickasaws, Alabamas, Taliboose and Abicaws and other nations of whose trade we were possessed of for above thirty years." [11]

They had an additional complaint in 1720, when Colonel John Barnwell acted as their spokesman in a report to Lord Charles Townshend. The French had established New Orleans in 1718 to strengthen their position in the interior. According to Barnwell, most of the French had been dispersed among the Indians where "they live after the maner [sic] of Savages." He and his associates were convinced that the object of the French strategy was to conquer Carolina. He recommended building several forts, including one near Fort Toulouse. [12]

No English fort was built in the Upper Creek country until the energetic Patrick Mackay, acting as Oglethorpe's agent, obtained consent from the Upper Creeks to construct a shelter for the traders' protection in 1735. Lieutenant Anthony Willy was in charge of the construction of the fort, which was little more than a stockaded trading post at the

Southern Colonial Frontier

TENNESSEE

NORTH CAROLINA

Overhill Cherokee **Middle Cherokee**

Lower Cherokee

Tennessee River

Broad River

Catawba R.

ALABAMA

Coosa River

Tallapoosa R.

R.

GEORGIA

Saluda

Ninety-Six

Saluda River

Santee R.

Upper Creeks

SOUTH CAROLINA

Augusta

Oconee River

Ogeechee River

Savannah R.

Charlestown

Fort Toulouse

Lower Creeks

Alabama R.

Chattahoochee R.

Flint River

Ocmulgee River

Altamaha R.

Savannah

ATLANTIC OCEAN

Satilla R.

St. Marys R.

Pensacola

Apalachicola R.

FLORIDA

St. Augustine

St. Johns R.

N

| 0 | 50 | 100 Miles |
| 0 | 50 | 100 Kilometers |

Present state boundaries are shown for reference.
Cartographic Services Laboratory, The University of Georgia.

Okfuskee village on the Tallapoosa River, a prudent forty miles from Fort Toulouse. For three years Willy commanded the three-man garrison. The outpost was within the jurisdiction of Captain Richard Kent of Augusta after 1739 but was not occupied. By 1742 the place was in ruins.[13] That year the English instigated hostilities between the Upper Creek Abihkas and the Choctaws. Surprisingly, because a novice trader was not supposed to influence major projects, the initiative in the chain of events that culminated in a new fort lay with Lachlan McGillivray.

Early in 1743 Lachlan McGillivray had begun trading in the Upper Creek village of the Wacocoys, situated on a creek that flowed into the Coosa. He wrote a letter to Alexander Wood, the partner of Archibald McGillivray. Wood enclosed McGillivray's letter with one of his own, dated March 20, 1743, and addressed it to Lieutenant Governor William Bull of South Carolina. The letters urged the government to rebuild a fort for the protection of the traders. Daniel Clark, a Strathnairn Scot trading at Coosa town, an old friend of Archibald's and a new friend of Lachlan's, had written the governor a letter even earlier, on February 7, but it was Wood's letter that brought action from William Bull and his council. The governor invited a delegation of headmen of the Upper Creek towns to meet with him in Charlestown. They not only consented to an English fort in their country, they offered to help build it.

A new urgency was felt when Daniel Clark's letter of October 31, 1743, told of the slaying of three white traders to the Chickasaws by the French-allied Choctaws. Bull and his council unanimously agreed to the necessity of building a fort and commissioned Wood to select a site and start work. Wood chose Okfuskee, the site of Anthony Willy's earlier stockaded post.[14]

Unfortunately for Wood, the Commons House of Assembly did not view the crisis in the same light as Bull did. The lieutenant governor was a popular figure in Carolina during the five years he acted as governor. The Commons House was so comfortable with his cautious use of authority that it did not hesitate to contradict him. On December 10, Bull informed the legislature of what he had done. Building tools and material to the amount of £250 had been dispatched to Wood. Bull did not doubt that the assembly would provide the funds.[15]

On December 15 the House Committee on Indian Affairs announced that it did not agree that a fort was necessary and advised Bull to tell the builders that they would get no money. Alarmed, Bull pleaded with the House to fund the project. A war with France was inevitable, and the traders' need for protection would then be even greater. The House grudgingly agreed to pay £250 but warned Bull not to expect any further appropriation for either building or garrisoning the fort.[16]

The matter of the fort was shunted aside as the assembly prepared to receive the long-awaited governor. James Glen arrived in Charlestown on December 17, 1743, to the acclamation of the crowds. The members of government were so concerned that he receive a proper reception that they forgot to thank the conscientious William Bull for his five years of service. An early South Carolina historian described Glen as "a man of considerable knowledge, courteous and polite; exceedingly fond of military parade and ostentation."[17] Oglethorpe's departure in July 1743 gave Glen control of Indian affairs on the southern frontier.

Alexander Wood, already in disfavor with the Commons House, got off to a bad start with the new governor. His letters of March 20 and 22, 1744, to William Bull described how he had sent out a hundred Creeks after Choctaw scalps. The French paid for Chickasaw scalps; he wanted the government to reward the Creeks for bringing in Choctaw scalps. Whatever William Bull might have thought of the policy of buying scalps, James Glen was shocked, and his council was "filled with equal surprize and displeasure." Wood's action was "unwarrantable," and he was ordered to report to Glen forthwith. Furthermore, the tools that were sent for erecting the fort were government property, and Wood was responsible for returning them.[18] Thus Lachlan McGillivray was introduced to the perils of public service. The traders on the frontier might do their best for king and country as they conceived it and then suffer from the mistrust and suspicion of those from whom they expected praise and gratitude. Alexander Wood, probably discouraged by the government's failure to support him, decided to retire from the trade in 1744, the same year Archibald McGillivray announced his departure from Carolina. Although these two giants of the company withdrew, the company remained in business under the leadership of Patrick Brown. Veterans William Sludders, George Cussings, and Jeremiah Knott were still active. Brown held the license to trade with seven Upper Creek towns, though he spent most of his time in Augusta. He continued to hold the license even after acquiring an indigo plantation on the Savannah River some miles below Augusta in 1747. Important recruits to the company were two traders licensed to the Lower Creeks, John Rae and George Galphin, both of whom became lifelong friends of Lachlan McGillivray.[19]

Although the company continued to do its importing and exporting through Charlestown merchants, it established its stores in Augusta. Oglethorpe's effort to wrest control of the Indian trade away from Carolina had resulted in a compromise. The king's Privy Council ruled in 1741 that one-half of the traders operating in Georgia could be licensed in Carolina and that those with Georgia licenses could trade in Carolina. By that year, the settlement around Fort Moore on the Carolina side was almost deserted. One reason for the rapid increase in Augusta's population at the expense of Fort Moore was that the excellent leadership provided by Captain Richard Kent contrasted with the arbitrary conduct of Captain Daniel Pepper at Fort Moore.[20]

James Glen had hardly settled comfortably in Charlestown when he was forced to listen to the complaints of the few remaining residents of the New Windsor district, in which Fort Moore was located. Martin Campbell, an employee of Samuel Eveleigh, and Jeremiah Knott of the McGillivray company were the leading traders with grievances against Captain Pepper. Pepper was accused of rustling cattle and changing the brands, "criminal conversations" with other men's wives, putting people in stocks for trivial offenses, and setting soldiers to work on his own farm. The governor and council decided to remove Pepper as justice of the peace, but they left him in command of the tiny garrison at Fort Moore. In a strained effort to be even-handed, they also removed Campbell from his office as justice of the peace. He was reprimanded for having waited until Glen arrived to press his charges, and this reflected a lack of confidence in Lieutenant Governor Bull.[21] Martin Campbell cannot be blamed for moving to Augusta, to be joined there by his partner Francis McCartan.

Augusta offered other attractions to the Carolina traders. Those embarrassed by debt were safely outside the jurisdiction of South Carolina. Best of all for enterprising individuals, there was a power vacuum in the frontier colony after the departure of the dynamic Oglethorpe in 1743. President William Stephens and his council in Savannah had only the vaguest notion of what went on in Augusta. The Trustees suspected with good reason that their regulations were not enforced there. On May 10, 1743, Benjamin Martyn wrote Stephens on behalf of the Trustees that he had done well to withhold the bounty on corn from the Augustans: "The Traders and Inhabitants are rich and have many Servants, nay and have (as the Trustees have great Reason to believe) unlawfully employed Negroes on their Plantations."[22] It was equally doubtful that the Trustees' ban on rum was honored before that restriction was removed in 1743. Augusta was a unique community in Georgia, and as happened with other frontier settlements, an orderly society gradually evolved. The first traders stopped quarreling and began cooperating. Under the leadership of Patrick Brown and John Rae, seven companies combined into one, styled Brown, Rae and Company. Rae, one of Augusta's pioneer settlers, continued to be active after Patrick Brown retired to his indigo plantation. Neglect by government proved salutary for the company. A law unto themselves, members were referred to as "the Gentlemen of Augusta" and were regarded with envy by the Trustees' representatives in Savannah and with annoyance by the authorities in South Carolina.

Augusta was Lachlan McGillivray's base of operations. He outfitted his packhorses there and followed the long trail across Georgia to the Upper Creek country. At the Wacocoys village on the Coosa River, he was beyond the protection of Richard Kent's company of rangers. The fort at Okfuskee built by his brothers of the company was useless without its own garrison, and it was miles away on the Tallapoosa. The French at Toulouse were nearby and represented a very real threat. McGillivray's village was a listening post for the distant British officials. The outposts of two empires met on the Coosa River.

Sieur de Bienville sailed for France in 1743, the year of Oglethorpe's departure from Georgia and Glen's arrival in South Carolina. He left New Orleans with a cloud over his reputation for the failure of his two costly expeditions against the Chickasaws. His successor, the Marquis de Vaudreuil, was quick to learn the intricacies of forest diplomacy. He wrote to his superior that the English traders had an advantage over the French because of the trifles they traded—mirrors, ribbons, belts, buckles, and the like. The English could afford to give better prices than the French. Where the French would ask for five deer-skins, the English would accept only two. Vaudreuil made the same complaint against the English which Barnwell had expressed about the French in 1720. The English traders, said Vaudreuil, "make alliance with them by marrying their daughters and drinking and eating with them very familiarly." Vaudreuil could not bring himself to believe that the Indians actually liked the English better than the French. It was their "insinuating behavior" together with their trade advantage that enabled the English to maintain their position among the Creeks.[23]

Vaudreuil was intensely concerned about the construction of the Okfuskee fort. He detected that the Tallapoosas living near Okfuskee began to behave arrogantly when the construction started. He considered the advisability of sending French traders among the Tallapoosa villages, but there is no evidence that he did so. The English traders in those villages must have influenced the Indians to reject any French overtures.[24]

Vaudreuil was convinced that Bienville's long campaign against the Chickasaws had brought that beleaguered nation to its knees. He was not ready to grant easy conditions of peace. He sent word to the Chickasaws that the expulsion of the Natchez was no longer the pre-requisite for peace. The Chickasaws must expel the English traders. Although the Chickasaws would never consent to such a demand, the Choctaws intercepted three Chickasaw traders and killed them. Daniel

Clark's report of these murders was the spur that hastened the building of the Okfuskee fort.[25]

Lachlan McGillivray became an expert on the machinations of the French. He and the members of his company saw themselves as servants to the cause of king and country. Only a lingering suspicion that they also served their own interests prevented them from being regarded as heroes in Charlestown and Savannah. There was some truth in the suspicion. Richard Kent was convinced that Jeremiah Knott, the trader, and Charles Jordan, a packhorseman, both employees of Archibald McGillivray and Company, were guilty of trafficking with the enemy. They sold goods to the French at Fort Toulouse which were picked up by the Spaniards and brought to Florida. Jeremiah Knott prudently maintained his base of operations in New Windsor and kept his distance from Kent.[26]

The traders had an opportunity to win Kent's approval when the celebrated Christian Priber wandered into Tallapoosa town on his way to Fort Toulouse. Priber, a German philosopher and adventurer, had lived among the Cherokees for five years, adopting their style of dress and imitating their behavior. He praised the Indians' way of life as superior to the European and warned them against succumbing to the white man's vices. The English trader James Adair admired Priber's erudition and noted that Priber had compiled a Cherokee dictionary.[27] In this and in urging the Indians to establish their own republic, he anticipated Sequoya and John Ross by almost a century. According to a letter in the *South Carolina Gazette*, Priber was "a little ugly man" who planned to establish a town called Paradise.[28] Criminals, debtors, and even slaves would be welcomed in this mountain stronghold. Runaway slaves were particularly welcome. Priber was said to be emulating the Paulists in Brazil in their missions. The *Gazette* reported that among the "whimsical priviledges" of this town was a dissolution of marital restrictions.[29] South Carolina sent an agent to arrest this man with such dangerous ideas, but the Cherokees refused to give him up.

In 1743 Priber and a few companions left his Cherokee sanctuary and made their way toward Fort Toulouse. When he was within a day's journey of the fort, he decided that he was safely within the sphere of French influence and lodged overnight at Tallapoosa town. The English traders of the neighboring towns convinced the Creeks that Priber was an enemy; they took him into custody and delivered him to Captain Richard Kent in Augusta. Kent escorted the celebrity to Frederica, where Oglethorpe made him as comfortable as a prisoner in a garrison town could be. Priber amazed his many visitors with his erudition. A correspondent for the *South Carolina Gazette* noted, "It is a Pity so much Wit is applied to so bad Purposes."[30] Priber died in confinement at Frederica, and his manuscripts were lost. They contained, according to Adair, "a great deal that would have been very acceptable to the curious."[31] The Priber incident was an example of the traders' service to king and country.

Oglethorpe's brief encounter with the mysterious Priber came at the end of the general's Georgia career. Since the virtual dissolution of the original Darien community in 1740, other Highlanders had been recruited and the settlement survived because of the pay the men received as soldiers in the Independent Company of Foot. Oglethorpe and the Highlanders became heroes to the English world in July 1742, when they repulsed a Spanish invasion at the Battle of Bloody Marsh near Frederica on the island of St. Simon. For Oglethorpe, Bloody Marsh was a demonstration of his personal courage and the high point of his military career; for the scattered members of Clan Chattan, it was retribution for Fort Mosa.[32]

Though the luster of Bloody Marsh was dimmed by the failure of a second Florida invasion, Oglethorpe deserves credit for a psychological victory that counted for a great deal among the impressionable Indians as well as the timid-hearted who were abandoning Georgia. He faced down a foe who had superior numbers. Then, too, it was no small achievement to organize a successful march to St. Augustine and back. Georgians tried three times to do the same thing during the American Revolution and never crossed the St. Johns.

On July 23, 1743, Oglethorpe sailed for England. He had every reason to be discouraged. The Trustees' experimental soldier-settler colony was a failure. The Trustees had already removed the prohibition on rum and would soon permit slavery and liberalize land grants. A subordinate filed charges against Oglethorpe in England, claiming that he had appropriated public funds for his own use. His mood must have improved when he was cleared of all charges by a military hearing. It might be expected that his happiness was restored when he married the wealthy Elizabeth Wright in September 1744 and moved from his ancestral manor house at Godalming to her estate in Cranham.[33]

He was not permitted to linger long in wedded tranquility. The Scots, under Prince Charles Edward Stuart, invaded England in November 1745. It was an ironic destiny that linked Oglethorpe's career with the Highland Scots. They had been his best allies in Georgia; now they were his enemies. It is not out of place, in this narrative about Clan Chattan, to follow Oglethorpe on his new adventure. Among the clans that marched to the bagpipes were the Mackintoshes and Clan Chattan. Oglethorpe's friend Aeneas Mackintosh, chief of the clan, was not with them because he was a captain in the first royal Highland regiment, dubbed the Black Watch.

The Scots penetrated deeply into England. On December 4, 1745, they reached Derby, only 127 miles from London. It was at this juncture that King George and his court were said to be as struck with panic as if the wild McGillivrays were in the Strand.[34]

Oglethorpe, at the head of a regiment that included a company of Georgia rangers and accompanied by the faithful George Dunbar, now his aide-de-camp, was ordered to intercept the invaders at a village called Shap. The light-footed Scots got away. When the Duke of Cumberland learned about it he called out to Oglethorpe, "General Oglethorpe, had you done what I ordered you to do, few of these People would have escaped."[35]

Oglethorpe demanded and received a court-martial. The testimony of Dunbar and others revealed that Oglethorpe had not slept for five nights before he reached Shap, that he was so ill that night that his officers feared for his life, that the duke's orders reached him late, and that weapons had to be put in order as the result of rain and sleet the previous day. Besides, the Scots slipped out at 4:30 in the morning before any attack could have been launched. Oglethorpe was acquitted and in September 1747 was promoted to the rank of lieutenant general.[36]

The exoneration and promotion did not improve Oglethorpe's status in the opinion of the Duke of Cumberland. As long as the duke lived, Oglethorpe would never again command British troops. When Oglethorpe offered to raise a regiment in America during the Seven Years' War, he was ignored by Cumberland. Angry and frustrated, Oglethorpe adopted a pseudonym and fought as a volunteer under Frederick the Great.[37]

The retreating Scots defeated an army under General Henry Hawley in a driving rain at Falkirk, near Edinburgh. Hawley had erected gibbets in Edinburgh to hang the rebels; he used them to hang some of his own men for failure to fight.[38] The Highlanders returned to their native hills without hindrance. On February 16, Prince Charles visited Lady Anne Mackintosh at Moy Hall, sixteen miles from Inverness, and rested briefly before joining his troops in Inverness. There he was met by Lord George Murray's column, which had taken a longer route through Aberdeenshire. The Duke of Cumberland, trailing Lord George, decided to spend the rest of the winter at Aberdeen, punishing all the Jacobites he could catch.[39]

By April the weather improved, and the duke's army marched again, keeping to the coast where supply ships were within sight. The royal army forded the river Spey on April 12 and no great natural barrier lay between it and Inverness. On the fourteenth the bagpipes sounded through the streets of Inverness summoning out the Highlanders. With colors flying and pipes skirling, the Scots marched out to Culloden moor in Strathnairn to await the invaders. Provisions were always scarce in the Highlands after a long winter, and the six thousand who followed Prince Charles had little to eat except pathetic oat husks. The prince took a position guarding the road to Inverness instead of crossing the Nairn and taking advantage of the high ground as he had done at Falkirk.

The Highlanders spent the night before the battle in a fruitless attempt to surprise the enemy but only made exhausting marches along the river Nairn. The McGillivrays were on their native soil and acted as guides. Starvation and exhaustion winnowed the prince's army to five thousand as he again awaited the duke on the field of Culloden. Clan Chattan occupied a place of honor, the center of the front line. Because her husband, Aeneas, was serving with the royal Black Watch, Lady Anne asked Colonel Alexander McGillivray to command the Clan Chattan regiment.[40]

The duke was resolved not to repeat the mistakes of Falkirk. The Scots had learned to take the bayonet thrust on their targets and slash with their swords. The duke gave orders that each soldier should thrust, not at the foe in his face but the next one to the right. Cumberland intended to use artillery for as long as the enemy waited. He would not charge first. When the royal army was within five hundred paces of the Highlanders, the duke called a halt and the deadly cannonade began. The Highlanders stood it as long as they could. With a shout, Alexander McGillivray led the center forward, followed by the Camerons, Stuarts, Frasers, Macleans, and the other clans. The Macdonalds, at the extreme left, were the only clan to hold back. The men of Clan Chattan, hoarsely yelling "Loch Moy and Dunmaglass," bore the brunt of the attack. A man on the English side recalled that "they came running upon our front line like troops of hungry wolves." The wild charge was met with grapeshot from the cannon, musket fire from front and flank. The Highlanders cut through the English first line but were impaled by the bayonets of the second line. Colonel Alexander McGillivray was mortally wounded by a musket shot in the side. He crawled to a spring and there he died; ever since it has been called the Well of the Dead. Major John Mohr McGillivray rushed on past the enemy's cannons. It is said that he killed a dozen men with his broadsword before he was slain by halberd thrusts. The duke, when he heard of it, stated that he would have given money to spare the brave man's life. The Mackintoshes and McGillivrays fell in scores. Lady Anne Mackintosh later told Cumberland's men who arrested her that only three of her officers escaped, but the clan history lists eight who survived.[41] The bodies were buried in a shallow trench on the battlefield. Later, his relatives reinterred their slain chief in the church at Petty, near his residence at Gask in Strathnairn.

The McGillivrays could take some solace in the knowledge that they had fought as bravely as Highland men knew how. In 1810, Bishop Donald Mackintosh reported meeting a veteran of the English regiment that absorbed the force of the Clan Chattan charge; he was told that only fifteen Englishmen survived.[42] The people of Strathnairn were bound more closely than ever by ties of grief as well as kinship. The place where Alexander McGillivray fell would always be sacred. It is marked by a rugged stone bearing the inscription "Here fell McGillivray, Chief of Clan Chattan."[43]

The chiefdom devolved upon William, the younger brother of Alexander and still a minor. His uncle William MacIntosh of Holme managed the young laird's estates until William came of age.[44]

Although Lachlan McGillivray was an ocean away and deep in the wilderness, he was deeply stirred by the drama and the bloodletting of Culloden. Within a few years he named his only son, Alexander, after his slain chief. He corresponded with his cousin William, the new chief, urging him to come to America and join his relatives. As William grew older, Lachlan lectured him on the need to marry and have a son who would succeed him. Lachlan could not have known when he gave that advice that the responsibility for rearing the future chief in the traditions of his ancestors would fall to himself. Though Lachlan McGillivray's post was on the edges of the British colonial empire, he was bound by the Clan Chattan connection.

The Scots were an envied group in Charlestown until Culloden. After that, April 15 and 16 were celebrated as double holidays, one for Cumberland's birthday and the other for the anniversary of his great victory. Peter Timothy's *South Carolina Gazette* carried insulting references to the Highlanders. One genealogy traced the ancestry of the Jacobites to the devil. Another florid tribute to Cumberland warned that if ever the Highlanders again came out of their mountains "with hideous cries" the sight of Cumberland would cause them to fly back to their fastnesses "and growl for hunger in a brutal cave." A twelve-year-old boy's poem ended with the lines:

> Fight drink and sing for great George our King
> and a f   t for a Popish Pretender"[45]

On the two holidays, it was the custom to wear sprigs of Sweet Williams in honor of Duke William and to illuminate houses. Even though the Highlanders in America had proven their loyalty and would do so again and again, the annual taunting they endured each April drew them more closely together. That so many brethren of the trade were also kinsmen of Clan Chattan bound them in a network which contemporaries understood but latter-day historians have not recognized. Ties of blood and memories of Culloden united them and, ironically, challenged them to prove anew their loyalty to king and country.

CHAPTER FOUR

Outpost of Empire

Lachlan McGillivray was an intelligence agent on an outpost of the British Empire. He forged lasting friendships with fellow traders such as Daniel Clark, James Adair, and George Galphin. They were bound by the brotherhood of a common cause: they represented the great King George himself. The flag they raised over their trading houses established Britain's claim to that portion of the frontier. When Lachlan McGillivray first hoisted his flag over the Coosa River villages, it was by no means certain whether the colors of England or France would prevail.

The Indians who lived along the Coosa above its confluence with the Tallapoosa in the time of De Soto were the Cosasti or simply the Coosa. Since that time the Abeikas had moved in to occupy the best sites. The once prosperous Coosa town was nearly deserted, but it was still important enough to warrant a trading post, and McGillivray held the license to the "Old Town on the Coosaw River." Above that town on a tributary of the Coosa was the village of the Wacocoys, and above that was the Puckantallahasee town, both of which were McGillivray's villages. To the east, between the Coosa River system and that of the Tallapoosa, was McGillivray's largest town, that of the Okchoys. These people had originally lived near the site of Fort Toulouse, and some of them still lingered there, which facilitated rapid communication of

French activities. The nearest town to the east of the Okchoy settlement was the most important in the Upper Creek Nation, Okfuskee, the site of the much bruited but undistinguished traders' stockade. The Okfuskees occupied both sides of the Tallapoosa River, but it was considered a Coosa or an Abeika town rather than a Tallapoosa one. The Tallapoosa Indians lived downstream of the river of that name. The principal town was Tuckabatchee on the great bend of the river. Tallassee was situated nearby and Muccolossus farther down, only seven miles from the confluence with the Coosa, where stood Fort Toulouse.[1]

The origins of the town that became McGillivray's residence are not known. It is possible that the people of Little Tallassee were the Okchoys who remained behind when the rest of their people moved north. The name Little Tallassee does not appear until about the time McGillivray established his residence there. John R. Swanton gives its earliest dating in the records as 1750.[2] In that year McGillivray's towns included "Old Town on the Coosaw River." Several years later he referred to the settlement as "Weetomkee Old Town" and, parenthetically, "Little Tallassee." The modern town of Wetumpka preserves the old name, but the original village was several miles up the Coosa, above the falls.[3]

Little Tallassee was only nine miles from Fort Toulouse and at the head of navigation of the great river highway, strategically located both to observe river traffic and to monitor the activities of the French. Rumor was rife and gossip a favorite pastime in every Indian village, and there was more opportunity for rumor at Little Tallassee because of its location. That must have weighed heavily in McGillivray's choice of the town as his residence. The site he selected was a mile or so inland from the river, among gently rolling hills of clay and sand, typical of the southeastern piedmont. Today a large red quartz boulder marks the place where McGillivray built his house and planted a grove of apple trees.[4]

If McGillivray selected the place because of its proximity to Fort Toulouse, it tells us something about the boldness of his character. In 1744, the year he obtained his license, France was officially at war with England. Two great empires met on the Coosa River, one represented

59

by a garrisoned fort, the other by a plantation house in an apple grove. The Alabama Indians whose villages stretched along the river of that name below Fort Toulouse were securely in the French interest. French officials, from the governor in New Orleans to the commander of the Alabama Fort, had the firm and fixed intention of driving the English out of the Creek country or, better, taking their scalps. The combination of policy and proximity spelled danger for McGillivray, the most exposed of all the English, with the possible exception of Chickasaw traders such as John Campbell and James Adair. McGillivray knew the risk when he selected the town, and in his letters he expressed an awareness of serving king and country at his outpost. There were some cynics in Charlestown, and Edmond Atkin on the governor's council was one, who suspected that McGillivray's purpose in locating so near the French was to carry on a clandestine trade, but there is no evidence, other than Atkin's accusations, that there was any commercial activity during wartime. But it would be surprising if some of McGillivray's wares did not find their way through his customers to the needy French.

If the Okchoys inhabited Little Tallassee, McGillivray's Okchoy license would have justified his residence there. The Okchoys were staunch friends of Alexander Wood and therefore of the English. The Okchoy king visited Governor Glen in the summer of 1748 and agreed to lead an attack on Fort Toulouse. Nothing came of it, partly because the Okchoy king lacked the clout to bring it off and partly because he drank himself to death.[5] McGillivray took Wood's place as chief trader to the Okchoys. These people produced three remarkable leaders, two at Okchoy and one at Little Tallassee, during McGillivray's residence among them. The Mortar, also called the Wolf of Okchoys, had the greatest influence at first and used it to maintain an independent stance between the French and the English. McGillivray suspected him of being unduly influenced by the French. A rapidly rising second man was Enochtonachee, whose English name was the Gun Merchant. Both men would be key figures in the game of empire waged during the first decade of McGillivray's career as a trader. The third great man of the Okchoys lived at Little Tallassee. His name was Emistisiguo, and out of respect, the English called him by his own name. Emistisiguo was a young warrior when Lachlan McGillivray built his house at Little Tallassee. A pleasant association with McGillivray was a factor in Emistisiguo's continued loyalty to the English. Another friend of McGillivray was Devall's Landlord, headman of Puckantallahasee. It might have been more than coincidence that, as McGillivray's star rose in Charlestown, so did the status of the Gun Merchant, Devall's Landlord, and Emistisiguo. All three chiefs were awarded great medals by John Stuart, the Indian superintendent.

Whether they were large towns like Okfuskee or small ones like Little Tallassee, the Muskhogee villages were laid out in a common pattern. The center of the village was the square, with four principal buildings around the sides. The house of the mico, or chief, faced east. The front of this and the other houses was open, the other three sides daubed with clay. The house which faced south was that of the warriors. The Great Warrior sat nearest the mico's house, and the others were placed according to their standing as warriors. The lodge facing north was that of the council of beloved men. These men were honored for their war service or their wisdom. The fourth cabin was reserved for the young warriors. The mico met with his counselors and warriors every day, drank their black drink, and smoked their pipes.[6]

Sharing the pipe with the principal men of the village was no problem for white traders like McGillivray. Participation in the black drink ritual was another matter. John Innerarity, a Scotsman with connections to McGillivray, recorded his experience at Tuckabatchee town:

> A seat was assigned to me next the Big Warrior and the Black Drink was handed to me by the Cup Bearer. This beverage of which they seemed uncommonly fond resembles somewhat strong tea in its taste and odour, tho' considerably darker and is of a deleterious quality. It is prepared by the Young King who acts as a kind of Master of the Ceremony, and is handed to each Chief by the Cup Bearer in a long Calabash. The drinker after retaining it a few minutes vomits it up in successive retchings.[7]

The ability to project the regurgitated tea was a source of manly pride. If not the most important of the cultural differences McGillivray encountered, it was among the most curious.[8]

Iappa
Ozur R.
and Soto
red the
1541.

Route of
90 M.

since few
Tapouchas
Witoupo

Indian Traders in 1690
250 m.

Coulsa
Abecochee
A b e e c a

Chacchumas

he Misisipi

Puckantalla

Patagahatché R.

Cahelan R.

Weypulco
U P P E

C R E E

on this Riv.
alliance with the
for which they have
red destroyed by the French

Bougfuka

Skanapa

Chactahatché

Cabo R.

Talapo

Cowachitow

Tkechipouta

Tombecbe

Ayanabé

Angola R.

Ochlanta
Puecanta
Jackifgi
Ceygay Or.

Octiboa

Concha

Okelousa

Black Bluff

A l i

b a m o u

Censatee

Little

Conchachitou

C H A C T A W S

Nitahauritz

Savannas

G

Chicachae

Chactaw chief Town
Youana Lovest
Vill. of the Chactaws

R. of the Chicacha-ws

Coulsa R.

The English have Facto
& Settlements in all the
of the Creek Indians
note, except Albama
was usurped by the Fr
1715 but established by
English 28 years bef

Estiquache R.

Naniaba

Albama or

About 150 M. by Land
180 by Water, from
Mobile to Albama

the
o.

Mobiliens

Jordan R.

Apalaches
Ft. Conde
or Mobile

Pascagoula R.

Spanish Branch

Penfacola
B. R. Governador
R. del Almirant

B. St. Rose
St. Andrews B.

Biloci

Red Bluff

R. Perdido

B. St. Jos
Deer Pt.

B. de Mobile

Lagoona
Penfacola E.
P. St. Rose

St. Rose

C. Escondido
or
C. St. Blaise

I. Dauphin or Majaure
Mobile

20 feet Water over the

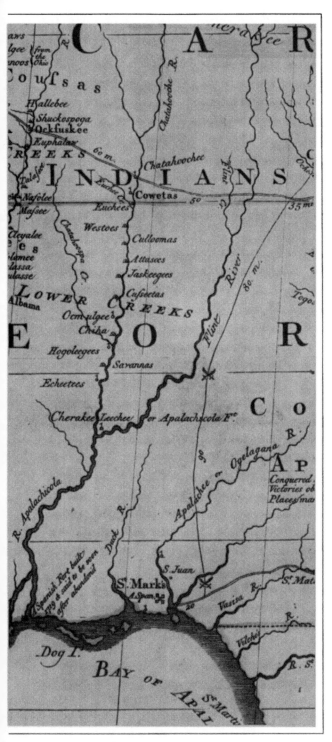

This John Mitchell map (1755) was the most accurate available at the time of the French and Indian War. (Hargrett Rare Book and Manuscript Library, University of Georgia)

Outside the square was the round structure which the traders called the "hothouse." The building was large enough to hold all the people of the village, who might assemble for dancing, singing, and gossip. A fire was kept alight in the center of the room.

Each year in May, the chiefs and headmen met at one of the towns. A large lodge was built for the occasion. Each delegate had an assigned place, and none could leave until the business before them was finished. The democratic nature of these assemblies impressed observers who returned to Europe to philosophize about universal natural laws and the rights of man.

The houses of the Indians themselves occupied smaller square lots. A more prosperous man would have buildings on all four sides of his lot. Like the mico, each had a summer lodge that served as a guest house for visitors. Couches of cane with cushions of skins lined the walls at a height of about four feet, high enough to be out of reach of the swarming fleas. What the Indians did about the ever-present southern cockroach, if recorded, is not known. The second structure was windowless and rounded with thick walls plastered inside and out, called the hothouse because a fire was kept burning during the winter. The third building was a storehouse for corn, potatoes, and other food; the fourth was a shed for deerskins and hunting equipment, or it might serve a different purpose such as a henhouse.[9]

Few Creek Indians bothered about gardens, but all of them worked in the fields outside the town. It was the job of the second man of the village (second only to the mico) to supervise the activities of the village. When he gave the appropriate whoop (there were whoops for every occasion), everyone turned out for the spring planting, and re-nowned warriors worked side by side with young boys and women. The warriors were careful, however, not to work up a sweat. Perspira-tion caused by work was somehow demeaning, but that which flowed from the stifling heat of the hothouses was purifying. After the general planting, the fields were marked off to each household. Cultivating and harvesting were done by each family on its own field. Little attention was paid to the crops, and weeds sometimes outgrew the corn, but the soil was good and the harvest ample.

Strawberries, grapes, and other fruit grew in abundance. Hogs, cattle, and chickens were plentiful. Indians were adept at fishing. They could spear fish with hand-held green cane sticks. Incredibly, they would hurl these canes like javelins and kill a swimming fish. They fished with their own kind of fishhooks, with nets and baskets.[10]

Their diet was varied by the yield of the forests. Wild turkey and deer were easy prey for the hunter. Bear and buffalo still roamed in great numbers. Barbecued bear meat was a delicacy, as were the tongue and hump of the buffalo. The Creeks, spoiled by the prodigal abundance of nature, were wasteful enough to kill the buffalo for its tongue and leave the rest to scavengers. They did their part in the extermination of the herds of the Old Southwest.[11]

Lachlan McGillivray had much to learn about the Indians' way of life. He knew the language, but he had to learn the rituals, become accustomed to the purgative black drink, the companionable rubric of the pipe, the meaning of the long silences, the hand signals, the grunts, and the superstitions. In time, he learned the art of conversation and became a master of it. Nothing was more highly esteemed by the Indians, except prowess at war, than the subtle intellectual give-and-take of a good talk. James Adair noted that "kind, persuasive language has an irresistible force, and never fails to overcome the manly and generous heart." [12] McGillivray was acknowledged by Adair as a master of persuasion.

Perhaps the most engaging quality of the Creeks was their hospitality toward strangers. A French visitor to the Abeikas wrote, "These Indians and their beautiful wives are very friendly. Upon landing among them you are greeted with a handshake and peace pipe. After you have smoked, they ask you the reason for your trip, the length of time you have been travelling, if you intend to stay a long time, and whether you have a wife and children." [13] The Wolf of Muccolossus was even more gracious to the Englishman Thomas Campbell. After the greetings, the chief required silence in order to rest and recollect, then he sent his visitors to bed. Questions would wait until morning.

McGillivray recognized and accepted the clan structure of the Creeks. It was similar to that of the Celts except that the Indian clans were matrilineal. Four of the principal clans were the Wind, the Tiger, the Bear, and the Eagle. The origin of the clan names was clouded in antiquity. The tribal storytellers explained that one time long ago a great cloud descended upon the land and the people walked in darkness. A kindly wind came down and dispelled the mist and gloom. The family that came out of the darkness before all the others and first saw the light of the sun became the Wind Clan, the most honored clan of all. When other families emerged from the fog, animals and birds accompanied them, and each family was named for the bird or beast that associated with it. Clan loyalty was stronger than town or tribal loyalty. The male was expected to select a wife from another clan, with the result that he was the only member of his family not a member of the clan. The brothers of the wife had a stronger claim on clan loyalty than did the husband. In one famous incident, a Chickasaw man, to avert a war, plunged a knife into his own throat because his guilty nephew, who had murdered a man, was afraid to kill himself.[14]

Because of intermarriage, there were people of all clans in every village. This was an incendiary condition which kept the Creek Nation poised on the brink of war. According to Adair, the Creeks did not like to go to war, and the beloved men would think of excellent reasons to avoid it. But all the best arguments would fail if clan members decided they had to revenge the death of a brother member. The Creeks believed that the shades of the dead would not be at peace until the death was avenged. According to Adair, the American Indians pursued revenge more avidly than any other people: "They say all nations not sunk in cowardice take revenge of blood before they can have rest." [15] The Indians understood perfectly well that one life taken meant another life forfeit. The English governors were coached by the traders to insist on a life for a life when treating with Indians.

The consuming desire for revenge played into the hands of the Europeans. If the French commander at Fort Toulouse wanted to provoke a war, he would bribe a few warriors to attack another tribe. The relatives of the slain would consider it a sacred duty to retaliate by taking the lives of the aggressors. If they succeeded, the clan members of the first party would keep the war going. Most war parties consisted of from two to twenty warriors. The head warrior would gather as many volunteers as he thought necessary (laggard volunteers were subject to scorn) and lead them through an elaborate ritual of fasting, self-painting, and invoking the Great Spirit which would have debilitated a white man. The warriors would set out, still fasting and resting only by sitting upright, along the trail to the enemy country. The greatest care would be taken to surprise the enemy, strike quickly, take a scalp, and run like the wind. Indians were capable of prodigious feats of endurance when their lives were at stake. Adair told of one brave who ran seventy miles at one stretch.[16]

Prisoners taken in war, if they were fortunate, would be adopted into the tribe to replace warriors who had been killed. Other captives might be forced to undergo a ritualized torture, fraught with meaning to the victim and his tormentors but excruciating nonetheless. The Creek treatment of enemy warriors was similar to that of the Iroquois and the Cherokees. The ceremony was conducted by the women of the village, who flayed and burned the victim in imaginative ways while he intoned his chant of defiance, even urging his enemies to inflict greater pain. The climax of the ritual occurred when, just before the victim expired, he was scalped and hot sand thrown on his exposed skull. Then he was dispatched with a blow of the hatchet. The religious significance was more obvious in the rest of the ceremony. The victim's flesh was boiled in kettles, and the whole village partook of the remains.[17] By McGillivray's time this treatment of captives had been virtually abandoned among the Creeks and Cherokees, and there is no evidence that McGillivray ever witnessed the grim ritual. Enemies were killed in battle, a terrible insult because their spirits were thus excluded from the villages of the dead. Scalps, not prisoners, were brought home in triumph.

The great object of war, other than revenge, was to live to boast about it. Rashness was expected in the young but not in the greatest warriors. If the expedition was a failure, the leader was blamed, if not for some obvious fault, then for some unsuspected impurity which of-

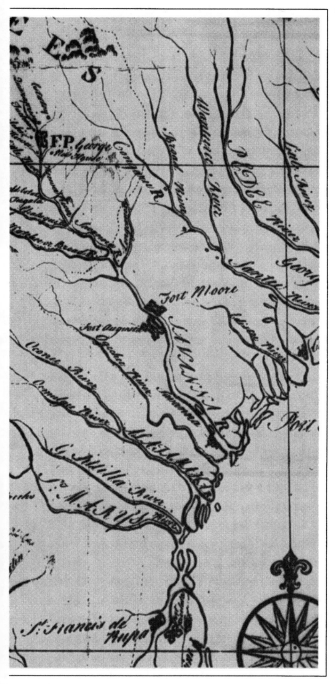

Taken from a 1766 copy of John Stuart's 1764 map, this map of the southern Indian country emphasizes the proximity of the colonial forts. (Hargrett Rare Book and Manuscript Library, University of Georgia)

fended the Great Spirit and brought bad luck. In that case, the leader would lose his badge of authority, the war whistle, and be demoted to a lower seat in the house of warriors.[18]

While learning the lore of his clients, Lachlan McGillivray must have found the lesson of love and romance of immediate interest. When he became the chief trader to his towns in 1744, he was twenty-five years old, tall, robust, and fair of complexion. We may assume that Indian women, like women everywhere, were attracted to handsome men. Handsome men who possessed the variety of presents that came in the trader's caravan had a decided advantage over the competition. McGillivray would not have lacked for female companionship. The micos of any of his towns would have provided him with young women as a common courtesy to an important visitor. It was no disgrace for an Indian maid to sleep with several men before marriage, but she had to be careful not to appear too promiscuous or she would not be chosen as a wife. When married, she was no longer free to bestow her favors on anyone but her mate.

The suitor would select the woman he wanted as his wife from a clan other than his. He was expected to follow a protocol as intricate as that practiced by the gentry of Virginia or Carolina. He never applied directly to the girl he admired. He would send his mother or sister or some other female relative to her female relatives. They, in turn, would consult his mother's brothers and uncles. As a courtesy they might inform her father, but his consent was not important because he was not a member of the clan. Neither would the prospective bridegroom be a member of the clan, but he would sire future clan members so he must be carefully screened. Almost as important as his ability to contribute to the gene pool was his ability to confer presents.[19]

The next step was the signal on the part of the girl's relatives that they were willing to receive gifts. The man sent whatever he could — furs, food, blankets. The more he sent, the better was his reputation as a provider. If his offerings were accepted, a great feast was prepared and the whole village invited. The next day the oldest man in the village presented the bride to her husband's parents. The husband might then take her to his house, but the marriage ceremony was not yet complete. He must plant a crop and harvest it and make a successful hunt and bring home the provender to prove that he was able to feed a family. During this trial period, the woman might leave the man without incurring blame, but once the crop was in and the hunt was over, she was bound. Adultery was strictly punished by cropping the ears of both parties and severely beating the woman. If the offenders could not be found, their nearest relatives were punished. The Wind Clan was especially strict in punishing adulterers.[20]

Divorce was a matter of mutual consent. In that case the woman kept her property and the children. The man could marry again immediately, but the woman had to wait until the end of the week-long ceremony of the busk at the end of the harvest season. All offenses were forgiven after the busk, and divorced women could make a new match.

The Creek custom of giving the mother absolute authority over the children must have been a problem to Scots like McGillivray, whose clans were male-dominated. He must have been of the same opinion as Benjamin Hawkins later in the century when confronted by an Indian woman who proposed marriage between Hawkins and her daughter. Hawkins explained that white men differed from red men in their treatment of children. If he had children, he would look upon them as his own, and the wife must allow him to bring them up as he pleased. She must accustom the children to obey him. "The woman I take must beside all this be kind, cleanly and good natured, and at all times pleasing and agreeable when in company with me or with those who visit at my house."[21] Lachlan McGillivray would have agreed with him, because he took responsibility for raising and educating his son and probably his daughters.

If there was more than a trace of calculation in a woman's choice of a mate, the same was true of the man's selection of the bride. It was in the best interest of the warrior, and more so of the trader, to marry into a prestigious clan and thereby to be assured of influential allies in the various towns. This calculation did not preclude the possibility of a genuine loving relationship any more than it did in the supposedly civilized parts of America. Lachlan McGillivray found both in Sehoy Marchand, a woman of the respected Wind Clan and the daughter of a French officer. Her brother was an Upper Creek chieftain named Red Shoes.[22]

There is some mystery about the identity of the man named Marchand. Albert Pickett, the Alabama historian, wrote that he was the commander of Fort Toulouse and was killed by his own men in a 1722 mutiny. Recent historians discount the story of his death. The officers were not killed by the mutineers, and there is no record of an officer named Marchand at the fort. There was, however, a Captain Marchand de Courtel who was commander of the Alabama district. He held this office from 1720 to 1723 and again from 1727 until 1729.[23] The Alabama Fort was in his jurisdiction, and he was probably the French officer who gave Sehoy Marchand her name. It was as common for Frenchmen in the Indian country to take Indian wives as it was for British traders. How well Sehoy knew her father or was exposed to European child-rearing habits is not known. Pickett obtained his information from Lachlan Durant, grandson of Lachlan and Sehoy, and penned a flattering picture of Sehoy as a maid of sixteen when she married, "cheerful in countenance, bewitching in looks and graceful in form."[24]

Although Sehoy Marchand is remembered in history mainly because she was a link between her famous son and the Wind Clan, she deserves mention for another reason. Unlike George Galphin, his friend in Coweta town on the Chattahoochee, who had wives in Ireland, in the Indian country, and at his plantation at Silver Bluff on the Savannah River, and unlike most of the traders who considered their Indian wives as temporary companions, Lachlan McGillivray regarded her as his mate and never took another. If she lacked some of the graces his Georgia friends admired, she made up for it by knowing how to entertain the many Indian friends who came to visit the McGillivrays. We can imagine that Sehoy possessed some of the qualities Benjamin Hawkins admired in the wife of the trader Richard Bailey. She shared the toils of her husband, even to the extent of swimming rivers while taking pack-horses to Augusta. She also presided at a neat, well-provisioned table. She was an efficient manager of her black domestics. She was kind to them all and firm when she had to be.[25]

The family tradition was that Sehoy, while pregnant with her first child, dreamed of piles of manuscripts, books, paper, and ink. The dream was prophetic because her son was to be the scholarly Alexander McGillivray. Lachlan gave him the name of the hero chief who died at the head of his clan at Culloden. In his own right, Alexander McGillivray was destined to become a greater chief than his namesake, though not so dashing a warrior. Pickett stated that Alexander was about thirty years old in 1778, which would have put his birth near 1748. Samuel Drake, writing in 1841, cited 1739 as the birth year. Historians have used various other dates. The matter is settled once and for all by Lachlan McGillivray's will, in which he gave Alexander's birth date as December 15, 1750.[26]

Was Alexander the first child? General Thomas Woodward, who was definite in all his opinions and wrong in some, believed that Lachlan's daughter Sophia was older than Alexander. Like Pickett, his contemporary, he obtained his information from Lachlan's grandchildren. His sources were Alexander's daughters, Margaret and Elizabeth. Pickett mentioned a second daughter named Jeannet. The name was appropriate because Lachlan's mother was Janet. The Frenchman Louis Milfort, Alexander's war general, married one of Lachlan's daughters, probably Jeannet. He described her as "a pretty girl, clad in a short silk petticoat, her chemise of fine linen clasped with silver, her earrings and bracelets of the same metal, and with bright-colored ribbons in her hair."[27]

Benjamin Hawkins, describing his tour of the Creek country in 1796, mentioned another sister. Her name was Sehoy, and she was the wife of Charles Weatherford and the mother of the Creek general of the War of 1812, William Weatherford. Woodward is positive that this Sehoy was not the daughter of Lachlan McGillivray but of his early associate Malcolm McPherson and that she was a blood relative of Georgia Senator John McPherson Berrien. She was reared in the house of Jacob Moniac, a trader, and lived for a time with Lachlan McGillivray's family. She first married David Taitt, deputy to Indian superintendents John Stuart and Thomas Brown. After Taitt left the Indian country in 1780, she married Charles Weatherford. She must have had a brother because Hawkins also mentions meeting a cousin of Alexander's named McFassion, the chief of the Little Tallassee people, who moved to a place called the Hickory Ground after Alexander's death. McFassion sounds like a Scottish rendition of McPherson. The chief and Sehoy McPherson were part of the extended family of Lachlan McGillivray, either because of his Clan Chattan connection with Malcolm McPherson or because of a clan relationship between Lachlan's Sehoy and the mother of Sehoy McPherson.[28]

Another source of confusion is Daniel McGillivray and his son the mixed-blood chief "Bit Nose Billy McGillivray." Daniel McGillivray is frequently mentioned in Alexander McGillivray's letters, chiefly as a messenger. When Hawkins met him, he was living with Alexander McGillivray's people at the Hickory Ground. Hawkins noted that the man was a native of Scotland, a former trader to the Choctaws, and, since the end of the Revolution, a resident among the Creeks. Again Thomas Woodward provides the answer to this McGillivray's identity. Daniel McDonald, who first accompanied Lachlan McGillivray to the Indian country, changed his name to McGillivray. There were McDonalds in Strathnairn who were members of Clan Chattan, and Daniel McDonald must have wanted to emphasize his kinship to the prominent McGillivrays. Lachlan remembered Daniel McGillivray in his will, made out in 1767, with a bequest of £100.[29]

The McGillivray household included black Polly Perryman, sold by the trader Theophilus Perryman to Lachlan McGillivray. Polly was a house servant when Lachlan's children were growing up and later lived with Alexander when he raised his family. After Alexander's death she was sold by William Panton to Jim Perryman. When the Creeks migrated to Arkansas in 1836, Polly was left with General Thomas Woodward. According to Woodward, she was very intelligent; she must have been a prime source for Woodward's intimate knowledge of the McGillivrays. Polly died in 1846 at the age of 115.[30]

The McGillivray family included relatives in Charlestown. Lachlan's brother Alexander married Elizabeth Patchabel, who bore a son in 1753, named William. Family tradition has it that Farquhar McGillivray became a Presbyterian minister, but there is no record of a McGillivray in the Scots Church records. Farquhar is mentioned as a cabinetmaker living on Elliott Street, Charlestown, in 1753.[31] When Lachlan's son

Alexander was fourteen, according to Pickett, he was entrusted to Farquhar's tutelage. Perhaps by then Farquhar had entered the ministry. Lachlan's brother Alexander must have made his part-Indian nephew welcome at his house. Early historians are as confusing as they are helpful in the details of Alexander's education. In 1841 Samuel Drake named the boy's tutors in Charlestown as Mr. Sheed and William Henderson. The latter taught Latin and later achieved some prominence as a literary critic in London. In 1855, Georgia historian George White repeated the names of the two teachers but located them in New York and said that the young Alexander went there to study. Actually, George Sheed was the writing master at the Charlestown free school and William Henderson the Latin teacher was in charge of the free school from 1753 to 1763. Alexander might have gone to New York with his father when the latter embarked for the "northward" in 1767, but there is no reason, other than White's reference, to believe that he went to school there. At age seventeen, Alexander was back in Savannah, working first with Samuel Elbert, a prominent Savannah merchant, and then with the firm of Alexander Inglis and Company.[32] By then, Lachlan had acquired a handsome plantation on the outskirts of Savannah, and Alexander resided there.

Most of those who attempted to describe Alexander McGillivray referred to his liberal education. He was said to be "well acquainted with all the most useful European sciences."[33] A visitor to Little Tallassee in 1791 referred to "an atticism of diction, aided by a liberal education."[34] Alone among those who described him, Thomas Woodward maintained that Alexander McGillivray could not write. According to Woodward, John Leslie wrote all McGillivray's letters. In this instance, Woodward relied too much on oral history. He did not have access to McGillivray's letters, including those to Leslie. John Pope marveled at the way McGillivray dashed off letters of elegant prose in the midst of many distractions.[35]

There is no doubt about Alexander's mastery of English. How well he knew the language of his mother is a question. Pickett said that sister Sophia could speak Muskhogean better than Alexander. Alexander was careful to employ an interpreter in important negotiations. Evidently he did not trust his own ability to translate English for his followers. This emphasis on a classical education means that Lachlan, unlike most traders, was intensely interested in his son's upbringing. The daughters would learn English, of course, but they would be treated much the same as if they had been reared in Strathnairn, that is, they would learn to manage the domestic affairs. Back in Scotland, Lachlan's sister Jean had to bring in the sheep at night because her husband considered manual work beneath him. (Lachlan scolded his sister for allowing that.) Lachlan's daughters in America would look after the livestock, work in the fields, and do the household chores. Sophia and the adopted sister Sehoy grew up to be strong-minded women who dominated their households. Jeannet, the pretty one who married Milfort the Frenchman, might have been more retiring; we hear no more about her after Milfort returned to France.[36]

The McGillivray family grew with the children's marriages. As mentioned, Jeannet married Louis Milfort, the adventurer. Milfort was Alexander's war general. In his account of his sojourn among the Creeks, Milfort puts his accomplishments in the best possible light and treats Alexander respectfully if not lovingly.[37]

Sophia married Benjamin Durant, whom Hawkins described as dark-skinned and a little stupid. Pickett painted a more favorable portrait, probably because his perspective was that of Lachlan Durant, Sophia's son. Benjamin Durant, a Carolinian of Huguenot ancestry, had a reputation for prodigious strength. Indians, as well as whites, loved tests of skill and dexterity. At Little Tallassee, Durant challenged a local champion, and an epic fight ensued. He won the match and also the affection of Sophia McGillivray, "a maiden beautiful in all respects," as Pickett saw her through her son's eyes. Although Pickett stated that Durant went on to become a wealthy man, his wealth was relative. Alexander stated that Sophia was rich only in Negro slaves. Benjamin Hawkins testified that neither the slaves nor Durant were much inclined to work. During the early years of their marriage, the Durants lived at Little Tallassee and for a while with Lachlan at his plantation outside Savannah. The Durants produced a tribe of children—Benjamin Hawkins counted eight survivors out of eleven in the year 1796.[38]

Sehoy, Malcolm McPherson's daughter, made a good match in David
Taitt. Taitt was one of the many Scots involved in the Indian trade and
may have been one of Lachlan's early associates, as Thomas Woodward asserted. Taitt was employed as a surveyor in West Florida from
1764 to 1767. After a two-year stay in England, he returned to become
John Stuart's deputy to the Creek Nation. In 1772, Stuart sent him on
an inspection tour of the Creek country. Taitt proved himself a loyal,
capable, and responsible agent; his journal is a classic study of the dis-
integration of the Indian trade on the eve of the Revolution. At the
outbreak of the war, Taitt remained in the Indian country as Stuart's
deputy and later as Thomas Brown's.[39] During this time he took Sehoy
as his wife and by her had a son who bore his name.[40] Although Thomas
Woodward was convinced that Taitt became deranged and died while
leading Indians to the relief of Thomas Brown's British garrison in
Augusta in 1781, Taitt's claim for compensation, filed in 1783, proves
that he survived the war.[41] He never returned to the Indian country,
and Sehoy took another mate, Charles Weatherford. Weatherford was
an unsavory character, but he fathered a famous son by Sehoy; William
Weatherford grew up to become the celebrated warrior Red Eagle who
fought against Andrew Jackson during the War of 1812.[42]

Alexander McGillivray took two wives: one was the daughter of
Jacob Moniac, the other the daughter of Joseph Cornell. Moniac and
Cornell both acted as interpreters for McGillivray, and both resided at
Little Tallassee. Alexander relied heavily on family connections when
he assumed the leadership of the Creek Nation. Taitt was a friend and
fellow deputy under John Stuart and Thomas Brown; Daniel McGillivray was a messenger; Moniac and Cornell were interpreters; Milfort,
his war leader. His mother's brother Red Shoes and the powerful Wind
Clan assured him of acceptance and support among the Upper Creek
towns. There was a subtle but powerful struggle in the soul of Alexander McGillivray between the two clans, that of the Wind and that of
the Cat, and two cultures, the Muskhogean and the Gaelic. Alexander
was unique, a successful misfit, too Scottish to be Creek and too Creek
to be British. His talents placed him far above the hundreds of mixed-
bloods in the Creek country. He admired his father and modeled his

plantation at Little Tallassee after Lachlan's. When Lachlan, late in life, returned to Scotland, he corresponded with Alexander and sent him gifts.[43]

This chronicle of the expansion of the McGillivray family in America must be balanced by a reference to the efforts of Lachlan to maintain contact with his relatives in Strathnairn. He cultivated the friendship of the new chief, William McGillivray, and urged him to come to America to build the fortune that he could never acquire in Invernesshire. William protested that family obligations held him in Scotland. As William grew older and remained unmarried, Lachlan scolded him for not doing his duty to the clan by marrying and producing a future chieftain.[44] Eventually, William took his cousin's advice on all counts; he became a Georgia planter, took a wife, and fathered an heir. Lachlan also encouraged William's younger brother John to come to America, promising to assist both men financially. Both William and John took advantage of Lachlan's generosity. John entered the trade under Lachlan's tutelage, and in time his wealth rivaled Lachlan's. Meanwhile, Lachlan maintained an interest in his native Strathnairn and bought property there. While the McGillivray family was growing in America, it remained anchored in Scotland by ties of blood and land.

Lachlan's service to king and country consisted of the intelligence contained in his frequent letters to the governors of South Carolina and Georgia. His service to himself and his family was the profit derived from his business. John Alden has analyzed the various transactions involved in the trade, based on figures used by Governor James Wright. Goods worth £12,000 were bought in England in 1764. After freighting and insurance were paid, the Savannah merchants charged 15 percent commission. Therefore, the Augusta storekeepers had to pay £15,360 for the cargo. Their share was 20 percent, raising the price to the traders to £18,360. The traders charged 30 percent to cover the cost of transporting the goods and expected an 18 percent profit. The final price on the £12,000 shipment was £28,000 in deerskins.[45]

McGillivray and others joined together in a company so they could manage the storekeeping in Augusta and the sale in the Indian towns and avoid the vicious competition that would later ruin the trading business. McGillivray's career consisted in moving along the ladder from trader in Little Tallassee, to storekeeper in Augusta, to import merchant in Savannah. Profits from the trade were invested in land for cattle raising, planting, and speculation. It was a path to success, and few followed it with as much determination as McGillivray.

One of the staples of the trade was the heavy cloth, usually a red color, referred to as stroud. The French called the cloth "limbourg" and had to buy it from the English to meet the demands of their Indian clients. The cloth was named for the English town of Stroud in Gloucestershire. During the seventeenth century the hilly country in the western Cotswolds attracted the woolen industry, which took advantage of the water power supplied by swift-flowing streams. Stroudwater scarlets became known throughout Europe and the East. In Turkey the cloth was used to make fezzes. Daniel Defoe, the writer, called Stroud cloth the finest in the world.[46] The clothiers who were responsible for manufacturing the cloth sold the product to London merchants, who exported it to merchants in Charlestown and Savannah. On the other end of the chain of trade, the best deerskins were sent to England for manufacture into leather products for sale in Britain and on the Continent. Thus the wool from English sheep was exchanged for the leather from American deer, and in the process many people became rich. Not the least of them was Lachlan McGillivray.

McGillivray spent a dozen years of his life in the Creek Nation, each year broken by winter and spring visits to Charlestown and Augusta to sell his skins, renew his license, and buy supplies. He was young, frontier life was exciting, and he enjoyed the respect of his Indian in-laws and his brothers in the trade. James Adair was intimately connected with the men who lived in the Indian country and he said of them, "The traders could not be reckoned unhappy; for they were kindly treated and watchfully guarded, by a society of friendly and sagacious people, and possessed all the needful things to make a reasonable life easy."[47]

By comparison with the period that followed, the years McGillivray resided with his family at Little Tallassee were good ones for him, his fellow traders, and the Indians with whom he lived. At this time the traders were "generally men of worth," as James Adair described them.[48] They were bound together by the knowledge that the French had put a premium on their scalps. On the frontier, the differences between Scot, English, and Irish disappeared. Scots might join the Jacobites at home, but in America they were regarded by the French and Indians as English. The traders served the king because their interests coincided with the government's. They were reasonably careful of their behavior, partly because they were competing with the French for the hearts and minds of the Indians.

McGillivray developed a thorough antipathy for his French neighbors. He was disgusted with what he called the "wicked and malicious lies" spread by the French agents. He wrote sarcastically of the arrival at Fort Toulouse of a boatload of "priest, popery and brandy."[49] He went with Devall's Landlord and the people of Puckantallahasee when they went to play ball with the Alabamas only half a mile from the French fort. The Creeks brought with them skins, bear oil, and tallow to trade with the French. They came away with brandy, powder, balls, flints, and knives. Devall's Landlord was aware of McGillivray's disapproval and in an unusual gesture of repentance remained drunk at McGillivray's house for two days.[50] The traders kept a restricted supply of rum for such occasions. McGillivray regretted the gradual increase in the amount of rum brought into the Indian country and warned the Charlestown authorities of its danger.[51]

McGillivray summarized his contributions to his country by stating that he kept the Indians of his towns in good order and "exerted himself for the public good even to the neglect of his own business," a fact recognized by his fellow traders.[52] Lachlan McGillivray exemplifies the various ways in which British traders influenced events on the southern frontier. By his constant correspondence with the provincial governors, he played a role in the game of empire. The flag that flew over his trading posts staked out the bounds of British hegemony. By his marriage into the powerful Wind Clan he gained important allies, and by his conduct he won the respect of the Creeks. Thus he was in a position to influence them at critical moments of decision. He and his fellow traders were instrumental in changing the life-style of the Creeks — changing, not destroying.

CHAPTER FIVE

The Choctaw Revolt

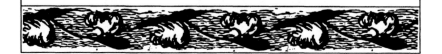

A dramatic example of the power of trade in influencing Indian affairs is the Choctaw Revolt of 1746–49. It was the first event of historic consequence in which Lachlan McGillivray was involved as a trader.

When Governor James Glen summoned Alexander Wood to Charlestown in April 1744, he was clearly annoyed. The ostensible reason for the governor's displeasure was Wood's request that Indians be rewarded for taking scalps. Wood's fort-building efforts at Okfuskee were discounted, even though Glen expended his energy in a vain attempt to construct another fort. In retrospect, he would have done better to reward Wood and improve the Okfuskee fort. Glen's suspicion of Wood was fed by members of his council who resented the power of the monopolistic Archibald McGillivray Company. Edmond Atkin was the most outspoken critic of the company. Atkin, a former trader, considered himself an expert in Indian affairs, and within a few years he would convince influential members of Parliament that he should be given the position of superintendent of Indian affairs for the Southern Department.

If Glen and his council looked askance at the veteran Wood, they very likely regarded young Lachlan McGillivray with the same mistrust at this early stage of his career. McGillivray almost certainly accompanied Wood on the journey to Charlestown. Wood's being in disfavor might have damaged McGillivray in the governor's eyes, but Archibald McGillivray and Alexander Wood had powerful friends in the Commons House of Assembly and an ally in Childermas Croft, the Indian commissioner. Lachlan got his license, and Wood retired from the trade to become a gentleman planter.[1]

While Wood and his party, which included several headmen, were still at Augusta and on their way to Charlestown, Captain Daniel Pepper relayed the message that fifteen Chickasaws, disappointed at Oglethorpe's absence, were also on the way to visit the governor. They brought word from the Lower Creek country that the French had offered rewards to any Indian who killed an English trader.[2]

The concurrent visits of two Indian delegations in July 1744 taxed the new governor's diplomatic skills. He talked grandly about expelling the French and requested the help of the Upper Creeks in taking Fort Toulouse. The Indians left Charlestown, pleased with this reception but troubled about Glen's message. Unfortunately, the trip was marred by the death of one of the headmen from a fever or from excessive drinking or both.[3]

Lachlan was back in the Creek country by mid-August and reported the sadness caused by the death of the headman. The Charlestown visit marked the emergence of Gun Merchant of Okchoy town as a leader of influence. He called for a general meeting of Creek chiefs at Tallapoosa. Realizing that there would be opposition to Glen's proposal about attacking Fort Toulouse, the Gun made the mistake of using ambiguous language which made it seem that the English were preparing to invade the Indian country. In McGillivray's words, "He gave them some small hints of it in such doubtful terms that they did not know what construction to put upon it, which put them in a small uproar."[4] The worst of their fears was that the English would send troops and they would become slaves, as the French had often predicted. They remembered how the Charlestown traders had sold captured Indians to planters in Barbados. The assembled headmen voted against Glen's schemes.

With that unpleasant news as preface, McGillivray could relay another, more favorable turn of events. The valiant and long-suffering

Chickasaws continued to resist French blandishments even as they repelled invasions. In July, while some Chickasaw chiefs were in Charlestown, others went to Fort Toulouse to inquire about terms of peace. The commander, Chevalier de La Houssaye, informed them that they must expel the English, allow the French to build a fort in their country, and afterward rely solely on the French to supply them with trade goods. The Chickasaws considered these words carefully and replied that they could not accept the terms. To do so would be to place themselves at the mercy of the French and to risk destruction. They preferred war to peace on those terms. McGillivray's letter captured the drama and even the cadence of the Chickasaw response.[5]

The French officer La Houssaye confirmed the substance of McGillivray's report. The Chickasaws refused to abandon the English, he informed Governor Vaudreuil. The Chickasaws trusted their English traders. "Neither the length of the road, nor the difficulty in bringing us the things we need ever rebuffs them," they said. It was just as well, Vaudreuil confided to his superiors; he was in no position to make peace with the Chickasaws because he had no trade goods for them. The French fell back on their old strategy of inciting the Choctaws to renew the war against the Chickasaws. By 1744, however, the Choctaws were weary of fighting. They complained that the French should do more; after all, it was the French who had started the war, not the Choctaws.[6]

The Choctaws' dissatisfaction was deeper than Vaudreuil realized. Since 1734, the Choctaw chief Red Shoes had flirted with the English. In that year he led a party to Savannah to meet Oglethorpe, only to be disappointed that Oglethorpe had left on his first return visit to England. In 1738, the Chickasaw trader John Campbell escorted Red Shoes and his warriors to Charlestown to see Lieutenant Governor Bull. Now, in 1744, Lachlan McGillivray was sought out by eight headmen of Red Shoes's faction. They wanted McGillivray and other English traders to bring goods to their towns. McGillivray realized the importance of this visit. "The Choctaw nation begins to groan under the French yoke and long for a correspondence with the English," he wrote to Governor Glen. Again McGillivray reflected the imagery of the Indian language: "Once they have tasted the sweetness of the Indian trade they cannot be contented but will long to have more of it."[7] McGillivray asked what advice he should give the Choctaws.

There would be several rival claimants to the honor of having initiated the schism that became known as the Choctaw Revolt. McGillivray did not enter that contest, nor did his role attract public notice. But his letter written at Augusta on January 14, 1745, marked the beginning of the Choctaw defection. The matter was of sufficient importance to cause Glen to call the letter to the attention of the South Carolina Commons House. The House referred McGillivray's letter to a special committee, which reported back on February 21 with the recommendation that McGillivray be commissioned under the great seal of the province to negotiate a peace with the Choctaws. No other person but McGillivray and his company would be permitted to trade with the Choctaws for one year from the date of the commission. The House concurred with the committee's report, noting that McGillivray would receive no other recompense than the year-long monopoly.[8] The attitude of the members of the House speaks volumes about their opinion of the young trader. McGillivray's only previous experience was as interpreter to James Bullock in 1741, and yet he was entrusted with this sensitive mission to the Choctaws.

If the House felt that McGillivray could do the job, the governor and council had other plans in mind, far more grandiose and ambitious. John Fenwicke, writing for the council, explained the strategy to the Duke of Newcastle. The French posed an immediate threat to South Carolina. The source of their machinations was the Alabama Fort; therefore, it must be destroyed. The province of South Carolina would require fifty to a hundred regular troops to lead an invasion. The soldiers would merely spearhead the effort; the Creek Indians would be mobilized under the leadership of the "linguisters" (the traders employed as interpreters). A liberal supply of presents would be required to persuade the Indians to go to war. When this force of soldiers, linguisters, and Indians was assembled, it would be an easy matter to take the Alabama Fort as well as the other French fort on the Tombigbee and to cooperate with the Royal Navy to lay siege to Mobile and New

Orleans.[9] The idea was magnificent in its scope; it was a precedent for a similar scheme during the next war. The one drawback was that it betrayed a woeful ignorance of the Indian mind. The Creeks would never permit an armed body of Englishmen to invade their country. In fact, Glen handed the French a propaganda weapon that they would use against him as long as he was governor. The French raised the alarm "the British are coming" long before Paul Revere.

The one realistic and typically Carolinian feature of Glen's strategy was that it did not place a single Charlestonian in jeopardy. Glen's request produced partial results. Three independent companies were dispatched to Carolina to guard the coast and garrison the frontier. The first contingent arrived in January 1746.[10]

During the latter part of 1745, Glen was confronted with Indian problems that distracted him from taking advantage of the Choctaw invitation. Daniel Pepper reported that the Chickasaws living on the Savannah River had become unruly. Fort Moore with its reduced complement would be useless against an Indian attack. Fort Augusta, garrisoned by Richard Kent's twenty-five men, was not much better. Only one one-pounder cannon was serviceable, and that would overset every time it fired. The garrison lived like the other inhabitants rather than according to any military code. There was no lock on the fort gate. The Chickasaws made fun of the fort and had even fired at it as they passed by.[11]

A new settlement of Shawnees, under the mixed-blood Peter Chartier, had settled in the Upper Creek country and had fallen under French influence. They were blamed for inciting the Lower Creeks to go looking for mischief. Malatchi, son of the Emperor Brims, was annoyed at the Georgians' failure to compensate his cousin Mary, who in 1744 had married Thomas Bosomworth. Pepper reported that the Creeks had made it known that all the land around Augusta was theirs and the houses in Augusta would soon be theirs. The Creeks were technically correct. Their cession to Oglethorpe in 1739 stopped at the tidewater line on the Savannah and Altamaha rivers. Augusta's Richard Kent ignored the technicality. When an errant party of Creeks attacked the inoffensive Yuchi Indians on the Savannah River and then demanded powder and shot from Captain Kent, the doughty commander told them that the only shot they would get was from the mouth of his cannon. Major William Horton marched his Frederica company to Augusta, anticipating a fight, but found that Kent had handled the crisis without help.[12]

All this French-inspired commotion, added to increased nervousness among the Cherokees, caused Governor Glen to stage a dramatic tour of the Carolina backcountry. Glen's ostensible reason, as he later explained to his superiors, was that he had received dispatches from various traders expressing the danger to which they were exposed because of French intrigue. If so, then Lachlan McGillivray and his friends played a role in the event. But Glen never left Carolina on his grand tour so it is hard to see how he might have soothed the fears of the traders on the Coosa frontier. Undoubtedly he wanted to resolve problems closer to home before tackling those farther away. Perhaps Glen's real reason for the expensive and controversial expedition was that he intended to advertise the fact that he was in control of Indian affairs now that James Edward Oglethorpe had returned to England.[13]

Glen decided on his mission before informing either his council or the Commons House. He instructed McGillivray to invite the Upper Creek headmen to meet him at Fort Moore. Similar notes were sent to traders among the Lower Creeks. He informed the Cherokee traders that he would see the chiefs of that nation at Ninety-Six and on his way he would visit with the Catawbas at Saluda. A joint committee of the Commons and council grumbled that Glen had not followed the proper procedure but recommended that expenses be paid for a two-hundred-man escort. In addition, forty to fifty gentlemen and their servants made the journey. In a later report Glen boasted, "I undertook it when nobody imagined I could live three days." [14] The traders who were within reach of the French fort might have wondered what danger Glen was in with an escort the size of a small army about him.

The great march began on April 21, 1746. Glen's first report was dated May 3 from Saluda. It had rained incessantly; his men made boats of buffalo hides to ferry the swollen rivers. Glen met with the Catawbas and promised protection, then proceeded to meet sixty Cherokees at Ninety-Six. He proposed building a fort in the Cherokee mountains to keep the French out; however, as he explained it, "they are pretty jealous of their liberty, they did not readily agree to it." [15] Glen was convinced that forts in the Indian country would solve most problems and he would keep trying. At Fort Moore, he addressed the fractious Chickasaws and "spoke roughly" to them. The once-feared Squirrel King was now an abject drunkard. He voiced a pathetic appeal to Glen to make his people respect him.

Glen was more conciliatory toward the Creeks who came to meet him but disappointed in their numbers. He invited them to come down to Charlestown in the fall and hoped for a better showing. His object, he told them, was to destroy the Alabama Fort. Would the Creeks help him do it? They could not answer him, but they would go home and think about it. [16]

Although Glen claimed to have pacified the Indian country in his month-long march of six hundred miles, neither the Lords Commissioners in London nor the members of the Commons House in Charlestown were much impressed. The Lords thought it would be less expensive to invite the Indians to Charlestown in the future. The Carolina Commons advised Glen to send experienced agents to do business with the Indians, implying that they could get better results. [17] The same body had proposed that young Lachlan McGillivray serve as agent to the Choctaws so it would appear that they trusted him more than they did the governor.

Glen used McGillivray as a messenger to invite the Creek chiefs to Charlestown. Though McGillivray's letters were lost with the entire volume of the Indian Book for this period, it is clear that he was responsible for delivering the invitation to Peter Chartier's Savannah Indians as well as the chiefs of his own towns. [18]

The October 1746 assembly of Indians in Charlestown taxed the ability of Stephen Forrest, the interpreter, and of the clerk who recorded the proceedings. An unprecedented effort was made to get the Indian names right; Invenaghe of Okfuskee, Poyhitchi of Wacocoys, Uchlepayhageo of Puckantallahasee, Enenawgy of the Okfuskees, Enochtonachee of Okchoy (alias the Gun Merchant), Poscogo Meeko of the Savannahs, among others, were McGillivray's clients. Malatchi, son of the Emperor Brims, and therefore especially honored among the Upper as well as Lower Creek towns, was a key figure at the meeting. The Wolf of Muccolossus, who had once saved John Spencer's life, was there as the most vocal friend of the English. Chigilly and Alleck of the Lower Creeks had gone first to Frederica and had been directed by Mayor Horton to Charlestown.[19]

While the Indian chiefs waited for their interview with the governor, the members of the council read three letters from Lachlan McGillivray, two of them dated September 10, 1746, one from John Eycott from Tallassee town, and one from George Galphin from Coweta. On the basis of these letters, the council decided that the time was right "to strike a stroke upon the French settled among them."[20] Further, the Indians should be prevailed upon to join in the reduction of the Alabama Fort, or at least not to oppose the English sending an armed force to destroy it.

Two of McGillivray's letters alienated Governor Glen and outraged Edmond Atkin. The council's report of the conference was almost certainly written by Atkin; it criticized "the man who hath been known to send the Governor two letters at the same time; the one enclosed in the other on the same subject and contradictory to each other."[21]

A full two years later, Governor Glen was still brooding about the incident of the two letters. Although he did not mention McGillivray by name in his letter to the Lords Commissioners, there was no doubt to whom he referred. A trader, he said, wrote two letters on a matter of consequence and suggested that Glen take the one he liked best. Glen laid the letters before the council, and "they were all sensible of the danger to permit such fellows to trade amongst the Indians."[22] This conciliar overreaction was fueled by the suspicion that McGillivray maintained a close correspondence with the commander of the French fort and even supplied him with goods. The result of this secret crisis in the career of Lachlan McGillivray was that the governor expressly forbade the Indian commissioner, Childermas Croft, to renew McGillivray's license. Instead, Croft, in Glen's words, "without hesitation granted him a license."[23] Glen counted the incident as another of the irregularities of the House which he was forced to endure.

It is hard to imagine what was the contradiction in McGillivray's lost letters. McGillivray routinely passed along the latest rumors, and it is entirely possible that the rumors were inconsistent. They usually were. A suspicious-minded person might have wondered if Glen's ire over the seemingly innocuous incident might have been fueled by a desire to cut Lachlan McGillivray out of the Choctaw trade after the legislature had spoken in McGillivray's behalf. James Adair, among others, accused the governor of self-interested motives.

Another reason for Glen's ill humor was that his Indian conference went badly. The council's report of the proceedings reflected disappointment that "only a few came to Charlestown at the governor's invitation." Of those, only the Wolf of Muccolossus was willing to cooperate. When Glen asked him privately if he would help pull down the Alabama Fort, he said he would; "it was a thing he long desired to see." He admitted that many were of a different frame of mind, but "his mouth was as strong in the nation as any."[24] In addition, the English could build a fort in his town, which was situated only seven miles from the French fort.

When Glen reported this good news to his council, he was advised to see how the other headmen felt about the matter. Malatchi, whose opinion was all-important, refused to cooperate. His father, Brims, had warned him never to let white blood be spilled on his ground, and he would honor his father's wishes.[25] If the English and French went to war in the Creek country, the Creeks would be the losers.

The other headmen deferred to Malatchi; they would not join in an attack on the French fort, but they would not object to an English fort in the Wolf's village, and they would be glad to accept powder and balls from the English. Glen showed his displeasure with Malatchi by exempting his village from the agreement to supply powder, an unfortunate decision that would inevitably force Malatchi to seek ammunition for hunting from the French.[26]

Presents were distributed; the Wolf was given a riding saddle for his daughter, and the mico of Puckantallahasee received a "genteel saddle." Poscogo Meeko of the Savannahs took away shoes and stockings for his young child. There was something for everyone.[27] Despite the presents, the chiefs went away in an uneasy frame of mind. They had been exposed to talk about destroying the French two years before and had not liked it then; they liked it no better now.

The first adverse reaction that came to the governor's attention was from Lachlan McGillivray, whose letter from Augusta was dated December 1, 1746. McGillivray wrote with the frankness of one who did not realize that he was blacklisted. He had met his friend the Gun Merchant on the trail and learned that he was displeased because the Wolf had consented to the building of an English fort without consulting the rest of the nation. If the English attacked the French fort, the chief would not be responsible for the consequences.[28]

Glen and his council decided that "no regard ought to be paid to this information" because it came from the man who had sent contradictory letters. The council acknowledged that Stephen Forrest, the interpreter at the recent meeting, reported that he spoke with several headmen when he returned to the Creek country and they would have nothing to do with any attack on the Alabama Fort. The council also noted that Old Bracket of Tuckabatchee, a loyal friend of the English, sent a note to Glen urging him to live peacefully in his own land. He wanted no disturbance in his country and no white men but traders. None of this unwelcome information changed the attitude of the governor's council. Stephen Forrest was suspected of being in sympathy with the French.[29]

It would take more than bad news to deter Glen once he had made up his mind. He announced to the assembly that his meeting with the Indians was a success; they had agreed to permit a fort to be built within seven miles of the French fort. He suggested that it would take a large number of men to build the new fort and implied that the same men might be used to attack and reduce the enemy fort.[30]

In April 1747, while the assembly was pondering the governor's message, a French deserter arrived in Charlestown with timely intelligence on conditions at the Alabama Fort. The garrison consisted of two officers and thirty-five men. There were only two cannon and one was useless. (An objective observer might have been amused by the two mightiest nations in the world opposing each other across a wilderness, represented by Fort Toulouse with one cannon and Fort Augusta with one that overturned when it was fired.) There was a ditch six feet wide on the land side of the Alabama Fort. The Coosa River bluff dropped off sharply on the other side. There were bastions at each corner, with powder stored in one. Did he think Indians could capture the fort? If led by the English, they might.[31]

Buoyed up by the governor's optimism and the deserter's responses, the Commons Committee on Indian Affairs recommended raising £3,500 to finance an expedition of three hundred men in addition to the three independent companies for the purpose of reducing the Alabama Fort and the Tombigbee fort. The House agreed on the absolute necessity of taking the French forts but balked at the cost.[32]

Lachlan McGillivray and his fellow traders in the Indian villages could have told the gentlemen of Charlestown that such belligerent talk was sheer madness. The Creeks were already fearful that the English would send an army of conquest, and the French were delighted to fuel that fear. Malatchi ordered his people to prepare to defend themselves with bows and arrows, the weapons of their forefathers, in case they could no longer rely on the English traders to supply them with powder and balls.[33] A group of concerned planters in St. John Parish, South Carolina, belatedly realized how successful the French efforts were. In a letter to the Duke of Newcastle, they reported that the French had spread the word that the English intended to take the Alabama Fort and then make war on the Creeks. The Creeks were so alarmed they actually sent out search parties to intercept the expected invasion. If they encountered twenty or more men, they would regard it as an act of war by the English and would kill all the traders in their villages.[34]

The French deserter, probably a young cadet named Lantagnac, who would become better known by both sides, could have painted a worse picture of the Alabama Fort than he did. Governor Vaudreuil was overjoyed at the Creeks' reaction to Glen's proposals. He reported to his superiors that the Shawnees, Alabamas, Tallapoosas, and Cowetas had refused Glen's requests and that Malatchi had said he would never permit anyone to attack the French whom he was keeping on his land. He was not so well pleased at a report of the condition of Fort Toulouse. The buildings were falling into ruins; the side of the fort nearest the Coosa River was dangerously near the edge of the bluff. It seemed likely that the fort would collapse without the assistance of the English. Vaudreuil ordered Commandant de La Houssaye to rebuild the fort. Thus both the French and English were resolved to put up forts at a distance of seven miles apart.[35] The French did theirs; the English continued to talk about it.

Meanwhile, the long-simmering Choctaw resentment against the French erupted into an open rebellion. As early as November 1744, a delegation of that nation had signaled Lachlan McGillivray that the Choctaws were ready to do business with the English. Since then, Governor Glen had become distracted by his grand tour and extravagant plans for fort building. Glen would later take credit for inciting the Choctaw Revolt by sending the Chickasaw traders James Adair and John Campbell into the Choctaw country with trading goods. Edmond Atkin broke ranks with Glen over the governor's handling of the Choctaws. He went to England in 1750 and wrote a tome under a title which suggested that the governor was making false claims: *Historical Account of the Revolt of the Choctaw Indians in the late War from the French to the British Alliance and of their Return since to that of the French In which are contained the Publick and Private Measures pursued on that Occasion in the Province of South Carolina and wherein the respective Services of the Several Persons claiming the Merit of effecting that Revolt are placed in their proper Light and the true Causes shewn of each Event.*[36]

Atkin, who asserted that Red Shoes started the revolt without any English instigation, was prompted to write his heavily titled account by Glen's claims and by counterclaims put forth by Charles McNaire and his associates under the heading *A Modest Reply to His Excellency the Governor's Written Answer to the Affidavit of Charles McNaire and Matthew Roche concerning the late Revolt of the Choctaw Nation.*[37]

One of those with a legitimate claim to credit was the veteran Chickasaw trader John Campbell. Campbell had traded to the Chickasaws for twenty years; with Nicholas Chinnery, he helped repulse the French invasions of 1736 and 1740. Since 1744 James Adair, formerly a Cherokee trader, had joined him in the Chickasaw country. Campbell and Adair conveyed small amounts of trade goods to the Choctaws when the French supplies failed. In 1746, Campbell learned that Red Shoes was ready to make a break with the French. By then, the Choctaws had visited Lachlan McGillivray with a request for trade goods. Although there is no direct evidence that McGillivray actually engaged in the Choctaw trade, he must have. According to James Adair, some "who had the fortune to get safe away made great returns." [38]

One reason for Red Shoes's defection was that since the official beginning of the war in 1744, the British navy had intercepted French supply ships and caused an unprecedented shortage of French trade goods and presents. A certain edge was added to Red Shoes's general feeling of dissatisfaction because a Frenchman at Fort Tombigbee had slept with his wife. The revolt began dramatically when Red Shoes killed three Frenchmen and gave their scalps to a party of Chickasaws to deliver to Governor Glen. The grisly gesture was meant to signal peace with the Chickasaws and an alliance with the English. It did not matter that the scalps did not reach their destination. The Chickasaws gave them to a party of Upper Creeks and the Creeks carried them to Fort Toulouse. The Creeks intended to fend off any war that would make their country a battleground. [39]

John Campbell, who was reluctant to appear in Charlestown because of his debts, asked James Adair to inquire whether the governor would recompense him if he succeeded in establishing trade with the Choctaws. Glen became excited about the idea and readily agreed that if Adair and Campbell could bring it off, he would see to their reward either from the province or the home government. It is not clear why Glen ignored the recommendation of the Commons that McGillivray's company be permitted a year's monopoly unless his conversation with Adair came after the two-letter episode of October 1746. [40]

Encouraged by the governor's response, Campbell delivered a caravan of trading goods to Red Shoes's village in the Tombigbee River country. The French were alarmed at the intrusion; Develle, the commander of Fort Tombigbee, offered a reward for the heads of Red Shoes and his confederates. Governor Vaudreuil extended the offer to include rewards for the heads of the English traders as well.[41]

These French bribes made life extremely precarious in the Choctaw country, as Campbell soon discovered. On a summer's night, Campbell sat in the open-front lodge of Red Shoes, with the Chickasaw wife of the chief beside her husband. A party of French Choctaws crept up unobserved and fired at Campbell and Red Shoes. Campbell was hit in the shoulder. The shot missed Red Shoes but killed his wife. When Campbell was well enough to be carried on a litter, Red Shoes escorted him to the safety of the Chickasaw country. On the journey Red Shoes became ill. One of his own people offered to sit with him; when the great chief turned his head to sleep, the cowardly assassin shot him dead to claim the French reward.[42]

Choctaw runners begged James Adair to bring a cargo of goods into their country but warned him of the French bounty on his head. While Campbell began a six-month recuperation, the intrepid Adair brought supplies to Red Shoes's faction. Adair did his best to carry out Glen's orders to persuade the Choctaws to storm Fort Tombigbee. The Indians were not so foolhardy as to take such a chance, but they were willing to risk flying raids on those Choctaw villages which remained staunchly pro-French. It is not clear exactly how many villages joined the rebellion; the English claimed that only four out of forty-six were loyal to the French. But there was a pervasive tentativeness about this rebellion. It was sustained only by the ability of the English to deliver the goods.

Adair was in the Choctaw country when the brother of Red Shoes returned from Charlestown. Mingo Pusscuss, or the Little King, had gone to see Governor Glen with an escort of forty-seven warriors. They were received with a ritual fanfare which Glen described to the Lords Commissioners. The Carolina horse and foot militia turned out in arms; the batteries of the Charlestown forts fired salutes as did the naval vessels in the harbor. The ceremony was calculated "to implant in these Savages a proper idea of our strength." The treaty was drawn up in the most solemn manner Glen could conjure. In return for powder and weapons, the Choctaws would seize the Tombigbee fort and assist the Creeks in taking the Alabama Fort. The Choctaw Nation and the English pledged perpetual friendship "while the sun gives light and while the rivers run."[43] The Little King was properly impressed and hurried back over the long trail to add his assurances that good things were to come.

Edmond Atkin was present for the treaty-signing ceremony on April 10, 1747. His disagreement with Glen began immediately afterward, when Glen introduced to the council Charles McNaire and announced that McNaire would take the ammunition to the Choctaws free of charge. As a reward, he was given a monopoly of the trade. Atkin objected to Glen's violation of procedure. The proper method of licensing was by the Indian commissioner. Glen was vexed at Commissioner Childermas Croft for disregarding his orders not to license Lachlan McGillivray and took it upon himself to license Charles McNaire; Atkin asserted that the governor's brother was forced on McNaire as a silent partner. McNaire, a North Carolina trader, was a surprise choice for the potentially lucrative franchise. He was a stranger to the southern frontier, as were his partners in the trade, Thomas Maxwell, Arthur Harvey, and John Vann. But as Atkin observed, he was "more sober and decent than the usual sort."[44] And he had the advantage of being in the right place at the right time.

The Charlestown merchants Matthew and Jordan Roche outfitted one of the greatest caravans ever to set out from Carolina. Beginning on June 10, 1747, it took a full two months to load two hundred horses with the government's ammunition and the company's trading goods. The government stock was meant to be distributed among the Creeks and Chickasaws as well as the Choctaws to induce them to act in concert against the Alabama Fort.

Atkin implied that McNaire was greedy in delaying so long to collect trade goods and faulted him for taking so much time on the trail. But McNaire's first caravan, which arrived in the Choctaw country on September 25, was speed itself compared to the pace of the second train of goods. McNaire's arrival among the Choctaws provoked a crisis. The Indians expected presents in addition to ammunition, and although McNaire had plenty to sell, he had nothing to give away. He blamed Adair and Campbell for raising the expectations of the Indians by promising duffels, strouds, shirts, paint, flints, and all kinds of goods and chided the governor for not choosing men of probity to do his business. Little King was acutely embarrassed; he, too, had expected presents in return for making war on the French. There was nothing for McNaire to do but hand out supplies and charge them to the government. In return, Little King promised to send a war party to attack Fort Tombigbee. He agreed to help the English build their own fort in one of his villages. In token of his good intentions, he sent eight scalps of French-allied Choctaws and promised more to follow.[45]

McNaire's letter, written October 6, 1747, reached Charlestown by November 13, a remarkably swift delivery. Governor Glen was in a sensitive position because he had written to the Lords Commissioners earlier in the year praising Campbell and Adair as enterprising individuals and recommending that they be given a reward of one hundred guineas each. Now, because of McNaire's critical report, the council wanted to reprimand Adair. Atkin's account makes it clear that the Charlestown gentlemen considered Adair a person of questionable character.[46] White men who looked and acted like Indians risked their reputation in Charlestown.

On December 14, 1747, another letter from McNaire was brought before the council. After two months, he was thoroughly annoyed with the Choctaws. They demanded all his goods as presents, claiming them as just payment for going to war. They made it clear that they had gone to war only because the English wanted them to; it was not their war. The Little King led an army of five hundred to attack the French faction but found the enemy strongly entrenched so he burned a few houses and returned. The Little King said he might go back and lay siege to the place, but McNaire doubted it. French Indians were lurking everywhere. One of McNaire's men, Henry Elsey, was killed ten miles from Fort Tombigbee. McNaire suspected that those "deceitful, treacherous People" did not intend to let him leave until more goods arrived.[47]

James Adair mocked McNaire for his arrogant airs and scorned him for not understanding Indians. Edmond Atkin criticized McNaire for allowing the Choctaws to think that they were fighting for the English instead of for themselves.[48] Despite growing doubts about the enterprise, the council recommended sending another huge shipment to the Choctaws and to the Creeks and Chickasaws as well. Eighty thousand pounds of powder and 160,000 pounds of bullets were packed for the Choctaws and 35,000 pounds of powder and 70,000 pounds of bullets were destined for the Creeks and an equal amount for the Chickasaws. Glen wrote to Lachlan McGillivray and two other members of the company among the Upper Creeks, William Sludders and Thomas Devall, explaining that the shipment to the Creeks was meant to entice them to destroy the French fort and to assist the Choctaws in their fight against the French.[49] A similar letter was sent to James Adair, asking him to involve the Chickasaws in the war against the French.

Matthew and Jordan Roche dispatched the horse train in late December 1747 or early January 1748. Despite the need for haste, the caravan was eight months on the trail. Glen was acutely embarrassed by the delay and by his inability to explain it to his superiors. In his letter of October 10, 1748, he could only state that the urgently needed supplies had not arrived by July and he did not know why but promised to get answers.[50] The delay led to a spate of anxious queries from the Lords Commissioners, and the matter was not settled until 1751, when Glen sent the deposition of the trader charged with conveying the goods, John Vann. Vann's problem was that the fifty-four horses he bought in February were in no condition to make the trip so he waited around Fort Moore and Augusta until spring, when the horses presumably felt better. Spring floods caused further delays. Eventually he reached the Wacocoys' village in the Upper Creek country. Fort Toulouse lay between him and the Choctaw country so he sent a message to Charles McNaire in the Choctaw country to send an escort. McNaire conveyed the message that a party of Choctaws was on the way, but they never came. Vann decided on a roundabout route through the Chickasaw country, but first he delivered the entire supply of Creek presents to the Wolf of Muccolossus at the Wacocoys' village in the presence of English traders. The Wacocoys' was one of McGillivray's villages;

he was undoubtedly among the traders present. Vann probably used McGillivray's storehouse to deposit excess trade goods.

In the Chickasaw country Vann persuaded John Campbell to accompany him to the Choctaw villages. The monumentally slow journey was completed when in late August 1748 he delivered the ammunition and supplies to the Little King in John Campbell's presence. Vann explained that he did not return to Charlestown until 1751 because of his debts.[51]

Glen and his council heard substantially the same story of the delivery of the supplies from John Campbell himself, who accompanied a group of Choctaws to Charlestown in January 1749. Charles McNaire, who had left the Choctaw country in August, just before Vann's arrival, was in Charlestown at the same time and both men were interrogated by the governor. Campbell confirmed that he went with Vann in August and that Vann distributed ten kegs of powder, twenty bags of bullets, and some guns. Vann's ten horseloads of trade items were quickly sold, and he went back to the Wacocoys, where he had stored other goods, to get more. Campbell met Vann in September as he was returning with twenty horses loaded with supplies.[52]

Campbell was paid £100 for interpreting during the visit of the Choctaw delegation, but he never received the reward promised by the governor. Campbell, who said he had "done all he could to serve King and Country," made an even greater sacrifice. He returned to his Chickasaw village and, while his friends were hunting, was surprised by a war party of French Choctaws, who shot him and carried his scalp in triumph to Fort Tombigbee.[53]

For three years the Choctaw civil war raged while an equally fierce battle of words was waged in Charlestown by those claiming credit for starting it. James Adair described the Choctaw war as "bitter beyond expression."[54] The friends of the English would beg for a stroud blanket or a white shirt so they might make "a genteel appearance" when they died. They died in great numbers. Governor Vaudreuil reported that his warrior chiefs had dumped one hundred scalps and three skulls at his feet with the comment that it was harder to kill brothers than strangers. Two years later, in 1751, he counted eight hundred dead among Red Shoes's party and three villages completely destroyed. In addition, the French had killed fifty survivors of a village on the Mississippi, "which we had undertaken to destroy without knowing very clearly why and without completely succeeding in doing so," said Vaudreuil.[55] The French strategy, with its single-minded emphasis on wiping out the Chickasaws, could hardly be called enlightened. Their only object in suppressing the Choctaw Revolt was to get on with the business of fighting the Chickasaws.

In September 1749, James Adair brought the Chickasaw chief Paya Mattaha to Charlestown. Adair expected to be thanked and rewarded for his role in the Choctaw war. Instead, he found himself a persona non grata. His companions, the Chickasaws, who deserved the best treatment for their long fidelity, were received coldly and soon left, bitterly disappointed.[56]

Adair could not resist a bit of mischief while he was in Charlestown. He read the February 26, 1750, notice of a reply to the governor's answer to McNaire's claim that he had started the Choctaw revolt. He sent an anonymous advertisement to the *Gazette* laced with broad sarcasm: "Shortly will be Published a Treatise Upon the Importance and Means of securing the Chactaw Nation of Indians in the British Interests . . . to prove that the year of Our Lord 1738 was several years antecedent to the year 1747, concluding with some scenes from a farce including dialogues between the several modest pretenders to the Merit of a Certain Revolt."[57] The notice, of course, was a reminder that John Campbell had brought Red Shoes to Charlestown long before Glen arrived in Carolina or McNaire was given the franchise.

Somehow Glen discovered that Adair was the author, and the governor was furious. His expanded ego was not balanced by a saving sense of humor. He told his council that the advertisement was "indecent and insolent" and "if such obscure fellows were permitted to insult the governor or government without punishment, there would be an end to all order, distinction and authority."[58] The council members agreed that the notice was "very saucy" and that Adair deserved to be punished but were not sure on what legal grounds. The unfortunate Adair probably never realized that the governor was aware that he had written the offending notice and continued to be mystified at the coldness he was shown.

If Adair's services were not appreciated in Charlestown, they were recognized at the Alabama Fort. He was the Englishman the French wanted most to kill. When he called at that place, he was arrested. Just before he was to be sent to Mobile by boat, he managed a dramatic escape.[59] Glen summarized his dealings with Campbell and Adair by reporting to the Lords Commissioners that the one had been killed and the other "has rendered himself unworthy" by insulting the governor and by offering his services to the French at the Alabama Fort.[60] Adair's contempt for his unfaithful patron is clear in the pages of his book. He deserved better treatment.

Charles McNaire, whose company was dubbed the Sphinx by Adair because of the secrecy surrounding it, flaunted his claim to credit. At first the Carolina Assembly agreed with him but awarded him only £150 and suggested that Glen ask the Lords Commissioners for £2,000. Glen disagreed and refused to forward the request. Glen's mood was further soured by a pamphlet by Jordan Roche which exalted McNaire at the expense of the governor. Glen branded the pamphlet "false and scandalous."[61]

Undaunted, McNaire carried his case to London. In a petition to the Lords Commissioners he described how he attempted to win over a considerable body of Choctaws to the British interest and that he "happily succeeded in this undertaking"; he described how he had made two tedious journeys of one thousand miles to the Choctaw Nation. In the first expedition he had some success, and with the second he gained the entire nation for the English. Here he glossed the truth. He had made two trips, but his second was without a cargo, and indeed he left before his partner Vann arrived. He also took credit for rescuing a lady in distress. The English Choctaws had raided a plantation on the Mississippi and taken a Mrs. Cheval and her daughter prisoner. They were escorted to Charlestown, and Glen had them conveyed from there to Mobile. The Lords were sufficiently impressed with McNaire's petition to grant him an audience. It was interesting that McNaire testified that he was told by the governor to give away his goods if necessary.

Earlier, McNaire had blamed James Adair for telling the Choctaws that goods would be given away. McNaire could not convince the commissioners to pay him the £4,000 he claimed, but he was awarded £1,000, considerably more than Governor Glen thought he deserved.[62]

During all this time, Glen was doing his best to boost his own claim to the credit for the Choctaw affair. In December 1751, he boasted to the commissioners: "It was entirely owing to me that any of the Choctaws ever declared War against the French." He acknowledged that this important Choctaw revolution had "made no great éclat" in Europe, probably because the governor in New Orleans was too prudent to send bad news to Paris. As for Glen himself, "An awkward modesty hindered me from claiming the merit that I knew was justly due to me."[63] If Glen did not receive the recognition he sought, it was not from the want of self-promotion. It was, rather, that the Lords never quite believed Glen's claims.

One of those who caused doubts about Glen was Edmond Atkin, who had left Charlestown for London in 1750. The McNaire claims provoked him to write the thesis with the weighty title which purported to set the record straight. *The Historical Account of the Choctaw Revolt* was addressed to James West, secretary to the Lords of the Treasury. It was critical of Glen, McNaire, and Adair and gave entire credit to Red Shoes and the Choctaws. Because Atkin had left Charlestown before the laggard trader Vann came out of the woods, Atkin's historical account was tantalizingly incomplete. He did not know what happened to the delayed second caravan.[64]

There was another claimant to the glory of serving king and country in the matter of the Choctaw allegiance—Lachlan McGillivray and his company. After the two enormous shipments, the McNaire Company was bankrupt and did no more business in the Choctaw country. Brown, Rae and Company quietly entered the trade. The seven partners in the company were on good terms with Captain Richard Kent in Augusta and with his constables in the Creek country. Elderly William Stephens, president of the Georgia Council, was grateful to the company for not bothering him, and he refused to interfere with its monopoly. If some of the partners or their employees did not come down to Savannah to renew their licenses, he assumed it was because they had licenses from Carolina. The company lost an advocate when Oglethorpe's regiment was disbanded in 1749 and Captain Richard Kent returned to England, and they sensed trouble when Stephens was replaced as council president by Henry Parker. Parker explained to the Trustees that Stephens had been replaced because of his "confused mind." Stephens had been asked by the company to make two of its number constables. Before he could grant what Parker considered an outrageous request, he was supplanted. Parker believed that the company had a "pernicious scheme" to enforce its monopoly of the Indian trade.[65] Parker and his friends in Savannah were irate because the company ignored Savannah and shipped its deerskins from Charlestown. An estimated 140,000 pounds of skins and 2,000 pounds of beaver fur came down the river annually, and practically the entire cargo went to Charlestown.

Parker's criticism alarmed the members of the company and moved them to defend themselves to the Georgia Trustees. They had heard that there was talk about denying licenses in the future. Observing that "our house is the best acquainted with Indian affairs of any," they said that they were responsible for keeping the Creek Indians on good terms with the English. Furthermore, the company had risked all to trade with the Choctaws. When the "great company went broke," their company supplied the Choctaws and prevented their going back to the French. The letter warned the Trustees of the potential confusion that would result from granting too many licenses and permitting an "inundation of raw unexperienced people among the Indians." As a concession, the company promised to do more business in Savannah in the future. The Trustees were advised to "let things run in the old channel."[66] It may not have been a coincidence that Savannah's first decent wharf was built in 1751, shortly after the company's letter went to the Trustees.

Lachlan McGillivray could have written the letter, which was signed simply "Brown, Rae and Company." None of the other partners were much given to writing. George Galphin wrote, but he did so very badly. William Sludders was ill and unable to leave his house at Puckantallahasee. Patrick Brown, John Rae, Daniel Clark, and Thomas Devall wrote sparingly. Whoever wrote it, there was wisdom in the advice to limit licenses and to let things run the old channel. When the British policy changed and trade was opened to all comers, a shocking deterioration of standards resulted. Brown, Rae and Company had become a monopoly, but it brought order into the wilderness.

The company did not enter the contest for credit for splitting the Choctaw Nation. Others could claim the glory; it had the trade. These traders maintained English ties to the Creek and Chickasaw nations and weakened the French hold on the Choctaws. They were a major influence in the shaping of the southern frontier during the first war with the French, known as King George's War, 1744–48.

CHAPTER SIX

The Powerful Company at Augusta

Henry Parker's complaint about the Brown, Rae monopoly was only one of several indications that the company had achieved dominance in the deerskin trade west of the Savannah River. The opinion was echoed by one of Parker's foremost adversaries. Thomas Bosomworth, writing in 1753, noted that "the powerful Company at Augusta seem to look upon the whole trade of the Creek Nation as their undoubted Right." The monopoly was never as complete as the members of the company would have liked, but it was too exclusive to suit its competitors. Henry Laurens, a shrewd young Charlestown merchant, estimated that Brown, Rae and Company accounted for 75 percent of the trade to the Creeks and Chickasaws. James Beamor, one of Roger Lacy's deputies in 1736 and a veteran of the Cherokee trade, was so impressed with the growing influence of the company that he warned Governor Glen "that company at Augusta notwithstanding they have the trade of the Creeks, Chickasaws and Choctaws chiefly, yet they will ruin us here." His complaint, written from the Cherokee town of Tugaloo in 1749, was that the company was granting licenses to traders in the Cherokee country and thus assuming the prerogative of the Carolina Indian commissioner.[1]

The frontier outpost of Augusta, situated in Indian territory, had become the fiefdom of the great company. To Scots such as McGillivray and Daniel Clark, it was much like the old country. Just as the Clan Chattan ruled Strathnairn, the lords of Indian commerce ruled Augusta. A policy of salutary neglect had been inaugurated by the founder, Oglethorpe. Because Augusta served his Indian diplomacy, he overlooked the flouting of the Trustees' regulations. Captain Richard Kent took a cue from his general and gave the traders wide latitude in organizing the trade. The company of seven brought order out of the confusion; uniform prices were established; sensible regulations were adopted. There was to be no trading in the woods but only in designated villages. Traders were assigned to specific villages; skins were to be properly dressed by the Indians before they were purchased. Rum was not supposed to be traded, according to the Rum Act of 1735, but the repeal of that measure in 1742 led to increasing use of rum as a trade item. Veteran traders knew the danger of the abuse of rum and attempted to limit its use.[2]

South Carolina's vigorous objections to Georgia's claim to the exclusive right to license traders doing business west of the Savannah had led to protracted negotiations between the Trustees and Carolina's agents and a compromise in 1741. The Privy Council approved an arrangement whereby half of the traders operating across the Savannah could be licensed by Carolina, and, in return, Georgians might trade with the dwindling Catawba tribe in Carolina.[3] The accommodation played into the hands of the traders. Some of the members of Brown, Rae and Company were licensed in Carolina, some in Georgia, McGillivray in Charlestown, Galphin in Savannah. If refused in one place, they could be licensed in the other. It is small wonder that officials in neither Charlestown nor Savannah ever knew who was legitimately licensed and who was not. It was even less wonder that the company became a law unto itself. The system worked. Its members cooperated with Captain Richard Kent in the government of Augusta. Traders

Isaac Barksdale and Rowland Pritchett were named assistants to Kent. Kent's constables out in the Creek country maintained a good working relationship with the members of the company. James Adair would look back on the era as a golden age, when the policies of government and traders were directed to the same end, the frustration of the French.[4]

When Oglethorpe's regiment was disbanded in 1749, the soldiers had the choice of staying in the colonies or returning to England. Augusta's permanent population was swelled by the discharged men, who claimed a bounty of fifty acres each. After twelve years at Augusta, Captain Richard Kent decided to return home. Captain George Cadogan was given command of the independent company at Fort Augusta as well as the small garrison across the river at Fort Moore. Although Cadogan attempted to exercise leadership for a brief period, he did not want a long commitment to the frontier town.[5]

In 1750 the people of Augusta petitioned for a conservator of the peace to be named to replace Kent. The council in Savannah recommended James Fraser, a trader, and the Trustees approved the appointment. John Rae and James Campbell were named assistants. It was no coincidence that complaints about the growing power of the company followed the appointment of traders to represent the government.[6]

It would be wrong to assume that the company was interested only in profit. Rather, its members displayed an interest in building up Augusta as a place to live. John Rae owned five hundred acres along a creek which subsequently bore his name. Patrick Brown cultivated an indigo plantation below Augusta. George Galphin settled on Silver Bluff plantation twelve miles below Augusta on the Carolina side and began to accumulate lands in Georgia across the river. On November 6, 1749, Lachlan McGillivray petitioned the council in Savannah for a hundred acres on "Kynion's Creek" near Augusta and announced his intention of building a mill to grind corn there. The council noted its confidence in the petitioner's ability to comply with his request and acknowledged that a corn mill would be of great utility to the inhabitants of Augusta. The land was granted.[7]

The petition indicated McGillivray's intentions. He had held a license for only five years and had taken a wife and built a house at

Little Tallassee. His son, Alexander, would be born on December 15 of the following year. Evidently, McGillivray intended to come in out of the woods. He would not, like some of his fellow Scots, make his permanent abode among his wife's people. Early in 1750 the company leased an estate of five hundred acres just above Augusta, where the main trail divided, one branch following the river to the Cherokee country, the other fork becoming the Creek trading path. The site was ideal for a supply depot, and apparently that is what the company had in mind. The signers of the lease were partners: Lachlan McGillivray, William Sludders, Daniel Clark, and Patrick Brown. They were described in the deed as storekeepers and traders. A stone house stood some eighty yards from the river and was called the White House. The building was destined to acquire fame as the site of a battle during the American Revolution. Twentieth-century Augustans confused the original house, destroyed during the battle, with a 1797 house built by the tobacco merchant Ezekiel Harris on the same tract.[8]

The company was in the forefront of the effort to introduce formal religion to the frontier town. On June 26, 1749, James Fraser reported that the people of Augusta were willing to build a church and provide a house for a minister. To prove their good intentions, the people proceeded to build the church under the protecting curtain of the fort. The Trustees seemed delighted at the unexpected display of edifying behavior and used their good offices with the Society for the Propagation of the Gospel to secure the appointment of a resident minister. On March 1, 1751, the Trustees were notified that the Reverend Jonathan Copp had been named to Augusta. The society sent a baptismal font with its blessing and good wishes. The font graces the vestibule of St. Paul's Church today. The Trustees, not to be outdone, dispatched books, altar linen, sacred vessels, and other essentials of the Anglican ritual.[9]

The Reverend Mr. Copp was not of the stuff of which martyrs are made. The Franciscans of Florida and the Jesuits of Canada who endured torture and death at the hands of the Indians were not his role models. The presence of Indians terrified Copp, and he listed many complaints in his first report to the Trustees. But candor forced him to acknowledge the leadership of the company, whose members he described as the chief promoters of the trade and of the "present flourishing State of this growing Town." They and those they employed "have demonstrated their hearty Zeal for the Good of this place."[10] They contributed more toward the building of the church and parsonage than all the rest of the town's inhabitants.

Attendance at Copp's services was good; he counted between eighty and a hundred people, although only eight were regular communicants. Copp was unhappy in his new ministry; his most heartfelt sentiments concerned the Indians. "We live at Augusta in the Fear for our Lives," he informed his superiors in London. "The merciless Savages and Indians (whose tender mercies are cruelty) have threatened us much of late." A party of Indians on the way to Savannah fired a friendly salute when they passed Fort Augusta. Copp, who was conducting services at the time, was greatly shaken.[11]

The Augusta traders were disappointed in Copp. They considered him fussy as well as fainthearted. John Rae resigned from the church committee after quarreling with the minister. Although Copp asked to be transferred shortly after he arrived in Augusta, he was forced to remain until 1756, when an invitation from a parish near Charlestown rescued him from his perilous ministry. The church in Augusta survived and became a parish in 1757, to the credit of the gentlemen traders more than to that of the unheroic minister.[12]

The company's quibbles with the first resident minister were the least of the concerns of the chief traders. A concert of crises occurred during the first year of the decade of the 1750s. The people in Savannah were critical of the company for not giving their town enough business. In addition, the Georgia authorities resented South Carolina Governor Glen's high-handed management of Indian affairs and blamed the traders who were licensed in South Carolina for ignoring Georgia's best interests. The Augusta traders had to be masters of diplomacy to gain the good graces of both Carolina and Georgia, and they largely succeeded. Another matter of engrossing interest was the viability of the colony of Georgia. The Trustees were discouraged and anxious to dispose of their unrewarding charge. Would Georgia revert to South Carolina or would it be maintained as a separate province?

Indian diplomacy was a continuing concern. Traders like McGillivray and Galphin came to be regarded as masters of their craft. The protagonists were, as always, the French, who by mid-1751 had completed a new and larger Fort Toulouse. The French, stung by the Choctaw Revolt, persuaded a band of Creeks to attack a Cherokee village and thus launched a typical Indian war. There were no massive invasions of either nation, but a series of surprise attacks and wilderness ambushes kept the frontier in turmoil. Glen of South Carolina was determined to stop the fighting between the allies of the English. The Georgia president and assistants disagreed with this policy, reasoning that while the Creeks were busy fighting Cherokees they would not bother Georgians. The Trustees' agents in Savannah were particularly worried about the Creeks because of certain outrageous claims on the part of Mary Musgrove Bosomworth and her husband, Thomas. The two were abetted by Thomas's brothers Abraham and Adam.[13] The Bosomworths played a critical if curious role in the shaping of the frontier, which deserves comment.

The Bosomworth affair embroiled both provinces in controversy. It represented a serious intrusion into the company's management of Indian affairs, and it taxed the adroitness of the traders' skill in maintaining good relations on all sides. If it were not taken so seriously by those involved, the Bosomworth saga might seem like high comedy. Lachlan McGillivray managed to weave his way through the intrigues and emerge in the good graces of Governor Glen and his council without alienating the Bosomworths or their friends.

The controversy stemmed from the conflicting positions of the English and the Creek Nation regarding landownership. According to English law, only the king could grant land to a British subject. The Creeks, understandably, did not consider themselves bound by English law. The land was theirs; they could dispose of it as they wished. They had allowed Squire Oglethorpe to settle the area between the Savannah and Altamaha as far as the tide moved the waters, reserving to themselves the Musgrove plantation on Pipemakers Creek and the islands of Sapelo, Ossabaw, and St. Catherine. Mary Musgrove Bosomworth claimed those places by virtue of her position as a surviving niece of Brims, the acknowledged head of the Creek Nation, and the acquiescence of the Creeks to her claim. Apparently Oglethorpe had led her to believe that the English would recognize her title to the places. If so, he did not speak for the Trustees or for their Georgia representatives. John Juricek, a historian who sifted through the conflicting testimony, noted, "Again and again the Creeks had granted them [the Bosomworths] the lands reserved under the 1739 treaty and again and again the Savannah authorities had thwarted them." [14]

In 1747 Abraham Bosomworth, an ensign in Oglethorpe's regiment, was dispatched on a mission to the Creeks. The Creeks were in an ugly mood, and no South Carolina agents would dare enter the nation at the time. Major William Horton asked Bosomworth to go up to Coweta with presents for Malatchi. Mary Bosomworth provided the supplies at the very real risk of never being compensated. Because of his connection with Mary, Abraham was well received by her cousin Malatchi. He prevailed upon Malatchi to go down to Frederica to confirm friendship with the English in Georgia. In return, Malatchi asked Abraham Bosomworth to go to England and obtain presents from the great king himself. [15]

The company now became involved. Shortly after Abraham departed on his errand, George Galphin circulated a letter with the signatures of his fellow traders disclaiming any connection with the Bosomworths. He was not sure what reason Abraham Bosomworth had for going to England, but if he claimed that he had the traders' support, he was wrong. Abraham and Thomas had tried to get the traders to concede that an agreement with Oglethorpe entitled Mary Bosomworth to three offshore islands. The traders refused to sign a statement to that effect. Galphin accused the Bosomworths of giving bad talks to the Indians. [16] Galphin's letter was sent to Glen rather than to the Georgia Council in Savannah.

Meanwhile, Abraham Bosomworth was successful in his mission. The secretary of state for the colonies, the Duke of Bedford, authorized annual presents for the southern Indians. Bedford wrote to Georgia and Carolina that he was sending £3,000 in supplies to be shared evenly between the two provinces. Bedford recommended Abraham Bosomworth as the proper person to act as the Carolina agent and left it up to Georgia to name an agent to cooperate in the distribution. Carolinians welcomed the unexpected bounty, but they chafed at the idea of sharing the goods on an even basis with the upstart province next door.[17]

When Glen attempted to make the case that Georgia did not deserve so much because the province dealt only with the Lower Creeks whereas Carolina had to maintain relations with all the other tribes, Henry Parker, the most feisty member of the Georgia Council, replied sharply that he and other Georgians had been dealing with Indians long before Glen arrived in America. "We can't be supposed to be unacquainted with them," Parker commented acidly. He went further and attacked Glen where he was most vulnerable, in his ego. Glen was then claiming all the credit for detaching the Choctaws from the French, but Parker said correctly that Choctaws were entertained in Savannah before they had any dealing with Charlestown.[18]

Like it or not, Carolina and Georgia were bound by Bedford's instructions to work together in disposing of the Indian goods. Patrick Graham went to Charlestown as Georgia's agent to work with Abraham Bosomworth in parceling out the goods. The two agents returned to Savannah in August 1749 to find the town in a turmoil and the Bosomworths in trouble. What had happened sounds simple in retrospect but was regarded with the utmost suspicion by the authorities in Savannah at the time. The straightforward version was related by Joseph Piercy, Thomas Bosomworth's "linguister," or interpreter. Thomas and Mary Bosomworth planned to follow Abraham's example and go to London. There, perhaps with Oglethorpe as advocate, they could obtain compensation for the supplies they had advanced in 1747 and also secure a clear title to St. Catherine, Sapelo, and Ossabaw islands as well as to the old Musgrove tracts above Savannah. Mary wanted Thomas to explain to Malatchi that she was going of her own free will and there was no truth to the rumor that she was being taken to England as a captive. On July 1, Bosomworth and Piercy left St.

Catherine on their ostensibly innocent errand, arrived at Coweta town on July 8, and delivered their message. Malatchi and two headmen of the Cussetas decided to pay Mary a friendly call before she left for England. They took along three young braves to hunt for food along the way. Another large party of Lower Creeks followed because they had heard that presents were to be distributed in Savannah.[19]

On July 21, Bosomworth and Malatchi's party arrived in Savannah. Bosomworth notified the president and assistants of the arrival of the important visitor, the successor to Emperor Brims as titular leader of the Upper and Lower Creeks. He explained that Malatchi was in Savannah to see that Mary went aboard the ship voluntarily.[20] Despite their above-mentioned boast to Glen, the Savannah gentlemen were amateurs in Indian diplomacy. Glen, at least, had a broader grasp of frontier politics.

William Stephens was in the last days of his presidency at the time. Henry Parker was the strongest member of the council, and he decided that Malatchi could not have made the trip for so light a reason. The real purpose, they concluded, must be to seize the lands claimed by the Bosomworths. The authorities were so convinced of Malatchi's treachery that they forgot their good manners. They deliberately ignored Malatchi. It was a stunning insult to a great chief whose own hospitality was legendary. A week later, Mary Bosomworth, embarrassed by the Georgians' silence, chided Stephens for not receiving Malatchi. The nervous council members finally agreed to invite Malatchi and the other two chiefs to a meal, but they instructed the interpreter, John Kinnard, to listen carefully to the Indians' conversation to discover the real reason for their presence in Savannah.[21]

The atmosphere of suspicion spoiled the gesture of welcome. Malatchi returned to Mary's house, and the council postponed all other business "in order to have a more watchful eye over the conduct of the Bosomworths and the Indians." Oddly enough, while maintaining a watchful eye, the council decided to cut a path from Mary's house to town to facilitate the Indians' coming and going. Why Indians who had walked through a wilderness should need an avenue to Savannah is not clear, nor was it comprehensible to the Indians then. When the five woodcutters trespassed on Bosomworth land, they were warned off. Henry Parker sent them back, explaining that the work was for the good of the Indians. This time the Indians seized the axes and put them across the property line. The minutes of the council express surprise over this "extraordinary behaviour" on the part of the Indians.[22]

The large band of Creeks, including women and children, arrived in Savannah ten days after Malatchi. As their canoes approached the town, they fired their guns in salute as they did routinely at Augusta. The Savannah people were alarmed, and the council minutes referred to the "menacing and insulting" manner of the Indians' arrival. Although the council blamed Bosomworth for bringing the Indians down for some mischievous purpose, the Creeks were actually interested in the expected presents. The militia was mobilized under John Milledge and ready for a fight.[23]

On August 10, 1749, the militia, foot and horse, marched out to the Indians' camp at the Bosomworths' place and ordered the Indians to lay down their weapons and follow along to William Stephens's house. The march was accompanied by the tattoo of a drum. At the head of the Indians were Malatchi, Mary, Thomas (in his clergyman's garb), and Adam. To the council it was a confrontation; to Malatchi it was a long-delayed ceremony of welcome. Malatchi made none of the threats or demands the council expected; rather, he enjoyed himself and departed, mellow with wine.[24]

The Indians consumed more wine later at Mary's house. Then Malatchi announced that he was going to take a bottle of wine to his new friend William Stephens. Adam Bosomworth accompanied him, and to add a touch of style, they brought along a drummer. Their only weapon was a bottle of wine and a glass. Nevertheless, the sound of a drum provoked a panic in Savannah. A hostile crowd surrounded Malatchi. Henry Parker, inebriated himself, ordered Adam Bosomworth arrested for leading the Indians in a hostile manner. When Malatchi told Mary what had happened, she flew into a rage and upbraided Parker for his stupidity. Parker asked her whether she was a white woman or an Indian. She answered that she was an Indian. "Madam," said Parker, "if I had called you that, you would have spit in my face."[25] He then put Mary in the guardhouse along with Adam.

In their extensive account of the affair, the president and assistants accused Mary of causing all the trouble; she was "Spirited up with Liquor, Drunk with passion and disappointed in her Views."[26] The next day she and her husband were severely reprimanded for their bad behavior and required to apologize in presence of the Indians. The council's official report conveyed the impression that the conference had gone rather well and that the Indians departed in good humor. In fact, Malatchi was disgusted with the treatment he received.

On August 16, Abraham Bosomworth arrived from Charlestown to find that William Stephens had already distributed most of the presents. It did no good for Abraham to explain that his instructions from the Duke of Bedford were to give some of the supplies to Mary to repay her for providing presents in 1747. The council decided that Abraham was in league with the others and that he had come "only to serve his own family." After careful consideration, the council concluded that the Bosomworths were legally entitled to presents but because of their bad behavior would not be given them.[27] Thomas Bosomworth summed up the episode by noting sadly, "This is a gloomy prospect of affairs." He had gone into debt to put a herd of cattle on St. Catherine Island and had no way of paying without the expected supplies. Adam Bosomworth swore before a magistrate that James Habersham, a member of the council, had been heard to say that some of the leading men had deliberately provoked a disturbance to get more soldiers in Georgia. Abraham Bosomworth registered a similar oath. The council displayed a marvelous lack of sensitivity by concluding that "the Board cannot conceive wherein Mr. Bosomworth or his wife have been oppressed or injured." Bosomworth called that statement "a Superlative Degree of Ingratitude as well as Disregard to Truth."[28]

On the last day of August 1749, William Stephens gave over the responsibilities of Indian commissioner to Patrick Graham. There was a large consignment of Indian presents left over, and Graham dispatched John Kinnard to invite the chiefs who had not received gifts to come down to Savannah. Kinnard's task was not easy. Malatchi spread the word that the Indians might expect hostile treatment such as he had received. A headman named Long Warrior persuaded ninety Lower Creeks to make the trip anyway. The Georgia Council attempted to recognize Long Warrior as emperor of all the Creeks instead of Malatchi. Long Warrior had more sense than to accept the honor and hastened to assure Malatchi that he would not consider accepting the offer.[29]

Henry Parker and his associates could not have conceived a better way of alienating the Creeks if they had set their minds to it. Malatchi rushed to the open arms of the French at Mobile, where he was "greatly caressed," as McGillivray might have phrased it. He and his chiefs returned to Coweta, hoisted the French flag, and invited the officers to Fort Toulouse to pay a friendly visit. Governor Vaudreuil in New Orleans was delighted at the turn of events. Governor Glen in Charlestown was horrified. The normal atmosphere of anxiety in which the traders lived became acute. George Galphin, the company's trader at Coweta, was caught in a tangled web. He had to maintain good terms with Malatchi as well as the council in Savannah. To show his displeasure at the French overtures, he refused to enter the town square at Coweta while the French flag flew.[30] In July, the Georgia authorities learned from two traders that Mary Bosomworth was expected at Coweta in the Lower Creek country any day. The rumor was that she was going to move her residence and her cattle into the Creek Nation. The council members suspected that the real reason was to mobilize Indians in her behalf.[31] George Galphin came to Savannah in September 1749 to renew his license and brought news that the Bosomworths were indeed in Coweta. Galphin, who did not realize that as a member of the monopolizing company he was in bad grace, made two requests of the council. Oglethorpe had promised him a tract of land in Georgia across from Silver Bluff. He asked for confirmation of the deed. At the same time, Galphin asked to be named constable in the Lower Creek country in place of one of Richard Kent's deputies, William Finlay, who had died in July.[32]

While the council considered these requests, one of the dreaded

Bosomworths arrived in Savannah. Adam Bosomworth presented a sworn deposition that he had asked Galphin why French colors were flying over Coweta. Galphin had answered that Malatchi's people had been dissatisfied since their return from Savannah. When Mary promised to take their case to the king in England, there was "a general joy in the face of the whole Assembly," and the French colors were taken down.[33]

Bosomworth also presented Mary's memorial in which she styled herself Coosaponakeesa, Princess of the Upper and Lower Creek Nations, the daughter of the sister of the Emperor Brims. The assembled Indians agreed that Mary had full authority to transact business "as firmly as if the whole tribe were present." The document was signed by Malatchi and six other headmen. It was witnessed by George Galphin, Adam Bosomworth, Joseph Piercy, and William Linden.[34]

The council regarded Galphin's act of witnessing as treachery, decided not to grant him any land, and thought his request to be made constable a sinister effort on the part of the company to further its monopoly. In a tight spot, Galphin squirmed as best he could. He explained that he had not wanted to witness the statement, but he was afraid that Mary's relatives would kill him if he did not. He stated, wrongly, that the memorial had not been interpreted to the Indians. His letter, couched in wretched English, reeked with repentance.[35]

The council decided that in spite of Galphin's "late double dealings" it would use him to frustrate the "wicked designs" of the Bosomworths. Patrick Graham would go up to the Creeks and force them to admit that Mary had no right to the land she claimed, and Galphin would assist him. Graham would then seek out the best linguist among the Upper Creeks and take his case to that part of the nation also.[36] The best man in the land watered by the Coosa and Tallapoosa was Lachlan McGillivray. While the Bosomworths were disturbing the peace of the Savannah functionaries, Lachlan McGillivray was busy improving his position among the Upper Creeks and in the council chambers of Charlestown. The Upper Creeks were oriented toward Charlestown rather than Savannah.

Mary Bosomworth's invitation to Malatchi to visit her in the autumn of 1749, coupled with the lure of presents to be had in Savannah, spoiled Governor Glen's grand conference at that same time in Charlestown. In his customary fashion, Glen advertised the meeting in superlatives. He intended, he told the Lords Commissioners, to settle a general peace among the Cherokees, Creeks, and Catawbas. He blamed the French at the Alabama Fort for instigating the latest rupture between the Creeks and Cherokees and still hoped to involve the Indians in an attack on that post. The meeting, he said, would be the biggest ever. Glen employed the company's traders to carry his invitation to the headmen. The excuses filtered back. Chigilly promised Parson Bosomworth to go to Savannah, so he could not go to Charlestown. Actually, he went to neither place. Malatchi went to Savannah with Bosomworth. Peter Chartier of the Savannahs visited the French instead of Glen. The Gun Merchant thanked Glen but said he had to build his house and care for his cattle. The Gun informed Glen that the headman employed by the French to provoke the Cherokees was called Acorn Whistler. In fact, Acorn Whistler's band was running amuck among the Overhill Cherokees while other Creeks prepared to go to Charlestown to listen to Glen's peace talks. Even that steadfast friend of the English, the Wolf of Muccolossus, decided to forgo this trip.[37]

Glen's meeting was somewhat less grand than he planned. It was a tribute to Lachlan McGillivray that some of the leading headmen were willing to accompany him to Charlestown. Among the eight Abeikas and eight Tallapoosas were Red Coat of the Okfuskees, Devall's Landlord of Puckantallahasee, and Alachi of Tuckabatchee. Glen made the most of it. The pomp and circumstance of his reception of the visitors contrasted strikingly with the farce being enacted in Savannah at the same time. Lachlan McGillivray solemnly introduced each chief, and the proceedings were carefully noted and inserted into the Indian Book, which was subsequently lost.[38]

Glen undoubtedly called for an end to the Cherokee war. He might have taken up the complaint of the Upper Creek traders. McGillivray brought with him a petition, signed by Patrick Brown, John Rae, Daniel Clark, Joseph Wright, Jerome Courtonne, and others, including himself, which complained of too many unlicensed traders infiltrating their territory and undercutting their prices. These vagrants bought poorly prepared, "green" skins, and as a result, Indian clients of legitimate traders were increasingly slipshod and the price of skins was declining.[39]

The meeting, which was disappointing to begin with, ended in disaster. Several of the visitors contracted a fever and some died. For McGillivray personally, the meeting was a success. The governor who had once doubted his integrity was won over. The House voted him £120 for acting as linguister on the occasion. McGillivray stopped in Augusta long enough to outfit his caravan from the company's stores and to plan new acquisitions of land. Then he joined his family at his plantation at Little Tallassee.[40]

On April 5, 1750, McGillivray sent a carefully crafted letter to Glen reporting a general assembly of the Upper Creeks called by the Gun Merchant at Okchoys. On behalf of the other headmen, the Gun thanked Glen for his efforts to bring about peace. He asked Glen to convey his good intentions to the Cherokees and promised to restrain his warriors, at least "until they kill some of us." Unfortunately, a large body of Lower Creeks had gone against the Cherokees for harboring northern Indians who had murdered some Cusseta braves. The Gun Merchant finished with a request that matched the name given him by the English. He wanted an English gunsmith sent to his village. As it was, his people had to go to the Alabama Fort to have their weapons repaired, and the French charged an excessive rate.[41]

Although the Upper Creeks were not involved in the furor over the French visit to Coweta, they were keenly interested. After all, they acknowledged Malatchi as their titular head, and Mary Bosomworth's town was the Upper Creek village of Tuckabatchee. For a while, it seemed that Mary would seek sanctuary with her relatives there.

When McGillivray, Patrick Brown, and Daniel Clark went to Charlestown to renew their licenses in 1750, they were immediately called into the council chambers for an interrogation. Glen was concerned about Malatchi's behavior. Had he told the French about Carolina's designs on the Alabama Fort? The traders could only answer that he went to that fort immediately upon his return from Savannah. Daniel Clark saw a French lieutenant, an engineer, an ensign, three private soldiers, and two blacks in Coweta by invitation of Malatchi. Did the French give presents? Only ammunition and paint. Had Malatchi gone over to the French? He leaned more to the French and Spanish than to the English. Should trade to the Lower Creek towns be stopped as a gesture of protest? The three traders were unanimous in their opinion that an embargo should be imposed. Would the Lower Creeks then molest the Upper Creek traders? The traders were certain of it. But wouldn't the Upper Creeks protect them? They would try. But the Lower Creeks would kill the traders and blame the northern Indians.[42] The traders' straightforward answers were more confusing than helpful.

Glen dutifully itemized the latest news to the Lords Commissioners. The French were building a new fort at the Alabamas. Malatchi obstinately opposed Glen's efforts to destroy that fort. Malatchi was not as great as Glen had thought; although he claimed to be emperor of all the Creeks, he was really just chief of the Cowetas. The traders wanted to deprive the Lower Creeks of presents for a year. Carolina should not have to share the Indian presents with Georgia. Glen's information was elaborated on by the Carolina agent in London, James Crokatt, who argued that presents should be distributed by the commander in chief of the military forces, and that officer was the governor of South Carolina. Crokatt contrasted the impressive reception accorded to Indian visitors in Charlestown with the poverty displayed in Savannah.[43] Glen was in trouble with the Lords Commissioners about his mishandling of the Choctaw trade, and his request to manage the distribution of the presents was rejected.

McGillivray, Patrick Brown, and Daniel Clark returned to Augusta for the annual outfitting of caravans and, very likely, to supervise the stocking of the storehouse on the company's five-hundred-acre tract between Rae's Creek and Augusta. They learned, if they did not know it already, that the company had enemies in Savannah. Some of the traders who were licensed in Savannah complained that they were excluded from the principal villages. Savannah merchants James Habersham and Francis Harris complained that certain employees of the company never came to Savannah or Augusta because they were supplied with goods in the Indian country. As a result, their creditors could not get them to pay their debts. Besides, the Augusta company shipped its skins to Charlestown instead of Savannah.[44]

The complaints against the company were made official in the colony's first assembly, which met in Savannah on January 14, 1751. The Trustees summoned the meeting as an experiment in self-government before yielding control of the colony to the king. Only two of the sixteen delegates were from Augusta, which meant that the company was poorly represented. After debating what to do about the monopolizing company, the assembly decided that storekeepers should not be licensed to trade. The business of storekeeper or merchant should be kept separate from the business of trade. This resolution reflected the interests of Francis Harris, Speaker of the assembly, and of James Habersham. Brown, Rae and Company, as merchants and traders, had an advantage over Harris and Habersham, who were merely merchants. Most of the other recommendations of the assembly concerned trade and navigation at Savannah. Finally, the assembly begged the Trustees not to allow Georgia to be gobbled up by the aggressive province of South Carolina when the Trustees relinquished control in 1752.[45]

The company took up its own defense in a dispatch from Augusta, which reads as though it were written by Lachlan McGillivray. The account expressed regret that the company's first letter addressed to the Trustees was a complaint, but the "late conduct of some envious and malicious" people forced the company to respond. The Trustees were reminded that the company had undertaken to supply the Choctaws. Its members were largely responsible for keeping the Creek Indians on good terms. The company should be considered a benefactor of the colony, "for we must say (and without vanity) that our House is the best acquainted with Indian Affairs of any in this Colony."[46] The letter was a subtle reminder that the Savannah merchants did not know what they were talking about in the matter of Indian affairs. The Trustees, bewildered by the labyrinthian politics of the Bosomworth affair and discouraged about the entire Georgia experiment, surrendered their charter to the king in 1752 and Georgia became a royal colony. Until a royal governor could be dispatched, Georgia was governed by the same council that had served the Trustees so ineptly.

In spite of its criticism of the company, the Georgia Council was forced to call on the services of the company soon after the 1751 assembly adjourned. Patrick Graham represented the council in distributing presents, first to the Upper Creeks and then the Lower. Unskilled in Indian diplomacy and a stranger to Indian customs, Graham relied on Lachlan McGillivray to organize a congress at Okchoys in May 1751. Twenty-six chieftains assembled, and the important traders were on hand for the occasion. Among them were stalwarts of the company: George Galphin, Daniel Clark, William Sludders, John Pettigrew, and Thomas Devall. It was a tribute to McGillivray's ability as a linguist that he was the official interpreter both for the Okchoys meeting and for the Lower Creek conference at Coweta on June 3, 1751.[47]

The import of Graham's message was that the Indians should disregard the malicious reports spread by the Bosomworths that the king meant harm to the Indians. He urged his listeners to pay no attention to the "foolish and idle" territorial claims of the Bosomworths. Instead, they should confirm the lands in question to the king. The Gun Merchant rose to reply on behalf of all the others. Rather surprisingly, he said that he and his people had no objection to the English occupying Sapelo, St. Catherine, and Ossabaw.[48] Graham went on to reenact the scene with the Lower Creek chiefs at Coweta. Malatchi was hospitable to visitors, even to those from Savannah, but he would not give Graham the satisfaction of agreeing with him. He was vague about whether the Bosomworths owned the lands in question; private ownership was an English concept. But he was certain that the three islands belonged to the Creek Nation and not to the English.[49] Graham had to be satisfied with that, and he brought away a good impression of the abilities and influence of Lachlan McGillivray. In the future the Georgia authorities would make use of McGillivray's services just as Glen of Carolina did.

McGillivray returned to his family at Little Tallassee for the fall and winter season. On December 18, 1751, he informed William Pinckney, South Carolina Indian commissioner, of the latest news from the

French fort nearby. The new fort was completed; it was "a pretty strong one." A large boat had come up from Mobile "loaded with a Priest, Popery and Brandy." The priest was to be stationed at the fort as a missionary to the Indians. A large reinforcement of soldiers had arrived in Mobile, causing concern among the Upper Creeks. The French governor had invited the Creek headmen to Mobile for a conference in the spring.[50]

The arrival of five new companies of soldiers at Mobile was part of a major French initiative. Thirty-seven new companies were distributed around Louisiana, most of them at New Orleans. Governor Vaudreuil was especially concerned about the security of Fort Toulouse. He knew that the English wanted to seize it in order to penetrate the French territory by way of the Alabama River. The officers at the fort were carefully chosen; "consummate experience and especial study" were required, according to the governor. Although it was official policy to rotate the garrisons at other posts, the men at the Alabama Fort were there on a long-term basis. They intermarried with the Indians and had families there. They cultivated the land and produced a surplus for the neighboring Indians. The Alabama Indians would object to their transfer.[51]

Although clever in Indian intrigue, Vaudreuil was in trouble with the government for his venality. He exacted one-third profit from all trade carried out at the posts. His wife was notoriously corrupt. Over the years she had purloined a warehouse full of government goods which her butler sold at a handsome profit for her. Vaudreuil decided that a successful expedition against the Chickasaws might redeem him in the eyes of his superiors. During the summer of 1752, Vaudreuil ordered fifteen hundred Frenchmen and Choctaw braves to march against the Chickasaw villages. John Buckles, a Chickasaw trader, described what happened: three hundred French and a large number of Choctaws attacked the Chickasaws, who hoisted English colors and fought with their usual resolution. The battle raged all day, but at a great distance, so there were not many casualties. Many of the Choctaws had only recently gone over to the French after their prolonged revolt, and their efforts lacked enthusiasm. Governor Glen later implied that he had something to do with the Chickasaw victory. His agent, Buckles, had warned the Chickasaws in time for them to call in their hunters and build a fort. He maintained the fiction that the English Choctaws were still loyal to him and that they only pretended to attack. The ignominious defeat sealed the fate of Governor Philippe de Rigaud de Vaudreuil. That year he was replaced by Louis Belouart de Kerlérec, who was destined to be the last governor of French Louisiana. Vaudreuil became governor of Canada.[52]

The burst of French activity, of enormous relevance to Lachlan McGillivray at his plantation near the Alabama Fort, was of surprisingly slight interest in Charlestown and Savannah, compared to the near panic caused by Bienville's earlier invasions. The English now took a Chickasaw victory for granted and, unfortunately for the French, so did the Choctaws. In 1752, the desultory Creek-Cherokee war was more important to the English, as were the Bosomworths.

The Bosomworths' response to Graham's 1751 mission was to take their case to England as they had planned to do in 1749, but that trip was again postponed because Governor Glen needed them for a difficult mission no one else would undertake. By chance, a party of Creeks visited Charlestown while a group of Cherokees lingered nearby. One of the Creek chiefs was the same Acorn Whistler who had instigated the recent Creek-Cherokee war at the behest of the French. Acorn Whistler sent word from Charlestown to some of his followers to ambush the Cherokees; the attack was carried out, and the guilty Creeks then returned to their own country, followed by Acorn Whistler. Glen could not tolerate the assassination of friendly Indians who were in the vicinity of Charlestown and under his protection. So he sent Thomas and Mary Bosomworth on a task no trader would try. They had to demand the death of Acorn Whistler.[53]

Thomas Bosomworth, who had originally come to Georgia to act as William Stephens's clerk, was never at a loss for words. He wrote a full account of the expedition. As his party was departing Charlestown on July 4, 1752, they met Lachlan McGillivray coming into town. Bosomworth regarded McGillivray as a member of the opposition, and he "taxed" McGillivray with circulating bad reports about the Bosomworths. McGillivray denied doing any such thing. Strictly speaking, it was Patrick Graham who spread the bad reports.[54]

Augusta was the stronghold of his enemies, according to Bosomworth. The "artful and designing" men there, with "their own sinister ends in view," put every obstacle in their way as the envoys attempted to outfit their party for the journey. The traders thought it a bad idea to try to execute a chief in his own country. The Bosomworths left Augusta on July 16 after one week, crossed the Oconee River on July 17, the Ocmulgee on the nineteenth, the Flint on the twentieth, and on the twenty-fourth they reached Coweta town, Malatchi's village. They were received with joy by old Chigilly and by Malatchi, when he came in from a raid he had conducted against the Cherokees.[55]

The chiefs were astonished at Glen's request. Chigilly said if Acorn Whistler had killed white people, he could understand, but he could not understand why a Creek chief should be put to death for killing his enemies. Mary used her influence, arguing that it was better that one or two should suffer death than that the whole nation should be punished. The chiefs consulted, but as they confessed, "for all their united wisdom," they could not determine what was best. The imperious Mary told them that their reply was weak and childish. Malatchi and Chigilly finally agreed that Acorn Whistler should die, but how to do it was a puzzle. His relatives would be honor bound to retaliate against the assailant, even if it were Malatchi. So the two leaders found a nephew of Acorn Whistler who had a grudge against him and bribed him to kill the guilty man. When the nephew reported that the deed was done, he was killed also so no one would discover that he was put up to it.[56]

Before the Bosomworths left Coweta, Malatchi conveyed a complaint to Governor Glen about the increasing number of white vagabonds in the Indian country. He wanted "all the strolling white people that are not employed in the Indian trade" ordered out of the nation.[57] It was the first of many such complaints, and they would grow in frequency and intensity.

While the Bosomworths were among the Upper Creeks, they noticed that the Indians nearest the French fort traded their English goods for French liquor. Most likely their goods came from McGillivray, the trader nearest the French fort. They learned also that a Chickasaw brave had killed a drunken white packhorseman. Malatchi, Gun Merchant, Devall's Landlord, and the Wolf agreed that the Chickasaw must pay with his life and sent a party after him. A poignant drama was enacted. When it was evident that the guilty man was afraid to die, his uncle said calmly that he would die for him. He went to find a gun, but his frantic wife hid it from him. The uncle then took a long French knife, returned to the village square, and in Bosomworth's words, "with greatest Undauntedness stuck the Knife into the Gullet and immediately dyed with the Wound." [58]

As with everything else, Governor Glen claimed credit for extinguishing the Creek and Cherokee war, which, in fact, continued sporadically. He related to the Lords Commissioners how he had brought about the death of Acorn Whistler, the "greatest warriour" in the Creek Nation. When he informed the Cherokees, they were overjoyed that Malatchi had given satisfaction in so striking and unexpected a manner. [59]

The governor instructed McGillivray to invite the Creeks down to Charlestown to celebrate and confirm the peace. As in most matters involving Indian relations, the confirmation of peace was not a simple matter. Many traders, James Adair for one, thought it a mistake. Continuing hostility between the two nations was the best guarantee of the traders' safety. Adair asserted that Lachlan McGillivray unwillingly engaged in this "pernicious affair" at the urging of the governor. McGillivray was successful in persuading the Creeks to make peace because they trusted him and his "steady, honest principles" and because of his "great natural sense." [60] He was master of their own figurative manner of expression.

McGillivray described the outcome of his debate with a group of headmen. When he had finished outlining the disadvantages of "frowning war" and the advantages of "smiling peace," an old chief responded, "You have made yourself very poor, by sweating, far and near, in our smoky townhouses and hothouses, only to make a peace between us and the Cherokee, and thereby enable our young mad people to give you, in a short time, a far worse sweat than you had yet had." [61]

The collective wisdom of the chiefs was that there should be no permanent peace between traditional enemies. How would young warriors prove their valor? It was no use arguing with McGillivray, they knew, because he was simply following orders from the great chief in Charlestown. Therefore, they said, "We will not any more oppose you in this mad scheme." [62]

Sixty-nine Upper Creeks and twenty-four Lower Creek chiefs accompanied Malatchi to Charlestown in May 1753. Peter Chartier, chief of the pro-French Shawnees, was with them. The Bosomworths were on hand, hoping that Malatchi would defend their claims. In fact, there were several agendas for this meeting. Governor Glen wanted to arrange a continental peace among English allies. Malatchi was concerned about settlers encroaching on Creek hunting ground. Although the Gun Merchant did not make the trip, his brother chiefs wanted a better rate of exchange for their deerskins. The Bosomworths singlemindedly pursued their elusive claims.

The Indians were escorted into town by three mounted companies, and the conference was conducted with the pomp and pageantry of which the Indians, as well as the governor, were so fond. The members of the council and "all the gentlemen of distinction," in Glen's words, were present as the talks began. Lachlan McGillivray's status as an expert interpreter or linguist was acknowledged by his appointment to translate the speeches. Five other skilled interpreters were called to attend and to correct him if the occasion demanded it. McGillivray was asked to swear that he would give the correct sense and meaning of each expression. It was a tribute to his skill that no one had to correct him and that after the lengthy talks, he swore that not only the sense and meaning were correct but the words themselves were precise and exact. As a result, the entire transactions of the conference were taken down and printed in successive issues of the *South Carolina Gazette*. Glen transmitted the minutes to the Lords of Trade with the comment that "they were interpreted by a person very skillful in their language." [63]

Malatchi conducted himself regally. Glen was greatly impressed; his speeches had all the dignity of a king's, he informed the Lords Commissioners. "It can hardly be credited," wrote Glen, "that People who are generally called Savages could make such proper pertinent Speeches and many of them without premeditation." Malatchi complained about Georgia and the Georgians. "They think, I suppose, that because we are Indians, they may do what they please." Too many of them were encroaching upon the lands reserved for the Creeks by the 1739 treaty with Oglethorpe. Malatchi had no complaint against South Carolina, which was a place of long standing. Georgia, however, was of very late standing. Sister Bosomworth had been there before the Georgians. Now the Georgians had taken her land. When he went down to Savannah, he was received in a rude and uncivil manner and was treated more as an enemy than a friend. He had heard that Dr. Graham pretended that Malatchi gave up the lands in question to the English. This was not true. Malatchi called upon Glen to set matters right. [64]

It became clear that though Malatchi might have been concerned about justice for the Bosomworths, the Upper Creek chiefs were more interested in lower prices for the trade goods they had to buy. Handsome Fellow of the Okfuskees, in the debut of a long and distinguished career, asked for the same rates the Cherokees paid. Governor Glen answered that Cherokee leather was thicker and of better quality. Besides, the Cherokee country was not as far from Charlestown as were the Creek villages. Many of the chiefs were so disappointed with that reply that they walked out of the chamber without waiting for their presents. The Wolf of Muccolossus was downright impertinent. It was no wonder the traders could not reduce the price of their goods when they gave away so much to their wives and women, he said. [65]

Malatchi apologized for the conduct of the others, commenting that they behaved like children. Glen loaded Malatchi up with the presents intended for those who had left. Two days later the chiefs sent Thomas Bosomworth to Glen to say that they were sorry and that they would each like a gun, a blanket, a flap, shirts, and boots. Glen admitted them to his chambers and administered a stinging rebuke. His dignity was salved and the Indians got their presents.[66]

After the meeting, Glen was full of praise for Malatchi, whose behavior, he said, "charmed everybody." More to the point, Glen informed the Lords Commissioners that he agreed with the Bosomworths that their land claims were valid. Glen's conversion to their cause was the turning point in their troubled campaign.[67]

Lachlan McGillivray came away from the conference with his status further enhanced by the confidence placed in him by both the governor and the Indians. While in Charlestown, he renewed family ties with his brother Alexander, the sea captain, and talked about Sehoy and the infant Alexander at Little Tallassee and about his plans to remove his residence to the slightly more civilized and safer environs of Augusta. The *South Carolina Gazette* reported a freak accident that happened to Alexander McGillivray's schooner, the *Elizabeth*, shortly after the great conference ended. A sudden squall dumped a heavy swell of water into the ship and it sank alongside the McGillivray wharf. Its cargo of seventy barrels of rice was damaged, but the ship was recovered.[68]

The Georgia authorities seemed more anxious about the Bosomworth claims than pleased with the general peace arranged by Glen. James Habersham expressed fear that the Indians might assume "that we unjustly resented her and her Husband's extravagant claims and Behaviour." His fears were entirely justified. Habersham confided to the Trustees' secretary that the Carolinians were jealous of Georgia's prosperity, and therefore "a great Man there takes every opportunity to place us in the most disadvantageous light."[69]

The ruling body in Georgia was the target for increasing criticism from within the province. On April 18, 1752, the freeholders of Darien signed a petition in the presence of John Mackintosh Mohr, once their chief, now their conservator of the peace. Several of the Scots who had come to fight the Spanish were now gentlemen farmers scattered along the Georgia coast. They complained about the arbitrary rule of the council in Savannah. "We are harassed with Warrants, Judgements and Executions," they said, contending that some were illegal.

Lower Georgia was almost defenseless, and the residents relied solely on the goodwill of the Creeks. For that reason, good relations with Mary Bosomworth were indispensable. Regardless of what her enemies in Savannah might say, they were very much aware of her assistance in thwarting the French.[70] The petitioners presented their complaints to Mary Bosomworth herself, to be carried over to England.

In 1754 the Bosomworths undertook their twice-delayed trip to put their claims before the Lords Commissioners of Trade. Mary presented the lengthening history of her contributions and grievances but was advised that her case must be processed through the royal governor now that Georgia had such an official. The irrepressible Bosomworths took passage for Savannah to make the acquaintance of John Reynolds.[71]

Georgia's first royal governor arrived almost without notice in Savannah on October 29, 1754. The *South Carolina Gazette* reported that word of his coming quickly spread and he was greeted by spontaneous demonstrations of joy. The gentlemen of the council were not popular, and the ordinary people of Savannah hoped for better things from Reynolds. According to the *Gazette*, "the lower class of people, not having the material to express their joy and unwilling to lose their share of rejoicing, set fire to the Guard House."[72]

Reynolds's first impression was that Savannah was well situated. Its 150 or so houses were all wooden, very small, and, in spite of the colony's short history, "very old." Even if some of Oglethorpe's first cottages were still standing, they would not have been twenty years old. John Reynolds, a sea captain by career, was a blunt, humorless, plain-spoken man. His letters reveal a mind that, though not unintelligent, was not cultivated. Nor did he display charm, wit, or the social graces that might have won the hearts and minds of the people. Charm and wit were dispensable qualities in sea captains but highly advantageous in governors.

When Reynolds first met with his council in the only large house in town, one end of the building collapsed. The incident was fraught with meaning, symbolic as well as real. Reynolds's report read simply, "one end fell while we were all there." Another opportunity for comment was that the tiny building used as a jail had no locks. Henry Ellis,

Reynolds's successor, would have written a humorous essay on a jail with no locks. Reynolds was content to note that he had ordered locks and bolts.[73]

He was impressed with his first sight of Indians who had come in quest of presents. He learned that the Spanish in Florida were a menace, no longer militarily but because they gave runaway slaves their freedom. Much of Reynolds's first letter to the Board of Trade was given over to citations from several letters from "Mr. McGillivray and others, Indian Traders of Reputation at Augusta."[74] The letters were addressed to Patrick Graham, who evidently had briefed the new governor on the good qualities of McGillivray and company. Perhaps it was because of Henry Parker's death in 1752 that no more criticisms were heard about the monopolizing company at Augusta.

The Bosomworths were well received by John Reynolds. He listened sympathetically to their long story. He then questioned the surviving members of the council, found their collective memory faulty, and concluded that they were not telling the truth. His opinion was that "Bosomworth and his wife have been very ill used by that Court of President and Assistants, who I think acted in a very injudicious, unwarrantable and arbitrary manner."[75]

In October 1755 Reynolds invited the Indian chiefs to Augusta, ostensibly to receive presents but at least partly to bolster the claims of the Bosomworths. Malatchi, their champion, was too ill to come. The Upper Creek delegation, led by the Gun Merchant, was never more than lukewarm in support of Mary's claim to the sea islands. The mediation of Lachlan McGillivray and George Galphin took on added significance. If they were hostile to the Bosomworths, they might easily influence the chiefs in Augusta. McGillivray's status was particularly important because he supplied the Indians with provisions, including thirty-eight bushels of corn, twenty-one kegs of rum, six cows, five pounds of sugar, and a barbecued steer, all valued at £242.16.[76] In addition to his role as chief interpreter, McGillivray was also host for the conference.

When he went up for the meeting with the Indians, John Reynolds was shocked at the decrepitude of Fort Augusta, the only fortification in the province. The walls of the fort had to be propped up. After waiting ten days, Reynolds left before the Indians arrived, naming William Little, his former first mate and general factotum, to distribute the presents. The Bosomworths remained in Augusta to gather depositions and testimonials. William Little asked the Gun Merchant about the validity of Mary's claims. The Gun and the others wrestled with the unfamiliar issue of private ownership before deciding that Malatchi had a superior right to the lands claimed by all the Indians and that his gift of the properties to Mary took precedence over any agreement they might have made with Patrick Graham.[77]

Lachlan McGillivray confirmed that Malatchi had given the lands to Mary. He had heard him say so in Charlestown. McGillivray, Galphin, and James Germany verified that Malatchi's people were disgusted with the treatment they received in Savannah in 1749 and therefore made overtures to the French. They denied that the Bosomworths had given out "bad talks" in 1749, 1750, 1752, or 1753. This admission required Galphin to retract his earlier statement to the council.[78]

The Savannah gentry were rapidly becoming disenchanted with the new governor, complaining that "there seems to have no other use been made" of the Indian conference in Augusta "than to Establish Mrs. Bosomworth's pretended Indian title."[79] The Bosomworths would not receive satisfaction until 1760, but after the conference in Augusta, it was only a matter of time. Even though Thomas Bosomworth had complained about the "powerful company at Augusta" and the "artful and designing" men there, it was in Augusta and with the help of that company and those men that he was able to achieve his final success.[80]

With the Bosomworth claims no longer a major irritant, McGillivray and company would turn their attention to greater threats to the security of the English frontier. Young Colonel George Washington had surrendered to a French force at a place called Fort Necessity near the forks of the Ohio River on July 4, 1754. The French and Indian War had begun.

CHAPTER SEVEN

Intruders on the Ogeechee

The Bosomworth affair was important because of its immediate consequences. The great Malatchi was offended, and he retaliated by cultivating the French and thereby creating anxiety among gentlemen of the trade and government. Even more significant was an episode that might be called the Edmund Gray affair. Gray was the most conspicuous among an influx of new arrivals in the backcountry. Though but a trickle in 1754, the movement of pioneer farmers into the area around Augusta would become a flood that would profoundly affect the shaping of the frontier. Gray, who was said to be a Quaker, assumed unwarranted authority in settling newcomers along the many tributaries of the Savannah River above Augusta.

Typical of the attitude of the settlers was a petition addressed to Governor Reynolds by Edward Brown and thirty-seven others explaining that they had come hundreds of miles to Georgia and had found unoccupied lands on the north side of the Ogeechee River, a hundred miles from its mouth. The petitioners asked that their title to the land be confirmed. They also demanded protection from the Indians. The squatters were indignant that some of the Indians had threatened them. In this instance the Indians had a much better grasp of recent history than the new Georgians. The treaty signed with Oglethorpe in 1739 specified that all the land above the tidewater belonged to the Indians.

Except for the town of Augusta, the Savannah River was the Indian boundary. The Indians thought of Augusta as a depot for the convenience of their traders, but this new encroachment of farmers into the traditional hunting grounds was a violation of their agreement with the English.[1]

The onset of the Reynolds administration forced Lachlan McGillivray to ponder where his loyalties lay. Was he a Georgian or a Carolinian? While at Darien, he was more a Scotsman than anything else; out in the Creek Nation he was simply British. His license was from Carolina, and Glen had become his patron. Now, however, Reynolds commandeered his services to convey a talk to the Upper Creeks. For yet a while, McGillivray would serve two masters, diligently informing both governors of the latest Indian intelligence. But 1755 was a watershed year in his career; he would leave his plantation at Little Tallassee to establish a residence in Augusta. Patrick Brown's death in July 1755 caused a reorganization in the company. Some property remained in the possession of the surviving members; there were new partners for new ventures. McGillivray took William Struthers into his employ and stationed him at Little Tallassee. Strictly speaking, McGillivray had no right to transfer his license. The licensee was supposed to reside in the Indian country. McGillivray and his friends considered that regulation too restrictive. They held the valuable license and sent someone else to the far frontier.[2]

McGillivray set out from Augusta on his errand for Governor Reynolds on January 11, 1755. He decided to keep a journal of his travels for the use of Reynolds and Glen. His friend George Galphin accompanied him as far as Coweta, Galphin's town, which they reached on January 22. Galphin, though a skilled linguist, deferred to McGillivray, who presented Reynolds's talk to Malatchi and other Lower Creek headmen. Malatchi was pleased that the king had sent his beloved man to replace the rude men in Savannah. McGillivray quoted him as asking "whether he was an agreeable, good natur'd and free spoken man." If Reynolds possessed these characteristics, he did not display them during his brief Georgia sojourn, but McGillivray answered in the affirmative. He explained that he had not yet met the new governor but that those who had gave him "an extraordinary character." Malatchi was satisfied and inquired politely about the health of his brother the governor of Carolina. In the course of their talk, McGillivray tried to discover what the French were doing, but Malatchi had nothing to say on that score. Nor did Malatchi say anything about a French report that his illness was caused by English poison. The French governor, Kerlérec, admitted, "We do not fail to second him in that idea."[3] Malatchi, however, was not as gullible as the French thought; if he had suspected that he was being poisoned by the English, he would have complained about it to McGillivray, but he did not. Malatchi, ill and with only a year to live, had dutifully followed his father Brims's advice. He had maintained a friendship with both the English and the French, though each would have set him to war with the other. More than anyone else, Malatchi thwarted the English plans to tamper with the Alabama Fort and to put a garrison of soldiers in his country. During his lifetime he was a shaper of the southern frontier. But forces were at work to change Malatchi's world. McGillivray's journal indicated what some of them were.

At Tuckabatchee, McGillivray was given the customary hospitality in the assembly lodge. Old Bracket was glad to hear Reynolds's promise of presents, but he quickly got to the point. He and the other chiefs were displeased at the new settlements on the Ogeechee. McGillivray assured the Tuckabatchees that only a few families from Virginia were involved, and he was certain that Governor Reynolds would abide by Oglethorpe's treaty with the Creeks. When Reynolds later read McGillivray's journal, he tried to find a copy of Oglethorpe's treaty and was unable to locate one. Reynolds confessed to the governor of South Carolina that he did not know what to do with "the lawless crew on the Ogeechee."[4]

McGillivray continued to gather information after he returned to his plantation and family at Little Tallassee. Most of the men were out on their winter hunts, but a sensible Indian by the name of Mad Wind, who remained at the village, visited McGillivray frequently and told him about the unusual efforts the French were making to win over the Upper Creeks. There had been an important meeting of the headmen at the Alabama Fort the past August, the purpose of which was to establish peace between the Choctaws and the Creeks. The French claimed that an English plot had been discovered. The recent peace the governor of South Carolina had arranged between the Creeks and Cherokees was a ruse and a deception. When the Creeks were least expecting it, the English and the Cherokees would attack the Creeks and destroy them, man, woman, and child. That attack would be followed by an invasion by the English. The French offered to assist their friends the Creeks as a tender parent would his children. They urged the Indians to notice how the English encroached daily upon their land from river to river until they would have it all.[5]

McGillivray asked the warrior what the English friends had to say in reply to the French. The Wolf, Devall's Landlord, Handsome Fellow, and the headmen of almost every Upper Creek town had remained silent. The story had been so adroitly told with such detail that it sounded plausible. The commander of the Alabama Fort then invited all the headmen to attend a great conference at Mobile to meet His Excellency the governor of Louisiana, their true friend and protector.

The headmen, worried if not convinced by the account of the English plot, journeyed to the rendezvous on the Alabama River, where they waited for ten days for the arrival of boats to take them to Mobile. They reached Mobile at midnight and had to wander about to find lodging; no one was on hand to greet them. Governor Kerlérec arrived the next day and made up for the inauspicious beginning by a surfeit of ceremony. His message was that he had received a letter from the English governor that it was his plan to take all the lands from the Indians. The English asked the French to help. Anyone who had eyes open could notice the advance of the English settlers, he said. Within two years the Creeks would be at war with the English.[6]

Several of the chiefs were discontented, partly because of what the French said and partly because they disliked their uncomfortable lodgings and the dearth of entertainment. Governor Kerlérec kept them there five days repeating his talk about the duplicity of the English and their "pernicious designs." Before distributing presents, Kerlérec asked the chiefs to confirm their peace with his faithful friends the Choctaws, who were engaged in destroying his enemies the Chickasaws. Although he said he did not have to explain why the Chickasaws were his enemies, he would do so. They had protected the Natchez from the "just resentment" of the French. The insufficiency of the reason was patent enough to McGillivray and perhaps to the Creeks.[7]

Kerlérec stayed at Mobile to wait for the arrival of the Choctaws. He heartily disliked these Indian conferences with their endless speeches: "It is work that is as difficult as it is unpleasant and disagreeable," he confided to his superiors.[8] McGillivray's journal reveals that Kerlérec's guests did not enjoy the party much themselves.

Kerlérec found the Choctaw meeting even more unpleasant and disagreeable than the Creek. The chiefs came singing and dancing up to his door, lifted him up, and carried him to the assembly house. They showered him with speeches. "I had to appear grateful for it," he wrote, "but after all, I knew them well enough to consider them deceitful, mendacious and very mercenary."[9] The Choctaws' worst fault was their chronic inability to achieve the French ambition of wiping out the Chickasaw Nation.

In February, McGillivray reported to Glen "all the little, low, mean, insinuating malicious Lies" that the French had broadcast at the Mobile meeting. Glen wanted to repair the damage by inviting the Indians to come see him at Charlestown, and Reynolds intended for them to meet him at Augusta. The Indians would go to Charlestown after they picked up Reynolds's presents in Augusta. Reynolds expected McGillivray to act as interpreter, which was a bit awkward because Glen had engaged his services; Reynolds issued a proclamation barring persons without Georgia licenses from trading in Georgia, and McGillivray's license was from South Carolina. "It is well known that I am at all times ready and willing to serve my country," he said, and tried to be loyal to both governors. He said that the French had caused great confusion and that he was doing his best to refute their lies. George Galphin reported to Glen how he and McGillivray had prevented the Twin, an influential Lower Creek chieftain, from going to Mobile by distributing £200 of their own goods.[10]

McGillivray's journal, which spans five months, reveals the major role played by the Gun Merchant in this year of intrigue. The Gun Merchant was preparing to meet a delegation of Cherokees to confirm the peace arranged by Glen at Charlestown. He was warned by the other headmen of the alleged English plot. The Gun answered that he could not and would not believe that their beloved friends the English had any such plans. He would put his faith to the test and go to the Cherokees.

The Gun's trip turned out badly for the English traders. He returned determined to get the same prices the English paid for Cherokee deerskins. Angry Okfuskees kept McGillivray, Lachlan McIntosh, James McQueen, and George Johnston "bound up" in the Gun Merchant's lodge. The traders said that setting prices was a matter to be decided by the governor of South Carolina and the new governor of Georgia. The Gun said that the Cherokees had told him that they got fair rates, not by begging the governor but by clubbing several traders. They had learned that the best way to get what they wanted from the white people was to treat them badly. The Gun stopped short of violence, but he sent word to Glen by McGillivray that he would not go to Charlestown until the governor agreed to lower the prices of trade goods and to send steelyards, or balancing scales, into his town so he could make sure he was not being cheated.[11]

To make matters worse, the headmen then went to the Alabama Fort and requested better prices for their skins. At this meeting, held May 1, 1755, the French captain granted their request without a quibble. Alabama Indians, who had traded with McGillivray, flocked to the French. McGillivray noted in his journal that "without the immediate interposition of Providence" the trade war would have fatal consequences to the British interests.[12]

The price of goods was one irritant, the encroachment of settlers another. The Lower Creeks were more troubled by trespassers than trade prices. When the ailing Malatchi was strong enough to travel to the French fort, he was loaded with presents and, in McGillivray's words, was "caressed in an extraordinary manner," with guns firing and drums beating at his coming and going. The French wanted to know why he put up with the settlements on the Ogeechee. Malatchi said he knew about them and that the war whoop would soon drive those people away. He was biding his time.[13]

By inviting the chiefs individually to his house and not counting the cost of the rum consumed, McGillivray convinced them that they should go to Augusta and Charlestown to voice their complaints. When McGillivray asked the Wolf if he did not think it would be unkind to decline Glen's invitation, the Wolf answered that he almost thought so himself. When McGillivray left the Upper Creek country, he was not certain that the chiefs would follow him to Augusta or Charlestown.[14]

Lachlan McGillivray brought his journal with him when he went down to Charlestown in August 1755. The journal created a stir in town. (In Georgia everyone seemed too preoccupied with internal politics to worry about French machinations.) James Glen was partly responsible for the French allegations because he had gone on another of his grand tours in pursuit of his favorite project, the building of a fort in the Cherokee country. The Raven of Toxaway came out to meet Glen's party and entertained them with the eagle's dance. In exchange for £100 worth of goods, the Raven gave Glen all the land he could see from where he stood. Glen set his builders to work on Fort Prince George near the Cherokee town of Keowee. Glen planned to build another fort among the Overhill Cherokees. The glory of his achievement was dimmed by the news that reached him in May 1755 that William Henry Lyttelton had been named to succeed him. Lyttelton set out for his new post promptly, but his ship was captured by the French and he was detained in refined captivity. He would not arrive in Charlestown until June 1756. The delay gave Glen an opportunity to embellish his achievements. His trip to the Cherokee country had attached that nation firmly to the English, he boasted; otherwise General Edward Braddock's defeat on July 9, 1755, near the French Fort Duquesne, would have disheartened the Cherokees and inclined them toward the French.[15]

Lyttelton's delay also gave Glen time for one last Indian meeting. Edmond Atkin, who was soon to return to Charlestown as England's first superintendent of Indian affairs in the Southern Department, accused Glen of trying "to finish out a puff at his exit." He suggested that Glen was eager to distribute presents to the Indians before Lyttelton could claim the credit.[16]

Glen convoked the assembly on September 15, 1755, and conveyed to that body McGillivray's long journal together with a letter from Lachlan McIntosh which contained the same information. On the seventeenth, the governor outlined the situation and recommended lowering trade prices. A committee of the House doubted whether the crisis was real and advised sending Henry Hyrne as an agent to determine whether McGillivray was telling the truth. Glen bristled at the suggestion. There was no need to send an agent because McGillivray said that there was no doubt of the Indians' coming to Charlestown. The committee's response bordered on the sarcastic. How could McGillivray have been "so barefaced" as to say that the Indians were coming after all the doubtful assertions in his journal? And if the governor held such a high opinion of McGillivray as to believe everything he said, why was the assembly called together?[17]

The curious debate continued with Glen defending the honor of the man he had once suspected. He knew that both McGillivray and McIntosh were men of veracity who would not impose on the public. Glen explained that McGillivray had been examined before the council and "delivered himself with so much distinctness and with such an Air of Candour that neither I nor any of the Members of Council could withhold our Assent to what he said."[18]

McGillivray was asked if lowering the prices would guarantee the friendship of the Indians. He declined to answer, saying that there were other traders in town and their opinion should be sought. When pressed, however, he stated that such an action would be beneficial; not to do it would be dangerous. "Even if we had not known McGillivray's character to be good we could not have doubted what he said," Glen opined. McGillivray did not believe the Indians would come down without assurance that prices would be lowered. If Glen were to give that assurance, would they come? Yes, they would. Any change in the Indian trading law required the assent of the House, and that was why Glen had called the assembly.[19]

The House was determined to be petulant and gave its collective opinion that the governor's letter would not be enough to induce the Indians to come to Charlestown. At the bottom of this scheme, as the members saw it, McGillivray was conniving to get a monopoly of the trade by setting prices so low that none but the largest traders could survive. Reluctantly, the House authorized a committee composed of the governor, the council, and a delegation of the House to regulate prices.[20]

On September 12, 1755, Governor Reynolds placed before his council a letter from Glen that stressed the danger from the frontier and the urgency of joint action in lowering the price of trade goods. Almost offhandedly the Georgia Council agreed but added the interesting stipulation that the reduction must not throw the trade "into too few hands." The Carolina Assembly had not yet met so it is doubtful that the Georgians were coached by the Carolinians in the economics of trade. The best guess by an experienced trader was that of the twenty-seven licensed traders working among the Creeks, about ten would survive the cut in profits.[21] The big storekeeping traders of Augusta would benefit, but the Savannah merchants would lose their small but growing share of the supply of trade goods.

The issue, which should have caused heated discussion, was quickly shunted aside because the Georgia Council members preferred to devote the session to venting their indignation on Governor Reynolds's right-hand man, William Little. By September, the members of the council had become disenchanted with their new governor and his first mate. To explain their feelings, it is necessary to examine the short but tempestuous career of Edmund Gray.

It was ironic that Gray and his friends among the recent arrivals in the Georgia backcountry were oblivious to the growing hostility of the Indians because of their trespassing and, instead, focused their animosity on Savannah. They accused the members of the interim council, James Habersham, Patrick Graham, Noble Jones, and Alexander Kellet, of unfair and arbitrary government before Reynolds's arrival. These men had given huge land grants to their friends and relatives, even to infant and absent persons, but denied grants to the deserving newcomers. In addition, it was said that certain members were Jacobites, supporters of the Stuarts, and had been heard to drink treasonable oaths.[22]

Gray allied himself with disgruntled Savannahians who had quarreled with the council, notably Charles Watson and Samuel Mercer, and began to talk about the need to fight for their rights as Englishmen against unlawful authority. They were disappointed when Reynolds retained the old members of the council in office and set their sights on capturing control of the first elected Commons House of Assembly, which met in January 1755, the same month in which Lachlan McGillivray began his journal out in the Indian country.

Gray and six of his faction, including a promising newcomer, Edward Barnard of Augusta, won seats in the House, but two Savannah candidates supported by Gray, Samuel Mercer and William Francis, were defeated. The losers were convinced that their enemies on the council were responsible for a fraudulent vote count. Gray argued for another election, but ten members of the House refused to go along. Thereupon, the seven Grayites boycotted the session, hoping to force the governor to call for new elections. Instead, the ten sitting members declared themselves a legal House and declared the dissenters rebels.[23]

Meanwhile, Gray had circulated broadsides summoning all friends of liberty to come to Savannah. The circulars had the ring of a revolution twenty years too soon: "If you regard the liberties of your Country" come to Savannah! Gray's spokesmen would later deny any rebellious intent, much less any insult to the governor. At the time, they were simply hoping for support in bringing about a fraud-free election.[24]

Reynolds was advised by the council that the situation was incendiary and that drastic action was required. Accordingly, Reynolds issued a proclamation forbidding people to gather in Savannah or anywhere else. He ordered the militia to stand by and sent to Charlestown for a warship.[25]

Edmund Gray was an organizer, not a martyr, and he and some of his followers left Georgia to settle in the disputed area between the St. Johns and the Altamaha. Future Georgia governors would treat them tactfully so as not to drive them into the Spanish camp. Other members of the faction remained in Georgia and bided their time until the next election.

The councillors had no time to celebrate their triumph because Governor Reynolds bestowed seven fee-paying offices, which they hoped to share, upon his friend William Little. Further, Little was seen to consort openly with members of the Gray faction and was heard to make derogatory statements about members of the council. Besides, Little proved "deficient and remiss" in the discharge of the duties of his seven offices. James Habersham signed the complaints against Little that were delivered to Reynolds on the same day Glen's letter regarding prices of Indian trade goods vainly tugged at his attention. The council, the governor, and William Little were much too caught up in their own argument to pay heed to other issues, even an impending Indian war. Little took pride in his ability to handle controversy and fired back at his accusers. His loyalty was well known after twenty years in the king's service; he was not sure the same was true of certain others. He had associated with the ousted members only to conciliate them and with Reynolds's permission. He named names. Alexander Kellet as provost marshal was cruel, haughty, and dissolute. Little's stinging rebuttal to Habersham's statement that he had insulted the council was that "I have labour'd to make no Man contemptible; alas the Deportment of Some People makes that Work altogether unnecessary."[26]

In a remarkable turnabout, the Gray faction won control of the 1757 Commons House and elected William Little as Speaker. Symbolic of the minor revolution was the seating of Adam Bosomworth as representative from Frederica. The honor of writing the "state of the province address" was given to Samuel Mercer, an old friend of the Bosomworths. The House passed a resolution stating that whoever advised the governor to issue his proclamation calling out the militia did it with "a Bad and Sinister design to Stigmatize those Members" who signed the circular letter "for no other reason but to procure a fair hearing in a disputed Election."[27]

Long before the political victory of their enemies in Georgia, the members of the council struck back where Reynolds was most vulnerable—in London. Alexander Kellet left Georgia in March 1756 to pour out the grievances of his friends, who were officeholders and "Planters of Substance and Character." The governor had turned over the entire administration to William Little, "a person unconversant in Business and of the most Despotic Principles." Kellet accused Little of extortion and falsification of minutes of the House. Almost lost among the litany of faults was a line criticizing the governor for mismanaging the Indian conference in Augusta in December 1755.[28] Kellet's mission was effective. The Lords Commissioners decided to recall Reynolds and send a new executive to introduce political order into a province not yet used to governing itself. Compared with the looming dangers from the frontier which threatened the young colony, the internal dissension was of minor importance, a comedy worthy of the pen of a master satirist. Georgians were so obsessed with themselves that they forgot that England and France were locked in an epic struggle that would determine the future of America.

Lachlan McGillivray was at the center stage of the backcountry drama. He brought the Indians to Reynolds's Augusta conference of December 1755, which gratified the Bosomworths and disappointed the Savannah gentlemen of the council. McGillivray was under instructions from Governor Glen of South Carolina to deliver the Indians to Charlestown after their stop in Augusta. Glen was willing to settle their complaints, including lowering prices of trading articles and clearing idle whites from the Creeks' hunting grounds.[29]

McGillivray had heard from John Spencer that some members of the Carolina Assembly suspected him of contriving the crisis about prices. It caused him great concern, he told Glen, that they should have such a mean opinion of him. He had served without fee or reward, often to the neglect of his business. He would continue to do so, but he wished the gentlemen of the assembly a servant more to their liking, and he wished for himself better masters. He thanked Glen for supporting his character.[30]

It was not easy to deliver Glen's message to the Gun Merchant.

McGillivray had to pay an Indian runner to go a hundred miles into the woods to reach him. The Gun Merchant took the matter seriously. He called the Upper Creek headmen together and delivered his answer to the traders present: Daniel Clark, John Spencer (who was McGillivray's messenger on this occasion), George Johnston, Lachlan McIntosh, James Germany, and John Ross. The Upper Creeks would go to Augusta in December to see Governor Reynolds. They would meet Glen at New Windsor. The traders were to tell Glen, his brother, "not to be lazy and fail not to meet him, as he expected." [31]

Malatchi was too ill to make the long journey to Charlestown. He said he would try to see Glen in April, but in January 1756 the great chief died. His son Togulki inherited the honorary title of chief of all the Creeks, but because he was a minor, his uncle Stumpe managed his affairs. The French wooed the new emperor as assiduously as they had Malatchi. As events proved, Togulki lacked his father's leadership qualities and voluntarily relinquished his title. [32]

It was not an easy trip to Augusta for the Gun Merchant, Devall's Landlord, the Wolf, and the other headmen. Snow and rain detained them, and by the time they reached Augusta in mid-December, Governor Reynolds had gone. He waited ten days and then left, apparently feeling that a longer wait was beneath his dignity. He gave as an excuse that a shipload of displaced Acadians had landed at Tybee and required his attention. By leaving early he forfeited his one opportunity to influence Indian affairs. Governor Glen was unkind in saying that Reynolds departed because Reynolds had heard that Augusta was only a stop for the headmen on their way to Charlestown, and he was jealous of Glen. [33]

Reynolds entrusted William Little with the lucrative task of distributing the presents at a 6 percent commission. The Lords of Trade were not pleased that Little neglected to take minutes of the conference, and the gentlemen of the council were bothered by all the attention paid to the Bosomworths and their claims. Lachlan McGillivray informed Glen that nothing of importance was transacted other than the distribution of presents, protestations of friendship, and some discourse concerning the Bosomworth claims. There was no discussion of the two burning issues, the trade prices and the encroachment of settlers. The Bosomworths, at least, were gratified that the Gun Merchant acknowledged their right to the islands.[34]

McGillivray hosted the ninety Indian visitors while they were in Augusta and gave them provisions for the journey to Charlestown. He went ahead of them, warning Glen that the Indians were expecting large presents, saddles in particular.

Glen's last conference was a replica of the others. He enjoyed the elaborate ritual as much as the Indians did and a great deal more than the haughty Kerlérec of Louisiana. McGillivray was again the master interpreter. And as usual Glen exaggerated the success of his meeting. It produced a treaty which he pronounced "the most beneficial for Great Britain that ever was concluded with any Indian Nation." He explained to his successor that he had agreed that the Creeks and Cherokees should be treated the same with regard to trade. Traders would make use of scales to measure just weights of the skins. He had obtained the consent of the six largest traders to abide by the Cherokee prices. In addition, they would carry up His Majesty's presents at no cost. Of the six, three were surviving members of Brown, Rae and Company, Lachlan McGillivray, Daniel Clark, and George Galphin. The others were James McQueen, David Douglass, and the firm of Francis McCartan and Martin Campbell.[35]

The Creeks were pleased at this important concession. When Glen attempted to exact a quid pro quo, they balked. They must have been astonished to hear Glen bring up the idea they hated most—the need for an English fort in the Upper Creek country. As a palliative, Glen suggested that, like the French fort, his outpost would exist solely for the purpose of distributing presents. The Gun Merchant remained as steadfastly opposed to a garrisoned fort as he had been ten years before. Glen could build a fort for presents, but he must not put soldiers there. When Glen asked the Creeks not to disturb the Georgians on the Ogeechee, they reminded him that their old agreement did not permit any settlements west of the Savannah. Glen then asked them to help the long-suffering Chickasaws. The Gun Merchant said that they had advised the Chickasaws to leave their villages and live among the Creeks, but the Chickasaws "were obstinate people and deserved whatever happened."³⁶ Glen salvaged something when the Creeks re-affirmed the peace with the Cherokees. All in all, the negotiations hardly qualified as the most beneficial ever.

Glen's chief critic, the newly appointed superintendent Edmond Atkin, mocked Glen's pretensions when he heard about the treaty. He was still in London when he wrote to William Henry Lyttelton on May 20, 1756, warning him about Glen's connivance with the traders. The unanimous consent of the Creek Nation would be required for any true agreement, not merely of "those of them in Charlestown headed by Mr. Glen's favorite interpreter, McGillivray." As for permission to put up a post in the Creek country, that had been agreed to in William Bull's time and again in 1746, and nothing had come of it on either occasion.³⁷ Before he returned to America, Atkin had made up his mind that he did not like Lachlan McGillivray.

The Indians left Charlestown in a good mood. Lachlan McGillivray escorted them as far as Augusta, gave them provisions for their journey, and sent them on their way "in high spirits and full of their new treaty." He presented his bill for entertaining the Indians to Glen.³⁸

McGillivray would undertake one more mission for Glen. He would apprise the Lower and Upper Creek villages of the latest agreement, though, as he pointed out to the governor, "I have very little encouragement to neglect my own business to serve the public (as I have often done) when the Gentlemen of the Assembly seem not to be disposed to pay but little regard to my remonstrances."³⁹ Their attitude would not deter him from serving his country, however. In this as in other letters, McGillivray showed that he knew the language of governors as well as that of the chiefs.

Glen continued to busy himself with Indian affairs until Lyttelton's arrival on June 1, 1756. In May, he sent a shipment of guns and ammunition to the hard-pressed Chickasaws in answer to their appeal. The headmen of the Chickasaws wrote to Glen that they were subjected daily to attacks by the French and Choctaws; no less than four expeditions had come against them that winter. They had not been hunting for three years because of incessant wars so they were unable to buy what they needed. They asked for guns. "We will never give up this land but with the loss of our lives," they said. Jerome Courtonne, who carried the ammunition to the Chickasaws, kept a journal which revealed that the weapons arrived just in time to thwart yet another invasion by the Choctaws. The Choctaws were careful to keep their distance, and therefore few lives were lost.[40] The disturbance on the far frontier contributed to the mounting tension in the Creek country.

Glen's third ascent into the Cherokee country with a large entourage was undertaken to fulfill a promise he had made to build a fort in the Overhills country as a symbol of English protection. The fort, named Loudoun in honor of the British commander in America, was of doubtful value and would be impossible to defend when the Cherokees turned against the English in 1759. One South Carolina historian has called its erection "an inexcusable blunder."[41] Even at its inception, it worried the Creeks. Lachlan McGillivray dispatched his man James Germany from Okfuskee town on June 10, 1756, to warn the Carolina authorities about the confusion caused by Glen's visit to the Cherokees. The Creeks now believed the French, who had said the English and Cherokees were conniving against them. The more they considered Glen's request to build an outpost in their country, the less they liked it. And the infiltrating whites along the Ogeechee showed no signs of leaving the Creek hunting ground.[42]

When Lyttelton arrived in Charlestown he was already prejudiced against his predecessor. He was greeted with more than the usual jubilation because of a general disenchantment with the high-handed administration of James Glen. The *South Carolina Gazette* reported that the new governor was received "with every possible Mark of Respect and unfeigned Joy."[43] Lyttelton summoned Glen back from the Cherokee mountains but adhered to Glen's plan to build the remote and inaccessible fort. The assembly immediately granted him the funds it had withheld from Glen.

Lachlan McGillivray was in Charlestown by late July or early August to pay his respects to Lyttelton and, undoubtedly, to apprise him of the Gun Merchant's acute displeasure that nothing had been done to lower the trade prices or remove the poachers on the Ogeechee; Lyttelton relayed that bit of intelligence to the Lords Commissioners. Lyttelton decided to send an agent to the Creeks to calm their fears and picked the former commander of Fort Moore, Daniel Pepper, for the job.[44]

By McGillivray, Lyttelton sent orders to Lieutenant White Outerbridge at Augusta to detach a sergeant and five privates to garrison Fort Prince George at Keowee. Outerbridge reported that there remained at Augusta, besides himself, one sergeant, one drummer, and eighteen private men. At Fort Moore, across the river, there were nine privates under command of a corporal. Neither Augusta nor Moore had matches to fire cannon on "rejoicing days." Outerbridge had to use firebrands. Both forts were as decrepit as they had been the previous December when Reynolds saw them.[45]

John Reynolds of Georgia wrote to welcome Lyttelton and to confirm the news of the official declaration of war with France. He took advantage of the opportunity to confess a perplexing problem. He thought that the Indians had good reason to complain about the forty or so families from North Carolina and Virginia, but he did not know how to go about removing the "lawless crew" from the Ogeechee strip.[46]

Five days after Reynolds wrote to Lyttelton, he received the worst kind of news from Edward Brown, chief of the "lawless crew." Brown was indignant that Indians had stolen his horses. He and eight others chased after the Indians and shot two of them. He wanted the governor to chastise the Indians. The message demonstrated the newcomers' ignorance of Indian customs. The code of the forests was a life for a life. The relatives of the slain were honor bound to avenge their deaths, otherwise their spirits would not rest. Brown was smart enough to withdraw prudently to Mount Pleasant on the Savannah River.[47]

At Augusta the news of the incident was greeted with outrage and alarm. The traders there realized that similar minor skirmishes had triggered the Creek-Cherokee war and the Creek-Choctaw war. The attack by Georgians would prove that the French were right and the English were in secret alliance with the Cherokees. A petition was quickly subscribed by the "Gentlemen of Augusta." Lachlan McGillivray's name was on the list, as were those of his partners, George Galphin, John Rae, Daniel Clark, and others, including David Douglass, Martin Campbell, John Williams, John Spencer, Edward Barnard, John Pettigrew, Isaac Barksdale, and William Bonar. There were twenty names, all of them traders or former traders. Their statement viewed the incident from their perspective. The French insinuations were taking effect; a war was a very real possibility; trading goods were stored in Augusta, making it a likely target; the fort was in such poor condition that it could not afford protection for anyone. If Augusta were destroyed, the province would be destroyed. The gentlemen did not explain that point; they assumed it. Finally, they expressed regret that anyone had been permitted to settle on the Ogeechee — the Indians saw it as a pretext for war and were "continually Exclaiming against it." [48]

The justices of the peace at Augusta, or magistrates as they were called, did not wait to be told what to do by the governor or by Lieutenant Outerbridge. David Douglass, John Rae, and Martin Campbell on their own authority issued a "hue and cry" for the apprehension of the "murderers." Panic did what Governor Reynolds could not do: it effectively cleared the Ogeechee strip of settlers. The backcountry was deserted as people flocked into Augusta. The fort was crowded with refugees. Somehow, the good soldier Outerbridge found provisions for them. The slogan of the hour belonged to the band of Chickasaws at New Savannah. They asked Outerbridge for a plot of land under the guns of the fort for their families. Then the warriors would go out and fight the Creeks; they were prepared "to live and dye by the English." [49]

The resourceful magistrates then dispatched a talk to "Our Good Friends, the Kings, Beloved Men and Head Warriors of the Cowetas and all the Towns of the Lower Creeks." They explained the Ogeechee incident, noting that the fleeing Indians had stopped and fired first. The magistrates had sent a search party after the whites who were involved. They hoped that the Indians would do nothing rash. The talks were well worded and sensible. The initiative was admirable. This was no time for the delay that would have ensued if they had asked the governor for advice. Reynolds and his council were sufficiently agitated about the incident but could think of nothing better than to authorize raising a troop of seventy rangers and to send another talk. [50]

The problem with sending the dispatch from Augusta, together with an equally conciliatory message from Lyttelton, was that nobody would dare visit the Indian country just then. George Galphin's caravan was ready to make its annual delivery of goods to Coweta, but Galphin declined to risk his goods. Outerbridge wondered if he could protect the four large trading boats, loaded with merchandise, drawn up at the riverbank under the shadow of the fort. It was fortuitous at that moment, when the town was gripped with anxiety, that two Creek chiefs happened to stroll in from Charlestown. The young chief of the Okfuskees called Handsome Fellow and another headman, the Captain of Okfuskees, were regarded as heaven-sent ambassadors. They were able to convey the Augusta position on the crisis, namely, that the shooting was an unfortunate mistake that should not spoil a working relationship. Thomas Ross agreed to go with them and carry the dispatches for a fee of £150.[51]

The talk from Governor Reynolds arrived in time to be taken up with the others. Reynolds again showed his inexperience in Indian affairs, if not bad judgment, by omitting any reference to the two Indians who were seen to fall when shot. "I think it will be best to conceal that part of the story," he confided to Lyttelton. One has to wonder if he thought the Indians had no other source of information than his dispatches.[52]

By September 22 all eight of the Ogeechee party were in custody. Reynolds knew of only six, but Daniel Pepper, about to leave Augusta on his errand, wrote Lyttelton on the same day that Edward Brown had been taken. Pepper was pleased with the unexpected cooperation of the Augusta storekeepers and had nothing but praise for Lieutenant White Outerbridge. The people were grateful for the care he took with refugees. A measure of calm had been restored, and people were beginning to return to their homes in the country.[53]

It was fortunate for the Georgians that the Creeks knew at least as much as the whites did about what had transpired. The Indians involved in the Ogeechee fracas had a reputation for being troublemakers. The response of the headmen was considerably muted as a result. Nevertheless, the Gun Merchant sent Handsome Fellow to Savannah to make sure justice was done. Handsome Fellow, another headman, and an escort of ten warriors arrived in Savannah on November 16, 1756. The occasion was the first real test of Reynolds's ability to deal with Indians. An interesting exchange occurred between the governor and the dark-skinned emissary. Handsome Fellow began by explaining that he was sent by the Gun Merchant to obtain satisfaction for the Indians killed. At Augusta he had heard things that made him worry. He admitted that the Indians involved were "a Parcel of Straggling runagates" and that it was natural for the whites to defend themselves.[54] Governor Reynolds and his council must have breathed a sigh of relief. The opposition had given in easily. But Handsome Fellow was not finished; he reminded the governor of the treaties between the English and the Indians which said that when an Indian killed a white man, an Indian would pay with his life and vice versa. That treaty must be obeyed.

Reynolds resorted to deceit. One white man had died of wounds received, he improvised. Another was missing and perhaps dead. Handsome Fellow knew Reynolds was lying; he was at Augusta when the search party returned, and they said nothing of any white blood spilled. He said that the old man who had carried the talks, Thomas Ross, had told them they would have satisfaction. Reynolds changed his tactics. It was permissible, he argued, for whites to kill a robber. Handsome Fellow was adamant. It was Indian law that bloodshed required blood in return. Reynolds was forced back to his original lie. Handsome Fellow decided that it was convenient to pretend to believe the governor. The headmen of the nation would have the final say.[55]

The best that could be said for Reynolds's first effort at Indian diplomacy is that he gained time at the expense of honor. Brown and his lawless crew were quietly released. They could not understand why they should be blamed for killing Indian horse thieves. It was unthinkable that they should leave the Ogeechee. They thought they needed the land to plant crops far more than the Indians needed it for hunting. They were the vanguard of a throng of others who saw Indians as an obstacle and a nuisance. The wonder of it was not so much that the Indians were overwhelmed but that it took the whites until 1790 to cross the Ogeechee legally. Alexander, the son of Lachlan McGillivray, would have much to do with that delay.

Lachlan McGillivray sent Lyttelton a dispatch which indicated that the crisis had passed. Lyttelton mentioned McGillivray's letter to Reynolds, who then fretted that he had not heard from McGillivray. Reynolds was irked that Peter Timothy's *South Carolina Gazette* was critical of his handling of the crisis and hinted at a lawsuit. The Ogeechee affair marked an inauspicious end to the less than distinguished tenure of Georgia's first royal governor. The *South Carolina Gazette* announced the arrival of Henry Ellis, Reynolds's successor, on January 27, 1757, in company with Patrick Graham, William Knox, and John Neufville. Ellis and Lyttelton got along famously from the beginning. Ellis conveyed his thanks in the graceful language of polite society and added that he had been received with tumultuous joy in Savannah, whereas his predecessor was insulted and neglected. He wondered if he would receive the same treatment when his turn came to quit the stage.[56]

CHAPTER EIGHT

The French and Indian War on the Southern Frontier

Avoiding a war is preferable to waging one if the results are the same. The main arenas of the French and Indian War were the great river valleys of the north: the Ohio, the Hudson–Lake Champlain, and the St. Lawrence. Although General James Wolfe's victory on the Plains of Abraham outside Quebec in 1759 proved to be decisive in determining the outcome, the French continued their intrigues among the southern Indians. They were successful in igniting the Cherokees' smoldering resentment against the British. During the winter of 1759–60, those Indians took up the war hatchet. The Cherokee War attracted British regulars into the South Carolina backcountry. The crucial question for Georgia concerned the stance of the Creek Nation: would it join the French against the British, as the agents at Fort Toulouse were determined it should, or would it retain its traditional neutrality? The movers and shakers of this war, led by the great William Pitt, planned a military invasion to snuff out the French nuisance at the Alabama Fort. As it turned out, there was no Creek war and no military excursion west of the Savannah River. The final results were the same as if a triumphant campaign had been conducted. The French lost Fort Toulouse of the Alabamas, Fort Tombigbee, Mobile—everything—and were expelled from the continent. Avoiding the war was a successful technique which required careful strategy, some of it directed at Indian diplomacy, some at the hawkish British authorities. Historians have noticed Henry Ellis's role in maintaining the peace and have lauded him for it. The role of Lachlan McGillivray, James Adair, and the traders has not drawn attention.

The reaction to the Ogeechee fracas of 1756 was immediate and unprecedented. Panic swept the exposed settlements and emptied them. Savannah and Charlestown were alarmed. The gravity of the matter was reflected in London, where the Lords Commissioners alerted the king. The idea of the septuagenarian George II puzzling over the name, location, and portent of Ogeechee defies the imagination. A Highland battalion was sent to Charlestown in anticipation of an all-out Indian war.[1]

Experienced traders and friends of the Creeks, even those such as McGillivray and Galphin, who had families of mixed blood, were so convinced of impending trouble that they remained in Augusta during the winter. McGillivray abandoned his pattern of shuttling back and forth between Augusta and Little Tallassee and became a year-round Augusta resident. He was immediately named justice of the peace, or magistrate, which indicates his prestige in Georgia as well as his permanent residency.[2]

If these professionals in Indian affairs were so certain that there would be trouble, why was there so little reaction from the Indians? Part of the answer is that the two Indians who were killed were not highly regarded. More pertinent was that the British navy prevented supplies from reaching French Louisiana, and therefore the larder at the Alabama Fort was bare. Governor Kerlérec sent a stream of complaints to France: in December 1756 he could not supply the Alabamas; in March 1757 all the king's warehouses were empty; August marked ten months without goods; by October the Choctaws and Alabamas were threatening to go over to the English. The crisis was relieved when what Kerlérec described as a "mysterious little vessel" arrived with a cargo of stroud cloth and other badly needed trade goods.³ The mystery ship was a Spanish vessel which picked up English goods at Charlestown and delivered the precious cargo to the French at Mobile. Kerlérec was convinced that if he could get enough supplies, his Indian allies would do as much for France as those in the north did for the Marquis de Montcalm.⁴

For Lachlan McGillivray 1757 was a year of transition from trader to planter, from Indian diplomat to Georgia magistrate. The change affected his family as well. Alexander was seven years old, the right age to begin his English education with cousin Farquhar in Charlestown and to make the acquaintance of uncle Alexander, the sea captain, and his new bride. Captain Alexander's first wife, Elizabeth Patchabel, died after the birth of their only child, William, in 1753. The captain married his second wife, Elizabeth Chandler, at St. Phillip's Church in 1756. The McGillivrays liked to retain family names. Young William was the namesake of his grandfather, Captain Ban; young Alexander bore the name of Captain Alexander and of his cousin the slain chief of the McGillivrays. It is likely that the mixed-blood son of Lachlan and Sehoy lived with his uncle and new aunt and played children's games with his younger cousin.⁵

The family circle was swelled by the arrival of another relative from Strathnairn who was destined to make his mark on the pages of frontier history. John McGillivray was the fourth son of Chief Farquhar. His brothers were Alexander, Farquhar's successor, who died at Culloden; William, the new chief; Farquhar, the carpenter and minister in Charlestown; and Daniel, a sea captain. John's career followed Lachlan's in its essentials. Lachlan was able to sponsor his cousin and introduce him to the trade, just as Archibald had done for him. John made his way to the far country, trading among the Upper Creeks and to the Mississippi Chickasaws. He took two wives in the Chickasaw country and by them fathered two sons, Samuel and William. He dutifully remembered them in his will, but what happened to them later is not known. John was in a position to expand his trading business after the French were expelled from the Gulf Coast. He entered into partnership with Peter Swanson and established his house in Mobile. Like Lachlan, he made a tidy fortune and was a member of the emerging society of that frontier town.[6]

The close-knitness of the Scots is evident in the will of Daniel Clark, the veteran trader and partner of Lachlan, who died in 1757. When he dictated his will in April, he remembered his brother, a resident of Strathnairn; then he listed Lachlan McGillivray, Alexander McGillivray and his wife, and John McGillivray, the new arrival. He left his books to William Struthers, Lachlan's partner in the trade, and to William McGillivray, the young son of the sea captain. The sum of £25 went to Mr. Morrison, minister of the Scotch Meeting House in Charlestown, and £25 to the Charlestown Library Society. Lachlan was named as one of four executors of the will.[7] The bond of clanship is evident, as are the tokens of a taste for the refinements of reading and religion. When the McGillivrays gathered in Charlestown, there must have been the same interest in literature and learning and in classical and current history. Young Alexander, with broad forehead and intelligent eyes, absorbed the civilization of his father and relatives, which set him apart from his sisters and his kind in the Wind Clan.

It is not known whether Sehoy and the girls, Sophia and Jeannet, came to Augusta with Lachlan in 1757. If they did, they would have felt more at ease in the frontier town on the Savannah than in Charlestown. Indians were constant visitors to Augusta, and McGillivray's house was always open to them.

At the beginning of the year, Lachlan listed himself as a trader. By the end of 1757 he referred to himself as a planter. In September 1756 he and Daniel Clark had been granted five hundred acres. On July 5, 1757, he asked for three hundred additional acres seventeen miles below Augusta between Spirit Creek and McBean Creek, citing the fact that his "family" included twenty blacks. The change in status from merchant trader to merchant planter was significant. His acquisition of twenty slaves in 1757 reveals that he was a participant in a profound social revolution newly under way in Georgia. On January 1, 1751, slavery was officially permitted by the Trustees. Within two decades there were fifteen thousand blacks in the colony. Before 1751 there was no talk of aristocrats or gentry. During the Reynolds administration, Edmund Gray and William Little rallied their followers by warning about the dangers of an "aristocratical" government. In spite of its brevity, the administration of Henry Ellis was memorable for many influences on Georgia history, not the least of which was that he served as a role model. He taught the upwardly mobile Georgians how to comport themselves like gentlemen.

A prerequisite for success was the ownership of land, and the more slaves one had, the more land could be granted. The head of the household was awarded one hundred acres, and for each member of his family, which included indentured servants and slaves, he could obtain an additional fifty acres. The system favored those with enough credit to purchase slaves in Charlestown in anticipation of making a profit. Georgia's first generation of traders, McGillivray, Galphin, and others, had excellent credit ratings in Charlestown.

A gentleman planter was expected to live in town, not out on an isolated plantation, and McGillivray acquired lot eleven in Augusta as designated on Oglethorpe's original plan of forty lots. The lot was located on the corner of Broad and Center streets in the very heart of town, just the location for one with social ambitions. By November of the same year, he was cultivating eight hundred acres and asked for a hundred more at New Savannah on Butler Creek. The ownership of that particular tract would embroil him in controversy with Edmond Atkin; for a decade at least, the Savannah River Chickasaws had occupied the site.[8] On December 6, 1757, McGillivray made two additional applications. Calling himself an "inhabitant and planter" and claiming eleven hundred acres and more than forty slaves, he requested four hundred acres on the Savannah at the Indian Old Fields next to George Galphin's lands. Galphin, too, had come in out of the woods and turned to planting and land speculation. McGillivray's second petition that same day was for five hundred acres near Augusta between lands of Daniel Pepper and Nathaniel Bassett originally granted to Rowland Pritchett. This request was denied on the grounds that Pritchett had heirs who claimed the tract.[9]

McGillivray pursued his quest for land into the new year, asking for a regrant of fifty acres on Briar Creek which he and Clark had obtained but never acted upon. In the rapid accumulation of property, McGillivray was interested in providing for his family connections, as well as profitable speculation. He had urged his cousin John to come to America, indicating that he would give him some of his land. He wrote to William, the chief of the clan, urging him to come also and establish the clan in Georgia. If he did, Lachlan would make him his heir. William felt obligated to care for his sisters in Strathnairn, but his cousin's entreaties would eventually draw him to the land of marvelous opportunity.[10]

Lachlan was entitled to the honor of attaching *esquire* to his name after February 1, 1757, when he was named justice of the peace in place of John Fitch. He thus joined the other "gentlemen of Augusta": John Rae, David Douglass, Martin Campbell, and Edward Barnard. Responsibilities followed rapidly. On February 8, he was named tax collector for Augusta and Halifax. Halifax was a sparsely populated and short-lived district below Augusta and opposite George Galphin's trading post at Silver Bluff, South Carolina. In July, McGillivray was appointed commissioner for security and defense. He thus joined David Douglass, John Rae, and Edward Barnard, who had taken matters into their own hands during the Ogeechee crisis of the previous September.[11]

As commissioners, McGillivray and his friends worked with the popular commanding officer of Fort Augusta, Lieutenant White Outerbridge. McGillivray's command of the Indian languages made him especially useful to Outerbridge, who had Indian visitors at Fort Augusta frequently. If the officer had an important message for them, he relied on McGillivray to interpret for him. On other occasions, McGillivray would pass along Indian intelligence which he gleaned from conversation with the resident Chickasaws or visiting Creeks.[12]

A typical visitor in July 1757 was the Mad Warrior of Okfuskees, an old friend of McGillivray's. He was on his way to Charlestown, but McGillivray suggested that he go to Savannah and meet the new Georgia governor instead. McGillivray paid his friend the compliment of accompanying him to Savannah and interpreting for him. When the Wolf of Tuckabatchees and sixteen others paid a friendly call on

Outerbridge in September, the officer asked McGillivray to provide for them.[13] Thus McGillivray's role after 1757 was different from before. He had been an advance agent of the English in the Indian country and a courier linking the Creeks and the English. He was now the Indians' trusted friend in the English camp, still a link between two civilizations.

The foremost actor in the drama on the southern frontier in this transition year was Georgia's new governor, Henry Ellis. During the year 1757 he changed Georgia from a hopelessly divided, pitifully weak, and generally ignored province to one that was taken seriously. If Oglethorpe was the colony's founder, Ellis was its restorer. William W. Abbot has painted an unforgettable portrait of Ellis in Savannah, carrying that recent invention the umbrella with a thermometer dangling from it so he could record the temperature for a scientific article.[14]

Born in 1721, Henry Ellis had taken to the sea at an early age. In 1746, he joined an expedition searching for the northwest passage. Like a precursor of Darwin on the *Beagle*, he noted everything he saw and speculated about that which he did not understand. His account of the voyage did not attract the attention Darwin's did, but it earned him a fellowship in the Royal Society.[15]

Henry Ellis is treated well by historians because his letters sparkle with wit and reveal a keen intelligence. Reynolds's correspondence is stodgy and dull by comparison. One has to avoid the temptation to cast Ellis as hero and Reynolds as villain purely on the basis of their personalities. For a large faction of Georgians in 1757, however, Reynolds was a champion. More accurately, William Little was their hero, and John Reynolds simply ratified Little's decisions. These Georgians considered the Savannah councillors a dangerous junta; they might be labeled democrats. They had gained control of the assembly, elected Little as Speaker, and were ready to enjoy the fruits of victory. Instead, their enemies conspired to remove their patron, and for all they knew, the new governor was an ally of the junta. William Little was their Patrick Henry. He composed an address to the assembly which anticipated the radicals of 1776. He warned that "an aristocratical form of Government is perhaps of all others the least eligible."[16] The bold

Speaker rudely intruded upon Ellis's privacy to warn him that it would do no good to dissolve the assembly because the same delegates would be reelected.[17]

Indeed, Henry Ellis was an aristocrat by preference; at least, he was not a democrat. He considered Little's friends "credulous and disposed to evil as readily as to good." The people in general were, he thought, "extremely indolent and unconnected." They were too lazy to support partisan politics. Ellis was too astute to reveal these feelings. He pretended not to take sides and dissolved the assembly to gain time to acquaint himself with the state of affairs.[18]

It was another piece of bad luck for the Bosomworths that the Reynolds faction supported them. Ellis tried not to be drawn into the dispute, but by his association with the gentlemen of the council, he was predisposed against the Bosomworth claims. Ellis did not like the way Reynolds had appointed his friends as officers in the troop of rangers called up after the Ogeechee alarm, but he did not interfere with the appointments. He quickly realized the frightening fact that Georgia was both exposed and vulnerable to Indian attacks. Therefore, he exerted most of his efforts to win the allegiance of the Indians by calculated diplomacy. During his first meeting with a group of Creek visitors, he offered twenty shillings for every scalp of a French-allied Indian and forty for every prisoner. He realized that his most serious problem was the renewed settlement of pioneer farmers on Indian land. He called these people "a kind of strollers from the back settlements to the northward."[19] He understood that his greatest advantage was the dependence of the tribes on English trade goods in the face of the French shortage of supplies.

To gain firsthand information about the state of his province, Ellis undertook a tour of the southern portion. He met and was intrigued by Edmund Gray, whom he considered an "odd character" but also a "shrewd, sensible fellow." Gray was reputed to be a Quaker; whether he was or not, he affected an austerity of behavior that impressed his associates as well as the Indians. Ellis agreed to give Gray a trading license for his post on the St. Marys. This innocent initiative caused Ellis some anxious moments. He had to apologize to Governor Lyttelton for interfering in South Carolina's jurisdiction because Carolina claimed the region between the Altamaha and the St. Johns. Ellis soon discovered that he had trespassed on sensitive diplomatic issues. William Pitt's ministry was anxious to keep Spain out of the war, and the governor of Spanish Florida considered Gray an unfriendly intruder. Ellis and Lyttelton were instructed to persuade Gray and his friends to leave the debatable land.[20]

Ellis's internal problems dissipated during the adjournment of the assembly when William Little left Georgia to assist Reynolds in pleading his case before the Lords Commissioners of Trade. Patrick Mackay was supposed to assume leadership of the Gray-Little faction, but he was not reelected to the new session of the assembly. Ellis betrayed an unbecoming note of condescension in describing the assembly's well-meant address to him as "foolish and fulsome enough" but pronounced himself well pleased at the disappearance of factionalism.[21]

Ellis's deference to Lyttelton at first bordered on the obsequious, but events conspired to sour their relationship. When Ellis met Lyttelton and Lieutenant Colonel Henry Bouquet at Beaufort in August 1760, he asked for some of the troops under Lieutenant Colonel Archibald Montgomery to be stationed in Georgia. Bouquet could spare one hundred Virginians, and those for a short time only. Ellis must have chafed over Lyttelton's demand that Carolina should have the lead in all Indian negotiations. By then, Ellis had entertained a constant procession of Creek Indians, whereas Lyttelton had not seen any Creeks since Ellis's arrival earlier in the year. Lyttelton told Ellis that his agent Daniel Pepper had been instructed to bring the Creek chiefs to Charlestown. Even though Ellis had sent Joseph Wright on a similar errand with invitations to Savannah, he deferred to Lyttelton's seniority. He explained to the Board of Trade that he was not interested in "pre-eminence."[22]

After their meeting, Ellis wrote to Lyttelton to reassure him that he did not want to be the chief Indian negotiator: "I have neither the abilities, or the means to support that character effectually." Ellis thanked Lyttelton for his hospitality at Beaufort: "A little more of that good living, as it is called, would have soon made me incapable of living at all."[23]

Despite his polite demeanor, Ellis clearly resented Lyttelton's claim to preeminence on the Georgia side of the Savannah River. For one thing, he objected to Daniel Pepper's mission to the Creeks as interference in Georgia affairs. Pepper took his job seriously and made a conscientious effort to investigate the condition of the trade and to propose reforms. After circulating through the Creek towns for six months, he advised that every trader be obliged to maintain a storekeeper in every town listed on his license and that the trader be required to visit his towns once a week to guard against any irregularities. The principal traders should remain in the Indian country from February 25 to October 25 of each year. When the Indians had gone out on their winter hunts, the traders might come down for their licenses. There were many more suggestions, some of them sensible, but the impracticality of the above and similar recommendations was enough to turn the traders against Pepper. Lachlan McGillivray, for example, had no intention of remaining in the Creek Nation during the stipulated period and visiting his towns on a weekly basis. He held the license and delegated the conduct of his business to William Struthers and, after 1757, to his cousin John McGillivray.[24]

Because Governor Lyttelton was not familiar with the Creek headmen, he had asked Pepper to compile a census of leading men from each town. Pepper categorized them on the basis of whether they leaned to the French. For example, the great Gun Merchant of the Okchoys was described simply as one who received no presents from the French. The Wolf Warrior of the Okchoys, better known as the Mortar, was put down as one who corresponded with the French. There were some dubious contentions on his list; Devall's Landlord of Puckantallahasee was listed as in the French interest. Even that stalwart supporter of the English the Wolf of Muccolossus was described as "a great Rogue and a true Swiss, much in favour with the French." Pepper concluded his extensive list with the comment that "there are Numbers of Others, not mentioned here, who might be of service, and of course would be necessary to bribe."[25]

The accuracy as well as utility of Pepper's observations is questionable. Veterans like McGillivray were skeptical about the value of the advice of troubleshooting agents such as Thomas Bosomworth in 1753 and Daniel Pepper in 1757. They were predisposed against the advent of the first royal agent, McGillivray's critic Edmond Atkin. In 1757 Atkin was making his way slowly southward from New York, where he had gone to see the Earl of Loudoun, the British commander in America.[26]

By July 1757 Henry Ellis had made up his mind that he did not approve of Pepper's mission. He hedged his opinion in a letter to Lyttelton, saying that Pepper was not well spoken of by either white people or Indians but that the reports might well be prejudiced. Ellis's disapproval was significant; it meant that Lyttelton's efforts to take the leadership in Indian negotiations were in trouble. It would do no good for Carolina to promulgate stricter trade regulations if Georgia refused to conform.[27]

Meanwhile, a competition for supremacy in Indian affairs was waged by agents of Georgia and Carolina. While Pepper spread the news that the headmen were summoned to Charlestown, Joseph Wright brought Ellis's invitation to a conference in Savannah. The shrewd Ellis had taken precautions to involve the traders. He requested their assistance in persuading the Indians to go to Savannah, reminding them that he intended to counter the overtures of the French.[28]

Ellis could not resist a chortle of satisfaction when the Creeks chose Savannah in preference to Charlestown. He noted to his superiors that in spite of Pepper's being sent up at great expense, he could not prevail upon the chiefs to go to Charlestown. He attributed Pepper's "miscarriage" to his having alienated the traders whereas Ellis had actively solicited their help.[29]

Ellis's meeting with the headmen of twenty-one towns was the grandest ever held in Savannah. Coincidentally, the one hundred men of a Virginia regiment loaned to Georgia by Lieutenant Colonel Bouquet were on hand to lend unprecedented martial dignity to the occasion. This stage show would be the Virginians' only contribution to the war in Georgia because Bouquet's battalion was ordered north by the Earl of Loudoun in November 1757.[30]

Borrowing on Glen's Charlestown ceremonial, Ellis sent Captain

John Milledge with his troop of militia out a mile to escort the visitors to town. As they entered, they were greeted by salutes from the bastions at each corner of the earthen fortification which Ellis had thrown up around the town. Ellis greeted the chiefs with an engaging address. He displayed a talent for the allegorical style of rhetoric the Indians loved. "Observe how serene and cloudless the Day appears," he said. "I hope you have come with hearts resembling it."[31] Unlike Glen, and later Atkin, who assumed an imperious attitude when talking to the Indians, Ellis stressed his brotherly love and affection. Fortunately, a supply of presents had arrived, and he was also able to display a noble generosity.

It was a master stroke of diplomacy for Ellis to invite the leaders to dine with him on successive evenings before he attempted to bring them to a treaty signing. Again unlike Glen, who habitually made his visitors uneasy by insisting that they attack the Alabama Fort, Ellis did not attempt to instigate a war with the French. He had been told by the traders that the Creeks would never agree to an attack on the French and so he did not pressure them. At the end of a three-week festival, the chiefs signed a treaty, reiterating their friendship for the English and, somewhat surprisingly, stipulating that they had never given any lands to the Bosomworths or anyone else but now they gave the same lands to the great King George.[32]

Ellis was exultant with the success of his diplomacy; he had outdone both Kerlérec of Louisiana and Lyttelton of South Carolina. He did not want to share the moment with the traders who helped bring it about, and the names of the interpreter and other traders present were not included in the records. We know George Galphin was there because he carried the news of the meeting to Charlestown. Joseph Wright, the hardworking agent who had coaxed the Creeks to Savannah, must have been the interpreter. Lachlan McGillivray and the principal Augusta traders were certainly present at an event of such immediate concern to them.

There were two repercussions of the October meeting which caused unforeseen problems for Ellis. The Indians who missed the party came to Savannah in a steady stream and exhausted Ellis's patience and his presents. By February 1758 Ellis confessed to the Earl of Loudoun that "this frequent intercourse begins to be inconvenient."[33]

Far more serious was the resurrection of the Bosomworth problem. Ellis was to learn the painful lesson that peaceful relations with the Creeks depended on maintaining harmony between the Bosomworths and the government of Georgia. Mary and Thomas were not pleased by the treaty of Savannah. They rightly believed that their interests had been betrayed. Just as formerly they had used their influence with Malatchi to promote their cause, so in November 1757 they invited Malatchi's son Togulki and his brother Stumpe to pay them a visit at St. Catherine. They convinced the two Cowetas of the justice of their claim and explained that the new governor Ellis was a tool of their old enemies. Togulki, or young Malatchi as the traders called him, was easily persuaded and reverted to the strategy practiced by his father. After leaving the Bosomworths, he went to see the French at the Alabama Fort and was received with the usual "caresses." An invitation from Governor Kerlérec to visit him in Mobile was the next step. That dignitary at last had gifts to bestow, and he lavished them upon young Malatchi and his entourage. He claimed that 150 Creeks accompanied Malatchi; if so, his numbers equaled those at Ellis's gathering. Kerlérec was determined to prove that the French were not poor and that the English were liars for saying so.[34] In taking advantage of the hospitality of the rival Europeans, young Malatchi was following the example of his father and grandfather.

The strategy worked well for the Bosomworths, though it did not seem so at first. Henry Ellis was angry at young Malatchi for going over to the Bosomworths. "These Savages are all mercenary," he exclaimed to his superiors.[35] He blamed the Bosomworths for poisoning the minds of the Indians and spoiling his good work. Again he used the traders to bring their influence to bear. As before, Joseph Wright was his agent, and the result was a hastily improvised and unnecessary treaty renewing the cession of the Bosomworth lands to the king. The document was drawn up on April 22, 1758, in the Wolf's town of Muccolossus and was more remarkable for the number of traders who signed than for the number of important Creeks. John McGillivray's name was there, as was John Spencer's; both, of course, were associates of Lachlan McGillivray. The veterans James Cussings, George Galphin, Lachlan McIntosh, and Stephen Forrest also witnessed the treaty.[36] Ellis's motive in securing this second treaty must have been to provide him with bargaining leverage in his negotiations with the Bosomworths. By June 1758, Ellis was exasperated with Thomas, whom he described as "cunning, industrious and desperate"; he was favorably impressed by Mary. She had two assets: the first was that she was "sensible," the other, and more important, was that she had the support of highly placed persons in Charlestown. The pragmatic Ellis asked and received permission from the government to reach a settlement. He then worked out an acceptable compromise. The Bosomworths would receive St. Catherine Island as a royal grant. Ossabaw and Sapelo would be sold and the couple would be compensated £2,000. On their part, they would relinquish all other claims. The scheme worked to the satisfaction of both parties. Sapelo brought £700 and Ossabaw £350. Ellis was fortunate in his timing of the settlement of the troublesome Bosomworth claims. When the Cherokees went on the warpath in 1759, Mary Bosomworth used her considerable influence to preserve the neutrality of the Creeks.[37]

A constant irritant to good relations with South Carolina was the enforcement of the Indian trade. Ellis did not care for Daniel Pepper's interference; he would like Edmond Atkin even less. A source of trouble was the increasing number of outlying houses where rum was sold to the Indians in exchange for deerskins. This barter was forbidden by the Indian policy of both provinces. When John Fitch of Augusta was accused of being involved in this illicit business, his excuse was that others did it. Ellis tried his best to eliminate the practice, but he could do nothing about the rum dealers in the South Carolina up-country except make strong appeals to Governor Lyttelton. An even greater source of tension between the two governors was Lyttelton's claim to command the garrisons of Augusta and Frederica. After enduring several instances of conflicting interests, Ellis wrote to Lyttelton as frankly as possible and still be tactful. He said he would have to distinguish between Lyttelton the governor and Lyttelton the friend, "for tho I revere the one, I may bear with impatience the encroachments of the other." [38]

Ellis as military commander experienced enormous frustration in getting the attention of the military commanders of the British forces in America. John Campbell, the fourth Earl of Loudoun and General Edward Braddock's successor as commander in chief, was the first Ellis had to deal with. On February 28, 1757, Ellis informed Loudoun of Georgia's helpless and exposed condition. Of four thousand white inhabitants, only about seven hundred were capable of bearing arms. He explained that his predecessor had raised a troop of rangers. The officers had been commissioned and forty men enlisted when he arrived in Georgia. Ellis's instructions as governor required him to secure permission from the commander in military matters. How was he to pay the rangers? [39] Instead of a reply, Ellis received Loudoun's circular letter requesting the attendance of the royal governors in Philadelphia. Ellis dutifully wrote back to say that he would have liked to have gone to Philadelphia but the invitation reached him after the meeting was over. Should he complete the troop of rangers? There was no reply. By May 23, 1757, Ellis reported that the credit of the captain of the rangers was "at utmost stretch"; all but twenty-five of the rangers had been disbanded. In June, Ellis wrote to Lieutenant Colonel Bouquet, who commanded the force of Highlanders and Virginians dispatched by Loudoun to South Carolina. He recited the history of the rangers to Bouquet. By then they were reduced to twenty men, and Ellis was embarrassed at his inability to maintain them. [40]

On August 10, Ellis wrote again to Loudoun, acknowledging that Bouquet had promised him a hundred men, but Georgia must pay their expenses. The assembly had approved his plan to build log forts in five districts, and he had raised a breastwork around the town of Savannah. Fascines of pointed logs protruded ten feet out of the earth embankments, and bastions were erected at each corner. Still he received no response to this effusion of information. [41]

Finally, in September, Ellis could not resist an uncharacteristic outburst directed at the distant commander: "It were greatly to be wished that you had more ample powers in what respects the defense of the southern provinces . . . especially as we are forbid to undertake any-thing of an expensive or military nature without the concurrence of your lordship." [42] Actually, by then Loudoun reluctantly had authorized £850 with which Ellis maintained his troop of rangers at forty men and four officers. He needed them because Loudoun recalled Bouquet's detachment, and the hundred Virginians had departed.

General James Abercromby, Loudoun's successor, was, if possible, even less helpful. In answer to Ellis's appeals, he replied in August and again in October 1758 that he could not approve expenses because he was not authorized to do so. [43] The ineptitude of the commanders and the inefficiency of the system explain the losses of Fort Oswego on Lake Ontario and Fort William Henry on Lake George to French forces under the leadership of the capable Marquis de Montcalm.

The accession of William Pitt to the office of principal secretary of state infused new life into the war effort and summoned the neglected southern provinces into the grand strategy for waging the war. Pitt's master plan was to nip the French at each extremity, at Louisbourg and Quebec in the North and Mobile and New Orleans in the South. He needed the advice of the southern governors on how to proceed. The two southern governors, Lyttelton and Ellis, relied on the traders for advice, and of all the traders the one they most depended on in this supremely important instance was Lachlan McGillivray.

The idea for an attack on the Louisiana French was a favorite of James Glen while he was governor. He emphasized Louisiana's weak-ness in a letter to the Duke of Bedford before he relinquished his office, in which he described how a Captain Colcock had carried a cargo to Mobile and could pilot the expedition if need be. [44] Pitt was intrigued by the notion of a southern offensive and broached the subject to Lyttel-ton on January 27, 1758, in a letter marked "secret." Pitt instructed Lyttelton to send Colcock to Halifax at government expense, there to confer with Admiral Edward Boscowen and give advice about the practicality of an assault on the French positions by a body of troops from Halifax at the onset of winter, when the weather would interrupt operations in the North. [45] In a follow-up on March 2, Pitt postponed the southern expedition until General Jeffrey Amherst completed his campaign against Louisbourg. He elaborated on his original plan by suggesting an overland march against the Alabama Fort to coincide with Boscowen's naval campaign against Mobile and New Orleans. From Pitt's perspective, with a map of North America spread before him, there was an irresistible appeal in the symmetry of a naval operation in the North combined with a land invasion by way of the Hudson River–Lake Champlain route and a similar two-pronged strategy in the South. Pitt couched his instructions in language that left little room for evading them. "Use your utmost endeavour," he ordered Lyttelton, "to set on foot and encourage an expedition from your province against the Alabama fort." Lyttelton was advised to engage the Indian nations to join the invasion. The routine courtesy phrase "in case you judge it practible [sic]" offered Lyttelton some room for independent judgment.[46]

Pitt's letter was dynamite, and it would have caused the utmost consternation in Charlestown if Lyttelton included others in his secret. Lyttelton needed advice. He had paid little attention to the confusing situation on the western frontier other than to sponsor Pepper's mission. He had been preoccupied with inducing the Cherokees to join General John Forbes's campaign against Fort Duquesne. Earlier that same year James Glen had recommended McGillivray to Lyttelton on another Indian matter: "If McGillivray be in town, he is a man of sense and substance and may be trusted and he knows ten times more of their affairs than any other trader."[47] In an effort to secure McGillivray's advice about the wisdom of an overland expedition, Lyttelton made a quick trip to Fort Moore in June 1758, ostensibly to visit the Savannah River Chickasaws and to inspect Fort Moore. James Adair happened to be there at the time, and he recorded his impression of Lyttelton: "We had great pleasure to see his excellency on his summer's journey, enter the old famous New Windsor garrison, like a private gentleman, without the least parade."[48] Lyttelton confided his secret mission to McGillivray and quietly left without giving out any presents. Lieutenant Colonel William Bull handled that chore, procuring what he needed from McGillivray's store—guns, ruffled shirts, coats, and boots for the men; petticoats and calico cloth for the women.[49] (Incidentally, he acquiesced in a land transaction proposed by McGillivray, about which more later.)

There followed a remarkable document of twelve folio pages dispatched by Lachlan McGillivray to Governor Lyttelton on July 14, 1758. After general comments on the state of Indian affairs, the writer came to the crux of the matter: "I infer that, for our own security, if success crowns our British arms in the present northern expedition, *Delenda est Carthago.*" He went on to say that because Lyttelton had commanded him to put his thoughts in writing as to how the objective could be attained, he would take up the question of a land attack first. An army of six thousand men would be needed to cut off the Alabama and Mobile garrisons; at least half of them should be trained in the tactics of Indian warfare. Moreover, a great number of horses would be needed to carry artillery and provisions the 450 miles from Augusta to the Alabama Fort. The rivers were at flood in the winter; even the traders, with their big leather canoes, had trouble crossing them. By the time the army reached the objective, it would have to deal with the French, Creeks, and Choctaws combined because all the Indians would resist such an invasion. After listing other problems, the writer concluded by commenting that Lyttelton's "sagacious wisdom" could foresee the fatal consequence of a land expedition without overt reference to Braddock's example.

If it was decided to risk a land attack, however, Mr. Atkin or someone else ought to go into the Creek Nation with presents. Supplies should be dispatched to the Choctaws and Chickasaws at least a month before the planned attack. Here McGillivray mentioned that "an old friend of mine" was ready and willing to carry the goods to the Chickasaws, and the sight of him "would warm the hearts of our brave, friendly Chickasaws." This friend, when asked, replied that he would gladly throw away the goose quill and take up the sword "as soon as honour sounds the trumpet." [50]

The reference was clearly to Adair, who was mentioned elsewhere in the rambling narrative. It was suggested that the bearer, Mr. Adair, would be glad to answer any other questions the governor might have. The letter was signed by Lachlan McGillivray. No stronger argument against a land expedition could have been written. The document itself is curious. It was not in McGillivray's handwriting, and the signature was misspelled "Laughlin McGilvery." The emotional, exaggerated style is that of James Adair. Evidently, Adair considered himself still under a cloud in Charlestown, and since the dispatch would probably be laid before the council, he signed McGillivray's name. Did McGillivray conceal Adair's involvement from the governor? On the contrary, he enclosed Adair's effort with a letter of his own and stated that he was sending "Mr. Adair's opinion" in regard to the projected attack on the French forts. He hoped the governor would question Adair; "he may be useful in his way." McGillivray made it clear that he had no other connection with Adair except compassion: "I pity his misfortunes."[51] Although the writing was Adair's, the ideas were McGillivray's.

What is remarkable about this letter is not so much the double authorship as Lyttelton's choosing to involve the two traders in this most secret affair. Lyttelton assured Pitt that he had not disclosed the matter to "anybody whatsoever," nor did he make the inquiries he would have had he "not apprehended that it would lead to a premature discovery of the business." In fact, Lyttelton had told somebody. He had asked McGillivray for advice on the feasibility of an overland attack on the Alabama Fort. Lyttelton sent extracts of the letter of July 14 to William Pitt so McGillivray's name, or at least his opinion, resounded in high places. Lyttelton referred to the document as the product of two traders of Augusta, "both very knowing in Indian affairs," but did not reveal their identity.[52]

Lyttelton did not much like the advice he received. It was obvious that he had sensed the opportunity to be at the focal point of history. He saw himself as another Braddock, this time with success crowning British arms. His covering letter to Pitt was a running argument against the points raised in the McGillivray-Adair letter. He believed two thousand men would be sufficient for the expedition; he could raise them in Carolina, plus a hundred men of the independent companies, some of whom had served under Oglethorpe and Braddock. He would send a proclamation ahead explaining to the Creeks that he came as a friend and intended to attack the French. He would invite the Creeks to join him; if they refused, he would order all traders out of their country. If they opposed, he would burn down their villages and put their women and children to the sword.

He would limit the number of baggage horses by building depots along the way. Fort Augusta would be strengthened and well stocked. The transportation of artillery, he admitted, was a problem, and he would require some small cannon and some good "matrosses" (gunner's mates adept at loading and firing artillery). In addition, he would need the services of an experienced engineer to strengthen the Alabama Fort after he had taken it with scaling ladders, presumably so that the French could not recapture it by the same means.

He would cross the flooded rivers on bridges of boats, hence boat-makers and carpenters would be enlisted in his expedition. If pontoons could be sent from England, he would transport them. Tents, muskets, and bayonets for two thousand men would also be required.

By the time Lyttelton had completed his list, his version of the invasion seemed as impractical as McGillivray's and must have appeared so to William Pitt. Lyttelton was too eager for action to realize the discouraging import of his requirements. He recognized that the McGillivray letter "represents an enterprise against the Alabama fort as likely to be attended with extreme difficulties," but he did not perceive that his own letter confirmed those difficulties.

The final curious part of this episode is that, after going to the trouble of seeking out and consulting McGillivray, Lyttelton dismissed the unwelcome advice by stating that he did not trust traders. Referring to the July 14 letter, Lyttelton wrote, "I do not give very much weight to that representation because I think it is the interest of the Traders to discourage the making any attempt upon that place as it would interrupt the tranquility with which they now carry on their trade in all part of the Creek nation should that country become a seat of war." [53]

In retrospect, the traders seem more sensible than the hawkish governor. The Alabama Fort, Fort Tombigbee, and Mobile would fall to the English without any attack, by land or sea, by virtue of the Treaty of Paris signed in 1763. Governor Lyttelton would have an opportunity in December 1759 to mount a war-horse and lead an expedition into the Cherokee country. He would discover that it is one thing to plan an invasion and another to execute it.

If the joint letter of McGillivray and Adair did not dissuade Lyttelton, it probably caused Pitt to have second thoughts. Meanwhile, the southern offensive was hostage to the siege of Louisbourg. While that operation lasted, Admiral Edward Boscowen's navy could not be spared for a campaign against Mobile and New Orleans. Lyttelton dispatched Captain Isaac Colcock, brother of the deceased mariner who had sailed into Mobile Bay, to confer with Boscowen in Halifax. On July 29, 1758, Boscowen wrote that Louisbourg had capitulated, but Colcock was no help in telling him how to navigate the Gulf waters. Why anyone thought that the brother of an expert would qualify as an expert was left unasked. Boscowen wanted to talk to an experienced pilot. By the end of August no pilot was forthcoming, and the admiral and General Amherst decided to postpone the operation.[54] Amherst explained to Lyttelton that he had received orders to detach General James Wolfe for an attack on Quebec by way of Louisbourg and that he was commanded to proceed with the rest of the army to Canada by way of Lake George. The war would be won in the North, not in the South.[55]

Nevertheless, the rumors of a British invasion, actively propagated by the anxious French at Toulouse, spread throughout the Creek country and caused confusion and consternation. Edmond Atkin's mission in 1759 was said to be the advance guard of a mighty army. The Carolina campaign against the Cherokees in that year was interpreted as an effort to enslave the Cherokees before doing the same to the Creeks.

Lachlan McGillivray and his friends would have to deal with the impact of the French propaganda. First, they had to confront the greatest challenge to their standing among the western Indians, the advent of the first superintendent of Indian affairs in the Southern Department and an open critic of Lachlan McGillivray, the Honorable Edmond Atkin.

CHAPTER NINE

The Mission of Edmond Atkin

One of the most curious episodes in the French and Indian War on the southern frontier was the mission of Edmond Atkin in 1759. The return of Atkin was of surpassing interest to the gentlemen of the trade in Augusta and especially to Lachlan McGillivray. Although the monopolizing company had dissolved by death and retirement, the former members, McGillivray, Galphin, Rae, and their associates, David Douglass, Francis McCartan, Martin Campbell, and Edward Barnard, had an agreement on trade practices and policies which worked well enough in the essential matter of preserving the goodwill of their clients in the Indian country. These veterans were uneasy whenever an outside agent came investigating, and there had never been an agent who bore the portentous title of royal superintendent of Indian affairs in the Southern Department, and there had never been an agent like Edmond Atkin, the man who proudly flaunted the title.

Atkin, born in England in 1707, lived in South Carolina most of his life. He and his brother engaged in the deerskin trade, and Atkin acquired an encyclopedic knowledge of the Indians of the west and of their country. As a member of the South Carolina Council, he was suspicious of the outlying traders and particularly of Lachlan McGillivray, Governor Glen's favorite interpreter. Nor was there any love lost between Atkin and Glen. Atkin's account of the Choctaw Revolt was an effort to spoil Glen's claim to credit in the affair.[1]

Atkin was a prolific writer, and after his treatise on the Choctaw schism, he wrote a pamphlet on what was wrong in the government of South Carolina, which prompted the Lords of the Board of Trade to ask him to put down his recommendations for regulating the Indian trade. He wrote the tract in 1754 and delivered it to the Earl of Halifax on May 30, 1755. On the basis of his exhaustive knowledge of the trade and the unqualified assertions about what ought to be done, Atkin was named as one of the first two Indian superintendents.[2] Sir William Johnson, wealthy and well-known trader to the Mohawks, was made superintendent of the Northern Department.

Atkin's report was filled with negative allusions to Lachlan McGillivray, though most readers then and later would not have recognized who was meant because no names were used. If Lachlan McGillivray read the report, which was unlikely, his reaction to Atkin's coming would not have been as polite as it was. Atkin pointedly criticized those who traded with the Alabama Fort during the last war and with the Choctaws after they had gone back to the French interests. He blamed the traders for the Creeks' opposition to an attack on the Alabama Fort, suggesting that the motive was to protect their trade with the fort. He accused them of giving false intelligence to serve their private purposes. He argued that traders who escorted Indians to Charlestown brought only their friends and told them what to say. He had McGillivray in mind for each accusation. It was significant that Atkin was concerned about the twenty thousand acres on the Carolina side opposite Augusta which had been given to the Chickasaws under Squirrel King. The Chickasaws made little use of the land, and whites were buying parcels of it. He intended to put a stop to that practice. Atkin may have known when he wrote that Lachlan McGillivray was one of the chief purchasers of Chickasaw land.

The extensive report, for all its verbosity, was a carefully reasoned statement which made the following points: traders could not be trusted to represent His Majesty's interests, none of the royal governors had wide enough jurisdiction to regulate the trade, and the only solution was to appoint an agent who would represent the crown in Indian affairs.[3]

Several influential Carolinians then in London, together with Sir George Lyttelton, the Carolina governor's older brother, helped secure the agency for Atkin. Atkin wrote to the Earl of Loudoun on May 14, 1756, informing him that he had received his orders from the Board of Trade that morning. An initial problem was that the Board of Trade referred Atkin to Loudoun for instructions and Loudoun was notoriously dilatory about giving instructions. Atkin had to go to New York to find Loudoun. The voyage was enlivened by a skirmish with a French privateer. When Atkin reached New York, he learned that Loudoun had gone to Albany, so he followed him there and finally had his audience and verified his pay, the same as Sir William Johnson's, £600 per year. Atkin's penchant for reaching beyond his grasp is evident in his statement to Loudoun that he intended to visit all of the tribes, including the 780-mile-distant Choctaws, every year.[4]

Atkin took advantage of his proximity to Johnson Hall to pay a visit to his northern counterpart and to sit in on a conference which Sir William hosted for the headmen of the Six Nations. Atkin would strive to emulate Johnson's style of management on the southern frontier. Unfortunately, he lacked the independent wealth to bring it off properly. Atkin and Johnson convinced the Iroquois to draw up a peace treaty with the Cherokees and Catawbas so as to concentrate their hostility on the French.[5]

In an attempt to secure the £2,000 he felt he needed to conduct his business, Atkin had to follow Loudoun about, from Albany to New York, to Boston, back to New York, and finally to Philadelphia. It was all for nothing because Loudoun referred Atkin to the southern governors for financial support.[6]

Atkin spent most of the year 1757 in Virginia, quarreling with various officials and displaying an imperiousness of demeanor that antagonized those he dealt with. He gained some success in consolidating the conduct of Indian affairs under the supervision of Christopher Gist, whom he appointed his deputy. Governor Robert Dinwiddie considered Atkin's services useful, if expensive.[7] It boded ill for Atkin's mission, however, that Dinwiddie declined to place control of the Virginia Indian trade in Atkin's hands or in Gist's.

Atkin's journey south was delayed by a long illness in North Carolina; he reached Charlestown on March 23, 1758, just as Bouquet's battalion was embarking for New York. Atkin obeyed Loudoun's orders to send a large party of Cherokees to join General John Forbes's campaign against Fort Duquesne at the forks of the Ohio River. By May, more than six hundred Cherokees were in Virginia, but they soon grew disgusted with Forbes's slow progress and returned to their mountains, plundering some frontier settlements along the way.[8] In the skirmishing that followed, some of the warriors were killed. The Indian code demanded that they be avenged, and the ever-alert French at the Alabama Fort made the most of that opportunity to separate the Cherokees from the English. The bitter fruit of the French intrigue would be harvested in the terrible winter of 1759–60.

After dispatching an agent to go north with the Cherokees, Atkin announced his plans to visit Henry Ellis in Savannah and then to proceed to Augusta and from there to the western Indians. He intended "to watch every motion and event" in the Creek country, and he hoped to be able to restore friendly relations with the Choctaws. He complained to General James Abercromby, Loudoun's successor, that he had not received a single shilling promised by Loudoun since he had been in Carolina. He had appealed to the South Carolina Assembly, but that body agreed only to pay the expenses of an interpreter and one assistant for six months. Atkin thought that an insult to his dignity, considering that Daniel Pepper had an escort of twenty men.[9] There was a cloak-and-dagger aspect to Atkin's mission. Lyttelton acted on the advice contained in McGillivray's letter of July 14. He briefed Atkin on Pitt's plan and instructed him to secure the cooperation of the Creeks and Choctaws regarding a possible invasion of their country.

Henry Ellis had long anticipated Atkin's arrival, as had the Augusta-based traders. Ellis told Lyttelton in May that he was unacquainted with the nature and extent of Atkin's commission. Finally, in October

1758 Atkin met Ellis.[10] He was accompanied by his secretary, George Mackenzie, and by one of his own servants who doubled as a drummer. His expenses included £2.26 for a walnut staff with socket, hook, and gilded head, on which Mackenzie carried Atkin's standard. Interestingly, the staff was made for Atkin by Farquhar McGillivray, Lachlan's cousin. Atkin's entry into Savannah with his standard and drummer conjures up images of Don Quixote and Sancho Panza.[11]

Atkin spent ten days in Savannah, conferring frequently with Ellis and complaining about being neglected in South Carolina. Afterward, Ellis wrote to the Board of Trade that he was not convinced of the necessity of Atkin's mission to the Creeks at a time when that frontier was quiet. If anywhere, Atkin should be in the Cherokee Nation. To Lyttelton, Ellis characterized Atkin as one who had a great amount of knowledge and undoubted abilities "but seems to want the address and the art of assimilating which are so highly necessary in our commerce with the world." In other words, Atkin did not know how to get along with people.[12] Despite his misgivings, Ellis accommodated Atkin with an escort of twelve rangers to Augusta.

Atkin was greeted at Fort Moore with a thirteen-gun salute by Lieutenant White Outerbridge. Outerbridge and his men then hurried across the river to repeat the ceremony at Augusta. Colonel David Douglass and Lieutenant Colonel Edward Barnard called out Captain John Rae's troop of horse and Captain John Williams's company of foot militia. With the detachment of Georgia rangers that accompanied Atkin from Savannah, they formed a ring outside the gates of Fort Augusta. After an artillery salute, the assembled militia fired several volleys. Atkin's commission was read aloud by his secretary, as were letters of endorsement from Ellis and Lyttelton. Atkin thrived on ceremony. Ellis commented that the superintendent had made a "very pompous entry" into Augusta.[13]

Atkin called the traders together and told them of his intention of fitting out a company of mounted troops to go with him into the Indian country. Although the traders "put a good Face upon it," Atkin was certain that they opposed his mission; "there is nothing they dread so much as the looking into the true State of the Trade," he reported to Lyttelton.[14]

He next sent Joseph Wright, who had been recommended by Ellis, into the Creek villages to announce his coming and to gather intelligence about the activities of the French. Atkin was displeased that no one had thought of providing him with an escort and that he had to recruit a troop himself. He complained about the great expense entailed in conveying the goods to Augusta and planned to send the supplies to the Indian towns in one of George Galphin's caravans to await distribution by himself. He commented snidely that he doubted if all the presents ever reached their destination when carried by the traders.

Among the proclamations he published was one forbidding traders to send any goods to the western tribes until he had distributed the presents. He warned against allowing anyone a license to trade with the Choctaws until he set the conditions. He remembered that during the Red Shoes revolt the traders scrambled for the deerskins without waiting for the government to act.

Within a month his escort was nearly complete. "I shall have such a troop as perhaps never was seen," he wrote.[15] There were plenty of men available, but he had a great deal of trouble enlisting a quota because of what he believed to be the underhanded insinuations and falsehoods spread by his enemies. He also ran into opposition in regard to the private purchasing of Chickasaw land. The two problems involved the same individual. He informed Lyttelton that he would supply details later because the governor would probably want to bring the individual before the council. The person Atkin had in mind was Lachlan McGillivray.

In Atkin's opinion the matter of the Chickasaw lands was so important that it had to be resolved before he resumed his mission to the interior. Accordingly, he called the Chickasaws of New Savannah together for a conference, which, though solemnly conducted, had overtones of a comic farce. The Indians gathered at the parsonage below the town of Augusta. John Pettigrew was sworn in as interpreter, as was London, Pettigrew's black servant. The Squirrel King had died;

Tuccatoby King was the chief and Nathlettoby, his head warrior. The Doctor and Mingo Stoby were among the oldest beloved men.[16]

Atkin opened the solemn session by lecturing the Chickasaws on the ethics of land transactions. The burden of his message was that the king had given them a fine strip of land on the Carolina side. Now Atkin found them living on the Georgia side at New Savannah. Why did they move? Tuccatoby King replied that they were afraid of their enemies over there. Atkin scoffed at that. He had heard of the Chickasaws killing their enemies but never the opposite. The Indians were silent.

Atkin continued that he had learned that when the white people first came to live in Augusta, the Chickasaws visited them, drank too much rum, and drowned trying to swim across the river. The Indians pondered the suggestion and agreed with it. "Tis true," said Tuccatoby King. "Had it not been on that Account partly, we might still have been living on the same Land." The Chickasaws, having received presents from Atkin, were in a mellow mood and willing to agree to almost anything.

How long had they been on the Georgia side, Atkin wanted to know. The Indians' collective memory was remarkably vague. They supposed it was about ten years. Atkin pressed on. He had heard that they gave leave to some white people to plant on the land they left. That was true, they said. Every white man who received a plot of their land promised to give them a keg of rum each year.

Was there a written agreement? Tuccatoby King did not know, but the old Doctor remembered that there was. Then Tuccatoby remembered that he had signed it.

Who were the white men who planted on your land? The question was embarrassing for Pettigrew the interpreter because he was one of those named, together with William Fraser, David Douglass, and others.

Did anyone buy the land? At first they only loaned the land, they said, but "at last . . . exchanged it by general consent with Mr. Lachlan McGillivray." That was the name Atkin was after. That was the fraud he was determined to expose. Was there an agreement in writing?

Yes; all put their hands to it. Atkin did not like that answer. He probed again and again. McGillivray had obtained a tract from opposite Rae's house down to a point across from the parsonage house. The riverfront measured about three miles. How far back from the river? They had no idea. Their land was never measured back from the river. McGillivray had many cattle and needed a great amount of land, they said.

What did he give in exchange? He gave the land below Augusta, around the bend of the river, called New Savannah, where they had been living, together with a piece of land on the other side of the river opposite New Savannah.

Who owned New Savannah in the first place? Their friend Billy Gray, they said. (Gray was Oglethorpe's captain who led them down to Florida to fight the Spaniards.) The Chickasaws were under the impression that Gray had given the land to them, but afterward he sold it to Alexander Wood, Archibald McGillivray's partner. The Indians did not know what happened next, but Atkin discovered that Wood had bequeathed the land to Thomas Pinckney, from whom McGillivray bought it. McGillivray acquired an additional one hundred acres in 1757.

Why did they give McGillivray so much when they received so little, Atkin wanted to know. "We are red people," was the answer, "we know no better. . . . That which Mr. McGillivray gives us, suits us, tho' small." Atkin then scolded the Chickasaws for selling their land. The king had given them the use of it; it was not theirs to sell. They should have asked permission of the governor before they sold it. They did send word by the governor's beloved man that they had exchanged land with Mr. McGillivray, they replied. The reference was to their conference with Lieutenant Governor William Bull on July 20, 1758.

That was too late. They should have asked first, Atkin scolded. "Our King don't allow his Children to sell or take his Lands to their own use." What would the Indians do when white people settled all around them? The Chickasaws saw no problem in that eventuality; they would move away.

Atkin's questions revealed the difference between the white man's attitude toward land and life and the Indian's. When he asked, "Where will you go then?" Tuccatoby King's answer was eloquent in its simplicity: "I am a Redman." He meant that he saw things differently from Atkin; his home was in the Chickasaw country to the west. He could not be excited about the Savannah River lands, which he regarded as temporary camping grounds. The Chickasaws were polite to Edmond Atkin, but they wondered why he was so worried about such a little matter. Atkin let them go with a warning not to sign any other papers but the ones he or the governors gave them to sign.[17] In his report to Governor Lyttelton, Atkin called the Chickasaw lands "a very troublesome affair" of which "I am now Master indeed."[18] He assumed that the matter would be laid before the council and that McGillivray's title to the land would be canceled. In this, as in other of his recommendations, he would be disappointed. Lachlan McGillivray was too experienced and too shrewd to carry out such an important transaction in a clandestine manner.

David Douglass began the division of the Chickasaw land in 1756; he told the surveyor that the land was vacant and produced a warrant for five hundred acres. John McQueen took a tract of three thousand acres in 1757. In April of that year, Lachlan McGillivray had a thousand acres surveyed under a warrant made out to his partner Daniel Clark.[19] There were other claimants to the land, including John Joachim Zubly, about which more will be said later.

Since there was doubt about the legality of the surveys, Lachlan McGillivray arranged a meeting between the Chickasaws and William Bull, the lieutenant governor, on July 20, 1758, at Fort Moore, New Windsor. The Chickasaws cheerfully signed away their Carolina land in exchange for two tracts of five hundred acres each owned by McGillivray. In August, McGillivray explained the transaction to Governor Lyttelton, emphasizing that the Chickasaws were pleased with the swap and that Douglass, McQueen, and the others would have title to the properties surveyed for them.[20] McGillivray obtained a warrant for fifteen hundred acres for himself on September 6, 1758, and the surveys were being done when Atkin arrived on the scene. The point to be made here is that McGillivray did not claim the extensive tract for himself and that what he did was done openly and legally. The governor, the gentlemen traders of Augusta, and the Indians were satisfied with the arrangement; only Atkin was displeased. His displeasure turned to outrage when John Spencer purchased five hundred acres and began to build on it, directly opposite the house in which Atkin was staying, right "before my face," as Atkin put it. He regarded Spencer's conduct as a deliberate act of defiance instigated by McGillivray.[21]

The matter of the Chickasaw land was one complaint Atkin lodged against McGillivray and his friends. Another was the shocking disregard of the Indian laws of both Carolina and Georgia. Atkin discovered that McGillivray had sold his license to William Struthers; John Rae sold his to William Fraser. David Douglass had three licenses and had never been in the Indian country. The traders ignored the regulation that they were supposed to live in the Indian country and that they were required to renew their licenses in person during certain months in Charlestown or Savannah. They claimed exemption from the law as a privilege. "Licenses on the present footing may as well be given to Men living in Cheapside," Atkin exclaimed in frustration.[22]

Atkin blamed the principal traders for delaying his recruiting of an escort; he secured his twelfth man only after two months in Augusta. Atkin felt that the traders themselves should have volunteered to go with him and swell his entourage. He confided to Governor Lyttelton that he had learned that they were not going to volunteer, but they did not know that he knew they would not. It did not occur to Atkin to ask them to accompany him. "I would willingly have done myself the pleasure of a trip to the Indian country with Mr. Atkin, but as he was not pleased to ask me, I could not imagine that my company would be acceptable," Lachlan McGillivray informed Lyttelton.[23]

The Augusta traders thought that Atkin should have let Lachlan McGillivray go in his place. James Adair noted that McGillivray never refused to serve his country on any important occasion and would certainly have gone if asked.[24] In December, McGillivray made a quick visit to Charlestown to see his brother Alexander, the sea captain, who was dangerously ill. Atkin thought it was a trumped-up excuse to spread malicious rumors about him so he published accusations against the traders in Robert Wells's *Gazette*. Captain McGillivray recovered, and Lachlan was back in Augusta within the month.[25]

It is to McGillivray's credit that in none of his letters to Lyttelton — and he wrote frequently during this period — was there any mean criticism of Atkin. He expressed regret that the gentlemen of Augusta "should deserve so severe and publick a censure from Mr. Atkin" as appeared in print. Instead, McGillivray's correspondence kept both governors acquainted with the stream of rumors and facts that he heard from his Indian visitors. McGillivray was an expert in winnowing out the substance of a story. He kept Lyttelton and Ellis abreast of events in the west. He told how the Savannahs left their villages near the French fort with the western Chickasaws hot on their trail. He explained that the French were intriguing with young Malatchi to join the Cherokees in an attack on Fort Loudoun. He revealed that the Choctaws were waiting impatiently at Wolf's town, Muccolossus, for Atkin's arrival and that the rest of the Creeks were anxious about Atkin because his ban on trade was beginning to pinch.[26]

James Adair was severely critical of Atkin for delaying so long in Augusta. According to Adair, Atkin "trifled away near half a year there . . . in raising a body of men with a proud uniform dress, for the sake of parade . . . with swivels, blunderbusses, and many other such sort of blundering stuff, before he proceeded on his journey."[27]

Because of the long delay, the traders appealed to Georgia's governor, Henry Ellis. Ellis passed their complaints on to Lyttelton. Their trade was held up, they said, for no good reason. Meanwhile, Atkin complained to Ellis about all the obstructions that were put in his way. Ellis relayed that to Lyttelton also, adding that Atkin brought most of his problems on himself. Atkin asked Ellis for authority to cancel the licenses of certain traders. Ellis balked. He doubted that Atkin would use his power wisely: "He is rather of too hasty and sanguine a temper to deal properly with the people he intends to reform." But if Lyttelton would agree to give Atkin that authority, he would go along. The issue was vital for the effectiveness of the Indian superintendency. The superintendent, to be taken seriously, should have control over the licensing process. Ellis, however, was not certain Atkin was the right person to exercise it. Lyttelton shared the doubts or was unwilling to lessen his own prerogative. In any case, the two governors retained the licensing power. On March 13, 1759, Ellis informed Atkin that he could not see any sufficient reason to comply with his request. In fact, Ellis did not see any need for Atkin's mission in the first place. As he told Lyttelton, the Creeks were satisfied; the system worked. Why tamper with it? [28]

The *South Carolina Gazette* followed Atkin on his slow march into the interior. By June, he was in Cusseta. He wrote to Lyttelton that the traders had been no help to him; the Indians brought him more intelligence than the traders did. He had not heard from McGillivray's two associates, William Struthers and John Spencer. Spencer, who had defiantly built the house on Chickasaw land opposite Atkin's house, put his cattle and horses in a legal trust managed by McGillivray and John Fitch before returning to his post near Muccolossus. [29]

Despite Lyttelton's statement to Pitt that he had not divulged the scheme of an overland attack on the Alabama Fort, he must have said something about it to Atkin because Atkin mentioned the plan to Ellis, who had not heard about it before that time. He also let the secret out to others so that the woods were full of rumors of an English invasion by the time Atkin reached the Creek towns. As McGillivray reported, the Savannahs fled northward, punished as they went by the Chickasaws under Paya Mattaha, and we hear no more about them or their chief, Peter Chartier, on the southern frontier. When Atkin told the patient Choctaws, who had waited all winter for him, that "when his king has a mind to attack the French, he will send his Great Ships and Warriors," he was telling the truth as he knew it. But there was something about Atkin that made it difficult for his listeners to take him seriously. James Adair referred to his "parading grandeur" and his "stiff, haughty conduct," which put off the Indians. Instead of being impressed that Atkin's king would send his ships and warriors, the Choctaws burst out laughing and said, "We wish we could hear and see that." Atkin signed a treaty with them, promising to reopen trade. [30]

Atkin made a serious mistake in dealing with the Creeks. They were ill disposed because of the Atkin-imposed ban on trade. When speaking in the great square of one of the towns, Atkin refused to permit the peace pipe to be passed to the Mortar of Okchoys, alleging that he was too friendly with the French. James Adair blamed Atkin for driving the Mortar to consort with the increasingly restless Cherokees.[31]

Atkin was pleased with himself for making an example of the Mortar. Ironically, Atkin called him "the compleatest Red man in principle, scorning a commission from any European power." Yet, in spite of the Mortar's neutrality, Atkin wanted to force the assembled Creeks to declare war on the French then and there and would have done so had not the traders present persuaded him otherwise. The Creeks' great law of survival was to avoid taking sides. Atkin followed his insult to the Mortar by taking the trading post out of the Okchoys, one of Lachlan McGillivray's old towns.[32]

Atkin's imperious manner got him in trouble at Tuckabatchee, where, in his words, "the greatest number of headmen ever known to have met together" gathered to hear his talk on September 28, 1759. An Alabama Indian called Tobacco Eater apparently had more than he could stand of Atkin's grand manner so he clubbed Atkin with a tomahawk. Atkin averted his head just in time and the blow was a glancing one. Before the shocked Creeks could react, John McGillivray intervened to shield Atkin from another stroke of the hatchet. The Indian country produced strange situations; one of them was that Edmond Atkin's life may well have been saved by a member of the family he disliked intensely. In the momentary panic, William Fraser, one of Atkin's uniformed guards, fled on his horse, spreading word that Atkin had been killed. Atkin was forced to dispatch John Reid to correct the story.[33] After Tobacco Eater was secured, the Creeks were extraordinarily amenable to anything Atkin said. They realized how near they had been to a complete ban on trade, if not a punitive war. Atkin put a positive interpretation on even this attack. Citing the newly chastened attitude of the Creeks, Atkin counted his mission a success after all.[34]

Henry Ellis disagreed. A month before the attack on Atkin, he had heard via McGillivray that the greatest men among the Creeks, the Gun Merchant, young Malatchi, and the Mortar, were inflamed against Atkin so he invited those chiefs to visit him in Savannah. The invitation was an obvious subversion of Atkin's mission, and Atkin never forgave Ellis when he found out about it.[35] Ellis entertained the Creek leaders in Savannah and listened to their bitter complaints about Atkin. They missed their winter hunt, they said, while Atkin loitered in the woods. When he reached Cusseta town, the headmen paid him the usual courtesy call. He rudely dismissed them, telling them that he would send for them when he wanted them. This was too much for young Malatchi, and he entered Atkin's lodge. He thrust out his hand in greeting. Atkin called the young emperor a Frenchman and told him to go talk to the French. Young Malatchi, burning with indignation, said that he had shaken hands with the governors of Carolina and Georgia. Was Atkin greater than they? Yes, Atkin replied, he was "the King's own mouth." The youthful chief, his uncle, and an entourage went to see McGillivray in Augusta, and he sent them to Ellis in Savannah. They were there when the news of the Tobacco Eater's assault reached Ellis. Young Malatchi said he was glad it was no worse, but he understood how such a thing could happen: "I would have served him so myself." [36]

On November 9, one of Atkin's most troublesome traders, John Spencer, brought a group of Choctaws to Savannah for an interview with Ellis. They were on their way to make a treaty with Ellis, they said, when they were halted in the Wolf's town of Muccolossus by a message from Atkin. Atkin wanted them to sign with him instead of with the governor, and Spencer thought Ellis ought to know about it. Spencer's appearance before the council helped his cause when Atkin pressed charges against him for illegal trading. His license was suspended, not removed.[37]

Old Bracket of Tuckabatchee, the aged and infirm friend of the English, sent a message to Ellis saying that when Atkin called the headmen together at Tuckabatchee, he called them all Frenchmen and refused to shake hands with any of them. Bracket chalked down every talk he heard about and calculated that Atkin gave forty talks in the Creek Nation. They could make no sense of any of them, except that they were filled with abuse.[38] The complaints of his Indian visitors confirmed Ellis's initial poor opinion of Atkin. He expressed an unusually strong negative judgment of Atkin's behavior to the Board of Trade;

Atkin was "very ill calculated for the employment he is in." Ellis could not resist a literary blandishment; he compared Atkin to the philosopher who put truth into the well so he could boast of having found it there.[39]

Atkin, however, thought he had done well in his mission. He reported his success in separate letters to Lyttelton, Amherst, and Pitt. Regarding the supposedly secret plans to attack the French posts, he said that the Creeks were now ready to cooperate with a British invasion. He brought an end to the Choctaw-Chickasaw war, he initiated trade with the Choctaws, he spoiled the Mortar's French strategy, and he left the Creek country "in the most desirable posture."[40]

In all his correspondence, Atkin lashed out at the traders, and particularly at Lachlan McGillivray. He accused McGillivray of making a fortune by trading with the Alabama Indians, who were in alliance with the French. Atkin liked literary allusions, whether appropriate or not: "Great was Diana of the Ephesians," he exclaimed to Lyttelton, "for by their craft her image makers gained their wealth."[41] Perhaps he meant Glen as Diana and McGillivray as the wealthy image maker. Among Atkin's grievances against McGillivray were the lack of cooperation from the Augusta traders, Ellis's interviews with the discontented Creeks, and an unauthorized (by him) trading caravan to the Choctaws; finally, he said that it was to McGillivray "that I must impute it that I have been hatcheted worse in Wells' *Gazette* by letters dated at Augusta than by the Tobacco Eater."[42] McGillivray's license, which was sold to Struthers, should be revoked, in Atkin's opinion.

Despite Atkin's claims, he seems to have done at least as much harm as good in his tour. The criticisms of the traders and the Indians, conveyed to London by Henry Ellis, put Atkin's superintendency in jeopardy. There is evidence that the Board of Trade seriously considered removing him.[43] Atkin's death in 1761 might have spared him that embarrassment. Lachlan McGillivray was better qualified than most to be named the second superintendent, but Edmond Atkin's campaign against McGillivray might have been a factor that removed him from consideration.

The southern frontier was not the focus of British interest in 1759, when the bells of London rang almost continually in celebration of victories around the world. Guadaloupe in the West Indies fell to the British; the French were beaten in India; a French fleet was destroyed at Quiberon Bay; Sir William Johnson's Iroquois helped capture Fort Niagara; and most wonderful of all, James Wolfe gained Quebec and immortality on the Plains of Abraham. Wolfe proved that battles can be won by military means if the armies engaged employ the same tactics. William Henry Lyttelton ardently wished for an opportunity to lead an army across the wilderness against the French. The fort of the Alabamas beckoned like another Quebec. He had an opportunity to practice his generalship during the winter of 1759 against the Cherokees. Lyttelton was on the march to the Cherokee country when Edmond Atkin reached Augusta, still grumbling about the recalcitrant traders.

CHAPTER TEN

The Cherokee War

When Edmond Atkin arrived in Augusta on December 23, 1759, hardly anyone noticed because attention was fixed on William Henry Lyttelton's march into the Cherokee country. As the traders saw it, Atkin had gone on a peacemaking tour to Indians who were already peace-minded, and he had ignored the inflamed condition of the Cherokee frontier.[1]

Lachlan McGillivray had warned Ellis in October 1758 that for "sometime past our affairs in the Cherokees seem'd to be on a tottering foundation owing to the unlucky management of affairs in Virginia." He reported that the Cherokee ambassadors had received no encouragement from the Creeks and still less from the Savannah River Chickasaws. Early in 1759, however, the pro-French faction among the Cherokees attacked settlers on the Yadkin and Catawba rivers, and nineteen whites were killed. Governor Lyttelton reinforced Fort Loudoun and Fort Prince George and cut off trade in arms and ammunition. The ban on weapons infuriated the Cherokees, and they retaliated against outlying settlers.[2]

Lyttelton decided on a punitive expedition. At the head of an army of fifteen hundred, he left Charlestown on October 27, 1759. On the march, Lyttelton visited the Savannah River Chickasaws and urged them to join his army. The problem in recruiting the Chickasaws was that the gentlemen of Augusta were reluctant to allow their defenders to leave the area, even if their mission was to punish the aggressors. Captain Ulrich Tobler of New Windsor carried Lyttelton's first message to New Savannah and was threatened by David Douglass and Edward Barnard with imprisonment for interfering in the internal affairs of another province.[3]

Some forty Chickasaw warriors followed Lyttelton under the captaincy of Ulrich Tobler. The Augusta traders complained to Henry Ellis, who immediately became their advocate. He explained to Lyttelton that the Augustans were aware that the militia of Fort Moore had been drafted for the expedition and were convinced that the Cherokees would seek the valuable stores in the traders' warehouses if the Chickasaws left. The argument was weak, but it was the best Ellis could improvise. Ellis stood on his authority to protest Tobler's interference: "I must confess to you, Sir, that it did seem a little surprising here, that any person from your province should affect to exercise a peculiar jurisdiction over a people who . . . had for some years past fixed themselves amongst us."[4] Gone was the fawning note that characterized Ellis's earlier letters to Lyttelton. Ellis directed Edward Barnard to raise twenty men for the defense of Augusta, now that Lieutenant White Outerbridge had to divide his attention between Augusta and Fort Moore. He sent instructions to McGillivray, Rae, McCartan, and the other storekeepers to interdict any trade with the Cherokees, or else the guilty would never get another license.[5]

The incipient friction between the two governors was aggravated when White Outerbridge, a good and patient man, told Lieutenant Colonel Edward Barnard that he could march his militia into Fort Augusta whenever he pleased, but Outerbridge would not give up command until he heard from Lyttelton. This led to a heated exchange between Ellis and Lyttelton in which Ellis questioned Lyttelton's authority over the independent companies stationed in Georgia: "Whatever right the Governor of South Carolina had to command the militia or regulars here during the Trustees' administration, they certainly have none at present."[6] Lyttelton's argument that Glen exercised that authority did not change Ellis's mind. Lyttelton's position could not be supported "with any degree of consistency or reason." Warming to his argument, Ellis declared that he would sooner command a cockboat than be the viceroy of Mexico under such degrading circumstances. Ellis complained to Amherst that "nothing can be more improper and preposterous than the present situation of things." [7] He wanted to move the Frederica garrison to Augusta and found that the troops would not obey him.

While the bickering went on at the higher level of government, the gentlemen of Augusta busied themselves with the long-delayed project, the rebuilding of Fort Augusta. Lieutenant Outerbridge admired their energy. "They work with spirit and alacrity," he said. Strong oak puncheons were used on the fort, and for good measure, the church was fortified similarly. There is reason to doubt whether the first fort was adjacent to the church, although that was the original intention of the builders. The reconstructed fort was to the east of the town about a mile from the church. Unlike the first, which was a square with bastions at each corner, its dimensions were 88 feet by 116 feet. Only three sides were stockaded with upright puncheons; the front was faced with horizontal plank. [8] Edward Barnard was in charge of the construction of the fort. It was completed just in time.

Meanwhile, Lyttelton's march proved more difficult than he had anticipated. For a man who savored the glory of commanding an expedition against the Alabama Fort, Fort Prince George should have been an easy trek, but he had not taken the weather into consideration, or measles, or smallpox. He had unfortunate experiences with all three. His exhausted troops reached Fort Prince George on December 9, 1759. Because he was unable to go farther, he let the Cherokees know he was willing to talk peace. He demanded that twenty-four guilty Cherokees be handed over for punishment to pay for the lives of twenty-four whites. Meanwhile, he held twenty-four friendly Cherokees hostage at Fort Prince George; they would be freed when the guilty ones were brought in. His stipulation was that the French and their adherents must be expelled from the Cherokee country; then trade would be resumed. The Cherokee headmen agreed to Lyttelton's terms and signed a treaty on December 26. Lyttelton could not have remained any longer at Fort Prince George if he had wanted to: smallpox spread among his men, desertion was rampant, and mutiny threatened. Lyttelton must have had second thoughts about the wisdom of an overland attack on the Alabama Fort.[9] He was lucky to get back to Charlestown with his army and reputation fairly intact. He was hailed as a hero when he returned on January 8, 1760, but kept his laurels less than a month. Before the end of January, Cherokee war parties were in full cry on both sides of the Savannah River.

The Cherokee raids on the Georgia side began in early December with an attack on Thomas Williams's house seventy miles above Augusta. Williams had been a source of trouble to Henry Ellis for selling rum to the Cherokees. White Outerbridge in Augusta thought that the robbery of Williams's store was not altogether a bad thing; it would put a stop to illicit trade. The Creeks considered the Cherokee attack an intrusion into their territory. Samuel Chew, a trader whose post was on Georgia's Broad River, reported that the Creeks threatened to kill any Cherokees who crossed a line near the Broad River.[10]

In late January the Cherokees launched an offensive, driving settlers before them and killing those they caught; 150 refugees from the Long Canes region, including the Patrick Calhoun family, tried to escape in heavily loaded wagons. They were overtaken as they crossed Long Canes Creek. The Indians killed twenty-three people and captured as many more. The terrified survivors sought refuge in Fort Augusta and Fort Moore. The church in Augusta had been stockaded as an additional place of safety. Traders piled their goods in the fort and church.[11]

The crisis shocked Edmond Atkin out of his hostility toward the Augusta traders. "All things round here now wear a wretched aspect," he reported to Lyttelton on February 5, 1760. "The Cherokees have drove all before them downward to a few miles from Augusta."[12] The Stephens Creek settlements were abandoned. The fort, the church, McCartan's, and other fortified houses were crowded with refugees. Atkin was at Fort Moore with only a sergeant and six soldiers. People from the up-country continued to flock into Fort Moore during February even though the fort was hardly defensible and had gaps in its stockade walls. The refugees had little to eat and could not be subsisted for a long siege.

On February 5, the Augusta traders learned that Thomas Williams's wife and child had been murdered and scalped and John Vann's house was under attack. Without waiting for orders, Lachlan McGillivray sent word to the Creeks to meet him at Little River and set out from Augusta at the head of fifty men. That trip is worth comment. This sortie marks the first time that citizens of Georgia had volunteered to fight since the Scots at Darien had turned out to follow Oglethorpe. Edmond Atkin had commented derisively on the lack of courage of the leading Augustans; he accused one of the magistrates of suggesting that Augusta remain neutral in the event of a war with the Cherokees.[13] McGillivray and his band put an end to talk of cowardice.

McGillivray found a hundred people fearfully huddled together at James Germany's stockaded house fourteen miles northwest of Augusta. McGillivray was told that John Burns and his wife were murdered thirty miles from there and that the Cherokees were in pursuit of Samuel Chew and other Broad River settlers. McGillivray encouraged the men at Germany's place to stand and fight and promptly sent to Augusta for guns and ammunition as well as axes and spades to build earthworks.[14] McGillivray's leadership in time of crisis earned for him a hero's status.

Other heroes were the Creeks under Escotchabie, the Young Lieutenant of the Cowetas and Talhichico, head warrior of the Cussetas, who rescued a party of refugees. The men, women, and children were lost in the swamps and canebrakes and near death from starvation and exhaustion. The Creeks found them and brought them to McGillivray at Germany's, and McGillivray escorted them to Augusta. The Young Lieutenant scouted the Cherokees and learned that war parties were approaching Augusta on both sides of the Savannah River. He believed that his Creeks had slowed their progress on the Georgia side.[15]

McGillivray entertained these Creeks at his house and treated them as allies and friends. The embittered Edmond Atkin could not bring himself to say anything good about McGillivray or the sudden appearance of the Young Lieutenant's band. He expressed the opinion that these thirty or so "renegades" were on their way to join the Cherokees when they met McGillivray.[16] But everyone else in Augusta was greatly relieved by the presence of friendly warriors.

The "gentlemen of Augusta" met with the Creeks and the New Savannah Chickasaws at Fort Augusta on February 11. It was significant that the man of the moment, Lachlan McGillivray, and not Atkin, delivered the talk on behalf of the white people. McGillivray told his Indian friends that he was glad to see them. The perfidious Cherokees had broken their treaty soon after signing it and were killing innocent people. He knew that the Creeks would want to keep the trading path from Augusta open and hoped they would help protect Augusta. The Young Lieutenant answered that it was the policy of his people to be neutral. He feared that the Mortar was under French influence and would cause many of the Upper Creeks to join the Cherokees. For himself, he would fight to keep the great road open from Augusta to his villages.[17] The Doctor spoke for the Chickasaws. The Chickasaws were the same as the English; the English fight was the Chickasaw fight. His people were prepared to live and die for the English.[18]

The advance parties of Cherokees reached Augusta and Fort Moore the day after McGillivray's meeting. Three men who ventured out of Augusta on the main trading path were attacked; one was shot, tomahawked, scalped, and left for dead. A different group of three leaving in another direction met five Cherokees who critically wounded one and sent the other two flying back to Augusta. A party of fifteen whites was attacked by sixty Cherokees the following day; all but one returned to Fort Augusta. The number of enemy Indians in the woods surrounding the town increased, and the forests were no longer the friendly shelters they had been.[19]

The fearless Creeks were able to slip past the Cherokees and rescue whites. On one such venture they took three children away from the Cherokees. On the other side of the river, Fort Moore was besieged. Patrick Calhoun and Captain Ulrich Tobler were riding from Tobler's house to Fort Moore at the head of a group of militiamen when they were attacked by at least thirty Cherokees. Tobler was killed; the war hatchet buried in his head was marked by notches for other victims.

Calhoun was wounded. Atkin, who was at Fort Moore, said that the residents of the area "were all running like sheep before a wolf." [20] They had reason to.

The refugees who crowded the fortified places in Augusta needed food desperately. McGillivray met that need, too. He had corn stored on his plantation on the former Chickasaw tract on the Carolina side of the river. His men were in the process of transporting the grain to Augusta when they were startled by the war whoop. Two horses were shot. McGillivray quickly collected his white neighbors and with several Creeks and Chickasaws who were guests at his house, he crossed the river and boldly pursued the enemy. It was a foolhardy act because he might have encountered a large war party. Instead, the Cherokees fled so rapidly that they left their blankets and other belongings behind. The Creeks rewarded themselves by plundering some abandoned houses. [21]

Reinforcements finally arrived from Savannah and Charlestown. Captain John Milledge with seventy men of the Georgia militia reported to Fort Augusta, and Lieutenant Lachlan Shaw relieved the weary White Outerbridge. Shaw was more the martinet than Outerbridge and had much to learn about life on the frontier. James Adair, who was at Augusta during the Cherokee crisis, referred to him as an "unskillful, haughty officer." [22]

Shaw thought that the frantic repair work at Fort Moore had insignificant results. Fence rails were inserted into the gaps in the stockade. Good timber for proper reconstruction was dangerously distant, and there were Cherokee tracks all over the neighborhood. There was no ammunition in Fort Augusta except what belonged to the traders, and Shaw indicated that he would use it, regardless of who would pay. The people were in great distress for want of food. He wanted to buy a wagon, but he needed Lyttelton's authorization before anyone would extend him credit. Even if he had a wagon, he could not find a volunteer to drive it outside the town. He complained, "If I was to give one hundred guineas to a person to cross the country to Orangeburg I could not get any person to undertake it." [23]

What surprised Shaw most was the proprietary attitude of the Creeks who came in answer to McGillivray's appeals and Ellis's summons. They took credit for lifting the Cherokee siege and saving Augusta. During his first two weeks at Fort Augusta, Creek parties constantly came and went, forcing him to post guards all night every night. The Indians would ride up to the gates of the fort, demand entrance, unsaddle their horses, ask for fodder for their horses and food for themselves, and generally make themselves at home. While Shaw wrote his report, three headmen sat at the same table, smoking companionably; twenty warriors were outside. Lachlan McGillivray would have enjoyed a pipe with the visitors; Shaw felt uncomfortable. The arrangement did not fit under military protocol. Besides, Shaw suspected the rescuers of perpetrating robberies and blaming the Cherokees.[24]

The Cherokees slipped away during the first days of March to turn their attention to Fort Loudoun in the Overhill country. The worst of the Augusta crisis was over. Henry Ellis had done his part by sending Milledge's militia to Augusta, by offering the Creeks £5 for every Cherokee scalp, and by furnishing muskets and swivel cannon to the forts erected by the gentlemen of Augusta. He was pleased that the Chickasaws and Creeks had gone out daily with McGillivray and others to scout the enemy. He acknowledged the assistance of his new friends, the Bosomworths, in turning out the Creeks, and he recognized that the relative immunity Georgia enjoyed was because of the Creek alliance. On March 7, when danger still threatened, he sent a brave message to Lyttelton: "I flatter myself the Cherokees will not drive us into the sea as they threatened." [25]

Indeed, the worst was over on the southern frontier. The Mortar's instigations would cause other anxious moments in Georgia, and Fort Loudoun would fall to the Cherokees under tragic circumstances, but the real crisis passed when the Creeks refused to join the Cherokees in the winter of 1759–60. Although not nearly so strikingly dramatic as the scene that unfolded on the Plains of Abraham, the pro-English stance of the Creeks was significant in the shaping of the southern frontier. The French waged a psychological war that prompted the Cherokees to revolt and caused a short-lived schism in the Creek ranks, but in the last analysis, the French were beaten in the war of intrigue as thoroughly as Montcalm was defeated by Wolfe's perfect volley. Oglethorpe laid the foundation for the final English victory; the Carolina and Georgia traders spun the web of trade that caught and captivated the western Indians and completed the work begun by Oglethorpe.

More immediately, Ellis, to a great extent, and Atkin, to a lesser, confirmed the attachment of the Creeks to the English. Among those who participated in the struggle for the minds and hearts of the Creeks, Lachlan McGillivray stands in the forefront. In the desperate, dangerous game of kill or be killed, McGillivray made his mark. That is why the Georgia Assembly paid him a unique tribute in 1760, the year of decision: "It is resolved by the Council in general Assembly met that the thanks of this House be given to Lachlan McGillivray, Esquire, for his Services to this Province in having during his Residence at Augusta and particularly in the late alarming Conjuncture, with great Pains, and private Expense, assisted this Government in the Management of Indian Affairs."[26] For the rest of his life, Lachlan McGillivray wore the laurels of a hero.

CHAPTER ELEVEN

The War Winds Down

The year of the Cherokee uprising was a time of transition for Lachlan McGillivray and for several of the principal actors in the Southern Department. William Henry Lyttelton and Henry Ellis were replaced; Edmond Atkin retired to his plantation; and after a brief crisis in the Upper Creek country and two punitive expeditions into the Cherokee mountains, the Great War for Empire came to an end.

In distant New Orleans, Governor Kerlérec persuaded himself that the Cherokee uprising presaged a French victory. He had an exaggerated notion of the number of English killed in the 1760 uprising and attributed the outbreak to his careful coddling of the Mortar and young Malatchi. Kerlérec had heard about Pitt's plans for an invasion of Louisiana at about the same time Lyttelton of Carolina did. So much for secrecy. He boasted to his superiors that he had frustrated that scheme by instigating the Cherokee diversion. But he continued to look out for English ships in the Gulf for another year.[1]

William Henry Lyttelton was the first to depart during this time of transition. He received news of his appointment to the governorship of Jamaica on February 13, during the worst of the Cherokee scare. Before he left, he welcomed Colonel Archibald Montgomery and twelve hundred men of the First and Seventy-seventh regiments. Montgomery's orders from Amherst were to strike swiftly at the Cherokees and return to the northward as soon as possible.[2] The instructions reflected the professionals' overconfidence in the effectiveness of European tactics in the wilderness. When Lyttelton departed on April 5, 1760, the situation was bleak.

Both of the Carolina forts in the Cherokee Nation were in trouble. Fort Prince George on the Seneca River among the Lower Cherokees was overrun in February during the Cherokee invasion of the Savannah River valley. Ouconnostotah, one of the head warriors of the Overhills, lured the commanding officer out of the fort on February 16; his concealed companions opened fire and mortally wounded the Englishman. Inside the fort, twenty-four Cherokees had been held hostage; now they were all killed. Such acts, as Lieutenant Governor Bull remarked, made peace difficult.[3]

The Overhill Cherokees focused their indignation on Fort Loudoun, which Governor Glen had built on the Little Tennessee River. Originally intended as a guarantee of British protection against the French, it was now a vulnerable target for the angry Cherokees, aided and abetted by French agents. Acting governor William Bull gained time for the garrison by sending up bundles of ribbons and other trifles which the garrison gave to Indian women in exchange for corn. Bull hoped that Virginia forces would cooperate with Montgomery in relieving Loudoun, but Montgomery's priority was not Loudoun but Fort Prince George. Montgomery burned the towns between Estatoe and Keowee and reached Fort Prince George on June 4, after marching sixty miles without sleep.[4] He sent talks to the Middle and Overhill towns, threatening similar treatment to those places if the Cherokees did not give up their siege of Fort Loudoun and make peace. The Cherokees did not believe an English army could penetrate their mountains, and indeed, Montgomery had decided even before the talks were sent that Fort Loudoun was inaccessible. Montgomery decided to attack the Middle towns with a select corps of three hundred men, leaving baggage and tents at Fort Prince George. The terrain was tortuous, the worst Montgomery had ever seen; the Cherokees lured the invaders ever deeper into their mountains before they attacked. The English beat off the Indians after a fierce fight at a cost of heavy casualties.

Montgomery burned the town of Etchoe, but, having lost twenty men and burdened by seventy wounded, he decided he could go no farther. With extreme difficulty and harassed by unseen Indians, Montgomery fought his way back to Fort Prince George. Satisfied that he had done what he could and unable to do more, he returned to Charlestown and embarked for New York. Bull tried to dissuade him and, failing to do so, commented acidly that Carolina was left in a worse state than before Montgomery arrived. Bull did not share his predecessors' confidence in the effectiveness of military might; he remarked that it was no use resorting to "spirited measures which show what we cannot do." [5]

Fort Loudoun was doomed. By August, the corn was exhausted and starving men climbed over the walls and subjected themselves to the doubtful mercy of their enemies. Some were tortured and killed; some were held as hostages against the ransom of Cherokee prisoners. On August 6, 1760, Captain Paul Demere and his officers decided to negotiate a surrender. Lieutenant John Stuart was named to arrange terms with Ouconnostotah, although he had little to bargain with. He offered the guns and powder in the fort, but the Indians knew that they would have the fort and its contents within a few days, regardless. Ouconnostotah agreed to permit the garrison safe passage to Fort Prince George. Despite his efforts to abide by that agreement, Ouconnostotah could not protect the soldiers. They were ambushed along the way, most were killed, some taken prisoner. Among the latter was John Stuart, who was ransomed by his friend Attakullakulla, the Little Carpenter. Stuart reached Charlestown on Christmas Day 1760, an object of wonder and admiration. His escape from Fort Loudoun was timely and would, within the year, win him the superintendency of the Southern Department, even though his experience in Indian affairs did not compare with Lachlan McGillivray's or George Galphin's. [6]

William Bull did what he could during the critical period following the fall of Fort Loudoun, although it must have been discouraging for him to learn by return mail that the Lords of the Board of Trade had gone to their country houses and could not respond to his frantic appeals. He sent supplies to Fort Prince George, repaired Fort Moore, reinforced Fort Augusta, and pleaded with Amherst to send another army. Amherst obliged by sending troops under Colonel James Grant. The Cherokee war assumed a pattern; in 1759 Lyttelton marched to Fort Prince George; in 1760 Montgomery repeated the exercise; and in 1761 Colonel James Grant, formerly second in command to Montgomery, led another invasion.[7] Expeditions into the Cherokee country were an annual event.

Grant arrived in Charlestown on January 6, 1761, with twelve hundred men. Bull raised twelve hundred provincials. This impressive force required 2,000 baggage horses and 250 wagons. The logistics confirmed McGillivray and Adair's estimates of the massive support a land expedition against the Alabama Fort would require. On May 18, Grant's ponderous army moved out of Ninety-Six and reached Fort Prince George on the twenty-sixth. Grant was met by Little Carpenter, Stuart's rescuer, who asked for peace terms. Grant felt that the Cherokees should be punished before any serious peace talks could be started, and on June 7 he set out on the trail taken by Montgomery— with the same result. The Cherokees allowed him to advance to nearly the site of the previous battle and then poured gunfire from the rugged hillsides. Grant lost eleven killed and fifty-two wounded. He burned Etchoe and fifteen other towns on the Little Tennessee River. He destroyed fourteen hundred acres of corn and beans, enough to feed five thousand people. He demonstrated that, although European tactics were inappropriate in Indian warfare, a scorched-earth policy was highly effective. The Cherokees were defeated not by bullets but by hunger.[8]

Grant's men were exhausted when they reached Fort Prince George. Like Montgomery, he could not prolong his stay in the mountain country. When Little Carpenter came again to plead for peace, Grant was more willing than before. He directed the chief to Charlestown, and the terms of a treaty were worked out. The assembly inserted a clause forbidding the Cherokees to come closer than twenty-five miles below Keowee without an invitation; the Indians successfully negotiated a forty-mile limit to preserve their hunting rights. The Little Carpenter had some trouble with his more warlike brothers before the treaty was secured on December 17, 1761. The treaty provided a fitting end to

Bull's difficult tenure of office. The new governor, a native of South Carolina and former governor of New Jersey named Thomas Boone, took office on December 24, 1761. Boone turned his attention to internal politics and boundary disputes and was less concerned with Indian affairs than his predecessors.[9]

The year 1760 was Henry Ellis's last in Georgia. When Lyttelton concluded his short-lived peace with the Cherokees in December 1759, Ellis believed that tranquillity had been restored to the southern frontier and applied for permission to resign his office. Meanwhile, the outbreak of the Cherokees kept him busy during the first four months of 1760. During April he entertained various war parties of Indians who came to collect the bounty he offered on Cherokee scalps. One band of Creeks proudly wore the enemy scalps on their heads as they whooped their way into town. The Savannah River Euchees, now reduced in number, brought in one scalp. They wanted Ellis to ask McGillivray to persuade the Creeks to go with them to get more. Another group of Cowetas brought Ellis English scalps which the Cherokees had sent to the Alabama Fort. John Spencer bought the grisly trophies and delivered them to Ellis for a respectful burial.[10]

This business of counting scalps was suddenly interrupted on May 26 by startling news from Augusta. One Robert French, a packhorseman, testified that on May 14, the Okfuskees had suddenly turned on the traders and killed several. He saw the bodies of William Rae, a trader, and William Robertson, a packhorseman, lying in the village square, with the Okfuskees engaged in their frenzied war dance. The chief called Captain of the Okfuskees concealed French and helped him escape to Augusta. Without waiting to hear other details, Ellis acted swiftly and shrewdly. He sent a talk to the Upper Creeks by the hands of his recent friend Thomas Bosomworth. "Though some of your people have done a mad thing," he said, "yet Friends may overlook it and make all straight again."[11] Ellis did not know how widespread the disaffection was at the time he sent his talk. He gambled that the incident was an isolated one and that he could contain it.

At least eleven traders were killed in other Upper Creek towns. The Wolf offered sanctuary for the English. The Gun Merchant and

Devall's Landlord protected their traders. Two Englishmen fled to the Alabama Fort, and five went down to Spanish Pensacola. William Bull agreed with Ellis's strategy of assuming that the Creeks did not intend to signal a war. For one thing, there were Creek visitors in Savannah and Augusta who had no inkling of trouble. Ellis wisely refrained from making hostages of them. McGillivray and his friends in Augusta prevented Lieutenant Lachlan Shaw from retaliating against the Creeks in Augusta, who were guests of McGillivray and Galphin. Bull was willing to stop all trade with the Creeks, but Ellis saw no need for that. The trade had stopped when the traders fled; to halt it indefinitely would force the Creeks to look to the French.[12]

On June 30, ten Creek ambassadors came to see Ellis. They brought talks from Gun Merchant and Stumpe, guardian of Togulki, son of Malatchi. The mischief was done by a few young fellows, they said; the headmen had nothing to do with it. They requested that Ellis send the traders back. Although the English and the French governors believed that the Mortar was behind the uprising, the other Indians did not blame him, and the Mortar stoutly denied any involvement. Ellis told the Indians that they must punish their guilty men for their own sake because the traders would not stay where they might be killed by any rash young men. The Indians promised to give satisfaction.[13]

The crisis passed, enabling Henry Ellis to turn a comparatively trouble-free colony over to his successor, James Wright, who arrived in Savannah on October 11, 1760. Lachlan McGillivray was an elected member of the assembly that greeted the new governor, and as a tribute to his ability with a pen, he was put on the committee that drafted the addresses of farewell and welcome. The address praised Ellis for his wise and prudent management of Indian affairs and cited the "amazing difference" in the current state of the province from that which he found at the beginning of his term.[14]

James Adair believed that Lachlan McGillivray and George Galphin shared the honor of keeping the peace during the recent crisis. At "their great expense and hazard of life," he wrote, "they allowed those savages to eat, drink and sleep at Silver Bluff and at Augusta."[15] It was common knowledge among the traders that these two had great influence over "the dangerous Muskohge."

It must have been a bit awkward for Henry Ellis that a fellow passenger on the ship out of Charlestown to New York was Edmond Atkin. Ellis departed that November to the plaudits of his countrymen, while Atkin left still nursing his grievances. Atkin revealed his bitterness in a letter to Amherst written aboard ship. He expected no friendly word from Ellis, he wrote. He had never had any help or cooperation from him; the "vilest trader who deserves severe punishment" (did he mean McGillivray?) "hath met with more countenance and credit" from Ellis. He asked Amherst to let him know what Ellis said about him. His litany of complaints included the mortification he felt while on the South Carolina Council of being outvoted by the majority although he was the king's agent; the fact that the Carolina Assembly was jealous of his authority; the disposition of the governors to believe the traders rather than him; the refusal of the governors to allow him to control the Indian trade. It did not occur to Atkin to blame himself. On the contrary, he continued to claim credit for the neutrality of the Creeks during the Cherokee war. None of his efforts were appreciated, he said, and after a final report to the Lords of Trade he would resign his commission: "I shall have no cause to desire to hold this invidious office any longer."[16] In spite of his accumulated injuries, Atkin could not bring himself to resign. In December 1760, he retired to his plantation near the Peedee River and wrote gloomy reports. In April 1761, he informed Amherst that the traders acted as though he did not exist. The one bright moment was a visit from the Wolf of Muccolossus. On this occasion, the Wolf was accorded hero status by the governors of Georgia and Carolina for having protected the traders at the time of the Okfuskee murders. James Glen once said of him that though he was not the first, second, or third among the Creeks and did not have as much good sense as some, "no man's mouth is heard in his towns but his own."[17] It was ironic that the Wolf was the one who called on Atkin because the Wolf was patron of John Spencer, whose post was near Muccolossus and whose life he once saved. The Wolf was an inveterate visitor, having been at it at least since 1739, when he gave William Stephens an opportunity to practice diplomacy in Savannah. The Wolf was Atkin's last Indian guest. The unhappy agent died on October 8, 1761. Thomas Boone was still in New York, not yet having taken passage to assume the governorship of South Carolina, when he heard about Atkin's demise. He hurried to see General Amherst and recommended John Stuart, whom he had known in Charlestown, for the superintendency. Amherst was easily persuaded and wrote his recommendation to William Pitt on November 27, 1761. On January 21, 1762, the Earl of Egremont notified Amherst that Stuart had the appointment. Seldom had the machinery of British bureaucracy worked so rapidly. Among the belated and disappointed suitors for the position was the celebrated Major Robert Rogers of Rogers' Rangers.[18]

Another aspirant to Atkin's position was the ambitious William Knox, who had come to Georgia with Henry Ellis to serve as provost marshal at the age of twenty-five. Three years later, he was bold enough to consider himself an authority on Indian affairs and shrewd enough to predict that Atkin would be fired. Among the qualifications he listed was that he had watched Ellis, "the second master in America," in his dealings with the Indians. Presumably, Sir William Johnson was the first master. Later, Knox revealed a better reason for his knowledge of the Indians and their country. He had made it a practice to consult with Indian traders. When Knox returned to England in 1762 as Georgia's agent, he was regarded by various high-placed officials as an expert in Indian matters.[19]

If the English system of patronage were based on merit rather than connections, McGillivray should have been offered the Indian agency. James Adair regretted that neither McGillivray nor George Galphin was chosen. It might have been some consolation to McGillivray that the new superintendent was a fellow Scot from Inverness. He could expect cordiality instead of animosity from the superintendent, and he would give Stuart support and cooperation in return.

McGillivray had an opportunity to introduce James Wright, Georgia's new governor, to Indian affairs and quickly earned Wright's respect and trust. Henry Ellis had invited the Gun Merchant, Devall's

Landlord, and the Captain of the Okfuskees, as well as the Wolf, to present themselves in Savannah and receive thanks. The Captain and Devall's Landlord and their attendants visited McGillivray in Augusta, and he accompanied them to Savannah. There he interpreted Governor Wright's first big conference. Wright dwelled on the theme that the French were totally ruined and destroyed and that they were base deceivers besides.[20]

McGillivray remained in Savannah for the legislative session. He was put on the committee to examine the state of fortifications of the town of Savannah. The earthworks erected by Ellis earlier in the year were a temporary expedient. It was decided to build four blockhouses, two on the south side, one on the west, and one on the east. The session allocated funds for finishing the fort in Augusta and building forts at Halifax, Midway, Newport, Darien, Ebenezer, and Ogeechee.[21]

McGillivray counseled the governor on the state of Indian affairs, and Wright showed a grasp of the situation in an early report to the Board of Trade. He was aware of the dangerous influence of the Alabama Fort. He was acquainted with the Mortar's pro-French stance and concerned about that chief's dalliances with the Cherokees. He seemed surprised that the Indians claimed all the land above the tidewater and that he was "hemmed in" in a small corner of the province. He was quick to recognize the importance of the debatable lands below the Altamaha River and put in a claim for that region, though Carolina claimed it also. He reported that the province was defended by two troops of rangers numbering 75 each and three regiments of militia numbering 896, besides 50 men of the independent company doing duty at St. Simon under the orders of the governor of Carolina. Like Ellis, Wright thought that arrangement was absurd. Finally, Wright took up the "Carthage must be destroyed" theme of the McGillivray-Adair letter of July 14, 1758, and urged the destruction of the Alabama Fort, not by a land campaign but by a naval attack on Mobile. His report showed an understanding of the essentials of the situation on the southern frontier. He would play an important role in the subsequent shaping of the frontier in the next decade and a half.[22]

News of the death of George II and the accession of George III required the dissolution of the sitting House of Assembly and the election of a new one. McGillivray and John Graham were reelected from the parish of St. Paul. McGillivray was appointed to the Ways and Means Committee and dealt with such matters as payment to Joseph Wright for his most recent errand to the Creeks, the reimbursement to Edward Barnard for guns and tools delivered to Germany's fort during the crisis, and relief for the refugees who had been forced to remain in Augusta during most of the year.[23]

Perhaps the most important piece of legislation considered by the assembly during its session involved the regulation of the Indian trade. McGillivray had an immediate interest in its formulation. The bill was an ambitious one for a novice governor and required the expertise of someone with McGillivray's experience. The plan was to return to the system that had worked so well for Brown, Rae and Company, with the legislature rather than the company assigning the traders to the towns. George Galphin was confirmed to the Cowetas, John Rae to the Cussetas, and McCartan and Campbell to the Euchees and Palachocolas on the Savannah River as well as two Lower Creek towns. James Cussings, George Mackay, James Hewett, and Richard Crooke were listed in other Lower Creek towns. McGillivray's associates in the Upper Creek country were well represented. John McGillivray's post was in the Abbecoochee village; William Struthers had Little Tallassee, Wewoka, and Puckantallahasee, all McGillivray's old towns. James Germany, an employee of McGillivray, had John Spencer's post at the Wolf's town, Muccolossus, along with several other towns.[24]

The regulation was too exclusive, and within a year, McQueen, Germany, and John Brown complained of competition by unlicensed traders.[25] In another year a royal proclamation would throw the Indian country open to unbridled competition, with tragic consequences. The golden years of the company's preeminence were past.

In August 1760, McGillivray supervised the formation of a new company consisting of his cousin John, his partner William Struthers, the veteran Chickasaw trader John Brown, and a storekeeper named William Trevin. According to the terms, Trevin would mind the store in Augusta and the others would be posted in the various Indian towns.

The partnership bought Lachlan's house, outbuildings, and stores. The house, advertised as the best in Augusta for its situation and convenience to the Indian trade, was fated to be the scene of a historic battle during the Revolution. McGillivray was a silent partner in the new company and continued to use the house in his visits to Augusta. When the property was put up for sale in 1764, prospective buyers were directed to Lachlan McGillivray in Savannah or Brown, Struthers and Company in Augusta.[26]

McGillivray continued to expand his landholdings. In January 1761 he owned 2,350 acres and was granted 1,000 more on the Altamaha. He claimed forty-nine slaves working on his plantation. In the following January, he asked for 500 acres which John Spencer had requested but never recorded. Lachlan provided for his son's future by obtaining two tracts of 100 acres each in Alexander's name.[27] He bought additional lots in Augusta, probably for speculation. But his career was at a transition point. He seemed uncharacteristically uncertain about where to establish himself and his family. Augusta had been good to him; his plantation and store to the west of town were convenient for his Indian visitors. He did not want to give them up just yet. Nevertheless, the recently available Bosomworth tract between the Augusta road and the river just outside Savannah was an attractive site, which appealed to him. Two plantations of 500 acres each, known as Rowcliff and Mulberry, were granted to Pickering Robinson on February 2, 1762. Robinson had no intention of keeping the properties and two days later sold the 1,000 acres to McGillivray.[28] McGillivray gave the tract the name Vale Royal; he built a house for his family, another for an overseer, and a barn for livestock. He devoted the low ground to rice culture and raised fine Chickasaw horses on the higher ground. The purchase of Vale Royal made McGillivray a Savannahian. The citizens of the coastal town welcomed him by electing him captain of the militia.[29] His recent forays in pursuit of painted Cherokees qualified him for that honor.

Vale Royal was only one of his acquisitions in the low country. Two tracts of rice land averaging 250 acres each on Hutchinson's Island in the middle of the river, an 800-acre estate known as Sabine Fields near Vale Royal, a 500-acre piece of land adjoining James Habersham's property on the Little Ogeechee River, a 350-acre tract two miles from Savannah with a house and other improvements — all were new additions to his already extensive holdings. Including his property in the Augusta region, McGillivray had over 10,000 acres, putting him among the largest landowners in the province in 1762. When the Gun Merchant, the Okfuskee Captain, and Handsome Fellow paid him a social call in December 1762, they must have been impressed with his social progress from Little Tallassee to Vale Royal.[30]

Just when it seemed that McGillivray was securely settled in Savannah, he startled his friends and neighbors by announcing that he was going to leave Georgia and would sell Vale Royal and everything else. He evidently had decided to return to Strathnairn and Dunmaglass. Fifteen years after Culloden, the Highlands still suffered from Cumberland's retribution. In 1746 the Disarming Act forbade the wearing of the Highland dress and the use of the tartan in any form. The bagpipes were proscribed as weapons of war. In 1747 the clan system was outlawed and the powers of the chief abolished. An Act of Attainder declared the lands of the leading rebels forfeit. Among those listed was Alexander McGillivray. Lachlan McGillivray's mother, Janet, at Dunmaglass managed to save from confiscation some cattle and a supply of corn. Her son-in-law William Mackintosh of Holme acted as regent for young William, the new chief. Mackintosh secured a good lawyer and in 1750 presented his case before the proper tribunal. He asked for the restoration of the McGillivray estate on the grounds that Alexander had died before the Act of Attainder was passed and that the law did not apply to him or his heirs. To the relief of the family, the estate was restored.[31]

In 1759, Lady Anne Mackintosh (the "Colonel Anne" of Culloden) secured for William a captaincy in the recently authorized Eighty-ninth Highland Regiment of Foot. William raised his company from among his kinsmen; there were fifteen John McGillivrays enlisted. When the company was ordered to India in 1760, his estates, including Dunmaglass, had no male manager.[32] Lachlan was concerned about his mother, sister, and other relatives. He felt that it was his duty to return to his ancestral estate. His brother in Charlestown, Alexander the mariner, had a similar responsibility, but Alexander died in 1763, leaving a wife and ten-year-old son. He was mourned by Lachlan and other members of his family and buried with honors in St. Michael's churchyard.[33]

In the November 29, 1764, *Georgia Gazette*, Lachlan repeated his notice that he planned to leave for England the following spring and called upon all those indebted to him to pay what they owed. He made it clear that he would sue anyone failing to meet his obligations. The same announcement appeared in subsequent issues of the *Gazette* through February 14, 1765. But Lachlan did not return to Scotland. What might have caused him to change his mind? Perhaps he could get no acceptable price for his extensive properties, but he could have left business matters in the hands of an agent. The likely reason for his decision to stay in Georgia was that his cousin, the chief, returned from India to take up his clan responsibilities. Lachlan maintained his interest in clan affairs and urged William to marry and continue the family line. William replied that he had too many people to take care of without the added responsibilities of a wife and children.[34]

During the period of uncertainty about whether to leave Georgia, Lachlan made a quick voyage to London to establish new trade connections. He imported goods through Charlestown merchants, one of whom was Henry Laurens. As he had moved from trader to storekeeper, now he intended to act as his own importer. James Cowles of Bristol was engaged to handle his account. Henry Laurens informed Cowles that McGillivray was taking passage for London and would see Cowles; he described McGillivray as "an honest man" and "a generous Merchant."[35] McGillivray sailed on May 10, 1764, on the ship *Polly*. He completed his business with dispatch and was back in Savannah by September.

While McGillivray was weighing his future, the map of the southern frontier was radically altered by the Treaty of Paris. France lost Canada and the land between the Mississippi and the Appalachians to the English. Spain, which had entered the war in 1762, was forced to cede Florida to the English. In compensation, Spain received New

Orleans and the Louisiana territory west of the Mississippi. The map was simplified: except for New Orleans, England had everything east of the Mississippi, including Canada; Spain had everything west of that river as well as the Isle of Orleans. The consequences for Georgia were extraordinary. Her western limits extended to the Mississippi and, after a brief struggle with South Carolina regarding jurisdiction over the debatable land below the Altamaha, the southern boundary was set at the St. Marys. Georgia, whose sons had done little in the way of actual combat, emerged from the war as a potential empire.

British mismanagement and French intrigue were responsible for the uprising of northern Indians led by an Ottawa chieftain named Pontiac, who attacked Fort Detroit on May 7, 1763. Detroit, Fort Pitt, and Fort Niagara held out against Indian assaults, but all other English posts on the northern frontier were taken by the attackers. Colonel Henry Bouquet led an army to the relief of Fort Pitt and defeated the Indians at Bushy Run on August 5, 1763. Pontiac remained defiant, and other armies would be sent against him.[36]

Thus the war died hard in the North. The French made a last desperate attempt in the South to involve the Creeks in a war with the English through the agency of the Mortar, who they hoped would be another Pontiac.

CHAPTER TWELVE

Reshaping the Frontier

The Treaty of Augusta in 1763 was a crucial watershed in the history of the southern frontier. Those historians who have acknowledged its importance have not noticed the pivotal role played by the traders. Although the spotlight of history has shone on John Stuart and the four distinguished governors, the great compromise at Augusta was worked out by the Indians and their trusted friends, specifically Lachlan McGillivray and George Galphin. The Indians displayed more initiative than the English.

The Indians were compelled to adjust their strategy when the French prepared to leave their outposts. For almost a century they had been able to play one European power against another. If thwarted at Charlestown, they would pay a conspicuous visit to Mobile. If insulted at Savannah, they would seek attention at Fort Toulouse of the Alabamas. The tactic had worked especially well for the Creeks. After the departure of the French, the Creeks were forced to seek advocates in the ranks of the English. They found natural allies among the veterans such as McGillivray and Galphin and some of the younger men who knew them well and did business with them. Their enemies were the poachers on their lands, those wanderers they called Virginians, who came across the Savannah River in ever-increasing numbers. The royal authorities, from John Stuart to James Wright, to the Lords Commissioners themselves, would have to decide whether to support the interests of the traders or those of the new settlers.

On the occasions when the governors found it necessary to persuade the Indians to agree to something they disliked, they would rely on the traders to convince their clients. The most persuasive during the decade that followed the war were Lachlan McGillivray and George Galphin. As it had done in 1760, the Georgia Assembly would officially tender its thanks to Lachlan McGillivray twice during the ten-year period, both times for his successful intercession with the Creek Indians in matters of major importance.

The most significant influence the traders exerted in the shaping of British policy was their unacknowledged and private advice to the southern governors. McGillivray and Adair's discouraging analysis of an overland invasion of French territory was a conspicuous example. There can be no doubt that the traders, McGillivray prominent among them, caught the ear of the urbane Henry Ellis during that gentleman's short stay in Georgia. Ellis adopted the traders' view that the aggressive settlers needed to be restrained. He sided with them against the officious Atkin and defended their management of the trade. The education of Henry Ellis paid handsome dividends after he returned to England. He was regarded by royal officials as an expert on colonial affairs, and, as he told Georgia agent William Knox, he became adept at "soliciting and dancing attendance upon people in office."[1]

In particular, Ellis's advice was sought by Charles Wyndham, Earl of Egremont, secretary of state for the Southern Department in the Grenville administration. It is generally acknowledged that Ellis was the author of two papers of enormous importance in the determination of frontier policy.[2] In a letter to Egremont later copied and entitled "Hints Relative to the Division and Government of the Conquered and Newly Acquired Countries in America," Ellis advised fixing upon some line for a western boundary "beyond which our people should not at present be permitted to settle."[3] The result would be a rapid population of Nova Scotia and Georgia at the extremities of the proposed line. The territory beyond the line would be an Indian sanctuary to which only traders would have access. Ellis's recommendations were passed along, virtually intact, through a confusion of ministers, Egremont to Shelburne at the Board of Trade and to Halifax, Egremont's successor as secretary and a longtime patron of Ellis. In the process a phrase was added, probably by Shelburne, who was something of an idealist, to the effect that there would be "full liberty to all your Majesty's subjects in general to trade with the said Indians."[4] That policy would have a devastating effect within a few years. By royal proclamation of October 7, 1763, the line of demarcation was drawn down the watershed of the Appalachians. In Georgia, where the mountains blended into the piedmont, the line was practically meaningless because the dividing line between the Atlantic and Gulf waters lay deep within Creek territory. A boundary acceptable to the Creek Indians would have to be negotiated.

Meanwhile, another of Ellis's papers prompted Egremont to take action even before the proclamation policy was announced. In a letter to Egremont dated December 15, 1762, Ellis noted that the French had often repeated the propaganda that the English wanted to remove them from Louisiana and the Spanish from Florida so as to conquer and enslave the Indians and that the Indians were inclined to believe them. Ellis advised calling a conference for the purpose of assuring the Indians that the French and Spanish had been banished because of their lies about the English. If the English retained the Alabama and Tombigbee forts, it was for protection of the trade, not military conquest. Past misdeeds would be forgotten, and fair trade would be maintained.[5] Egremont incorporated Ellis's ideas into his own advice to Amherst on March 16, 1763. The governors of Virginia, North Carolina, South Carolina, and Georgia were instructed to meet with John Stuart and the southern Indians at Augusta. Egremont saw no need to maintain Forts Loudoun, Toulouse, and Tombigbee; they could be demolished as a token of British goodwill. The advice marked a contrast with the policy in the Northern Department, where isolated outposts invited attacks during Pontiac's uprising in 1763. Egremont dispatched presents valued at £5,000 to be distributed in Augusta.[6]

Meanwhile, John Stuart, whose appointment dated from January 5, 1762, had much to learn about the complexities of the Creek-Chickasaw-Choctaw region. He was an expert in Cherokee affairs but a novice in the western arena. Although there are no documents to prove it, he must have consulted with his fellow Scot from Invernesshire, McGillivray, and with other leading traders. Stuart learned that the Mortar had returned to the Upper Creeks after a sojourn near the Cherokees and was up to some mischief. The Mortar announced that the French lands would revert to the Creeks, not the English. He contended that the land was only loaned to the French, not ceded.[7]

Stuart realized that the new situation would affect the Georgia trade. Georgia had enjoyed primacy in the Creek trade because of its proximity to that nation. The profits to be made had attracted men of character and ability, who were an asset to England in its contest with the French. With Mobile and Pensacola in English hands, Augusta would have competition for control of the trade. There was a very real danger that too many persons would take advantage of the new opportunities and enter the trade.[8] Stuart began a dialogue with Amherst about the problem. The general warned Stuart that he did not want a parcel of "worthless people" to spoil Indian relations. That was the reaction Stuart wanted, and he took the next logical step. Would it not be a good idea to impose some regulations upon the new traders at Mobile and Pensacola? Why not allow Stuart the authority to license the traders in the newly ceded territories? Such a power would give Stuart clout among the Indians. The idea seemed feasible and would have made an essential difference in the future course of the trade.[9] But Amherst would have none of it. His answer was almost indignant: "I cannot think it right to grant you an exclusive privilege to give licenses as I have always considered everything of that kind as inconsistant with the freedom and liberty that ought to be indulged to every British subject who conforms himself to the rules prescribed for carrying on trade in general."[10] In ideal conditions, Amherst's philosophy was correct, but on the southern frontier it would cause an intolerable situation to develop. How could John Stuart keep out the "worthless people" Amherst warned about if he could not regulate the trade? With the two new provinces of the Floridas, there would be six governors in the business of granting licenses, and the direct result would be chaos.

Having contributed that unfortunate advice, Amherst made another suggestion that would cause an equal amount of trouble. To Governor Boone of South Carolina he expressed the opinion that Indian land should be purchased as soon as possible, "for by dispossessing them we secure to ourselves what seems to be intended for us." [11] This advice contained the seeds of Manifest Destiny.

Considering the circumstances, it was surprising that the Augusta Congress took place at all. The French, with their American empire trembling on the verge of dissolution, were still capable of bedeviling the English. Pontiac did their work in the North; the Mortar was their agent in the South. Both the French and the English were convinced that the Mortar was under French influence. Most likely the powerful chief was under no influence other than his own determination to preserve his tribal rights. On April 5, 1763, he sent a strong talk to Governor Wright stating that the Savannah River was the rightful boundary of his nation. Now his woods were full of white people and there were no buffalo, bear, and deer to hunt. He demanded that the governor remove those Virginia people from the Indian lands. A month later, the Gun Merchant joined the Mortar in a threatening message. They had heard that the English intended to take their lands and reminded the governor that "it made their hearts cross to see their Lands taken without their Liberty." They were tired of the English telling them to kill the French and the French telling them to kill the English. The chiefs warned that those who told them to use sharp weapons might get cut. They loved their land: "The Wood is our Fire, and the grass is our Bed." The best answer that Wright could give was that all problems would be worked out at the great meeting at Augusta. [12] The Mortar's attitude seemed to doom any hope of land cessions the governors may have had.

A more serious impediment to the meeting was the sudden rash of killings. English traders had grown accustomed to French efforts to buy their scalps. John Spencer had nearly lost his twenty-three years earlier, when the Wolf interceded for him. In May 1763, Spencer was struck down by a party of Upper Creeks on the great trading road to Augusta. Spencer was a turbulent personality, often in trouble with the governors and an enfant terrible to Edmond Atkin, but he was a friend to Lachlan McGillivray and in good standing with the gentlemen of Augusta. His death disturbed them greatly. Next, a trader named Pierce was murdered; then, in October, on the eve of the congress, three other traders were killed. Governor Boone favored strong measures of retaliation, but Wright preferred Ellis's earlier strategy of blaming only a few, not the nation. The generals were too busy with Pontiac to bother about a southern war. Although the Mortar did not prevent a delegation of Creeks from going to Augusta, he discouraged the greater chiefs by reminding them that the English took hostages of innocent Cherokees and later killed them. The Gun Merchant, Devall's Landlord, the Okfuskee Captain, and the Wolf decided upon the prudent course and stayed away from Augusta. The Wolf went down to Pensacola and warned the new English officer there that the land belonged to the Creeks. According to John Stuart, the Wolf wanted to confine the Pensacola garrison to a garden plot.[13]

The factionalism among the Indians had a counterpart in the bickering among the governors, who were as jealous of their prerogatives as any Indian chief. On October 4, Francis Fauquier of Virginia, Arthur Dobbs of North Carolina, and Thomas Boone of South Carolina met together in Charlestown and decided they would rather not go to Augusta. Besides the inconvenience of getting there, they could not put the Indians under guard in "so straggling and ill-settled a place as Augusta." Governor Wright objected to the slight to the second town of Georgia. Although not as elegant as Charlestown, Augusta "affords sufficient houses, plenty of provisions and accommodations of every kind," he said. Perhaps they were misinformed about Augusta, replied the three governors. Even so, they did not want to go there. Besides, Wright was overly concerned about the Creeks; the governors doubted that the Creeks would dare show their faces at the conference. It was obvious that the governors' primary motive for attending this congress was to satisfy Lord Egremont, not to deal with the Creeks. Wright's response was testy. He was concerned about the Creeks because Georgia would be devastated if they went on the warpath, a problem the other three governors did not have. Given the mood of the Creeks, Wright doubted that they would take orders to go to Charlestown, and if they would not, he would meet them at Augusta even if he had to go alone. The trio argued that the Upper Creeks would not come and Stuart should be able to compel the Lower Creeks to go to Charlestown. The Creeks might not like to follow orders, but they should not be indulged. The debate ended when Stuart informed the governors that the Upper Creeks had indeed come in and seemed determined not to go one step further than Augusta. Their reason was that they much preferred a straggling town in which they were safe to a comfortable one in which they would be put under guard. The visitors were annoyed that the governors were not at Augusta and said they would give them ten days to get there. The Lower Creeks expressed concern about the rumors that the governors intended to take their land away from them.[14]

The governors had no choice but to go to Augusta even though they were convinced that the congress would fail. They did not want to be held responsible by London for causing the failure. They sent an advance notice to Stuart to assure the Indians that it was "evil news" they had heard; taking their land had never occurred to the governors: "No such intention is harboured in the breast of any of us."[15]

John Stuart was uneasy in his role as general manager of the conference. It was his first major responsibility as superintendent. He felt comfortable with the Cherokees, who were led by his friend the Little Carpenter; he had no reason to worry about the docile Catawbas; the Chickasaws were time-tested friends of the English. Only two Choctaws came to Augusta, not enough to occupy him long, but the Creeks were an enigma to him. Although Stuart did not entirely trust the traders, he was forced to rely on their good offices. Governor Wright urged George Galphin to assist Stuart, and Galphin's help was significant. The Lower Creek delegation headed by Togulki, or young Malatchi of Coweta, Captain Alleck of the Cussetas, and Tallechea of Chiaha arrived in Augusta on October 20, and Galphin invited them to Silver Bluff. On that same day, Governor Wright and several gentlemen left Savannah. They were escorted by Captain Lachlan McGillivray's mounted troop and must have made an impression on the Indian visitors when they entered Augusta two days later.[16]

The Upper Creeks camped at a place called Indian Springs, on the hill to the west of Augusta, only a short distance from McGillivray's plantation. McGillivray welcomed the Upper Creek chiefs to his house. He was especially glad to see Emistisiguo, now the headman of Little Tallassee, McGillivray's former post. For Emistisiguo as for John Stuart, this was a debut on a major stage. Both men became adept performers. Because the other governors did not reach Fort Moore until November 2 and Augusta a day later, the traders had ten days to confer with the visiting Indians. The essential business of the Augusta Congress was accomplished in these comfortable sessions marked by pipe smoking, rum drinking, and interminable talks of the sort that Indians loved, traders understood, and the governors found tedious.[17]

By November 3, 1763, when the laggard dignitaries finally reached Augusta, there was a throng of nearly nine hundred Indians in town, of whom about seven hundred were men. With some solemnity and to the discharge of cannon the governors announced that the congress would begin on the following day. They were astonished when the Upper Creeks asked for a delay of one day while they consulted with the Lower Creeks. The governors could not imagine why; the Indians were merely supposed to listen to a routine ritual of platitudes. The Lower Creeks convinced the Indians from the upper towns that the only way to repair the damage done by Upper Creek transgressions was to give up land as far as the Ogeechee.[18]

Stuart's opening talk on behalf of the governors on November 5 was filled with the usual rhetoric. Past offenses were buried in oblivion, he said, thus giving away a potential negotiating point. The former French forts would be occupied only for the convenience of the Indians, not for oppressing them.[19] After the redoubtable Paya Mattaha spoke for the Chickasaws, asking only that the trade to his country be limited to his friends John Highrider and John Brown, the Creeks spoke through the veteran interpreter Stephen Forrest. Tallechea dropped a bombshell by calmly announcing that the Creeks were willing to give away a huge tract of their hunting ground and then explained in detail where the boundaries would be—the Little River to the northwest, the Ogee-chee River to the west, and then a line to the Altamaha. The boundary at Pensacola would be the tidewater. What did the Creeks want in return? Only that past misdeeds be forgiven. Stuart and the governors had agreed to that, without a quid pro quo. The governors were so surprised by the gratuitous offer that they requested a day off to prepare their response.[20]

It is clear that the deal was made before the governors arrived and probably without John Stuart's knowledge, and it is interesting that the Indians saw the advantage of a line before the Proclamation of 1763 was known in America. If Ellis, the putative author of the proclamation, and the Indians agreed about the necessity of a line, it may have been because both reflected the views of the traders. The Indians understood perfectly where the line was to be run. Stuart later asked them if they were certain that they knew the boundaries, and twice they answered that they did know. They had worked it out while waiting for the governors. The Indians did not negotiate with Stuart; they presented him with a fait accompli. The negotiations could have been made only with trusted white men who knew the country as well as the Indians themselves. The conclusion is inescapable that Lachlan McGillivray and George Galphin were the party of the second part. Emistisiguo later referred to McGillivray's discussions of the boundary line at Augusta. When the line was actually marked, McGillivray and Galphin accompanied the Indian observers, who did not trust the official surveyors. McGillivray and Galphin had enough prestige to convince the Indians that the line was drawn in the places agreed upon at Augusta.[21]

The pedantic wording of the treaty conceals the satisfaction the governors must have felt in being handed this unexpected bonus. The limits to the south would have to wait until the boundary between Georgia and Florida was determined. The Cherokees and Catawbas agreed to boundaries in their territories. The Choctaws were promised trade. The Chickasaws were told to limit their business to their two preferred traders. The treaty was signed, and the guns of the fort fired a salute of celebration.[22]

The governors reported their great achievement to Secretary of State Egremont. They harbored a doubt as to whether the absent Creek chiefs would agree to the terms when they heard about them. They suggested that the Choctaws be supplied from Mobile, to free them from the necessity of crossing Creek country. Finally, they suggested that the time was right to impose a general regulation of the trade.[23]

In retrospect, the governors contributed little except dignity to the great congress. They were wrong in their prediction that the Creeks would not appear at Augusta. They were not prepared to bargain with their one asset, the forgiveness of past misdeeds. They had given no thought to any comprehensive settlement beyond the first instructions from Egremont to notify the Indians about the French and Spanish cessions and to assure them of the goodwill of the English. The Indians knew about the French evacuation long before the conference. The Indians and traders handed the governors a package already neatly wrapped.[24]

Just why the Creeks and the traders should have reached the agreement they did is a matter of speculation. It is certain that the Creek chiefs came to Augusta with a reluctance amounting to dread regarding the possibility of losing their land. It is also obvious that the Augusta traders were aware of the potential danger of indiscriminate settlement. Regardless of Indian title, people were moving into the backcountry around Augusta as far as the Ogeechee, some forty miles to the west. One can guess that Galphin convinced the Lower Creek chiefs that the Savannah was no longer a realistic line, that the governors were angry at the recent killings, and that the Creeks would do well to compromise on the Ogeechee line. The boundary would be well marked and would be like a stone wall, never to be crossed. Lachlan McGillivray persuaded Emistisiguo and the Upper Creeks of the wisdom of the plan.

John Stuart lingered in Augusta to distribute presents. His careful accounts reveal the following numbers: 312 Cherokees, 305 Creeks, 45 Upper Chickasaws, 113 Lower Chickasaws, 69 Catawbas, and 2 Choctaws for a total of 846. Among the presents were strouds, duffles, vermillion, shirts, guns, powder, balls, calico, hoes, hatchets, brass pans, greatcoats, gun flints, belts, looking glasses, garters, trunks, gunlocks, saddles, bridles, stirrup leather, and cutlery. No wonder they went away "with all the Marks of contentment and good humor," as Stuart put it. He took the two Choctaws with him to Charlestown for their own protection and had them carried to Mobile by ship. Presents for the tribe went with them.[25] Stuart's list of presents was an index to the various ways their association with the British traders had affected the Indians' life-style. The year 1763 was a watershed in frontier history in several ways. It marked the beginning of the influx of settlers into the new cession and the proliferation of unscrupulous traders into the Indian country. It also marked the beginning of a slow decline of the Creeks from a condition of proud independence to what Benjamin Hawkins at the end of the century would describe as beggary.[26] Hawkins blamed the annual effusion of presents by the British government rather than any abuses of the trade. Although there had been sporadic distribution of gifts in 1753, 1755, and 1757, gift giving became a habit during John Stuart's tenure of office.

Another feature of the treaty signed at Augusta was also a harbinger of social change. The Indians were promised a reward of goods equal in value to fifty pounds of half-dressed deerskins for every fugitive slave they returned to the authorities. Though comparatively few slaves had sought refuge in the Creek country, the clause in the treaty demonstrates that the number was enough to cause serious concern. As the number of Georgia slaves increased during the two ensuing decades, the number of runaway blacks increased.[27]

The great question, as the congress broke up, was whether the absent chiefs would concur with the cession of land. It was significant that the Upper Creek headmen did not sign the treaty at Augusta; they felt that they must consult the absent headmen before they gave their consent.

On December 24, 1763, seven Creeks who had been living among the Lower Cherokees murdered fourteen people in the Long Canes area, near Ninety-Six, South Carolina. Stuart blamed the Mortar for the deed, suggesting that his intention was to spoil the treaty. The incident shocked the Creek leaders in both the Upper and Lower towns. Togulki made a hurried visit to Galphin at Silver Bluff to assure him that the deed was done by people who had lived among the Cherokees for four years. Galphin hoped that Wright would not hold the nation responsible. Wright's first reaction was to stop the trade. Boone of South Carolina favored strong retaliation "to bring the insolent Nation to Reason."[28] Boone suggested that Wright send notices to St. Augustine, Pensacola, and Mobile that trade would be cut off. By that time, Wright had second thoughts. Was Carolina ready to support Georgia if a war started? Would General Thomas Gage be willing to send troops? While he hesitated, other peace messages came in. The Wolf of Muccolossus sent word that none of the Upper towns knew of this mischief or had any hand in it. He believed that the Mortar was innocent. The Lower Creek chiefs begged for time and promised satisfaction. The White King of the Cussetas said that two of the culprits were his own sons and they would die. On March 26, 1764, Handsome Fellow, the Okfuskee Captain, and other headmen went to Augusta and appealed for the return of their old traders to the nation.[29]

General Gage's advice was not very helpful to the peace process. On January 27, 1764, he encouraged Stuart to "foment the fears and bickerings of the several tribes against each other" to keep them from combining against the English. On May 1, 1764, his solution to the latest problem was to find some bold Cherokee who would knock the Mortar on the head. Stuart wisely declined to take this advice.[30]

The cautious policy of wait and see paid dividends. A meeting of Upper Creek headmen, including the Mortar himself, was held at Little Tallassee on April 10, 1764. Lachlan McGillivray's partner William Struthers was there, as were James McQueen, Joseph Cornell, James Germany, George Whitfield, and William Gravis. A sign of Emistisiguo's growing influence was that he and not the Mortar or the Gun Merchant was chosen to make the talk. Not all of the headmen had been present at Augusta, he said. All were present now. They agreed to the land cession made by the Lower Creeks, "providing you keep your slaves and your cattle within those bounds." He asked that the English build no forts in their country.[31] The Upper Creeks' confirmation of the Treaty of Augusta was as important as the original treaty. It marked the submission of the most troublesome man in that nation, the Mortar. On August 13, the Mortar sent his own talk to Augusta by Handsome Fellow. He asked forgiveness for any past misconduct and promised thereafter to be a faithful servant of the king. His main desire was that the great old path between Augusta and the nation be kept white and clean and that his people be supplied by that path and no other.[32] The Mortar reflected the Upper Creeks' unwillingness to rely on Mobile or Pensacola; those trails led through Alabama and Lower Creek territory. With the disappearance of the French, the Mortar's influence declined. Because of his rapport with the English, Emistisiguo's prestige increased.

The opening of two important points of entry into the Indian country had significant repercussions on the dynamics of the southern frontier. The Choctaws, when supplied by Mobile, would be freed from dependence on the Creeks. The Lower Creeks could play off the Pensacola traders against those from Augusta, much as they had done the French against the English. On August 6, 1763, Lieutenant Colonel Augustine Prevost, a Swiss of the Royal American Regiment, occupied Pensacola, and on October 20 of that year, Major Robert Farmar took over Mobile from the French commander d'Abbadie. The latter wrote to Kerlérec how galling it was to have to deal with people who were intoxicated with success and who regarded themselves as masters of the world. Like a good soldier, d'Abbadie met with a Choctaw delegation and, in the presence of Major Farmar, asked them to accept the English as friends.[33]

Fort Tombigbee was occupied by thirty men detached from Farmar's command, and he intended to post soldiers at the famous Alabama Fort. The Indians, however, had other ideas. The Alabama Chief Tamathlemingo burned the fort rather than let the English have it and then took the people of his village to Mobile.[34] Carthage was destroyed at last.

Among the opportunistic English traders who decided to move their base of operations to Mobile was John McGillivray. He reaped the advantages of the early start, and his personal wealth approached that of his cousin before the decade was over. During 1764, the first year of peace, there was an unusually brisk commerce on the overland trails between Augusta and the two new British possessions. The traders of Augusta were busy establishing branch offices in those places. A British officer, in Augusta to inspect the fort, was surprised that "the gentlemen at Augusta often make trips to Mobile and Pensacola." They offered to carry messages to the military officers there. He had not heard about this new channel of communication before but promptly informed General Gage. Gage wrote back that he was glad to hear about this "easy communication" and would send dispatches by that route.[35] These were hardy travelers indeed who could consider the Augusta-Mobile trek easy.

British Mobile resembled Augusta during the rawest of its early years and Major Farmar encountered the same problems that had beset Richard Kent. Whereas Kent silenced the "jangling" among traders by his courage and good judgment, Farmar managed to alienate almost everyone by his harsh application of military discipline. In his recent biography of Farmar, Robert Rea described a confrontation between the major and a gang of John McGillivray's hirelings who were accused of behaving "in so riotous, debauched drunken manner of life that they were a nuisance to every family . . . and a pest to society." Farmar had the whole lot of them arrested. The men were tried by a military court, which acquitted all but the chief offender, one Richard Jones. Jones, whom Farmar described as "a wretch, bred among Savages and a Scourge to Society," was sentenced to 250 lashes. On another occasion Farmar imprisoned, then tried to banish a merchant for selling a damaged brass kettle to an Indian. The other Mobile merchants refused to do business with the military and forced Farmar to rescind the order of banishment.[36]

The merchants of Mobile were glad to see the new governor of West Florida, George Johnstone, who arrived with John Stuart on December 1, 1764. The crusty Farmar refused to shake hands with Stuart and was soon locked in an acrimonious struggle for power with Governor Johnstone.[37]

The scrape between the military and John McGillivray's men underscores a new and growing problem in the postwar Indian trade, namely the inability of the principal traders to regulate the conduct of their employees. There was no indication that any of Lachlan McGillivray's men had ever run amuck in similar fashion. Brown, Rae and Company policed its employees effectively. The episode that so disturbed Major Farmar was attributable in part to the absence of law on the new frontier, but it was mainly the result of the new British policy announced in the Proclamation of 1763 opening the trade to all who would enter.

Stuart called a conference of Choctaws and Chickasaws to Mobile, and the traditional enemies sat down together at his generous table. Stuart lavished them with food, rum, and presents. He borrowed an idea from the French, who rewarded their important friends with medals. Henceforth, Stuart distributed "great medals" to the most influential headmen and smaller medals to lesser chiefs. In the Treaty of Mobile, April 27, 1765, the Choctaws ceded a generous strip of land along the coast for settlements. A significant innovation of Stuart's was the introduction of his deputies or commissaries into the Indian country. The Indians were bound by the treaty to protect these agents. After Mobile, the Choctaws cooperated in assisting a British expedition under Major Farmar to pacify the Mississippi Valley as far as the Illinois country.[38]

Stuart's next problem was to define the limits of settlement around Pensacola in the Creek country. Chiefs who had been reluctant to go to Augusta in 1763 came in with their followers to Pensacola in May 1765. Five hundred Creeks attended the congress from May 12 to 28 and enjoyed Stuart's hospitality. The Mortar was present, more to limit any English land acquisition than to display friendship. The Gun Merchant, Devall's Landlord, the Wolf of Muccolossus, and Emistisiguo were the most prominent of the Upper Creeks. Because Togulki had voluntarily resigned his inherited title as "emperor," Captain Alleck and Escotchabie were recognized as spokesmen for the Lower Creeks. Escotchabie was called Young Lieutenant by the English and had fought beside Lachlan McGillivray in Augusta against the Cherokees. John Stuart's tactics in the winning of the Mortar were in striking contrast with the recriminatory methods employed by Edmond Atkin. Stuart named Montaut de Monberaut, a former commandant of the Alabama Fort and now a resident of Pensacola, as his deputy. Monberaut was an old and trusted friend of the Mortar and acted as intermediary in calming the Mortar's fears about the English intentions. Stuart cleverly used a new form of persuasion on the Mortar. He showed the chief the French medals which the Choctaws had given up as an indication that that entire nation had turned its back on the French. He then explained his idea of recognizing and rewarding the very greatest men with the king's medals. The Mortar, being human, was intrigued by the idea. He indicated that he was not averse to receiving a medal. Stuart tantalized him a few days before conferring a great medal upon him. Among the Upper Creeks, the Gun Merchant, Devall's Landlord, the Wolf, and Emistisiguo were similarly honored. The award to Emistisiguo indicates how rapid was his rise to prominence and is evidence of the important part he played in securing the acceptance of the Augusta land cession.[39]

Stuart came away from his meeting with the Mortar with the same high regard Atkin felt toward him. The Mortar was "a sensible manly Indian, and seems to have been actuated in his opposition to us, more by principles of love of his country, and jealousy on account of their lands and independency, than by love to the French, to whom he adhered for purposes of his own."[40] It was unfortunate that such a man was so often regarded as an enemy.

The Creeks ceded the coastal area around Pensacola as far as the tidewater and agreed to accept Stuart's commissaries. Stuart looked to his fellow Scots to act as these agents. McGillivray's partner William Struthers was the Mortar's choice and was acceptable to Stuart as commissary to the Creeks. John McIntosh, one of the Strathnairn-Darien connection, was named commissary to the Chickasaws. Charles Stuart, John's cousin, was appointed to the various small tribes on the Mississippi and soon promoted to deputy to replace Monberaut, who proved too temperamental for his post.[41]

The dismissal of Monberaut obliquely involved John McGillivray. Apparently the Frenchman first heard that he was in trouble from his son, who had it secondhand from McGillivray. Monberaut penned a long letter to the feisty governor George Johnstone, asking for the truth of the rumor. Johnstone gave him no satisfaction. He considered Monberaut's letter a "long, vain, tedious, puffing memorial." McGillivray had no authority to speak for Stuart or the governor. Indeed, he said, McGillivray had spent too much time "among the creoles of Guadaloupe; he is at present delirious." The remark is interesting in that it reveals that the enterprising Scot was already exploring new mercantile opportunities with the French merchants who had been relegated from New Orleans to the island of Guadaloupe. Governor Johnstone went on to admit that McGillivray had guessed correctly and that Monberaut was indeed sacked and that if he did not leave the country he would be arrested.[42]

After his successes in establishing boundaries at Mobile and Pensacola, Stuart had one last bit of tidying up to do. The lower portion of the Augusta line had been left vague because of the uncertain provincial jurisdiction. By 1765 the territory to the St. Marys was confirmed to Georgia and the line could be finished. James Grant of Cherokee war fame was governor of East Florida and host to a conference of Lower Creeks at Picolata, Florida, on November 18, 1765. Captain Alleck was present as the recognized "mouth" of his people. The line of 1763 was extended from the Ogeechee to the Altamaha opposite the place where Finholloway Creek joined the Altamaha and from that point to the St. Marys and along the St. Marys to the tidewater mark.[43] Alleck confirmed the line with Governor Wright in January 1766.

Thus by the end of 1765 the reshaping of the southern frontier seemed complete. Architects of change had done their work in London, Paris, Augusta, Mobile, Pensacola, and Picolata. Whether the physical structure that had been so carefully framed would accommodate the various inhabitants of the southern country was the question. The answer was soon obvious. The components of the 1763 package were incompatible. Regulation of the trade was impossible with an open-door policy regarding the licensing of traders. Permitting Indian traffic through a region settled by Indian-hating pioneers was a mistake. The seeds sown in 1763 would bear bitter fruit. By comparison, the impact of the Stamp Act of 1765 on the southern frontier was inconsiderable.

In an indirect way the Stamp Act did have an effect on the frontier. Funds raised by the tax were to be used to implement a plan proposed by the Board of Trade under Lord Hillsborough in July 1764.

After seeking the advice of the two superintendents, William Johnson and John Stuart, the board proposed a plan for dividing the departments into districts, with deputies, commissaries, and lesser employees scattered throughout the Indian country. Civil authority was granted to the superintendents. The delighted superintendents began to carry out the plan as soon as they received notice of it from the Board of Trade. The experiment was short-lived. When the Stamp Act was repealed, so was the funding system. The plan, which might have imposed some degree of order during the critical period ahead, was aborted.[44]

CHAPTER THIRTEEN

The Aftermath of 1763

The difficulty in regulating the Indian trade stemmed from a visionary principle contained in royal Proclamation of October 7, 1763. The trade was declared to be open to all British subjects, provided only that they obtain a license from any of the six southern governors and obey the regulations set by the proper authority. The ministry was not certain who should have that authority. At first, the superintendent set the rules; in 1766 the governors were given that responsibility.[1]

Regardless of who made the regulations, they were much the same as the time-tested principles which Carolina and Georgia traders followed: trade was confined to Indian towns; purchase of green skins was forbidden; false weights and measures were outlawed; no blacks, mixed-bloods, or Indians were allowed to engage in business; a price schedule was to be adhered to; the names of a trader's assistants were to be listed on his license; and the sale of rum was limited. Though these rules had been infringed upon, they were generally followed before 1763 and increasingly ignored after that.

After the proclamation, the six governors refused to impose any restrictions on the number of persons who could be employed. The licensed traders hired assistants, the assistants subcontracted with others, and the Indian country swarmed with people. The Chickasaws, who had asked for only two traders at the Augusta meeting, had seventy-two working in their towns within two years.[2]

James Wright of Georgia was one of the chief critics of the royal policy. He was bold enough to tell the Earl of Shelburne that "the person who wrote that proclamation was unacquainted with Indian affairs." The new packhorsemen and servants of traders were "generally the very worst kind of people."[3] William Knox, who like his patron Henry Ellis had returned to England to act as adviser to a succession of secretaries of state, wrote a pamphlet in 1768 in which he described the current state of Indian relations. He began by stating how the Indians were when the British first treated with them: "Vagrant in their manner of life, without social intercourse even among each other, jealous in the highest degree of their liberty and independency and attached to their customs and nation with more than Spartan pride and tenacity." Knox was brutally frank about what had happened: "We eradicated their notions of honesty." British traders and Indians now mutually deceived each other. Both expected to be cheated and complained only when they were cheated too much. Knox, a good Presbyterian, thought religion might provide a solution. He advised adopting the methods successfully employed by the French Roman Catholics. Protestant missionaries should adopt the Indians' customs, learn their language, and gain their trust. The missionary should be well versed in the use of medicines. Knox anticipated Thomas Jefferson and Benjamin Hawkins when he outlined a plan for converting the Indians from a hunting to an agricultural economy. Above all, he concluded, the Indians should be treated as brothers. In other comments, Knox revealed himself as a man of his times, for example, in his suggestion that silk culture be introduced to the Creeks or in his belief "that man was intended for polished society."[4]

Ironically, religion would be used to segregate and expel the Indians rather than foster any feeling of brotherhood. The pioneers who poured into the 1763 cession brought with them the evangelical religious attitudes associated with the Great Awakening. The distinction between the good person and the wicked was the experience of a personal salvation. Indians, by this definition, were wicked and doomed to exclusion from the heaven of the Christians. The exclusion, in fact, began on earth. Had not God made Christians the lords of nature and all that was in it? Good Christians, not the heathen, should possess the land and use it the way God intended, that is, in farming.

The invasion of settlers into Georgia's backcountry was a major development in the shaping of the frontier. Discouraged from crossing the mountains by the Proclamation of 1763, these hardy folk moved down the mountain valleys and infiltrated into the new Georgia cession. By Wright's count there were fewer than 6,000 whites in the province when he took office. In 1766 there were 10,000. The number of blacks had doubled from 3,578 to 7,800. In 1761 only 42 vessels were loaded at Savannah. In 1766 the number was 153. Lord Adam Gordon visited Savannah on his tour of America in 1763 and commented that the town was "extremely well laid out, and the buildings increasing in Number and Size." Exports in that year alone were valued at £50,000. He predicted that Georgia would become "one of the richest, and most considerable Provinces in British America and that in a very few years, provided peace continues."[5]

The council was deluged with requests for land on the Ogeechee and below the Altamaha. The old Georgians did not permit themselves to be overlooked in the distribution of land. Lachlan McGillivray obtained 392 acres in the new parish of St. Andrew, formerly the Darien district, in 1764. In 1765, he claimed more than sixty-eight persons in his "family" and obtained 100 acres on Beaver Dam Creek below Augusta. In 1767, he purchased "sundry vacant lots" in Savannah.[6]

The grandest scheme hatched during the post-1763 era was the brainchild of McGillivray and the other two surviving partners of Brown, Rae and Company, John Rae and George Galphin. On January 1, 1765, the three partners, animated with "true Patriotism," as they said, and persuaded that the young colony needed settlers, asked for fifty thousand acres of vacant land on the Ogeechee River, centering on Lambert's Big Creek. They were convinced that a large number of Irish Protestants would cheerfully come to Georgia if land were available. The request from these giants of trade was surprising in that the interests of traders were not generally those of settlers. The three,

however, saw themselves as rising above the narrow and selfish and acting the part of statesmen and shapers of the future. They undoubtedly
were, and they were also possessed of huge, scattered tracts of land that
would rise in value as people moved into the colony.[7]

After lending his prestige to the request, McGillivray devoted his
efforts as a member of the House of Assembly to securing the necessary legislation. On March 6, 1766, an act "for encouraging settlers
to come into the Province" was passed, and provisions were made for
raising £815 for that purpose.[8]

John Rae's letter to his brother Matthew in County Down, Ireland,
was published in the local papers there. Rae described how a firm and
lasting peace with the Indians had been arranged. Industrious people
who wanted to better their lot in life were needed on the frontier.
Clergymen and schoolteachers were encouraged to come; there were
too few in Georgia. They were cautioned that there were no social refinements on the southern frontier, no markets or fairs, "but we have
plenty of good eating and drinking," Rae promised. "I bless God for
it," he said. "I keep as plentiful a table as most gentlemen in Ireland,
with good punch, wine and beer." Those who could afford to should
buy a slave or two, he advised, "that they may live very easy and well." [9]
The lure of the good life made possible by an economy based on slavery
had built up Carolina and stamped its society with a unique blend
of hedonism and commercialism. After 1763, Georgians emulated the
Carolina model.

Galphin, for whom writing was a chore, contributed promises of
milch cows from his plantation on the Ogeechee and free transportation from Charlestown in his riverboats. In February 1768, Rae and
Galphin asked for a year's extension of the incentives and were granted
it. At the same time, LeRoy Hammond requested the same terms on
behalf of a group of forty families from North Carolina, many of them
Quakers. The assembly readily agreed and granted a large tract on
the Little River, only to find that the ministry disallowed the Georgia
Act of 1766, which encouraged immigration. The government was not
averse to settling the frontier, but it did not want to do so at the cost of
depopulating the home islands.[10] Caught in a dilemma, Wright and his

council decided to proceed with the promised aid to the two townships but not to initiate any new such projects.

The ship the *Prince George* landed 107 passengers on December 2, 1768, most of them bound for the Ogeechee and the newly labeled Queensborough township. Lachlan McGillivray was on the committee that distributed the land to the new arrivals. The township on the Little River attracted seventy families instead of the anticipated forty. Two of the leaders, Joseph Maddock and Jonathan Sell, asked for more land and a road connecting their settlement to Augusta and Savannah. Again McGillivray was in a position to be helpful, and again the legislature agreed. The governor was honored by the decision to call the town Wrightsborough. Though a minority of the residents of Wrightsborough were Quakers, the leaders came from members of that denomination, and the Quaker meetings gave the community a coherence and continuity that Queensborough lacked.[11] Queensborough, however, attracted more people. The initiative of McGillivray, Rae, and Galphin was responsible for a steady flow of irish immigrants between 1768 and 1774.

If all the newcomers were as law-abiding as the Wrightsborough Quaker-led community and as industrious as the Irish, there would have been less trouble in the Georgia backcountry than there was. The dichotomy between the open-trade policy enunciated in the Proclamation of 1763 and the governors' efforts to regulate trade was one source of friction. Another inconsistency that was fraught with graver consequences was the policy that attracted migrants to a region open to Indian traffic. The Proclamation line funneled the westward-trekking pioneers down the mountain valleys and into the Indian cession of 1763. These pioneer folk had in common a craving for land, a stubborn independence, and a dislike of Indians. Governor Wright had hoped that the "middling sort" of persons would occupy the territory to the Ogeechee. He was pleased that many good, hardworking people migrated to the backcountry, but there were too many of those called variously vagabonds, strollers, stragglers, banditti, and crackers. The Indians referred to the type as "Virginians." They flocked into the countryside, squatted on the land without bothering to ask the authorities, built crude huts, and lived off the abundant game. The Indians complained that they killed the buffalo, bear, and deer and ruined the land for hunting.

Through the heart of the cession ran the Upper and Lower Creek trading paths, which merged before they entered Augusta. As a reward for the Creek cession, or perhaps as an afterthought, the Creeks had been promised at the Augusta Congress that they could continue to come and go along this trail, which they called the great white path. The high-placed British ministers who should have provided oversight to the frontier problems were rotated too frequently to establish a comprehensive plan for the southern frontier, or for the colonies as a whole, for that matter.

Thus there were reports of ugly incidents almost at once. One Indian was killed in October 1765. In November of the same year, three whites were killed. Wright complained to the four great medal chiefs, the Mortar, Gun Merchant, the Wolf, and Emistisiguo. In turn, the Lower Creek chiefs, including the White King of the Cowetas and the Young Lieutenant, accused the "straggling people" of crossing over the line.[12] Wright ordered Colonel Edward Barnard to take a few militiamen and ride along the line to see if there were any trespassers. Barnard reported finding none, although there was an Indian camp just across the Ogeechee that might cause trouble. Wright advised the Creeks to remove those people "for the White People sometimes get drunk as well as the Indians and it is not good that they should live too nigh each other." In July 1767 the Indian town became the focus of the settlers' displeasure. Thirty-one persons living near the Indian line signed a petition stating that Indians had stolen some horses. Five men chased the thieves to the camp on the Ogeechee, but there were too many Indians for the whites to deal with. Traders, who were accustomed to Indian ways, would have ridden into the camp and negotiated the problem. The settlers peered from behind trees and ran when a dog began barking at them. The petitioners asked the governor to send assistance because they had heard that a war party was on its way and they did not want to be left "to the Mercy of Savage Fury."[13] James Wright barely had time to dash off another talk to the Creek chiefs when he received news from the Augusta magistrates that the settlers had taken the law into their own hands. They went up to the Ogeechee camp and burned all seven huts there. Wright sent another talk on the heels of the first, blaming "Straggling White People" and promising that they would be prosecuted.[14]

Though the Ogeechee fracas of 1767 did not cause the alarm that followed the Ogeechee incident of 1756, it attracted attention from Governor James Grant in East Florida, who wrote General Gage about it. In his opinion, the settlers were at fault: "It is just as likely that the Horses were carried off by some of their Brother Crackers."[15] He hoped East Florida would not be disturbed. On November 14, 1767, General Gage in New York and Lord Shelburne in London gave their verdicts. Gage thought Georgia should pay the Indian damages: "It is highly unreasonable that the Crown should be put to an expense for the unruly proceedings of every lawless banditti upon the frontiers." Shelburne was equally annoyed: "The back settlers have been too much addicted to this practice already and therefore it cannot be too much checked."[16]

The excitement subsided when the Creeks displayed moderation and indicated that they would settle for one keg of rum for each house burned. The Creeks were more interested in stemming the encroachment of whites than in retribution. John Stuart called the headmen to Augusta in May 1767 to discuss the final marking of the boundary line. Where there was no river or stream, the trees would be marked so that white men could see clearly where the line was and not go across, and Indians would not bother them on the white man's side. The chiefs promised to send observers to make sure the line ran true.[17]

While in Augusta, Stuart arranged a schedule of fair prices for trading goods between the leading traders of Augusta and the Indians. The traders initiated the request for a price list because they were undercut by the many new traders. Among those who asked Stuart to regulate the trade were veterans James McQueen, Theophilus Perryman, John Francis Williams, John Ladson, and George Mackay, and younger men who would make their mark, notably Andrew McLean and Robert Mackay. Unfortunately, Governor Grant of East Florida stubbornly refused to enforce the schedule, and Governor Fauquier of Virginia continued to distribute licenses regardless of whether the traders agreed to observe Stuart's prices.[18]

General Gage was not optimistic about the benefit of marking the line, commenting that the frontier people were not likely to be limited by any bounds, visible or otherwise. The commanding officer at Fort Augusta reported that some Virginia people were trying to make a road through the Creek Nation to Mobile. In June 1768 George Galphin was worried about the increasing friction on the trading roads, stating that the settlers and the Indians "keep Robbing one another."[19]

Thus conditions were unsettled, at best, when the marking of the line began in June. The Creeks were represented by the Coweta Lieutenant, Selechee, the Blue Salt, and others. George Galphin and Edward Barnard were the British observers, and Samuel Savery was the surveyor. Roderick McIntosh was John Stuart's deputy; he was a hot-tempered Scot of the Clan Chattan–Darien connection. There was no problem while the line followed the Little River. The first quarrel concerned the location of the fork of the Little River mentioned in the treaty as the point where the line departed in a southerly direction. The Indians wanted Upton Creek to be considered the fork instead of the true fork twenty-five miles upriver. According to Governor Wright, Galphin explained matters to the Creeks, and they permitted a compromise, using Williams Creek as the point of the line, still six miles short of what the whites considered to be the true fork. In reality, the quarrel was not so easily resolved and nearly resulted in a fatality. "Rory" McIntosh upbraided one of the chiefs, whereupon the Indian raised his gun and pulled the trigger. The weapon misfired, and Galphin barely managed to reconcile the angry parties. If the deputy had been killed, the British and the Creeks would have been plunged into a crisis.[20]

The matter was serious enough for Stuart to include a reference to it in his report to Shelburne's successor, Lord Hillsborough. The Creeks "blame my deputy to whose warmth of temper they objected," he said. Therefore, "I shall take care to send a proper person with them now."[21]

Stuart asked McGillivray to undertake the important assignment. In spite of being ill, McGillivray agreed.

The incident was important enough to bring Emistisiguo down to Savannah to confer with the governor. Before he joined the surveying team, McGillivray acted as interpreter for the interview. Emistisiguo had a gift of eloquence, and McGillivray's translation showed him to his best advantage. As was usual with Indian talks, Emistisiguo began circumspectly, speaking about distances being no barrier to friends and the necessity of frequent intercourse to keep fresh the memory of treaties. He gradually approached his point. What happened on the Little River, he wanted to know; did those running the line get lost in the woods?[22]

Governor Wright said that he remembered seeing Emistisiguo at Augusta and was glad to see him again. Wright explained about the disagreement on the Little River and said that the surveyors had extended the line to the Canoochee, where there was another difference of opinion, and whites and Indians had decided to go home and wait for cooler weather. In a few days, McGillivray and the surveyors would resume the work. Lower Creek chiefs were expected to join the party. Wright would do everything he could to make the line like a great stone wall, not to be crossed by whites.[23]

Emistisiguo accepted Wright's explanation and took up the other troubling topic. When Stuart or Wright sent talks, the Indians took them seriously, but the white men who traded among the Indians ridiculed the talks and threw them away. The rule against the purchase of raw skins was broken every day, there were too many traders, too much rum, too great a quantity of goods, and Indians were employed as factors, all contrary to the rules. It was stated at Augusta, Emistisiguo continued, that the path from the nation to Augusta should be as it had always been, straight and open. Now the Virginians continually robbed the Indians' horses and did them other injuries along the trail. "There never was so much ill will between them and the white people," he said, "as since the Virginians came into the province."[24] At the congress, the Indians were told not to take matters into their own

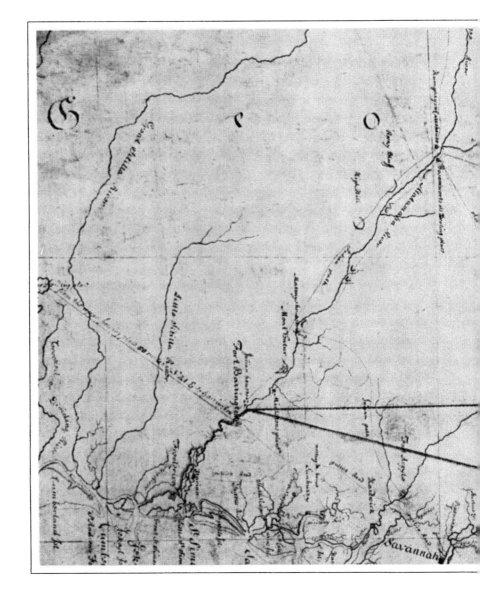

A map of the 1763 cession by Henry Yonge and W. B. de Brahm. The line from Ebenezer to Fort Barrington marks the limits of settlement set by Oglethorpe's treaty of 1739. (Courtesy William L. Clements Library)

hands but to complain to the governor. Now Emistisiguo was talking to the governor. Wright was in an awkward position. He was supposed to handle the Indians' grievances, but he could do nothing to solve them. He could not prevent the settlers from coming into the province, and he dared not close the great white road to the Indians. For lack of a good answer, he gave Emistisiguo an honorary commission.

The great medal chief assured the governor that although it was not their custom for chiefs to dress according to their rank, and indeed he was not dressed differently, he was of the Tiger Clan and therefore of royal descent and the headmen permitted him to speak for the whole nation. Wright came away from the talk impressed. He wrote to his superior that Emistisiguo was "a man by far of the greatest consequence, weight and influence of any in the Creek country."[25]

After Emistisiguo's party left, McGillivray began his job of marking the lower line, and Wright attempted to bring order to the trade business. He wrote to Lord Hillsborough on October 5, 1768, suggesting that the tribes be assigned to specific governors, the Choctaws and Chickasaws to West Florida, the Lower Creeks to East Florida, some of the Lower Creeks and all of the Upper Creeks to Georgia, and the Cherokees and Catawbas to Carolina. The scheme seemed worth trying, but the Earl of Hillsborough was afraid it would interfere "with that freedom of commerce which the subject is entitled to."[26] If Hillsborough could have seen how some of His Majesty's subjects were abusing this freedom, he might have thought differently.

Lachlan McGillivray, James Mackay, and the surveyor Samuel Savery found the stretch from the Canoochee River to the St. Marys the most difficult of all. Savery's map showed the line crossing "deep ponds . . . and terrible bogs." The tidewater side was described as containing low pine barrens and cypress ponds, suited only for a cattle range. One of the wildest and most mysterious places in Georgia even today is the Okefenokee Swamp, a vast watery wilderness, the residue of an ancient ocean. As their bad fortune would have it, the line veered directly across a twelve-mile corner of the great swamp. McGillivray had the diplomatic task of maintaining a working relationship between the whites and Indians. One member of the party was convinced that the Indians had led them into the most dangerous part of the swamp. The fifty-year-old McGillivray, who was not well when he began the expedition, wondered if he would survive. He assured John Stuart later that in all his lifetime of traveling through the wilderness he never encountered a more difficult challenge. Nevertheless, they ran the line "so far as circumstances and the temper of the Indians would possibly permit."[27]

The inscription on Savery's map reveals something of the mysterious quality of the Okefenokee. He labeled it "A great swamp called by the Indians Ekanphaenoka or the Terrible Ground. This swamp is supposed to be bottomless, having been found impassable by all who have attempted to cross it. The Indians (from ancient tradition) have a notion that it is inhabited by a race of Immortals which they call the Este Fatchasicko or invisible people of whom they tell many marvelous and absurd stories."[28] One can imagine the Indians telling their marvelous tales around the camp fire, enhanced by an increasing feeling of dread as they penetrated the terrible ground.

At last the St. Marys was reached, and the line was finished. It took thirty-one days for McGillivray's team to mark the boundary from the Canoochee to the St. Marys. Considering the terrain, that was good time. McGillivray was a hero again. Insiders such as James Adair gave him and Galphin most of the credit for the success of the undertaking. The *Georgia Gazette* sang McGillivray's praises, describing the "uncommon address" he exhibited in dealing with the Indian deputies and stressing "the ardour, unwearied diligence and unanimity" with which he and Captain Mackay conducted their business. The public owed them thanks and lasting honor. The Commons House of Assembly added its congratulations on December 23, 1768, extending thanks to McGillivray, Galphin, Mackay, and Edward Barnard for their "extraordinary care and trouble in seeing the Running of the Indian Line executed."[29]

It seems odd that the marking of the line attracted as much attention as the original agreement in 1763. It was regarded as an affirmation of the treaty of 1763 and a pledge to abide by its terms. To add to the solemnity of the occasion, John Stuart convoked another congress in Augusta to celebrate and confirm the agreement. Captain Alleck voiced the same misgivings expressed by Emistisiguo two months before to Governor Wright. Alleck said that he had long been accustomed to Englishmen and "Scotchmen," but the Virginians were very bad people who paid no regard to laws. Alleck wondered how the English could expect the Indians to control their young people when the whites could not manage theirs. He blamed the back settlers who gave rum to the Indians for stealing horses. It was doubtful that the marking of the line would stop those practices.[30]

The line of 1763 was destined to loom large in Georgia history. It remained the boundary between whites and Indians throughout the revolutionary war and, despite Georgia's efforts to change it, it was in place until 1790. The man who played the most prominent role in maintaining the line after the Revolution was the recognized head-man of all the Creeks, Emistisiguo's successor, Alexander McGillivray. It was fitting that the son of the man who marked the line should defend it.

With the final ceremonies of the line finished, James Wright had every reason to congratulate himself on successfully ending the negotiations begun at Augusta in 1763. His satisfaction was short-lived. He received a rude jolt when he was notified that General Gage had ordered all regular troops in the Southern Department to report to Quebec. Wright considered a post at Frederica important and a garrison at Augusta essential to the security of Georgia. His struggle with General Gage to maintain these forts began in 1764, when three companies of Royal Americans were sent to Charlestown to replace three independent companies and Gage asked Captain James Mark Prevost to investigate the forts at Augusta and Frederica and find out "of what use they are."[31]

Prevost carried out the assignment promptly and reported that Fort Frederica was in ruins and without ammunition. The ten men of the independent company stationed there had to provide for themselves because neither Carolina nor Georgia supported them. Fort Augusta was not much better. It is difficult to reconcile Prevost's description with the fact that the fort had been rebuilt as recently as 1759. Prevost said "it is almost entirely ruined." Its guns lacked carriages, and the powder was the property of the province, not the garrison. Fort Moore, though in bad condition, was better than Augusta. The men at Fort Augusta were there to guard the few things in the fort, not anybody or anything else. Besides, there were three stockaded posts in the country manned by rangers. Prevost concluded that it was useless to maintain both Forts Augusta and Moore.[32]

James Wright admitted that Augusta's fort was in poor condition, but he assured Gage that it would be repaired and asked for a complement of an officer and thirty men. Wright prevailed, and Gage ordered Prevost to dispatch that number of men to Augusta on the condition that the fort would be repaired. Wright's request for fifty-two men at Frederica was fanciful, and Gage cut the number to twenty. Fort Moore would be abandoned in favor of a more suitable location upriver.[33]

After dispatching Ensign Matthew Keough and all the men fit for duty to Augusta, Captain Prevost joined his battalion in the Ohio country and was replaced by Captain Gavin Cochrane. Cochrane made a tour of the backcountry, noting the distress of recent French immigrants in the New Bordeaux community on the Carolina side of the upper Savannah River. He selected the site for a stone fort fifteen miles above New Bordeaux; the place was named Fort Charlotte.[34]

Cochrane's report affords a rare description of the fort and town of Augusta. The thickly settled part of town was west of the fort; the church half a mile west or upriver; half a mile farther was Francis McCartan's fortified house with a ditch around it. It was armed with ten cannon and had a garrison of a lieutenant, a quartermaster, and thirty rangers. Two miles above McCartan's was Rae's stockaded house. The frontier was about twenty miles beyond that. He wondered if it would not be better to build a new fort on the frontier rather than repair Fort Augusta.[35]

Cochrane carefully examined the fort in company with Edward Barnard and James Jackson. It measured 88 feet by 116 feet. The powder magazine was in disrepair, as were the fort's gates and the barracks. Bedding and cooking utensils were lacking. The officers' house had no tables or chairs, and windows were papered over. Moreover, its walls were propped up to prevent collapse. There was "a kind of bastions" at

Cahuitta or Couetta

Tavofsee

Path from Oakfoskee

Okeser

Okonee

Collamee

Cullomes

Joskage

Great Ogechee River

Little Ogechee River

Great Jones's Creek & Creek

Great Buffloe

Town Creek

Town Creek Oconee

Little River

Branc

Ha

Lambells Creek

Trading Path from Cufoitau

Oakmolgee River

Rr.

from

Old Trading Path

Gitasee

Hogolegees
Savannahs

Ockmulgo

Lower Creeks

Apalaches and Timookas

Great Satilla River

Indian Fort

The Great

Swamp

Owaquaphenogaw

St.

Coastal Colonial
Georgia, 1763. Drawn
by University of
Georgia Cartographic
Services from the
original Thomas
Wright map in the
British Public Record
Office.

the corners. The front wall of the fort was faced with horizontal planking, and the three sides consisted of upright posts. It was armed with four four-pounder cannon, one three-pounder, one two-pounder, and eleven one-pounders. The guns were "indifferent" and the carriages rotten.[36]

Despite the uncertainty about the utility of Fort Augusta, the provincial assembly wanted a fort there and authorized payment for repair work. The actual construction dragged on as Captain Lieutenant Ralph Phillips replaced Cochrane and Captain Lewis V. Fuser succeeded Phillips. Phillips was a mild-mannered man who planned to retire in Augusta, but Fuser proved to be as critical as Cochrane. Fuser accused Edward Barnard of inventing crises to cause people to believe that a fort was necessary. Barnard profited from the fort in two ways, according to Fuser: he supplied the garrison with corn and he contracted to do the extensive repairs. Barnard's work was so badly done that the new powder magazine collapsed in 1767.[37]

The continued presence of the military was jeopardized by the Georgia Assembly's refusal in 1767 to pay for the support of the troops as required by Parliament's Mutiny Act of 1767. Governor Wright complained that Georgia could not afford the cost and observed that "acts of the British Parliament will I fear for the future, have very little weight in America." Lord Shelburne was furious with the Georgians and stated flatly to Wright that the assembly would indeed pay for the support of the troops. He was astonished that the province "so lately erected and which has been so singularly favored and protected by the Mother Country" could be so ungrateful.[38]

Wright tried to explain that it was not insubordination that caused the Georgians to neglect their duty, but poverty. The province was too poor to support itself, much less His Majesty's troops. Wright's argument magnified the importance of Augusta and stressed the need to maintain the garrison there. "Augusta, my Lord," he addressed Shelburne, "appears to me to be a place of some consequence . . . it is a receptacle for goods of considerable value for the Indian trade and the general resort of Indians themselves and in the neighborhood of a set of almost lawless white people who are a sort of borderers and often as bad if not worse than the Indians."[39] Wright's argument was more than a plea to leave the soldiers at Augusta. Though he might not have realized it, he succinctly summarized the contradictory policy of allowing Indian traffic through a country rapidly filling with Indian-hating pioneers. Wright, Shelburne, and Gage were too narrowly focused on whether barrack necessities would be supplied to contemplate the larger result of their policies.

The argument about the forts had many elements of a farce. Captain Fuser accused the people of Augusta of tempting the soldiers to desert. Wright denied that and asked for proof. Fuser said that Fort Augusta was not needed because everybody in Augusta went around armed, and the gentlemen had better forts than the king's. In that instance, Fuser was not far off the mark. There were thirty rangers stationed in Francis McCartan's stockaded house virtually in the middle of town.[40]

The solution to the problem of two forts where Fuser thought none was needed was solved by the policy of inadvertence that dominated British colonial administration. Gage received orders to disband the two troops of rangers in Georgia. He relayed the information to Wright, saying that he knew Wright would not like it, but there was nothing he could do. Gage retained Fort Augusta, even though he confided to Fuser that there was not the least necessity for keeping it. When the rangers were disbanded, the outlying forts to the south were closed down, Barrington on the Altamaha, Argyle on the Ogeechee. Ironically, the Georgia Assembly, which balked at the Mutiny Act, appropriated funds for Fort George on Cockspur Island, which could not be garrisoned with rangers and which Gage refused to staff.[41]

Fuser continued to complain about conditions at the Augusta fort throughout 1767. The soldiers had to eat corn instead of wheat; they made their own beds of straw; they fetched their own fuel. Wright debated each point. Corn was as good as wheat; he had furnished "platform" beds at his own expense, although one room was not yet so equipped; and the wood for fuel was just outside the fort and fetching it offered no inconvenience.[42]

Wright seemed to win a complete victory in October 1767, when the assembly agreed to provide the "barrack necessarys" for Augusta and

Frederica. Several months elapsed before the resolution was funded. By June 1768 even the hard-to-please Fuser commented that the men at the frontier forts, Augusta, Prince George, and Charlotte, were as well provided for as those in Charlestown.[43]

The year 1768 was a troubled one. The seaboard towns complained about the Townshend duties. Frustrated by the government's refusal to establish courts in the Carolina up-country, and determined to put an end to increasing lawlessness, self-appointed vigilantes calling themselves Regulators formed posses and waged war against outlaws. In Georgia, the hostility between the Indians and backcountry people continued unabated and the condition of the Indian trade steadily deteriorated. In light of all this unrest, it was a shock to Governor Wright to receive a letter from General Gage saying that the troops were to be withdrawn from the South. Gage's letter seemed petulant; the Georgia Assembly need no longer worry about the expense of supplying His Majesty's troops according to law, he said. "They will now be eased of that Burthen as Captain Fuser will receive Orders soon to withdraw the Garrisons in South Carolina and Georgia and embark for the Northward with the Three Companys under His Command." Gage told Fuser to turn Fort Augusta over to the local militia, which would need it in case of an Indian attack. He did not care what happened to Forts Frederica and George.[44] John Stuart was embarrassed that he did not have earlier notice of the decision to abandon the forts. He vented his displeasure upon Fuser in a shouting match on the streets of Charlestown. William Bull, acting as governor again after the transfer of Thomas Boone, informed Gage that Carolina would maintain Forts Prince George and Charlotte at the expense of the province.[45]

Georgia was completely disarmed for the first time since Oglethorpe founded the colony, and James Wright was distraught. He might have been thinking about the contradictions in the policies of 1763, the inconsistencies of the efforts to regulate trade, the whimsical decision to disband the rangers and to close Fort Augusta just after it was rebuilt, and more when he wrote to Gage: "I cannot help lamenting when I reflect on the whole British policy respecting America for between 2 and 3 years past, which I conceive has been extremely mistaken, and

they will probably be convinced of it when it is too late or near it."
Two of the most flourishing colonies in America, he concluded, were
left without a single regular soldier.[46]

In addition to the contradictions in the Indian policies, Wright must
have had in mind the passage and repeal of the Stamp Act. For a time
in early 1766, he was afraid that agitators from Charlestown would stir
up trouble. He expected a mob of country people to march on Savannah, but nothing came of it. Some well-disposed gentlemen went out
into the country and quieted the malcontents. At that time, Wright
still had the rangers if he needed them. By 1768 that resource was taken
from him.[47] The only protection Georgia had left was the imaginary
wall from the Ogeechee to the St. Marys built by Lachlan McGillivray, George Galphin, and the Creek Indians and supported by their
mutual trust.

CHAPTER FOURTEEN
A Savannah Gentleman

Lachlan McGillivray demonstrated his business acumen by taking advantage of the opportunities at hand. He had a knack for being on the cutting edge of crucial changes in the shaping of the frontier. He left Scotland for a better life at Darien when Georgia was struggling for survival under Oglethorpe. When that settlement declined, he entered the thriving Indian trade. He left the wilderness to become one of the first merchant-storekeepers in the frontier town of Augusta. Finally, he settled in Savannah, where the merchant planters were building a society. McGillivray joined John Graham, one of Georgia's wealthiest men, in a mercantile partnership.[1] They imported goods on commission; among their customers were the Indian merchants and traders. Thus McGillivray moved up the economic ladder, from trader in the Indian country, to storekeeper in a frontier town, to importer in the colonial metropolis.

Lachlan McGillivray's move to Savannah put him squarely in the midst of a major reshaping of Georgia society which followed the legalization of slavery in 1751. Peter Wood has argued persuasively that there was a time during the first quarter-century of Carolina's existence when black people were employed in useful trades and were regarded as equal members of the community, at least potentially.[2] Alden Vaughan has made the same contention about Indians before the mid-eighteenth century but asserts that Anglo-Americans never believed that blacks were assimilable.[3] The argument is interesting, but in the case of blacks it had been settled by the time slavery was permitted in Georgia. When Carolinians turned to a staple economy built on the cultivation of rice, blacks became the majority and the nervous white establishment enacted the harsh Barbadian slave code. Blacks were, by definition, chattel and therefore unassimilable.

Historians Betty Wood, Alan Gallay, and Darold D. Wax have focused their attention on the mass movement of Carolinians into Georgia after 1751 and the formation of a plantation elite in Georgia.[4] Between 1746 and 1766 South Carolinians accounted for more new settlers in Georgia than Europe or any other American colony. Jonathan Bryan was conspicuous among these newcomers, who knew exactly what they wanted when they came. They intended to emulate the life-style of successful Carolinians such as Benjamin Smith, Miles Brewton, and Henry Laurens. They wanted land on which to grow rice with the object of living comfortably in town. Charlestown was the preferred town, but Savannah would have to do.

The acceptance of plantation slavery united Georgians of different cultural origins. The Darien Scots, who resisted the movement to the interior and managed to cling to the land during the difficult decade of the 1740s, were quick to take advantage of their proximity to the best rice lands. In January 1775, the residents of St. Andrew Parish, headed by Lachlan McIntosh, drew up a series of resolutions supporting the people of Boston. One of the resolutions was a denunciation of slavery reminiscent of the Dunbar statement of 1739. None of the slaveowners, however, freed their slaves.[5] A community of Puritans from Massachusetts by way of Dorchester, South Carolina, established the town of Midway above Darien, and the community dispersed into plantations. The Salzburgers at Ebenezer adapted their views regarding slavery to the times. Historian William Withuhn has noted that good Pastor Johann Martin Bolzius was conspicuous among those who joined the Darien Scots in their antislavery petition of 1739. By 1748, however, most of his people decided they needed the help of slave labor, and Bolzius wrote to the Trustees asking them to ignore his last position on the subject and to permit slavery under certain restrictions.[6] Like the Midway Puritans, the Salzburgers began to scatter onto individual farms. Neither Midway nor Ebenezer survived into the next century.

The dramatic influx of Carolinians into the low country has obscured the fact that slave labor was used in the Augusta area from the time of the first settlement in 1736. The so-called malcontents of Savannah complained that it was "absolutely certain that if these Negroes were not indulged them, not one trader would settle on that side of the river."[7] They maintained that Augusta's vaunted prosperity was owing to slave labor. Thomas Causton, the Trustees' storekeeper, admitted that sixty bushels of corn were harvested at Augusta for every ten in Savannah. In 1746 William Stephens wrote that the Augustans had employed slaves for so long that there was no use doing anything to stop it.[8]

A representative backcountry plantation was advertised for sale in 1769. The five-hundred-acre estate included the main house with a central hall and two rooms on each side, an attached kitchen, and a storehouse. Nearby structures included a smokehouse, as well as a "meathouse" and "milkhouse" with brick foundations, a chicken house, a barn, and a storage building large enough for a wagon, cart, and chaise. In addition, there was a stable for eight horses. Three new corn houses could each hold a thousand bushels. There were an overseer's house and slave cabins. Thirty slaves, thirty head of cattle, and seventy sheep were included in the sale. In addition to extensive apple and plum orchards, corn and indigo were produced on the plantation. The owner was selling because his other business took up too much of his time.[9]

In the ownership of plantations and management of slaves, the backcountry gave the example to the low country. During the first four years of royal government, from 1755 to 1759, all of the following Augustans possessed enough slaves to warrant at least five hundred acres of land: Martin Campbell, Francis McCartan, John Rae, Daniel Clark, John Fitch, George Galphin, William Newberry, James Parris, Thomas Red, Alexander Shaw, William Struthers, John Pettigrew, Edward Barnard, and, of course, Lachlan McGillivray.[10] Economic differences fueled a rivalry between the low country and backcountry.

Savannahians pointed to the way Augustans flouted the Trustees' regulations; later, they complained that the trade of the interior went to Charlestown. The factional bickering that brought down the Reynolds administration was regional in nature. It was partly regional one-upsmanship that led Edward Barnard to donate an organ to Savannah's Christ Church in 1765.[11] Augusta's St. Paul's had its organ two years earlier.

It could be argued that in the spirit of regional competition the low-country planters merely emulated those of the interior. Actually, the first Augustans were Carolinians and Carolina values shaped their conduct from the beginning. Although historians have focused their attention on the tidewater rice lands, in fact the Carolinization of Georgia began in the backcountry and, after 1751, spread to the rest of the province.

While he was ascending the economic ladder, McGillivray made progress along the political and social scales. When he moved to Savannah, more affluent Georgians were engaged in establishing what was then referred to as "society" and what modern social scientists like to call an elite. The model was that of the Carolina merchant-planter, who owned scattered rice and indigo plantations but preferred to live in a handsome house in town. Plantations were given titles reminiscent of old English manors. Some of those near Savannah were Hermitage, Valambrossa, Hope, Isle of Hope, Cedar Grove, Mulberry Hill, Wild Horn, and, of course, McGillivray's Vale Royal. These merchant-planters traveled about in phaetons and riding chairs. They dressed in silk breeches, lambskin gloves, painted hose, and powdered wigs, the finest London could provide. They sniffed smelling salts from crystal bottles, carried silver toothpick cases, and calculated time with sand-glasses that measured from two hours to a quarter of a minute. They enjoyed dances, horse races, and celebrations such as St. Andrew's Day, Guy Fawkes Day, and the king's birthday.[12] Savannah was a different town from the cluster of shacks McGillivray had seen when he first came to Georgia.

McGillivray's exploits in running the line through the swamps enhanced his celebrity status in Savannah. In addition to being elected captain of militia, he was made justice of the peace and returned to the Commons House of Assembly representing Christ Church Parish. He comported himself like other members of Georgia's new gentry. He had his riding chairs and horses, his house and range of lots in Savannah, his scattered plantations with names like Springfield and Sabine Fields, in addition to Vale Royal with its thousand acres. He bred prize Chickasaw horses and raced them on Savannah's race days.[13]

James Wright, whose twelve plantations set a mark for other aspiring gentlemen to match, introduced McGillivray to Lord Hillsborough in London as a man of "very considerable property."[14] McGillivray must have been well off indeed to impress the governor. As a gentleman of very considerable property, McGillivray could afford an occasional beau geste. He presented Bellamy Roche, daughter of former trader and deputy provost Matthew Roche, with a slave girl named Cassandra because of the "good will and affection" he had for her. He gave two servant girls to Tamar Oates, the daughter of the manager of Vale Royal, on the occasion of her wedding. He gave his godson James Fraser Barnard, son of Edward Barnard of Augusta and grandson of James Fraser, 350 acres of prime land outside Savannah because of his "love, friendship and great regard" for young James. Later he presented the same godson with a manservant. To George McKenzie, son of his friend William McKenzie, he gave a town lot in Savannah.[15] Clearly, McGillivray was a man of generous impulses and was wealthy enough to indulge them.

McGillivray's will, drawn up in June 1767, is an index to his closest connections. John McGillivray, then in Mobile, was the heir to Vale Royal and the Hutchinson Island tract. The reason for this preferred treatment was that Lachlan had promised John an inheritance to induce him to come to America. If John died without heirs (and he did) the two plantations would pass to William, the chief of the McGillivrays. In case William had no children, the properties would be divided between the oldest son of Lachlan's patron, Archibald McGillivray of Daviot, and the son of Farquhar McGillivray of Dalcrombie. These stipulations reveal Lachlan's determination to perpetuate the clan with Vale Royal as an American Dunmaglass.

Lachlan's son Alexander, then seventeen years old and employed at the mercantile house of Inglis and Hall, would receive £1,000 in addition to the properties Lachlan had purchased in Alexander's name. A thousand pounds was willed to the oldest son of his sister Jean, very likely the nephew called "Dunie." Cousins mentioned were James and Alexander McIntosh of Mobile; Lachlan, Archibald McGillivray's third son; and Daniel McGillivray, formerly known as Daniel McDonald.

The oldest sons of John Graham, Edward Barnard, and David Douglass were generously remembered, as was Elizabeth, daughter of Thomas Burrington, clerk of assembly. William Struthers, merchant at Mobile, and George Galphin were mentioned as "loving friends." John Rae of Rae's Hall, his wife, Catherine, and their daughter Jean Somerville were included. John Oates, his overseer, and John's daughter Tamar were remembered. The rest of Lachlan's extensive possessions were to be divided five ways, one part to son Alexander, one to cousin John in Mobile, one to cousin William in Strathnairn, one to sister Jean, and one to his friends and fellow merchants Alexander Inglis and John Graham. Executors of the will were John McGillivray, James Habersham, and John and James Graham, his business partners. Lachlan's will testifies to his devotion to his family, his loyalty to old friends, and his comfortable association with Savannah's gentry.[16] Conspicuously absent from his will were Sehoy and his daughters Sophia and Jeannet. They would be taken care of by the Wind Clan.

The records do not reveal Lachlan McGillivray's attitude toward his slaves. We know that some household slaves occupied a privileged position in the McGillivray household, notably Charles and Polly, both of whom served Lachlan and later his children. In the first year after he moved from Augusta to Savannah, McGillivray hired out fifty of his slaves to Charles Wright for a pittance of fourteen shillings a month, with the stipulation that John Oates go with them as overseer and that they be given adequate food and lodging. Incidentally, one of these slaves was named Adair in honor of McGillivray's old friend.[17] Later, John Oates managed Vale Royal and from time to time advertised for the return of runaway slaves. Oates lost his wife in 1765; he posted a notice in the *Gazette* that she had run away.[18] Oates later lived with

Rose, one of McGillivray's slaves. In 1780, Oates gave Rose one-half of the lot he lived on in Savannah and four slaves for her own use. Trustees for Rose were Lachlan's son Alexander and James Robertson, the attorney general.[19]

Lachlan McGillivray's attitude toward slavery was the same as that of other Georgians. He accepted the institution as a fact of economic and social life. If a planter wanted to grow rice, he regarded black labor as essential. When he joined John Graham's mercantile house, McGillivray entered the business of trafficking in slaves. Curiously, from a latter-day vantage point, no stigma attached to the merchant importer of slaves, either in Charlestown or Savannah. The New England merchants who subsidized slave ships and the captains who transported the human cargo on the terrible "middle passage" were regarded as squalid individuals engaged in a cruel enterprise. The merchants were merely doing an essential service for the planters, and the planters were easily persuaded that the slaves were better off under their care than they would have been anywhere else. The most active Savannah firm dealing in slaves was that headed by West Indian newcomers Basil Cowper and William and Edward Telfair. Inglis and Hall, the firm in which Alexander McGillivray served as an apprentice, was next most involved. Scots Graham and McGillivray and Yorkshire-born James Habersham and Joseph Clay were also importers of slaves. Charlestown supplied almost all of Georgia's slaves between 1750 and 1764 and transshipped slaves in increasing numbers after that. Beginning in 1765, Georgia merchants established their own connections with English firms for the direct importation of slaves from Africa.[20] The risk of scurvy and other diseases was great on the long voyage, and in 1766 the assembly took Governor Wright's advice to establish a lazaretto near the mouth of the Savannah River to impound slaves who had contracted contagious diseases while on ship.[21] Even with the risks involved, the direct trade with Africa was preferable to importing slaves from the West Indies. The Georgia Assembly imposed a tax on blacks "from the West India islands" in 1761 because such slaves were likely to be criminals or refractory.[22] The Keith Read Collection in the University of Georgia Special Collections contains an interesting memorandum

written in 1775 and signed by James Wright, John Graham, Joseph
Clay, Lachlan McGillivray, William McGillivray, William Struthers,
and Stephen Deane asking a London firm to confine the purchase of
slaves to the west coast of Africa from Sena Gambia to the Gold Coast
but not to buy "Ibos, Conga's, Cape Mounts and Angola Negroes." It
was stipulated that two-thirds of the contingent of 200 to 250 should
be males not exceeding thirty years of age. Women should not be older
than twenty-five.[23] The instructions reveal Georgians' preference for
Gambia slaves capable of doing arduous work. It also reveals the well-
placed circle of business associates with whom Lachlan McGillivray
worked and into which he introduced the recently arrived chief of the
McGillivrays, William.

The busiest season for slave sales was between April and September.
Sales were brisk because the demand was high. Graham and Com-
pany advertised the arrival of a shipment in May 1770: "To Be Sold,
In Savannah on Thursday the 13 instant, A Cargo Consisting of Three
Hundred and Forty Healthy New Negroes, Chiefly Men, Just arrived
in the Ship Sally, Capt. George Evans, after a short passage from the
Rice Coast of Africa. N.B. The Sale will begin at 11 o'clock in the
Forenoon and no Slaves sold or bargained for till the gun is fired."[24]
The notice hints that buyers should curb their eagerness.

Georgia merchants risked little or no capital of their own and vended
slaves for a commission of 5 percent of the gross sales. The real importance of the slave trade, as Darold Wax has pointed out, was that
customers were attracted to buy various commodities on sale. Planters
who bought slaves on commission were likely to purchase whatever
else they needed from the same importers.[25]

Both as an importer of slaves and a planter who employed slaves,
Lachlan McGillivray was at the center of Georgia's social revolution.
By 1775 there were fifteen thousand black persons in Georgia, and the
ethnic composition of the colony was fundamentally altered.

McGillivray continued to acquire land: 500 acres in St. George
Parish in 1768, 750 on each side of the Altamaha in 1769, and another
1,000 of potentially valuable rice land on the same river later in the year.
Alan Gallay has documented Jonathan Bryan's "obsession to accumu-

late land" as a characteristic of the emerging planter elite. Like Bryan, McGillivray bought and sold properties almost continually and retained a princely amount. His most valuable property was Vale Royal's thousand acres, valued at £6,000. Three tracts of rice land on Hutchinson Island were worth £4,154. He acquired substantial holdings in the region between the Altamaha and the St. Marys, which was opened after the expulsion of the Spanish in 1763. Eight tracts there totaled 7,100 acres. He owned 950 acres on the Ogeechee and 1,000 acres in the Halifax district. He maintained a house and two lots in Augusta and 400 acres outside that town, two houses and four lots in Savannah, and a lot each in Hardwicke and on Tybee Island. McGillivray estimated the value of his holdings at £21,504. In fact, they brought £23,084 when sold as confiscated property by the state of Georgia.[26]

McGillivray had property in South Carolina also. I have noted Edmond Atkin's intense aversion to McGillivray's acquisition of the Chickasaw reserve on Horse Creek, South Carolina. He retained a comparatively small farm of under two hundred acres there and rented it to Daniel Wallicon. His interest in the old Chickasaw tract led him to become involved in a highly public and protracted debate of the sort that resulted in duels at a slightly later date in Georgia's history. This duel was fought with pens, and the stage was James Johnston's *Georgia Gazette*. McGillivray's adversary was the Reverend John Joachim Zubly, whose pamphlets denouncing British colonial policy would soon make him famous.

Zubly was a native of Switzerland whose family was among the first settlers of Purysburg, South Carolina. Zubly was ordained in London and arrived in Carolina in 1745. He married Anna Tobler, the sister of Ulrich, the New Windsor surveyor, who was killed in the Cherokee war of 1760. After serving as pastor of a Congregational church near Charlestown, Zubly was called to the Independent Presbyterian Church in Savannah.[27] Lachlan McGillivray was a member of the congregation. There is evidence that McGillivray, a good Scottish Presbyterian, considered Zubly's Congregationalism too radical and that the religious differences led to the open rupture.

The extended controversy made tedious reading for those who were not involved, and it is impossible to say who was right and who was wrong. Zubly asserted that part of McGillivray's land belonged to him, and he also claimed a portion of George Galphin's property and a tract belonging to the widow of his brother-in-law Ulrich Tobler. McGillivray denied Zubly's right to the land and chided him for conduct unbecoming a minister. Zubly replied that although McGillivray had done great services for his country and was universally held in high esteem, he was wrong in this case, and Zubly had no choice but to bring the matter to a court of law. As a result of a court decision, McGillivray, Galphin, and Mrs. Tobler were ordered to pay a small amount of compensation for encroaching on Zubly's land.[28] McGillivray appealed the decision and posted signs around New Windsor stating that the titles were still under litigation. Zubly wrote an open letter saying that McGillivray, who had the reputation of being an honorable man, had not dealt honorably with him. "Money can do so much," he wrote, "but it cannot alter the nature of things or make right what is wrong."[29]

McGillivray, his dander up, accused Zubly of being "an avaricious, grasping man," and the debate ended on that strident note.[30] It was a pity that so much rhetoric was devoted to a matter of such little consequence to the general public. The same pages of the *Gazette* carried arguments of greater moment such as the successive installments of John Dickinson's "Letters from a Pennsylvania Farmer," which maintained that the Townshend duties on imports were unconstitutional because their purpose was to raise revenue. If not fraught with any profound political significance, the debate reveals the intense concern of Georgians about the absorbing matter of land acquisition. McGillivray's manner and tone were those of one of the first citizens of Savannah society, loyal to his friends, sensitive about his reputation, skilled in the classic prose of his day, and exhibiting an imperiousness of expression not seen in his earlier writing.

The debate put an intolerable strain on the relationship between Zubly and McGillivray. One does not call his minister a greedy, grasping person and then sit down before him to hear God's word of a Sunday. The tension that already existed between the conservative Scottish Presbyterians and the more radical dissenters reached a breaking point.

Zubly complained that the Scots allied themselves with the Anglican establishment and "even effect a difference between Presbyterianism and my people, whom they call Dissenters."[31]

McGillivray was joined by his partner, Councillor John Graham, Councillor Lewis Johnston, Attorney General William Graeme, Commissary General George Baillie, his old friend John Rae, John Simpson, John Jamieson, and John Glen in a committee to sponsor the building of a Presbyterian meetinghouse. They had in mind a building modeled after James Gibbs's St. Martin-in-the-Fields of London with its classic portico and handsome steeple. Subscriptions for the erection of the church were handled by the firms of Inglis and Hall, and Cowper and Telfair.[32] Nothing came of their effort so McGillivray and his friends had to endure Zubly or attend services at Christ Church. Interestingly, a building such as they envisioned was erected in 1816 after the plans of John Holden Greene for the Independent Presbyterian Church, and it stands today as one of Savannah's architectural treasures.

Contemporary materials provide brief glimpses of McGillivray's activities as a merchant. His two visits to London in 1764 and 1770 were for business purposes, as was his trip to "the northward" in 1767. He imported merchandise through the firm of Cowles and Company of Bristol. Henry Laurens of Charlestown described him as a responsible, honest merchant. James Wright was one of McGillivray's clients. Wright exported his huge rice crop through McGillivray and bought what he needed in London through McGillivray.[33] To cut middlemen's costs in his import-export business, Lachlan joined John McGillivray in purchasing half-interest in the ship *Inverness*. London merchants John Clarke and David Milligan owned the other half. As further evidence that Lachlan looked after his own, the ship was captained by Daniel McGillivray.[34]

The portrait of McGillivray, the gentleman merchant-planter, becomes atypical when one considers his family. What did Sehoy and her children think of this kind of civilization, as far removed from the life-style of Little Tallassee as the province of Georgia could offer? Unfortunately, the records are mute on Sehoy's role, nor do we know the date of her death. We know that her daughter Sophia and Sophia's husband, Benjamin Durant, lived in Savannah for a time and that Durant replaced Oates as manager of Vale Royal.[35]

Alexander McGillivray grew into young manhood at Vale Royal. He was six when McGillivray left Little Tallassee for Augusta, ten when his father moved to Savannah. It was common knowledge among his contemporaries that Alexander studied in Charlestown. It may be assumed that family tradition is correct in ascribing his education to Farquhar McGillivray. In 1767, Alexander's name appeared on a number of his father's legal transactions for which he acted as a witness. Doubtless this was part of his education, too. In conveying two servants to Tamar Oates, Lachlan stipulated that if Tamar's "heir" died, one servant would go to "my natural begotten son." During this time Alexander supposedly worked as a clerk in Samuel Elbert's mercantile firm and certainly clerked with Inglis and Hall.[36]

His ties to his family and the chain of trade linked Lachlan to the Creeks on the distant frontier. In spite of his new status as merchant-planter, he was known as an expert in Indian affairs and continued to serve as a consultant to royal officials in that capacity. According to James Adair, McGillivray and Galphin argued with John Stuart about his attempts to maintain peace between the Choctaws and Creeks. The point was sensitive because Stuart and Gage were under orders from Lord Shelburne to reconcile the various Indian tribes. Adair referred to "two respectable, intelligent old Indian traders," gave their initials, and said that they had frequently dissuaded Stuart from "ever dabling [sic] in such muddy waters." It was their firm opinion, which Adair shared, that the best defense against the Indians was to permit the tribes to continue their habit of sporadic war against each other. Adair acknowledged that some clergymen in England might try to persuade the king's ministers to follow a policy of brotherly love, but those reverend gentlemen had never witnessed the horrors of an Indian war.[37]

Adair completed the manuscript of his history of the American Indians in 1769 and in the introduction acknowledged the part played by McGillivray and Galphin. "You often complained how the public had been imposed upon, either by fictitious and fabulous, or very superficial and conjectural accounts of the Indian natives—and as often wished me to devote my leisure hours to drawing up an Indian system." He stated that his completed work "was composed more from a regard to your request than any forward desire of my own." [38] Their encouragement had inspired him to write, and he was especially pleased by their approval of what he had written. If his book afforded Englishmen a better knowledge of the Indians, McGillivray and Galphin should share the credit. Adair's praise of the two soared as he celebrated their public spirit, social and domestic virtues, and zealous service to their country, which had made their names more illustrious than high-sounding titles. In the conclusion of his dedication, he wished them continued calm and prosperity so that "the widow, the fatherless and the stranger may always joyfully return (as in past years) from your hospitable houses." [39] George Croghan, Sir William Johnson's deputy in the Northern Department, was included in the dedication, but the references in the introduction and in the text were to the two southern trading partners.

Adair's narrative reflects his personality; it is effusive, imaginative, and exaggerated. Nevertheless, it is valued by historians as a realistic insight into Indian customs. What was Adair's point in writing it? What was McGillivray's point in urging him to publish it? Adair had three important recommendations to the ministry: permit industrious settlers to colonize the Chickasaw country on the Mississippi so as to secure that frontier against the Spaniards in New Orleans; abandon free licensing, which had almost ruined the Indian trade, in favor of a restricted number of orderly traders; and introduce the Indians to a more diverse economy so that they could become productive and self-sufficient. Adair did not advocate the removal of the Indians but seems to have in mind the kind of civilization the Cherokees of Georgia adopted after 1820. He realized that the independent Creeks (he called them Muskohges) would not readily change their ways. He thought they could be influenced by Lachlan McGillivray or George Galphin if either were made superintendent. "Every Indian trader knows from long experience," he wrote, "that both these gentlemen have a greater influence over the dangerous Muskohge, than any other besides." [40]

Adair's personal story was a bitter one of services unrequited and a lack of official recognition. His most recent misfortune was his effort to adhere to John Stuart's policy of fixed prices and the limitation on rum, and as a result he had been ruined by the competition of the many unsavory people who disregarded the regulations. He complained to the governor of West Florida; his complaints were verified, but nothing was done.[41]

McGillivray must have hoped that Adair's book would help reform the trade policy. He would have been equally concerned about the ministry's erratic shifts regarding Indian relations. After 1763, the various ministers condoned a policy of encouraging the tribes to fight one another. The leading agitator in America was West Florida's feisty governor, George Johnstone. Johnstone believed that the Upper Creeks were too arrogant and intractable, and he encouraged the Choctaws and Chickasaws to annoy them. Johnstone had the full support of the traders in his district, particularly James Adair. John Stuart's cousin Charles went along with the policy even though John was not enthusiastic about it. John McGillivray was Charles Stuart's confidant and sometime emissary.

John McGillivray exploited his opportunities in Mobile as successfully as Lachlan did in Augusta and Savannah. In partnership with a merchant named Peter Swanson, he established warehouses at Manchac on the Mississippi and operated a trade network between the Mississippi and Alabama rivers. When the peripatetic William Bartram arrived in Mobile in 1777, he entrusted his precious collection of specimens to the house of McGillivray and Swanson, to be shipped to the learned Dr. John Fothergill in London. Like his cousin Lachlan, John McGillivray was a source of valuable information on Indian affairs. John Stuart and his deputies learned to rely on McGillivray's advice. In May 1766, he told Charles Stuart that James Colbert was following orders to foment a Choctaw attack on the Creeks and that soon the Creeks would have it "hot and warm."[42]

That same month a distinguished delegation of Upper Creeks paid a visit to West Florida Governor Johnstone. Emistisiguo, the Mortar, and the Gun Merchant, all three bearers of Stuart's medals, headed the party. Emistisiguo's status was confirmed when the Gun Merchant stated in the presence of all that Emistisiguo was their king. Curiously, Johnstone did not forward Emistisiguo's talk to his superiors but only the Gun's and the Mortar's. The latter was so annoyed at the English that he resigned his medal. He was angry that the English should attempt to set Indians against one another. Emistisiguo was more diplomatic and logical. John Stuart summarized the points the chief made to Johnstone: the English supplied arms to the Choctaws, Chickasaws, and even the small tribes on the Mississippi; the English acted as incendiaries in provoking the Indians to fight; and prices had not been lowered as agreed to. Stuart sent the complaints to London with the remark that it was bad policy to appear to instigate war.[43]

Johnstone lost the little patience he had when two traders were murdered by a party of Creeks, and he called for a war of extermination. He said that all the money spent on the various conferences was wasted and blamed "the imbecility of government."[44] Stuart employed the best method of disarming the fiery governor; he sent Johnstone's letter to London. In 1766 the Earl of Shelburne was the secretary for the Southern Department, and he took umbrage at Johnstone's attitude, particularly to the "imbecility" reference. Shelburne's first decisive action was to remove Johnstone as governor.[45]

Shelburne then scolded John Stuart and the southern governors for fomenting trouble and instructed them to inform the Indians that the king loved them alike and that they should stop fighting. Shelburne's Indian policy was as high-minded and as visionary as his policy of opening the trade to all comers; he wanted the Indians to look to the English as "their Guardians and Defenders . . . the only Refuge they will think of seeking in their Distress." Their boundaries must be respected, and trade must be conducted fairly. Such a policy was superior to "that of spiriting up one Tribe to cut the throat of another." Shelburne informed Stuart on February 17, 1767, that he had written to all the governors instructing them to restore peace and harmony among the tribes.[46] John Stuart and his brother dutifully adopted the new line, to the disgust of James Adair and to the dismay of Governor Wright and the McGillivrays in Mobile and Savannah. The policy of telling the Indians not to fight was almost as bad as telling them to fight. Either way, it was interfering in the internal affairs of the nations involved.

The peace policy continued to prevail under Hillsborough, who was appointed to the powerful new post of secretary of state for America in 1768. "I am taking steps to accomplish a reconciliation between the Chactaws and the Creeks," Stuart assured Hillsborough on April 14, 1769.[47] Stuart called the Upper Creek chiefs to Augusta to persuade them to stop their war against the Choctaws. Emistisiguo, for whom visits to Augusta had been routine since 1763, agreed on behalf of his people. In Mobile, Charles Stuart secured the consent of the Choctaws: "I had made every Choctaw throw away his war stick," he reported proudly.[48]

Emistisiguo kept his word to John Stuart. He went to see Charles Stuart in Mobile and told him that some northern Indians had tried to incite him against the Choctaws, but he told them that he had promised the great beloved man of Charlestown that he would bury the hatchet. General Gage confirmed the success of the policy and credited the mediation of Stuart.[49]

When Charles Stuart learned that John McGillivray intended to travel to Charlestown, he conveyed a message through him to John Stuart about his progress in reconciling the Choctaws and Creeks.[50] John visited his brother Farquhar, whose illness may have been the principal reason for John's going to Charlestown. Farquhar died in August 1770, soon after Lachlan sailed for England. John McGillivray saw Lachlan in Savannah before the latter's departure. They must have talked of Lachlan's plans to see his sister in Strathnairn and to attempt to persuade the chief of the McGillivrays, John's brother, to come join them in America. The cousins would have agreed that the deplorable condition of the trade should be brought to the attention of the ministry, and they saw eye to eye on the dangers of the policy of restraining the Indians. Governor Wright gave McGillivray a letter to be delivered personally to Lord Hillsborough and sent another letter introducing McGillivray as one who was thoroughly familiar with Indian affairs and whose judgment could be trusted. Wright even recommended McGillivray to His Majesty's attention for appointment to Wright's council.[51]

Hillsborough replied that he was looking forward to his meeting with McGillivray and conversing about Indian affairs. He was open to suggestions and would be glad "if that conversation shall furnish any hints that may be improved for the further advantage of the King's service."[52] Wright wrote again in July to say that McGillivray had embarked. He used the letter to convey his misgivings about the peace policy. The Creek leaders had been summoned to Mobile to confirm the peace with the Choctaws, and "the Indians will now have nothing to amuse themselves with . . . it is highly probable that they will pick a quarrel with us."[53]

Although Hillsborough made no direct reference to McGillivray's visit, he adopted the policy advocated by Wright and McGillivray. He warned Stuart of the danger of "promoting union among the savages" and thereby endangering neighboring provinces. The new policy was "to avoid interfering in the Quarrels and Disputes between one Nation and another" and to observe the agreements already made.[54] Nonintervention became the new watchword. Once more John Stuart was forced into an embarrassing change of tactics. He put the best face on it in a letter to Hillsborough. Arranging peace between the Choctaws and Creeks was not what he had in mind, he explained. He saw the possibility that the Creeks and Choctaws would settle their differences without his mediation and did not want to appear to oppose their reconciliation.[55] The sudden shifts from warmongering to peacekeeping to nonintervention added to the confusion of the post-1763 era.

McGillivray's unheralded mission was a high point in his career. He was a trusted counselor of English lords as well as of Indian kings. In the past he had influenced British policy subtly through governors. Now he brought his powers of suasion directly to bear on a king's minister.

McGillivray did not dally long in London after his conference with Hillsborough. He received notice that his mother was near death at Inverness and took passage for the northward. His return to Inverness must have brought forth a mixture of emotions—anxiety for his mother, nostalgia for reminders of his boyhood, anticipation about renewing old acquaintances. As his ship sailed past the battery at Fort George into the great bay called the Moray Firth, he would have watched the green hills closing in on each side as the firth narrowed in its approach to the River Ness. On the east shore was the church at Petty, where the warrior-chief Alexander was buried after Culloden. Finally, there was Inverness town with its characteristic red stone buildings clustering on both sides of the river and the fort on Castle Hill dominating all. It had been thirty-five years since Lachlan had seen Inverness.

Janet McIntosh McGillivray died before Lachlan's arrival so his homecoming was more somber than it might have been. Highland wakes were long and wet, with relatives gathering from far and wide. With all the waking and welcoming, McGillivray had to apologize to an acquaintance for neglecting business, explaining that he had been kept drunk since he reached town. The acquaintance, a Mobile-based merchant, admitted that Lachlan's condition was one "he could hardly avoid." [56]

Lachlan was a celebrity in Invernesshire. A man who lived with and fought alongside Indians and who was fabulously wealthy besides was noticed in his native shire and strath. There were happy moments with Jean, his sister, and with William, his cousin and chief of the McGillivrays. There were poignant moments when he visited the field of Culloden and saw the Well of the Dead, where Alexander McGillivray fell.

Lachlan lingered in Scotland throughout 1771 and part of 1772, taking a keen interest in Inverness politics and in his family's business. He finally convinced his cousin William, who was still a bachelor, to put his affairs in order and join him in Georgia. He promised to donate some of his property to William to get him started as a Georgia planter. To provide the proud William with ready cash, he bought parcels of William's holdings. One of his purchases was Ballanagarek, the farm rented by his sister Jean and her husband, Duncan Roy McGillivray. Lachlan soon became impatient with the men who, like Duncan, used their family ties to claim exemption from manual labor. In the days before Culloden, when tackmen were responsible for raising warriors for the laird, there might have been some excuse for idleness. There was none now that the Highlands were demilitarized. "Be assured that

I have no pleasure in throwing away money to no purpose," he wrote to Jean from Inverness. He expected the farm to produce. If so, he would be encouraged to invest more in cattle and improvements. He had become thoroughly disgusted with his brother-in-law, Duncan Roy McGillivray, and called him a "despicable, worthless wretch." If he would not work, Lachlan would turn him out. It outraged Lachlan to learn that Duncan and a tenant of his could not be bothered to put up the sheep one recent evening. Instead, they waited until Jean returned from a visit to Anne at Dunmaglass and obliged her to go out after dark to bring in the sheep. "I find that you are so weak and silly to let that husband of yours do what he pleases," he scolded.[57] Lachlan was generous in his attention to Jean's children and arranged to take young Duncan or "Dunie" back to America for a visit. Farquhar McGillivray of Dalcrombie was charged with looking after the family estates as William prepared to leave the Highlands. Lachlan gave Farquhar instructions regarding the supervision of Ballanagarek. According to the clan history, Dalcrombie was "arrogant, callous and cruel." But Farquhar respected wealthy men and did what Lachlan and later what John McGillivray asked him to do.[58]

Lachlan returned to America by way of London and there settled accounts with the merchants James and William Cowles. Henry Laurens reported seeing McGillivray in London in September 1772. On October 27, Lachlan and his nephew Dunie boarded the Georgia packet bound for Savannah. A few months later, William McGillivray followed them to America and became a Georgia rice planter. Lachlan turned over his Hutchinson Island estate to William.[59] William had every reason to expect that America would be as good to him as it had been to his cousin Lachlan and his brother John. It seemed that Lachlan's wish for him would come true, that the clan would be perpetuated in America and the seat of the clan would be transferred from Strathnairn to Georgia. It must have given deep satisfaction to Lachlan to introduce his cousin, the chief of the McGillivrays, to the gentlemen of Savannah.

CHAPTER FIFTEEN

The Second Congress
of Augusta, 1773

If Lachlan McGillivray visited with Governor Wright when he was in London in September 1772, and it is hard to imagine that they did not see each other when both were in town, Wright would have told him of a startling development. The Cherokees had offered to surrender a huge area of land in north Georgia in return for the cancellation of debts they owed to traders. Wright had come to England to obtain the consent of the authorities.

Upon his return to Georgia, McGillivray found everyone agog with news of the possible cession. They spoke of an extension of the boundary to the Oconee River. The line that was to be like a stone wall would be erased. The year 1773 was a fateful one; the chain of events that followed the Boston Tea Party is well-known. On the southern frontier the great land cession of 1773 would just as surely lead to revolution.

McGillivray's friend George Galphin was involved in the affair from the beginning. In December 1770, he and the other gentlemen of Augusta learned from some Cherokee traders that the Indians, despairing of paying their debts, were willing to give their land in exchange. Galphin, Edward Barnard, and the other merchants told the traders that the Indians should make the offer to Wright and Stuart. Andrew McLean, an Augusta merchant and a close friend of Stuart's deputy to the Cherokees, Alexander Cameron, told Cameron that the Augusta merchants did not instigate the transaction but were heartily in favor of the idea. Since it was likely to transpire, Cameron suggested that Stuart might want to take charge of the negotiations.[1]

Stuart was in an awkward situation again. He knew that Hillsborough frowned on any changes in the boundaries already set, but he also knew that Governor Wright was eager for the acquisition and was prepared to go to London to press for it. Stuart therefore informed Hillsborough that the Indians had proposed the cession and the traders "greedily grasped" at the offer. There and then the traders gave the Cherokees all the goods they had in the nation. And all of this happened without Stuart's knowledge.[2]

At first, Hillsborough was opposed to the plan. He told Stuart that the king was against it and the scheme should be quashed. "His Majesty does entirely disapprove such Proceedings," were his words. Seldom has a direct order of a high minister been so unavailing. It was not John Stuart's fault; he dutifully passed the message along to the merchants, traders, and Cherokees that the deal was off. The Cherokees, however, were determined to see it through. It was their land, they said, and they could do what they wanted with it.[3] Governor Wright was as eager for the exchange as the Cherokees were. Wright sailed for London on July 10, 1771, with his arguments ready. Wright proposed to raise £62,500 from the sale of the land. That was more than enough to redeem the Indians' debt to the traders. The traders could then pay the Augusta merchants, who in turn would pay the London exporters. The London merchants jumped on the bandwagon. Nine of them signed a memorial to the king urging favorable consideration of Wright's request.[4]

The great advantage of selling the land rather than giving it away in the usual manner was that people of property would settle the cession. Wright put it bluntly: "And, my lord, . . . they will, of course, be something better than the common sort of back country people." There would be enough money left over after all debts were paid to raise two troops of rangers and to build forts, churches, schoolhouses, and jails. From Georgia, acting governor James Habersham added a notion that had fascinated Parliament for years: silk could be grown in the new cession, he said.[5] Hillsborough was won over by the brilliance of the scheme. He told Wright to be sure to include John Stuart in the talks, and he wrote to Stuart that although he was loath to alter the Indian line, this particular cession "is in every light in which it can be viewed, an object deserving attention."[6]

Wright's imagination soared beyond the limited confines of the Cherokee cession in upper Georgia. If the Creeks could be persuaded to yield the strip between the Ogeechee and Oconee, then the backcountry settlers would have three fine rivers to carry their crops to market, the Savannah, the Ogeechee, and the Oconee; the latter flowed into the Altamaha. The mouth of the Altamaha at Darien was too shallow, but the projected new port city of Brunswick, just south of Darien, would serve as the outlet for the Oconee traffic. Wright saw himself as the master architect of the Georgia frontier.[7]

The rub was whether the Creeks would go along with such a splendid idea. Hillsborough was aware of that problem and made his approval conditional on the Creeks' acceptance. John Stuart and James Wright already knew of that potential shortcoming. When he first broached the matter to Hillsborough, Wright confided that he dared not tell the Creeks that he had anything to do with the plan but would intimate that the Cherokees were wholly responsible.[8] Another potential problem was posed by the infiltrating "borderers," who had already camped on the Cherokee cession. James Habersham warned Hillsborough that idle people, some of them great villains, had built their crude huts on the lands in question. Those who lived by hunting and plundering were "by no means the sort of people that should settle those lands." He did what he could; he issued a proclamation banishing the trespassers. Habersham had no way of enforcing the edict short of calling out the militia so it did little good. John Stuart shared Wright's and Habersham's opinion that these "crackers" would cause more trouble with the Indians and that industrious people from Britain, Ireland, or Germany should be given preference in the settlement.[9]

Stuart had deep misgivings about the project, yet he did not want to appear as a spoiler. He tactfully explained to Hillsborough that the last war had left the Cherokees destitute; they had no skins on hand with which to buy supplies. As a result, they had been forced to borrow from their traders. The situation was different with the Creeks. They continued to hunt during the war, and their traders made handsome profits. The Creeks claimed the same land the Cherokees were willing to give up, and because they were not debtors, they had no reason to cede.[10] Stuart's demurrer was lost amid the general clamor of approval. The Lords of Trade secured the king's blessing on the proposal on November 9, 1772. James Wright, the sponsor of the plan, was made a baronet. Hillsborough's successor, the Earl of Dartmouth, advised calling the Indians for another great congress at Augusta and wrote the following flattering words to Wright: "His Majesty, relying upon your zeal and integrity, has thought fit that you should have the principal direction of this important business."[11]

The single individual other than Wright who had most at stake in the unfolding drama was the great medal chief of Little Tallassee. If Wright was the architect of the cession of 1773, Emistisiguo had been the architect of the settlement of 1763. He had persuaded the reluctant headmen of the Upper Creek towns to accept the terms of the Augusta treaty over the vociferous objections of the Mortar to any yielding of territory. Each year subsequent to the treaty, Emistisiguo represented his people in reminding the English to adhere to their agreement. In June 1770, he went to Pensacola to tell Charles Stuart that the Virginians were encroaching on Creek hunting grounds and that traders were dealing with Indians in the woods for raw skins.[12]

In May of the following year Emistisiguo sent Stuart a talk in which he cited the many instances of interference with Indians who traveled the road to Augusta and reminded the English that the path "should be always free for their friends the Indians to pass and repass upon." While other chiefs followed the Mortar's lead and sulked in their tents, Emistisiguo documented each violation as though the English were not aware that the terms of the Augusta treaty were being ignored. "We are informed that the white people have encroached two days march over the land that was given them. We suppose that these people by coming over the Great Water have not seen the path which Mr. Stuart said should be like a mountain, not to be passed, or they certainly would not have done so," he told Stuart.[13]

Emistisiguo remembered that Lachlan McGillivray had come to live in his village at a young age and was satisfied to eat the same coarse food the Indians ate. This was his way of saying that McGillivray could be trusted. He went on to say that at Augusta in 1763 McGillivray had said that the line would be respected; the white men's cattle would stay over the line. Now cattle were being driven through his country. One man, he said, had started a plantation with forty black people beyond the line. He came at last to his main point. He had heard that the Cherokees had given the white people a body of land at the head of the Oconee. He did not threaten, but his clear implication was that this was another violation of the Augusta agreement.[14]

In December 1771 Emistisiguo delivered his most eloquent appeal to Stuart at a congress in Pensacola. "Everything goes now contrary to our agreement," he began. He was speaking as the mouth of the nation. He had gone to great lengths to gain acceptance for the treaty, and now it was coming apart. It was agreed that all persons found trading in the woods should be considered violators of the treaty and treated like the French or Spanish. Emistisiguo caused some of these traders to be plundered to show them the error of their ways. For that, he was reprimanded by the governor of South Carolina and by his own people. Stuart's reply sounded lame. He admitted that Emistisiguo was right but said that enforcement had been taken out of his hands and given to the governors; "although my intentions were good," he said, "yet they were frustrated."[15]

The chief then named the traders who drove cattle into his country, beginning with George Galphin. James McQueen had brought slaves with him and established a plantation. "I am now far advanced in life," the chief said, "and this is the first time I ever saw plantations settled in my nation."[16] Finally, he broached the topic of the Cherokee cession. The trader John Miller had said that Governor Wright would stop their trade if they did not agree to the land transaction. John Stuart denied that Wright had said any such thing and promised to report Miller for telling a lie. Emistisiguo returned to Okchoys to tell the Cherokees who gathered there for his answer that his nation had come to a decision. The land the Cherokees wanted to give away was Creek land also. The Creeks would not let the English have it.[17]

At this point, John Stuart, whose gout made him increasingly sedentary, dispatched David Taitt on a fact-finding mission to the Creek country. Taitt was a Scotsman who had been employed as a surveyor in West Florida. If he was the same man General Thomas Woodward referred to as "John Tate," and it seems that he was, he was the husband of Sehoy McPherson and the father of her son Davy Taitt. Sehoy was so close to Lachlan McGillivray's family that Benjamin Hawkins thought she was Alexander's sister.

Taitt was to be Stuart's eyes and ears. Stuart had only a dim notion of the geography of the Creek country, and existing maps were barely adequate. Taitt was to put his skills as a surveyor to good use and make a map of the region. He was instructed to discover any French or Spanish intrigues. Stuart gave him talks to deliver to Emistisiguo and Captain Alleck and sent him on his way.[18] Taitt was accompanied by Joseph Cornell, Stuart's paid interpreter to the Upper Creeks. They left Pensacola on January 30, 1772, and made their way up the Alabama River to the Coosa. The first trader they met was James Germany, McGillivray's former employee, whose plantation on the Tallapoosa was one of those which Emistisiguo complained about. Taitt and Cornell were received with the usual hospitality at Tuckabatchee, where they remained for several days.

Francis Lewis, a trader employed by George Galphin at Tuckabatchee, met the Indians when they came in from hunting, plied them with rum and exchanged goods for skins, then his Indian wife bought back the goods with more rum. He sold the same goods again and kept the profits. Taitt discovered that this had become a common practice. The Indians, of course, were left with neither skins nor goods.

Taitt's next stop was McGillivray's old town, Little Tallassee. Emistisiguo lived four miles away at a place called Hickory Ground and invited Taitt to come see him. He told Taitt he was going off to war—

nothing big—there was a man he had to kill. When he returned, he would call a conference of headmen to hear the talk sent by Taitt. He told Taitt that the Augusta merchants had promised to reduce their prices if the Creeks would agree to go along with the Cherokee cession. He said that this "was just like a man telling a fine story to his children to make them Merry at Night but in the Morning would be foregot."[19]

Taitt talked to the now venerable Wolf of Muccolossus on his return to Tuckabatchee, then went to the Okchoys town to see the Gun Merchant and the Mortar. Each one expressed concern about the talks from Augusta. Taitt indicated that there was a "jealousy" among the Tallapoosas of Emistisiguo's ascendancy. Taitt thought that their attitude had something to do with Emistisiguo's being "of a slave race." Emistisiguo had boasted to Governor Wright of being of the royal Tiger Clan; Taitt's reference indicates that the chief's father was an Indian from another tribe taken captive in some bygone war.[20]

Taitt found that James Grierson of Augusta had sent talks to some of his clients, promising cancellation of debts and future rewards if they would support the proposed cession. George Galphin was busy promulgating the same message among the Lower Creeks.

Taitt's journal is a geographical atlas of streams, rivers, and towns and a directory of the cast of characters in the Indian country. It is interesting that Taitt's guides were Joseph Cornell and Jacob Moniac. Alexander McGillivray later took the daughters of both men as his wives. Cornell and Moniac would serve Alexander as interpreters just as they served Taitt. Among other whites, the veteran Stephen Forrest was still active. Taitt mentions a "Mr. Cuzens," a trader to the Natchez, who was probably Archibald McGillivray's associate, George Cussings. The old men among the Indians were the Gun Merchant, Devall's Landlord, the Wolf, and the Mortar. Taitt's records reveal the power wielded by the Augusta traders in their effort to coerce their clients to agree to the new cession. Above all, Taitt's journal is a sad chronicle of an industry in decline. Francis Lewis kept a whole town drunk while Taitt was there. Hugh Simpson told Taitt that he would not obey the governor or the superintendent or anyone but his employer. Most of the traders in the Creek country were, according to Taitt, "Deserters, Horse thieves, half breeds and Negroes," who obeyed no regulations.[21]

Taitt concluded his journey at Augusta on June 2, 1772. On June 4, the king's birthday was celebrated by a muster of the local militia under Captain James Grierson. "The men made a very sorry Appearance," Taitt noted, "some having old rusty firelocks, others Riffles, and some being well Clothed and Others with Osnaburgh Shirts and Trousers." Their use of their weapons was as badly coordinated as their uniforms.[22] John Stuart was pleased with Taitt's performance, if not with the news he brought. At Stuart's request, Acting Governor Habersham and his council named Taitt justice of the peace in the Creek country. It was not likely that the gesture would awe those who refused to obey the governor or superintendent. The Georgia Council further resolved that John Stuart should call a meeting as soon as possible at Augusta and persuade the Indians to cede all lands to the Oconee River.[23] After conferring with Taitt, Stuart concluded that the Creeks would not permit an extension to the Oconee; whether they would agree to the Cherokee cession above the Little River was doubtful.

James Wright was welcomed upon his return to Savannah like a conquering hero. Few would have imagined that in three years' time some of the same people would place him under arrest. The assembly prepared an address which hailed Wright as a "faithful servant of the crown and a sincere friend to the true interests of the people."[24] Wright's excitement was tempered by his conversation with John Stuart in Charlestown. Stuart felt that pushing for the Oconee was a mistake and cautioned Wright, but Wright confided to the Earl of Dartmouth that he still had hopes of getting the Oconee strip. He reported that six hundred families were eager to buy the land and settle on it.[25] In anticipation of the conference scheduled for May in Augusta, Wright had a map prepared showing the province of Georgia as he would like it to be. The boundaries were set at the Oconee River, with the section above the Little River labeled "Cherokee Lands" and the area to the west of the Ogeechee marked "Creek Lands."[26] For the Upper Creeks the proposal meant an abrogation of the Treaty of 1763, and they were determined to oppose it. The Lower Creeks were wavering as they journeyed to Augusta. Their recent debts were greater than those of the Upper Creeks, and George Galphin had done his persuasive work well.

Lachlan McGillivray's role in bringing the Upper Creeks to the talks is not clear. John Alden, a careful historian, gives McGillivray equal credit with Galphin. A resolution was introduced in the Georgia Commons House of Assembly thanking both men for their services in arranging the conference.[27]

The records are silent as to who was present when the talks began in late May 1773. The occasion was important enough to attract a coterie of gentlemen from Savannah. McGillivray was certainly among them if the legislature thought to thank him. Nor do we know the names of the Indian delegates, but Emistisiguo must have been there for the Upper Creeks, Alleck for the Lower Creeks, and the Little Carpenter for the Cherokees. It did not bode well that the ever-suspicious Mortar chose to confer with the anti-English Cherokee chief Ouconnostotah while the Augusta talks were taking place.

The gentle Quaker William Bartram happened to be in Augusta when the congress began. The negotiations "continued undetermined for many days," he noted. The "powerful and proud spirited" Creeks were unwilling to yield any land, "and their conduct evidently betrayed a disposition to dispute the ground by force of arms," he noted. Liberal presents by the superintendent and the influence of the older chiefs brought the opposition into line. Bartram was of the opinion that the treaty was concluded "in unanimity, peace and good order." [28]

He did not mention that the Creeks forced Governor Wright into a compromise. Wright could not get his coveted Oconee strip. Instead, the Creeks gave up about 500,000 acres of pine barrens in the low country between the Ogeechee and Altamaha. The most valuable region was the Cherokee cession above the Little River, a tract of 1,616,298 acres. The Creeks acquiesced in yielding that area, even enlarging slightly on the Cherokees' original proposal.[29]

Governor Wright admitted to the Earl of Dartmouth that he could not prevail upon the Creeks to cede the Oconee lands, "which they said was their beloved hunting grounds for bear and beaver." He would bide his time until another opportunity offered. Wright's enthusiasm for the project was only slightly diminished by his failure to obtain the whole loaf. He told Dartmouth about the great numbers of people who had already applied from Pennsylvania, Maryland, Virginia, and North and South Carolina. There was only one source of anxiety; the "temper of the Creeks" troubled him. Fortunately from his point of view, the Choctaws renewed their war against the Creeks during June, while the Creeks were still angry about the treaty. Wright hoped that the Choctaw war would divert the attention of the disaffected Creeks from the Georgia frontier.[30] John Stuart shared Wright's concern about the surly mood of the Creeks. He advised young William Bartram that it would not be prudent to go gathering flowers in the Creek country just then. Bartram decided to accompany the surveying party that set out immediately after the treaty to mark the new northern territory under the leadership of Edward Barnard. Philip Yonge made a detailed map, which emphasized the attractiveness of the cession. Governor Wright broadcast a proclamation advertising the newly ceded land and invited purchasers to take advantage of this unparalleled opportunity.[31]

The Creeks were among the potential spoilers of the brighter day Wright had in mind. Another source of trouble were the crackers who were already usurping some of the most valuable sites. Hezekiah Collins was typical of many of these frontier "sooners." Two young Cherokees, who were with Barnard's boundary-marking expedition, called at Collins's cabin on the Broad River for some refreshment. They were not armed and were not looking for trouble. Collins's wife invited them in and gave them something to eat. When Collins returned to his cabin and found them there, he killed both of them, the second with an ax. As was true of many other frontier people, Collins's hatred of Indians was blind and unreasoning.[32]

Governor Wright and John Stuart posted rewards for Collins's arrest but knew it would do little good in a land where his neighbors thought him a hero. Wright put out another proclamation, ordering all trespassers to leave the ceded lands. More effectively, he raised a troop of rangers captained by Edward Barnard to patrol the area. He himself led an expedition to explore the region and clear off any of the "banditti," as he called them. Wright built a fort for the rangers at the confluence of the Broad and Savannah rivers and laid out a town nearby; he gave the fort and town the name of the colonial secretary, Dartmouth. After the Revolution, the place was called Petersburg.[33]

By December, Wright was able to report that he had sold 55,650 acres to buyers accounting for 1,413 white settlers and three hundred blacks. Wright was pleased with the growth of his province. He counted 18,000 whites and 15,000 blacks and estimated that there were more than that. He had presided over an increase of 12,000 whites since 1761. He wondered if Dartmouth would represent to His Majesty "the insufficiency of my present annual income to support me . . . in the rank His Majesty has been graciously pleased to place me."[34] The Georgia legislature congratulated James Wright for his role in bringing about the Treaty of 1773 but could not bring itself to acknowledge the contributions of George Galphin and Lachlan McGillivray. A resolution of thanks was introduced and debated but fell short of passage by a vote of ten to nine. That the measure was introduced indicates that Georgians believed that the two men were still very influential with the Creek Nation; the failure of the resolution was probably owing to disappointment in not obtaining the Oconee strip.[35]

A faction of the Creeks was so embittered by the Treaty of 1773 that not even a Choctaw war could distract them from retaliation. On December 25, nine days after the Boston Tea Party, Creek warriors massacred a white family near the headwaters of the Ogeechee on the newly ceded lands.[36] On January 14, another war party attacked a stockaded fort near Wrightsborough. In a day-long battle, seven of twenty whites were killed and five were wounded. As best as could be determined, the Creeks suffered only five casualties. Edward Barnard's troop of rangers and Colonel James Grierson's regiment of militia were called out to search for the hostile Indians. The Indians found the militia on January 25 and routed them. The *Georgia Gazette* ridiculed the frightened militiamen and called their excuse that they had to return home to protect their families a "silly speech."[37] Governor Wright explained ruefully that Grierson's men were "struck with such a Panick that neither fair means nor threats could prevail on them to stay."[38]

The Creek war parties effectively cleared the ceded lands of banditti and everyone else and brought an abrupt halt to Wright's promising experiment in colonization of the frontier.

In his address to the Commons House, Wright called for the erection of stockaded forts in the backcountry and asked for money to build them and to maintain the militia in service. The House responded so promptly to Wright's leadership that no one could have predicted that a revolution against his authority would begin in the next year. Wright begged General Gage to send down troops as Amherst had in 1760 and Loudoun in 1756. In the bitter spirit of what might have been, he told Dartmouth that there would have been ten thousand souls on the ceded lands had it not been for the Indian outbreak.[39]

Wright would have had a less difficult problem if it were not for the Indian-hating element among the frontier people. Afraid to do battle themselves, they welcomed the idea of the king's troops removing the Indians; "exterminating" was a word they used. The traders, however, wanted simply to restore the status quo. William Goodgion was an Indian trader and son-in-law of Edward Barnard, who was friendly with a chief called Mad Turkey. The Indian agreed to go with Goodgion to Augusta to help arrange a peace settlement. Augusta was filled with refugees from the backcountry, and a crowd of them were in the public house when the Indian entered, unarmed. As Mad Turkey raised a bottle to his lips for a drink, one Thomas Fee crushed his skull from behind with an iron bar. The peace-seeking emissary died instantly. Fee left Augusta with a reward on his head from Governor Wright. He was arrested and jailed in Ninety-Six, South Carolina, but a mob broke open the jail and set him free.[40] Fee like Collins was a hero in the backcountry. Such conduct was calculated to stoke the fires of war.

Georgia was at the crossroads of history in 1774. If the Creek war continued, the backcountry likely would have remained loyal to Governor Wright and dependent on the king for protection. If Gage could have spared troops from the northward, the disaffected in Savannah and St. John Parish on the lower coast might have been intimidated.

Three men made a difference in the course of history. One of them was Emistisiguo. The great chief took the exceedingly grave risk of meeting Mad Turkey's fate by taking the trail to Augusta and thence to Savannah, where he advised Governor Wright that a curtailment of the trade was the only way his mad young men could be brought to the peace table.[41] Wright had lost control of his banditti, and Emistisiguo could no longer restrain his warlike people. When Emistisiguo conversed with the governor, it is likely that it was through the medium of Lachlan McGillivray, as it had been in the past.

The second man of the moment was James Wright. He obtained Dartmouth's reluctant permission to impose a general stoppage of Indian trade. Dartmouth instructed the other southern governors to cooperate with Georgia in the emergency. Dartmouth thought the move was dangerous, and Wright admitted that it was "rather bold and somewhat hazardous."[42] The lawless element among the traders defied the ban until Wright authorized Barnard's rangers to interdict all trading caravans.[43] The people of the backcountry were delighted at Wright's bold move. Here was evidence that the government was on the side of the people and against the Indians and those who did business with them.

The backcountry attitude was tested in a striking manner. On July 14, a group of irate Savannahians gathered at Tondee's Tavern and protested the British Coercive Acts. The friends of government in Savannah replied with a statement of loyalty; the names of James Habersham and Lachlan McGillivray headed the list. Every backcountry district protested the Tondee's Tavern document—the town and district of Augusta, St. Paul Parish, Kiokee and Broad River settlements, St. George Parish, Queensborough, the western part of St. George Parish, and the town and township of Wrightsborough. The gist of these petitions was that the people relied on the king for protection against the Indians; the Tondee's Tavern signers were not exposed to the bad effects of an Indian war and did not speak for those who were.[44]

The third person who influenced events during the crucial year was John Stuart. As soon as he heard of the January hostilities, Stuart conferred with his cousin Charles and with John McGillivray, both of whom were in Charlestown at the time. Stuart asked both men to go back to Mobile and instigate the Choctaws to attack the Creeks. Stuart explained to Brigadier General Frederick Haldimand, the commanding officer in West Florida, that the Creek uprising stemmed from "our incessant requisitions for land."[45]

John McGillivray was instrumental in carrying out Stuart's strategy, and Lachlan acted as counselor to James Wright. The twin efforts had their effect. Robert Mackay was entertaining David Taitt at his house in Augusta when nine Okfuskee Creeks startled them by knocking on the door. They had come unobserved by trigger-happy whites to ask for peace and a resumption of trade.[46] The Lower Creeks signified their readiness for peace by putting to death two of the Indians involved in the attacks on settlers. Governor Wright was relieved and jubilant. "Thus your lordship sees that I was right in my plan," he wrote to Dartmouth.[47] He invited Upper and Lower Creek chiefs to come meet him in Savannah to ratify the peace.

All those people who were disappointed that the cession of 1773 did not include the Oconee strip saw the Savannah meeting as a second chance to get what they wanted. The legislature reflected this expectation by advising the governor to exact the Oconee boundary as a condition of peace.[48] Captain Samuel Elbert's Grenadier Company escorted Emistisiguo and seventy Upper Creeks into Savannah in October 1774. The Pumpkin King and Chehaw King led the Lower Creek contingent. A total of 137 Creeks sat down to talk with Governor Wright and John Stuart on October 18.[49]

The dilemma facing Wright was whether to press for additional lands and risk another angry Indian reaction or simply to restore the peace and resume the interrupted settlement of the ceded lands. Wright chose the latter course. Right or wrong, the people who had recently signed the loyal petitions blamed the Indian merchants and traders for influencing the governor to maintain the Ogeechee boundary. The faction of settlers accused those representing the traders of acting from "self-interested views" by prevailing on the governor to preserve the Oconee strip as a hunting ground for the Indians.[50] Lachlan McGillivray was certainly among the gentlemen of trade who had access to the governor. It is possible that he opposed a new cession. John Stuart was also against any acquisitions, and he was on hand to voice his objections.

The backcountry people who believed that the Creeks were willing to yield more land had some evidence to support their assumptions when Jonathan Bryan met with some of the chiefs in Savannah and persuaded them to agree to the lease of a huge tract of land along the Gulf Coast of northern Florida.[51] In his biography of Jonathan Bryan, Alan Gallay credits the Creeks with being farsighted and arranging the Bryan lease along the Appalachicola to secure an alternative to "British" trade.[52] The Creeks may have recognized in Bryan a maverick who was willing to flout the trade restrictions—there were many others who made a business of doing that—but it would have required unusual prescience on their part to predict that there would be a revolution and that Bryan would not be on the British side. There were alternatives to Georgia trade already in Mobile and Pensacola. None of the great chiefs, Emistisiguo, the Gun Merchant, Devall's Landlord, or Alleck, participated in the Bryan transaction. The unreconciled nativist the Mortar was apparently engaged in seeking a genuinely non-British source of trade during the Savannah conference by what John Alden described as "an amazing plan to secure a trade with Louisiana."[53] The Mortar was on his way to New Orleans when he was killed in a skirmish with the Choctaws. Unlike Emistisiguo, he had never accepted the finality of the settlement of 1763.[54]

Bryan's lease was another of those illegal private transactions which so annoyed John Stuart. He opposed similar concessions by the Cherokees to Richard Pearis and Edward Wilkinson and by the Catawbas to William Henry Drayton.[55] Governors Wright in Georgia and Patrick Tonyn in East Florida vehemently opposed the Bryan transaction, and the Revolution put an end to Bryan's plans. The region in question must have been considered disposable by the Lower Creeks, however, because they gave approximately the same tract to John Stuart's successor, Thomas Brown of the King's Rangers.[56]

The October 20, 1774, treaty marked the turning point in Governor Wright's relationship with his people. Wright attributed the disaffection to the settlers' hunger for land: "Every man thinks and says he has not only a right to Hunt on Indian lands but to purchase them and do just what he pleases." On December 9, 1774, a Savannah Whig expressed the opinion that Georgia would now join the other colonies in the Continental Association against trade with the mother country because "two of the back Parishes which made the most noise are now coming over to us."[57]

Even the most loyal Georgians were disheartened by the failure of the royal government to send any substantial aid to their endangered province. The Commons House of Assembly couched its disappointment in the formal language of the day: "We cannot but with horror reflect on the dreadful crises to which this province must have been reduced had we experienced no other resources than those dilatory succours which administration meant conditionally to afford us."[58] South Carolina radicals fanned the fires of revolution in Georgia by spreading fantastic rumors. It was said that the king planned to raise an army of slaves and set them against their masters. John Stuart was accused of plotting to bring an Indian war to the frontier. In May 1775, he was forced to flee from Charlestown and seek refuge first in Savannah, then in St. Augustine.[59] When a young gentleman from Yorkshire named Thomas Brown answered Governor Wright's invitation to settle on the ceded lands and arrived in Georgia with seventy-odd indentured servants, it was rumored that he was the illegitimate son of Lord North, come to spy on the disloyal.[60]

Then, in May, Georgians heard about Lexington and Concord. On May 11, 1775, the royal powder magazine in Savannah was broken into and some of the gunpowder was shipped to the patriots at Boston. The *Georgia Gazette* of June 21 contained a summons to a meeting at the liberty pole to discuss a course of action. It was a crucial moment in the history of the southern frontier. There was no doubt now that there would be a war; it had already begun. What the war was about was still a matter of debate, and whether Georgia would join in the protest by arms was at issue. Savannah's leading citizens gathered at the liberty pole on June 26, 1775. The group included future Whigs Joseph Clay, Noble Wimberly Jones, John Glen, Edward Telfair, George Walton, James Habersham, Jr., Oliver Bowen, William LeConte, and Andrew Elton Wells. Future Loyalists were John J. Zubly, Basil Cowper, William Struthers, Thomas Netherclift, John Jamieson, William Young, John Mullryne, and Josiah Tattnall. It was a distinguished assemblage of Georgia's best and brightest, and the group paid Lachlan McGillivray one of the highest compliments in his career by electing him to chair the meeting. It was McGillivray's name, therefore, that was ascribed to the resolutions printed in the *Georgia Gazette*, and we may assume that they reflected his personal position in this crisis moment:

1. That the present acts of Parliament tending to raise a revenue in America are grievances.
2. That we will do all that we legally and constitutionally may to obtain redress of those grievances.
3. Resolved to meet June 30 at Mrs. Cuyler's to consult methods.[61]

It was still possible for faithful subjects of the king to protest and petition their government for redress of their grievances. In November 1775, Lachlan McGillivray was elected to the extralegal provincial congress and at the same time nominated by Governor Wright to the Royal Council.[62]

It was a critical moment in the lives of McGillivray and the men of his generation. The nature of the colonial relationship with the mother country was to be decided, of course, but at stake also was the subsequent shaping of the frontier. What would be the future relationship of European Americans and native Americans?

The relationship with Indians was intertwined with the desire for land. Since Oglethorpe's time Indians were regarded as clients. The Indian trade was a vital part of the economy of Georgia and, before that, of South Carolina. It was the main business of the new Florida provinces. South Carolina had developed a diverse agricultural economy in which rice and indigo production had become more important than the Indian trade. During the ten years following the Great War for Empire, Savannah diverted an increasing amount of deerskin and peltry exports from Charlestown.[63] The question for Georgians in 1775 was whether the Indian trade should continue to set political priorities. Merchant traders like McGillivray were aware that if the frontier advanced in Georgia, they would lose business to the eager entrepreneurs in Pensacola and Mobile.

The newest Georgians did not intend to do business with the Indians. They were impatient with the argument that the Indians needed land for hunting. They answered that their need for farmland was greater. Many of them cultivated the blind, unreasoning hatred of Indians exhibited by Hezekiah Collins and Thomas Fee. David Hackett Fisher has observed that there was a cultural basis for the attitude of the frontier people. Most of them were Scots-Irish, with roots in the border counties of north Britain. They had practiced fighting and hating for four centuries. In the old country they were independent, restless, and prone to violence. They continued to exhibit these traits as they followed the Appalachian Valley roads into the southern backcountry.[64] There was no love lost between the borderers of the lowlands and the Scottish Highlanders. Georgia newcomers would have been inclined to side against the Georgia Highlanders, even if the latter were not in league with the Indians.

Another source of division was that the people of the British borderland were dissenters in religion. In America many were enkindled by the fervor of preachers of the Great Awakening. The inhabitants of Augusta were accustomed to a more civilized moderation in religion. James Seymour, rector of St. Paul's Church in Augusta, reflected the opinion of many of his parishioners when he complained in 1772 that upper Georgia was "overrun with ignorant preachers who call themselves Irregular Baptists. They travel from place to place and pretend to miraculous conversion and inspiration but are men of very abandoned characters and live in adultery."[65] By contrast, Augustans regarded themselves, in the words of one of them, as "very worthy and respectable people."[66] They set a good table, entertained in the Charlestown manner, and traveled about town in coaches and riding chairs. From that day to this, rural Georgians have suspected that city folk regard themselves as "a better sort."

All these divisive influences pale in comparison to the Indian question. The old Augustans were accustomed to dealing with Indians, and the newcomers had no intention of accommodating themselves to the Indians. Lachlan McGillivray knew Indians better than most men of his time. He was aware of their vices as well as their virtues. Since 1742 his letters and advice to the governors of South Carolina and Georgia had helped formulate Indian policy. He could not support a movement that regarded Indians as enemies and ostracized John Stuart as a traitor. The other and more important reason for McGillivray to preserve his ties to the Creek Indians was that his family belonged inseparably to the Wind Clan of the Creek Nation. His son Alexander was now a man of twenty-five. He made his decision to return to his mother's people at Little Tallassee, Emistisiguo's town. He was ready to take his place as a beloved man in the council house.[67]

Ironically, George Galphin had many of the same reasons McGillivray did to side with the trading interest and oppose the aggressive frontiersmen, but he accepted the position of commissioner of Indian affairs when the revolutionary provincial congress of South Carolina offered that important post to him. He exerted his enormous influence to keep the Lower Creeks neutral. He despised the backcountry banditti who clamored for a war of extermination against the Indians. "They have every reason to break with us," he said of the Indians, "and yet I think I could keep them peaceable, if it was not for the people on the ceded lands."[68] When Galphin used the epithet "those damned villains" he meant the whites, not the Indians. He was suspect by many of those who thought a war with the Indians was preferable to neutrality. He and McGillivray remained friends; Galphin named McGillivray as one of the executors of his will. And when the British recovered control of Georgia and Galphin was arrested as a rebel, McGillivray pleaded for pardon for him, arguing that Galphin had merely tried to prevent the horrors of an Indian war. Galphin's death in 1780 did not resolve the issue but made it moot.[69]

Most of the Scots who were involved in the trade remained loyal to the king. That fact was so obvious to contemporaries that later in 1782 the Georgia revolutionary legislature took the extraordinary step of barring any further immigration of people from Scotland. It was the legislators' way of saying that the new Georgia would belong to farmers, not traders.[70]

CHAPTER SIXTEEN

Return to Strathnairn

The American Revolution was the final decisive factor in the shaping of the southern colonial frontier, not that the shaping was complete, but the colonial phase was at an end. As the region slipped away from British control, the Indian traders lost place and power. McGillivray returned to Georgia with the restoration of royal rule in 1779, only to watch the passing of the old order. His influence was limited to advising Governor Wright and serving in the ineffective royal assembly.

For a time, fortune seemed to favor the loyalist cause, and during that time McGillivray assumed his former role as intermediary between the Creek Indians and the government. The occasion was the unexpected arrival in Savannah in April 1779 of a contingent of Creek Indians led by David Taitt and Alexander McGillivray. Before John Stuart died in March of that year, he had instructed Taitt to lead the Indians to Augusta and there join forces with Lieutenant Colonel Archibald Campbell's Seventy-First Regiment. Taitt did his best, but his orders had come far too late and Campbell had been forced to withdraw from his exposed position long before the Indians reached the Ogeechee River. The British retreated as far as Briar Creek, then turned and routed their pursuers on March 3, 1779. Thus the lower half of the province was under British occupation.[1]

Most of Taitt's party turned back after learning that Campbell was no longer at Augusta, but Taitt, McGillivray, and a few companions crossed through enemy territory and reached Savannah. According to Jacob Moniac, who was with them, McGillivray had to make a run for it between two lines of fire.[2] It is passing strange that Alexander McGillivray, who never considered himself much of a warrior, should have risked his life to get to Savannah, where he was not needed in any military sense. It is even stranger that he lingered more than a year in Savannah. He left in June 1780 because his Creek companions were growing sickly in the summer heat and were anxious to return to their country.[3] We can surmise that the desire to see his father after the lapse of three years drew Alexander to Savannah and that he felt comfortable enough at Vale Royal to stay there. We can assume that David Taitt was welcomed as a member of the family. We do not have to guess or assume that Lachlan McGillivray provided for the Indians during their stay; his account for their provisions is a matter of record.[4]

The tug of family ties is evident in Thomas Woodward's testimony that Sophia attempted to join Lachlan and Alexander at Vale Royal but was unable to get through enemy lines.[5] Her inability to communicate was symbolic of the way this war severed the connections between British merchant traders and their Indian clients.

The war came perilously close to the McGillivrays in Savannah. The sudden appearance of a French armada off the Tybee coast was a shock to loyal Georgians. Governor Wright spoke for them in his report to Lord George Germain: "We have met with a very unexpected, alarming and serious scene, especially in this part of the world, for no man could have thought or believed that a French Fleet of 25 Sail of the Line, with at least 9 Frigates, and a number of other Vessels, would have come on the Coast of Georgia in the month of September, and Landed from 4 to 5000 troops to beseige the town of Savannah, but My Lord amazing as this is, it is certainly Fact."[6]

General Benjamin Lincoln's American army joined forces with the French and set up siege lines around Savannah. McGillivray's Vale Royal plantation was dangerously exposed between the enemy lines, but McGillivray was able to secure the protection of a British warship that anchored at his wharf. Another of McGillivray's properties, the 945-acre Springfield plantation, became historic ground when it was the focal point of the allied grand assault on the British Springhill redoubt on October 9, 1779. An authority on land surveying in Georgia believes that Count Casimir Pulaski was struck down on the Springfield tract.[7] The allies suffered 752 casualties in the attack. General Augustine Prevost's British, loyalist, and Hessian defenders lost 18 killed and 39 wounded. The British press made much of the victory. King George III ordered salutes fired from the Tower of London and in St. James Park. In New York, Sir Henry Clinton, British commander in America, was jubilant. He wrote to the Duke of Newcastle, "Tis certainly the greatest event since the beginning of the war!"[8]

The disheartened French sailed away, Lincoln's army withdrew to Charlestown, and the war receded from McGillivray's doorstep. Sir Henry Clinton brought his army down from New York and trapped Lincoln in Charlestown. When that proud city surrendered, resistance collapsed all over Georgia and Carolina. Thus it seemed that the war had been won when Alexander McGillivray and his homesick companions left Savannah in June 1780. The new Indian superintendent, Lieutenant Colonel Thomas Brown of the King's Rangers, had work for them to do in the Indian country. Lachlan resumed his interrupted import-export business.[9]

The war affected Lachlan's cousins in different ways. Captain William McGillivray left Georgia at the beginning of the Revolution. While waiting in Charlestown for passage, he made no secret of his loyalty to the king and as a result had to endure insults and even threats to his life. His military experience qualified him for the rank of lieutenant colonel, and he was confident that he could raise a regiment among his kinsmen in Strathnairn. Bad luck plagued him. He tore a tendon in his leg when he finally arrived in London and had to wait until it healed. In September 1779 William informed Farquhar, who was managing the family estates at Dunmaglass, that General Amherst had assured him that if any new regiments were raised, he would recommend William for command.[10]

Although William was safely, if reluctantly, out of the war, his brother John in far-off Mobile was unexpectedly thrust into it. In 1778

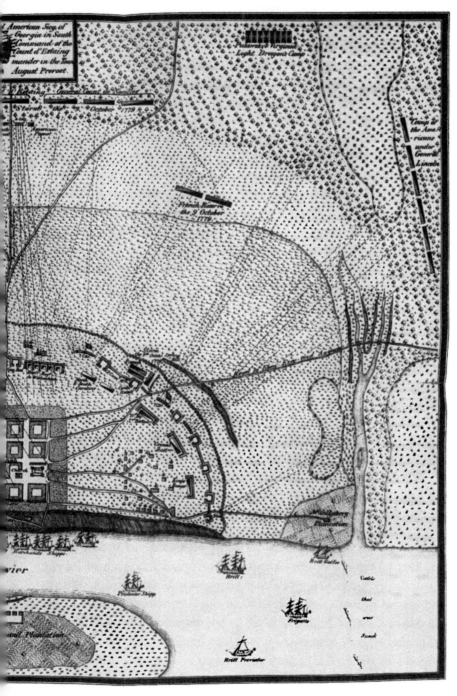

The only two plantations shown on this sketch of the siege of Savannah are Lachlan McGillivray's Vale Royal and William McGillivray's Hutchinson Island Plantation. (Hargrett Rare Book and Manuscript Library, University of Georgia)

an American expedition under maverick James Willing plundered loyal subjects on the Mississippi and alarmed the inhabitants of British West Florida. On March 25, West Florida Governor Peter Chester reported to Lord George Germain that John McGillivray had volunteered to raise a hundred men to defend the Mississippi frontier. Chester noted that although McGillivray had greater influence around Mobile and with the traders in the Indian country than anyone else in the province, he did not believe a hundred men would turn out. Less than a month later, John Stuart had informed Germain that McGillivray had exceeded the quota of a hundred men. Stuart called McGillivray "a gentleman of fortune intimately acquainted with the Choctaw and Chickasaw Indians." McGillivray was "the fittest person" to manage the two nations, and Stuart authorized him to employ those Indians on his expedition. Stuart confided that he had used his influence to induce McGillivray to undertake the operation.[11]

Lieutenant Colonel McGillivray and his little army marched seven hundred miles to Natchez. He captured or killed thirty of Willing's men and helped put an end to that threat. More adventure was in store when he returned to Mobile and took passage to Savannah. His ship was captured by a Spanish man-of-war, and he was taken to Havana, Cuba, and thrust into prison for ten months. Officers were not usually accorded such treatment; a parole on their word of honor not to fight until exchanged was the general rule. Evidently, the Spanish authorities considered John McGillivray especially dangerous. When he was exchanged, he made his way to Charlestown and from there proceeded to Augusta, where Lieutenant Colonel Thomas Brown commanded.[12] Brown had opened the great white road to Indian traffic and cleared settlers off the Oconee strip. Augusta was again an Indian town. Brown's deputy to the Upper Creeks was Alexander McGillivray, and one of Brown's first directions to the Creeks was an order to assist Major General John Campbell in the defense of Pensacola against a Spanish siege.[13] John McGillivray was familiar with the trail from Augusta to the Creek Nation and thence to Pensacola. He had followed that path after cousin Lachlan helped him get started in the trading business. He took the road to Pensacola and defended the town as lieutenant colonel of volunteers. There must have been a pleasant reunion between John and Alexander—both had fascinating stories to tell. Unfortunately for their cause, Campbell was an inept officer, and he surrendered Pensacola to the Spanish forces in May 1781.[14]

John McGillivray then joined Lachlan in Savannah. These were dark days for the British cause. Lord Charles Cornwallis's invasion of Virginia had left the loyalists in the South practically defenseless. Thomas Brown was forced to surrender Augusta to Nathanael Greene's troops in June 1781. By the end of the year, royal Georgia was limited to the coastal area. Brown's Rangers patrolled the perimeter, and in answer to Governor Wright's desperate urging, Brown called on the Indians for help. The gallant Emistisiguo responded. At the head of three hundred warriors, he attempted to break the American lines in a surprise night attack. Emistisiguo engaged General "Mad Anthony" Wayne in hand-to-hand combat and would have dispatched Wayne but was shot from behind. Most of his warriors broke through and joined Brown's rangers. Thomas Brown mourned "the brave, gallant Emistisiguo." His adversary, Anthony Wayne, described him as "our greatest enemy and principal warrior of the Creek Indians."[15] The greatest chiefs paid for their policies with their lives: Red Shoes of the Choctaws in his attempt to be free of French domination, the Mortar in his efforts to balance the power of the British, and Emistisiguo in his loyalty to his treaty promises to the agents of the king.

History nearly dealt Lachlan McGillivray another hand in the fateful game being played out upon the frontier. When Thomas Brown was made superintendent of the Creeks and Cherokees in 1779, Alexander Cameron, John Stuart's deputy, known to the Indians as "Scotchy," was put in charge of the Choctaws and Chickasaws. After the fall of Pensacola to the Spanish, Cameron went to Savannah, where he died on December 29, 1781. Lachlan McGillivray was uniquely qualified to succeed him. We can guess that he did not want the honor or the £500 per year that came with it. Governor Wright, McGillivray's friend and patron, nominated McGillivray's partner John Graham for the post.

Although Graham was one of the least qualified by experience, he was awarded the superintendency.[16] Wright and Graham would not have snubbed McGillivray; he must have decided not to seek the job.

It was in the waning days of the British occupation of Savannah that John and Lachlan McGillivray reached an unusual agreement. Citing his "years and infirmities," Lachlan decided to turn over his extensive landholdings to John and in return asked John for £300 per year as a pension. John willingly agreed but volunteered to increase the annual stipend to £500. Thereupon Lachlan transferred Vale Royal and twenty-two other properties to John. The deeds were dated September 10 and 11, 1781.[17]

John McGillivray assumed ownership of Vale Royal and employed Archibald McGillivray's youngest son, Lachlan, to manage it.[18] This younger Lachlan barely had time to harvest one crop of rice before Savannah was surrendered to Anthony Wayne's troops. The American terms were generous. Loyalists were given six months to settle their business affairs. Lachlan the elder sailed for England in May 1782. On May 4, his estates were confiscated by the Georgia General Assembly. His name appeared fourth on the list behind those of Governor James Wright, Lieutenant Governor John Graham, and Alexander Wright, the governor's son. William's name was seventy-third on the Chatham County list; John's was ninety-sixth. John McGillivray was among the last loyalists to leave Georgia. With Governor Wright as a fellow passenger, he sailed for Jamaica on April 8, 1783.[19] He then joined Lachlan and William at a residence on Northumberland Avenue in London, where John and William applied to the Commissioners of Claims for compensation for their losses. Sir James Wright and John Graham were on hand to vouch for the validity of the claims of the McGillivrays. John Wereat of Georgia supplied an affidavit that Lachlan's former Georgia properties had been sold by the state for £23,084. John McGillivray sought compensation in that amount in addition to losses of his own amounting to a total of £27,462. Meanwhile, John established a plantation in Jamaica and Lachlan the younger went there to manage it.[20]

It seemed that fate frowned on the McGillivrays. The American

Revolution brought an abrupt end to Lachlan's dreams of establishing the clan in Georgia. John might have continued to trade in Mobile, but the Treaty of Paris in 1783 transferred the two Florida provinces to Spain. The clan would continue, but not in Georgia. Captain William married Johanna Mackenzie of Fairburn, Scotland, in 1780 and probably did not return to Georgia during the brief restoration of royal government. Their first child was a girl, Barbara Ann. In 1783, the year of peace, an heir was born and named after the two men who were his benefactors, John Lachlan. If anything could compensate Lachlan for the loss of his American estate and the separation from his natural children, it was his delight in the birth of John Lachlan. The family spent a happy summer in sunny Cornwall in the year of John Lachlan's birth. John McGillivray wrote to Farquhar of Dalcrombie that William's family and Lachlan were at Tavistock, just north of Plymouth. William had been ill but was recovering. Goat milk was considered a sovereign remedy in the Highlands, and William had gone to Wales to sample the goat milk there. John described Lachlan as "fat and hearty" at the age of sixty-four.[21] The family affectionately called him "Lachlan Lia," Lachlan the Gray. That summer's happiness was short-lived. William's health grew worse. He sought the warmer climate of Portugal and died there, leaving his wife and the two young children. From 1783 to 1786 Farquhar McGillivray of Dalcrombie managed the family estate in Scotland. He does not enjoy a good reputation in the McGillivray clan history. Farquhar reported that many of the farms were without tenants in 1785, but he was just as glad: "Really its better having lands lay than possess'd by such misserable obstinate creatures." Farquhar blamed the tenants for the poverty of the Strathnairn farms, but the weather was mainly responsible. The winter of 1784 was one of the worst in history. It was remembered later as "the year of the white pease" because the principal source of food was white peas imported from Holland.[22]

John McGillivray invested heavily in the improvement of the McGillivray properties. He became increasingly annoyed by Farquhar's inefficient management of the draining and planting. He scolded Farquhar for taking the advice of people who did not know what they were talking about. John told his cousin that he wanted to approve all future projects. In 1786 John's claims against the government were allowed, assuring him and his heirs of a comfortable future. John made out his will in 1786, leaving his fortune to John Lachlan. Having completed his business in Britain, John took passage for Jamaica. He built a plantation house at Bath and settled down to life as a West Indian planter. John represented one option taken by many loyal southerners who were reluctant to test the cold climate of Nova Scotia. Jamaica was the preferred location; the Bahamas proved too barren. Lachlan McGillivray was an example of an alternative taken by other loyalists, a return to Britain.

Unfortunately, John's new career was cut short. He died in early February 1788, after taking passage on a ship bound for England.[23] Lachlan McGillivray the younger was saddened by the death of his employer and disappointed at not getting a legacy. He informed the colonel's executor that he had worked for McGillivray for ten years and was owed £3,200 in back pay. He was willing to continue managing the plantation, but if the executors preferred another overseer, he suggested hiring someone from America because the local whites tended to treat slaves too harshly.[24] John McGillivray's Jamaica possessions were sold and the profits went into a trust fund for young John Lachlan. The agreement with Lachlan Lia was honored after John's death; each year Lachlan received £500 from John's estate. The annuity was a small fortune compared to the annual income of many Scottish lairds.[25] In 1784, the year of the white pease, Lachlan moved north to Inverness and took lodgings with Anne, sister to John and William. Anne lived part of the year at Dunmaglass, as did Lachlan. In 1790, Anne died and Lachlan was named "cautioner" or trustee of the estates of seven-year-old John Lachlan. There were seven estates to manage: Dunmaglass, Easter Aberchalder, Inverairnie, Wester Gask, Easter Gask, Faillie, and Lairgs. Lachlan was determined to carry on the improvements contemplated by John. He applied the lessons he had learned in America to the breeding of livestock and cultivation of crops. His correspondence in 1790 indicates that he supervised the planting of trees at Easter Aberchalder, the selection of crops for Gask and Dunmaglass, diking and draining of other properties, and the repair of the corn mill at Gask.²⁶ He inventoried the household effects of Anne's house in Inverness and conducted a "roup" or auction of the contents. These roups were social events, proclaimed in all the parish churches in Invernesshire. On this occasion Lachlan ordered a half anker of whiskey, two dozen bottles of port wine, and an ample supply of beef and bread.²⁷ "Miss Anny" McGillivray had given permission to various persons to cut wood on one of the estates. Even before her death, Lachlan informed her that no more trees would be cut down. He was determined to follow a re-forestation program, a new and radical idea in the Highlands, where trees were regarded as a refuge for the birds that ate the seeds and young shoots. He planted on a grand scale; on November 11, 1791, he ordered twenty thousand trees "for the present." ²⁸

A perceptive clergyman noted the effects of Lachlan Lia's conservation efforts. He described the naked rocks and heath-covered hills in Strathnairn and the large areas of peat moss and barren moor in the low ground. Those areas had never been cultivated, but "Mr. McGillivray of Dunmaglass" had begun planting forest trees "with flattering success." If the other landlords would follow his example and that of one or two others, the appearance of the valley would be changed and the lands would acquire great additional value.²⁹

It seems appropriate that Lachlan, who had worried so about the perpetuation of the clan, was the one into whose hands fell the responsibility of rearing the future chief. William died during John Lachlan's infancy and apparently so had Johanna, the child's mother. Colonel John, the benefactor, died in 1788, and Anne, the last of the aunts, died in 1790. So little John Lachlan and pretty Barbara Ann grew up at Dunmaglass under the care of Lachlan Lia. Lachlan taught them lessons of grammar and civility, just as he had taught his own son Alexander. And he followed tradition. His father had placed him with a tutor in Inverness, and Lachlan did the same with John Lachlan. His concern for the boy is reflected in his letters. He called him "my Johnny" and sounded like an anxious parent in inquiring about the child's health. When Johnny's tutor became ill, Lachlan wrote that he wanted Johnny "here with me" in Dunmaglass.³⁰ That was in the autumn of 1791, when

John Lachlan was eight and his sister was ten. Lachlan's life had come full circle. He was once more in his boyhood home of Dunmaglass at the southern end of the valley of the river Nairn. It was the residence of his ancestors, the seat of the chiefs of the McGillivrays. He was a good custodian of the estate, repairing the mansion, rethatching the roof, introducing agricultural reforms, supervising the tenants. In short, he was a Georgia planter, bringing energy and innovation from the New World into an ancient setting. His continuing interest in his clan during the forty-odd years in America made it possible and even easy for him to return to Strathnairn and serve his clan. He was not, like many other loyalists, a displaced person who had left the mother country originally because there was no future for him. Those loyalists began life again in the strange new environments of Nova Scotia, the Bahamas, or Jamaica. Lachlan, who, like his father, had been promised a residence at Dunmaglass, came home again.

Still, he had invested forty years of his life in the shaping of the southern frontier. He had ties of blood and affection which bound him to the land and people he left behind. He corresponded with Alexander, his son, and sent him mementos of Scotland.[31]

Alexander McGillivray was true to his clan, the Wind people, as Lachlan was to Clan Chattan and the McGillivrays. Alexander's prestige was based on birth and bolstered by his appointment as John Stuart's deputy to the Upper Creeks in 1778 at the height of the revolutionary war. Alexander served Stuart well, and his importance increased during the superintendency of Thomas Brown. During the summer of 1783, his people paid him their highest compliment by electing him "Head warrior of all the Nation" in place of the great Emistisiguo.[32] When the British abandoned their Indian allies, Lieutenant Colonel Brown suggested that McGillivray might strike an alliance with the Spanish authorities, who had returned to Florida after a lapse of twenty years. McGillivray had no particular love for the Spanish, nor did the Spanish governors of East and West Florida ever completely trust him. But the Creeks and Spaniards were joined in a common cause that took precedence over petty suspicions. They opposed the efforts of the aggressive Georgians to push back the Indian boundary. The Spanish government granted a franchise to the firm of Panton, Leslie and Company to supply the Creeks with trading goods formerly brought over the great white road from Charlestown through Augusta to the nation.[33]

The frustrated Georgians could not coax, cajole, or threaten McGillivray into ceding anything beyond the line of 1763. The fact that his father had marked the line would have been of nostalgic interest to Alexander, but he would certainly have opposed any extension of the line in any case. He stood on the same ground as the Mortar and Emistisiguo and had the support of his people. Only a few minor chiefs were willing to negotiate with the Georgia authorities; Alexander contemptuously dismissed them as "roving beggars" and disregarded the treaties they signed.[34]

The argument has been made that Georgia entered into a stronger federal union with her sister states because Alexander McGillivray refused to bargain for the Oconee strip and instead launched a war in 1786 to clear white trespassers from those lands. Georgia desperately needed the area to redeem the bankrupt credit of the state. So Georgia's delegates at the Constitutional Convention collaborated with the nationalist faction there in establishing a strong central government that could deal with the stubborn McGillivray.[35]

One of George Washington's first initiatives as president was to dispatch Colonel Marinus Willet to the Creek country with an invitation to Alexander to come to New York. McGillivray gathered some thirty of his chiefs and made his way on horseback and in wagons to the seat of government. In Baltimore, McGillivray was entertained by a Scot by the name of Collin Douglass. The evening was mellow, marked by good fellowship and nostalgic singing. "Sweet Jim of Aberdeen still vibrates in my ear," Alexander recalled when he later wrote to thank his host. The spectacle of a famous Indian chief locked in song with Scotsmen might have seemed bizarre to the curious, but it provides an insight into a soul formed by two cultures.[36]

If the whites thought it strange to see an Indian acting like a Scot, the Creeks must have wondered at the garb of the group that welcomed them to New York. The Sons of St. Tammany, wearing their version of

Indian costumes, turned out in force, presumably to make the visitors feel more at home. Their host in New York was Secretary of War Henry Knox, who escorted them to Washington's residence, where they were warmly received. Abigail Adams, who was capable of making caustic observations about famous persons, was impressed by McGillivray; she commented that he "dresses in our own fashion, speaks English like a native . . . is not very dark, [and is] much of a gentleman." [37] For once, it would seem, the legendary hospitality of the Creeks was matched by American officials. The occasion was historic, and the implications equally concerned the British and Spanish governments, which were represented in New York by anxious observers, fearful that a Creek-American alliance would upset the balance of power on the southern frontier.

Alexander McGillivray and his chiefs signed their names to the Treaty of New York, which moved the boundary for the first time since 1763 and fixed it at the Oconee River. A faction of Creeks was disturbed that McGillivray had given up anything at all, but the Indians' annoyance paled in comparison with that of the expansionist Georgians, who had hoped for much more. In their opinion, the Oconee should have been theirs long before. They felt betrayed by the federal government and assumed an antifederalist stance, which characterized much of Georgia's subsequent history. George Washington undertook an exhausting southern tour, which included Charlestown, Savannah, and the state capital in Augusta and placated at least some of the critics of the Treaty of New York.

We get a glimpse of Alexander McGillivray at home at Little Tallassee through the eyes of John Pope, a traveler through the frontier country in 1791. The son of Lachlan was at the zenith of his power and influence among his people. He held a brigadier's commission from the United States as well as a commission from Spain, both of which carried substantial stipends. McGillivray's house was near Little Tallassee, about five miles from the site of Fort Toulouse. The general was not there, however, and Pope was told that he had gone six miles upriver to his "upper plantation." This was the same place where Lachlan had lived and was Alexander's birthplace and childhood home. Alexan-

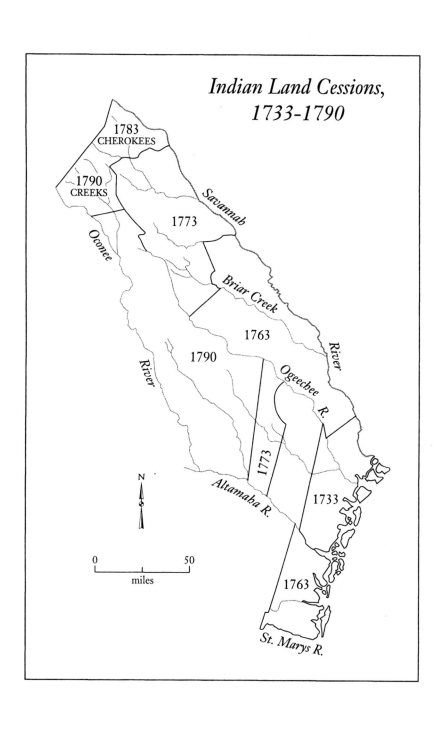

Indian Land Cessions,
1733-1790

1783
CHEROKEES

1790
CREEKS

1773

Savannah

Oconee

Briar Creek

1763

1790

River

Ogeechee R.

River

N

1773

Altamaha R.

1733

0   50

miles

1763

St. Marys R.

der, or "the General" as Pope called him, was busy erecting a log house with dormer windows on the very site of Lachlan's house. A grove of apple trees planted by Lachlan almost a half-century before crowned the gentle hill and made a "venerable appearance" in Pope's opinion.[38]

McGillivray received his visitor with impeccable courtesy; he said that his house was Pope's house. Pope guessed that the chief was only thirty-two years old, though he looked forty-five. Actually, McGillivray was forty-one. He suffered from a chronic headache, but his disposition was placid and serene and at times joyous. Pope commented on the correctness of McGillivray's diction and his fund of wit and humor. McGillivray's wife attracted Pope's admiration. He called her "A Woman loveliest of the lovely Kind, Perfect in Body and complete in Mind." The two children, Alexander and Elizabeth, were well mannered and spoke English as well as any white child. Benjamin Hawkins identified Alexander's wife as a mixed-blood woman by the name of "Mcrae," a Scottish name. She would bear another daughter for Alexander before his death in 1793.[39]

Alexander emulated Lachlan in his life-style. He had several plantations, employed more than fifty slaves, and was said to have double that number in the Spanish West Indies. McGillivray kept a gentleman's table and his sideboard displayed a connoisseur's selection of wines and spirits. One of the chief's most prized possessions was a collection of gilt-edged books given him by President Washington in New York. Another was the president's own golden epaulet, which he had worn throughout the war and which he gave McGillivray as a souvenir. Alexander told Pope that he received presents every year from his father, Lachlan, in Scotland. He said of Washington's gifts that they came from his political and adopted father, and Lachlan's were from his natural father.[40]

Pope was amazed at Alexander's ability to dash off beautifully composed letters in the midst of a circle of chieftains "whose Garrulity would have confused any other Man than McGillivray."[41] Pope's account provides a rare insight into the character of Alexander McGillivray. This giant of his times and shaper of history was a loving son, a good father, a generous, sensitive, and sophisticated man. Above all, he was loyal to his people in the tradition of Malatchi, the Mortar, and Emistisiguo. As John Caughey observed, he found his people in 1783 abandoned by the British and discouraged, and "he won for them territorial integrity and a favored position with their neighbors." He was "the very soul of the Creek Nation."[42]

During the last years of his life, Alexander wrote a history of his people and sent it to a renowned historian, Professor William Robertson of the University of Edinburgh, for a new edition of his *History of America*, first published in 1777. Robertson died before he could revise his history, and McGillivray's manuscript was lost.[43]

In April 1793 Alexander was taken ill on a journey to Pensacola. William Panton gave him all the care he could, but Alexander died after eight days of suffering from pneumonia and an ailment Panton described as "gout on the stomach." The *Gentleman's Magazine* of London reported his death and described how a large number of his people attended him in his last illness and accompanied his body to the grave with cries of "unaffected grief." The *Magazine* noted that he was "by his father's side a Scotchman, of the respectable family of Drumnaglass [sic] in Invernesshire."[44]

Panton informed the Spanish governor at New Orleans that McGillivray had no papers of importance with him, only a letter from his father and one or two others. That Alexander saved a letter from Lachlan is indicative of the bond between them even though they were an ocean apart. William Panton wrote to Lachlan to tell him how much he esteemed Alexander and how Alexander had helped in securing the success of his firm. As Panton had meant to share his good fortune with Alexander, he now intended to do for the children. "They have lately lost their mother, so that they have no friends, poor things, but you and me," he said. Apparently there had been an understanding between father and son that Alexander's remains would be sent to Scotland for burial with his ancestors of Clan Chattan. Emma Hulse Taylor, a descendant of William Panton, cited a family tradition that Sophia Durant took Alexander's body to Alabama for interment.[45] Thus the women of the Wind Clan claimed their own.

They claimed more than Alexander's remains. According to Creek custom, a man's children had no right to his property; it belonged to his relations on the maternal side. So Sophia Durant and Sehoy Weatherford took possession of Alexander's land, slaves, and livestock. The Wind Clan claimed the girls also. Benjamin Hawkins tried to persuade the sisters to allow him to take the daughters under his own roof to further his "plan for civilization." He wanted to teach the girls spinning and weaving in the hope that they would become examples to other Creek women, but "their family did not accord with the idea." [46]

Another agreement worked out by Lachlan and Alexander was that young Aleck would be educated in Scotland under the watchful eye of his grandfather. Lachlan had insisted that Alexander be given a British education, and evidently Alexander wanted his son to have the same experience. William Panton honored this wish of his friend and dispatched Aleck to Inverness by way of London. John Innerarity, Panton's brother-in-law associate in London, was charged with the care of the boy. Davy Taitt, several years older than Aleck, went with him as a companion. Aleck was nearly the same age as John Lachlan, and we can imagine that the two boys enjoyed each other's company when visiting Lachlan at Dunmaglass. Lachlan Lia must have felt that he was entrusted with the future of the two clans. John Lachlan was chief of the McGillivrays, and it was assumed that Aleck McGillivray would become the leader of the Creek Nation. [47]

Aleck and Davy Taitt were sent to Banff to study under a tutor named Robertson. The older boy chafed under Robertson's restrictions and soon returned to America. Aleck, like his father, was adaptable and got along well with his tutor. John Innerarity wrote a glowing report of Aleck's progress in 1798: "As for Aleck the accounts I have of him are of a pleasing nature and he bids fair to make a good scholar and what is better a good man, and as for David's being taken away from him, I don't think it will make any great difference to him." [48] Davy went home to take advantage of the generous legacy Sehoy Weatherford provided him. In 1809, Benjamin Hawkins reported that the young man lived on the Alabama River, "is careful and conducts himself well." [49]

The McGillivrays of Strathnairn, from Archibald the great trader to Alexander the Creek chief, had played vital roles in the shaping of the

southern frontier. They were displaced by the revolutionary generation, which had a different agenda for the future. But there were other
frontiers, and the energy of the McGillivrays was not nearly spent.
There was another William McGillivray, born in 1764 and very likely
named after the then chief of the clan. He was the eldest of twelve children born to Donald McGillivray of Clovendale, the estate neighboring Dunmaglass. This Donald married Anne McTavish, whose brother
Simon made a small fortune as a trader in the Mohawk Valley of
New York and transferred his operations to Canada after the American
Revolution. Simon offered to sponsor young William in the trade, just
as Archibald had sponsored Lachlan long before. In 1783, nineteen-
year-old William left Inverness with much the same expectations that
had motivated the pioneers of the Darien settlement in 1735; he was
off to seek adventure and his fortune. Like his predecessors, he found
more than enough adventure in the Canadian wilds, and like Lachlan
he made a fortune in the Indian trade. He took an Indian wife and
fathered mixed-blood children and had them baptized in Montreal.
When he returned to Invernesshire in 1793, he was hailed as a celebrity.
The town of Inverness tendered him an official reception and made
him an honorary burgess. As a dutiful member of his clan, he called
upon his chief, the ten-year-old John Lachlan, at Dunmaglass.[50] One
can imagine the interesting stories told around the supper table, with
Lachlan Lia reminiscing about his forays against the Cherokees in 1760
and young William describing the terrible winters he spent at Ile a la
Crosse some twenty-five hundred miles by canoe from Montreal.

Though the southern frontier was closed to McGillivray and his
friends, the great northern frontier beckoned. Scots who were forbidden by angry Georgians to enter their state, at least until their
war-inflamed emotions cooled, would help form a new country. The
bagpipe and the tartan would become symbols of modern Canada.
William McGillivray earned the title bestowed on him by his biogra-
pher, "McGillivray, Lord of the Northwest." Under his leadership the
North West Company rivaled the Hudson's Bay Company for control
of the fur country. Alexander Mackenzie of Stornoway and Inverness
became the first white man to reach the Pacific by an overland route.

Simon Fraser of Clan Chattan matched the exploit in 1808, shortly after Lewis and Clark's epic trek for President Jefferson and the United States. William's brother Duncan McGillivray took a special interest in exploring the recesses of the Canadian Rockies until death stopped him in 1808.[51] The Highlanders stamped their names on the rivers and passes of the West and in the pages of Canadian history.

Lachlan Lia played a role in perpetuating the traditions of the Highlands. In 1782, the law proscribing bagpipes and tartans was repealed as an acknowledgment of the loyalty of the Scots during the American war. In January 1788, Charles Edward Stuart, the "King over the Water" to many Highlanders, died, a victim of boredom and dissipation. His death removed any vestige of a possibility of another uprising. For the Highlanders who could never forget the forty-five, the death of the man they would always remember as Bonnie Prince Charlie was an incentive to preserve the memory of the past. Thirteen gentlemen, one of whom was Lachlan McGillivray, met at the town hall in Inverness on June 11, 1788, to form a club that would assemble once a year for a week of traditional games and social events. Thus was founded the Northern Meeting, an organization devoted to the preservation of Highland piping, dancing, and games. Two hundred years later, the Northern Meeting celebrated its bicentennial at its own park in Inverness.[52]

Lachlan died at Dunmaglass on November 16, 1799, rich in years and satisfaction. His attitude was expressed in a letter to his factor in Inverness: "I thank God that I enjoy as much health as I can expect at my time of life."[53]

It was just as well that he was spared the sorrow of mourning for the lovely, nineteen-year-old Barbara Ann, who died in Edinburgh a few months after Lachlan's death. And it was merciful that he did not know that his grandson, Aleck, outlived him by only two years and never returned to claim the place waiting for him at Little Tallassee. William Panton's partner John Leslie visited Dunmaglass in 1799 and kept in touch with Aleck's progress. In 1802 he reported sadly to Panton that the youth was suffering from pneumonia. The doctors gave him three months to live.[54]

A happier fate was in store for seventeen-year-old John Lachlan. No

McGillivray chief ever owned as much land in Strathnairn as he inherited. Thanks to the conservation efforts of Lachlan Lia, the estates had never been so productive. In 1800, John Lachlan purchased a cornetcy in the Light Dragoons and later a lieutenancy. He acquired the reputation of being a skilled swordsman. He was also extravagant as a young man but settled down after marrying Jane Walcott of Inverness in 1805. John Lachlan lived until 1852, and in the words of the clan historian, he was "a chief greatly loved and respected by his clansmen and deeply mourned" at his death. He had no children and left a fortune of £40,000 to the tenants of his estates. He was the last of the line to live at Dunmaglass. After his death the chiefdom passed to the Canadian branch of the clan.[55]

Epilogue

Lachlan McGillivray died as the century ended. The southern frontier was still plastic, but most of the questions Oglethorpe's pioneers might have posed were answered. The French were gone, leaving a cultural residue in the dialect, diet, architecture, and folklore of Louisiana. The Spanish were back in Florida after a lapse of twenty years, but they posed no threat as they had in Oglethorpe's day. They were nervous neighbors, worried about rumors of invasion by aggressive Georgians. They were right to be worried. The British had left the southern frontier, but their influence was still strong in the Northwest.

Georgians were restless behind the Oconee River barrier, already demanding more land as theirs by right of their victory in the American Revolution. The formative forces were nearly complete in determining the kind of society the mature state would have. The commercialism and pragmatism they learned from their Carolina mentors reached new heights in the bizarre Yazoo land fraud episode. The worldly, pleasure-bent life-style associated with the Charlestown ethic was diluted by the infusion of evangelical religion, which reached rural Georgia before the Revolution and spread into towns after the war, benefiting from the identification of Anglicanism and Toryism. A third influence was the class-conscious agrarianism of the Virginians, who moved into the Georgia piedmont before the Revolution and in larger numbers afterward. They were shocked by the crassness of the Yazoo and other speculations and joined a reform movement which attempted to bring a degree of honesty into politics. These three influences, meeting and melding in Georgia, would in time shape the society of the states of Alabama and Mississippi and even Texas.

What of that other society to the west of the Oconee? The Creek Nation was still powerful, but the revolutionary era had a lasting impact. An estimated three to four hundred loyalists fled into the Indian country, bringing slaves with them. Many of them established plantations. Creek war parties captured slaves on raids into Georgia and Carolina. Kathryn Braund has noted the merging of aspects of African culture with that of the Indians.¹ Mixed-blood chiefs followed Alexander McGillivray's lead in establishing plantations, growing cotton, and raising livestock. Daniel Usner has counted thirty-five hundred black slaves and two hundred free blacks among the thirty thousand Creek, Choctaw, and Chickasaw Indians in 1795. He credits the Indians with a "resourceful adaptability" not generally noticed by historians.² It was the policy of the United States government and its agents to foster that adaptability. During the Washington administration government "factories" or trading posts were established in an effort to counteract the influence of foreign traders but also to reform and "civilize" the Indians. In practice, the American policy was remarkably like that suggested by William Knox in 1768. Knox's plan consisted of eradicating the tradition of warfare; furnishing seeds, tools, cattle, and poultry to lure the men away from hunting; supplying locks and hinges to introduce the notion of private property; and preaching the message of Christianity. Knox was convinced that "man was intended for polished society" and that the Indians should learn good manners.³ Thomas Jefferson would have differed with Knox only in the degree of polish that might be expected. It was a settled policy at the government posts that Indians should put on the trappings of white society.

Benjamin Hawkins, the conscientious agent among the Creek Indians, was convinced that this "plan of civilization" was working. He wrote to James Madison in 1803 that warfare and talk of war had been banished from the Indian country: "Tell Mrs. Madison that we are all Quakers in the Indian agency." He went on to say that hunting had been reduced in importance to an amusement for young men. "We shall in future rely on stockraising, agriculture and household manufactures," he reported.[4] William Knox, growing old but still active as agent for Nova Scotia, would have been pleased with this progress. The pious Knox would have applauded the goals of the Indian trade as enunciated by Thomas McKenney, the superintendent of trade: "It is enough to know that the Indians are men and that we have the power not only to enhance their happiness in this world, but in the next also."[5]

Many of the Creeks, especially the older men, were not pleased with this civilization. Chief Efau Haujo spoke frankly to Hawkins: "We must tell you there are many of our Chiefs who think much of times past and are constantly talking of them. They think the present times and the future prospects arising out of them won't do."[6] In spite of this cautionary admonition, there was a pervasive conviction that changes were inevitable. At the turn of the century, no one knew what the results of the cultural interaction would be, but it seemed that the future held reform, not removal. The insatiable appetite of the frontier people for land would nullify the government's efforts to transform hunters into sedentary farmers.

Historians of American Indians and ethnohistorians have given much attention to the question of responsibility for the damage done to the colonial environment. It has been decided that Indians and Europeans alike contributed to the destruction of wildlife and the depletion of the forests. In fact, the first human beings who crossed into North America began the process. (One is tempted to look back further into the evolutionary struggle among species.) Timothy Silver has studied the colonial environment and suggested that we should stop trying to assign guilt to either colonists or Indians and should "view the destruction of wildlife as the understandable, although lamentable, result of a complex contest of cultures played out in a land of plenty."[7]

Ever since Frederick Jackson Turner there has been an assumption that Indian traders were unsavory characters who broke down Indians' resistance by fashioning a chain of dependency that was a preliminary step toward removal. To what degree were they culpable? If we use the career of Lachlan McGillivray as a yardstick, the answer is not simple, but a judgment can be made.

During the period of the 1740s and 1750s, which was dominated by the two wars with France, McGillivray and his fellow traders enjoyed a positive relationship with the Indians. They were guests who lived in Indian villages because their hosts wanted them there. They were on their best behavior because they were aware that the French had put a price on their heads, and they depended on the friendship of the local Indians for protection. Their marriages and their mixed-blood children forged lasting bonds. There can be no doubt that the Creeks among whom he lived liked and respected Lachlan McGillivray. It would be a mistake to imagine that he manipulated the Indians into doing something they did not want to do. He had influence because he talked their language and respected their customs but especially because they recognized him as a good man. At that time the number of traders was restricted, as was the use of rum. If McGillivray got rich by his trade, it was because his post was favorably, if dangerously, situated.

In his role as emissary of the various governors, McGillivray mainly arranged conferences and acted as interpreter. His swapping of his property at New Savannah for Chickasaw land in Carolina was judged harshly by Edmond Atkin, but it was done openly and aboveboard. The Chickasaws could have nullified the transaction if they wished, but they refused to do so. He played an important part in the cessions of 1763 and 1773, but the initiatives came from the Indians, the Lower Creeks in the first instance and the Cherokees in the second.

In Augusta, McGillivray was a responsible leader and builder as a member of Brown, Rae and Company and later as a magistrate and member of the assembly. His friendship with the Creeks and Chickasaws paid dividends when he led them against Cherokee war parties outside Augusta and later when he was instrumental in drawing the boundary line of 1763.

McGillivray was in Savannah after 1763 when the Indian country was thrown open to traders indiscriminately. As an importer of goods, McGillivray was removed from direct involvement in the Indian trade. His services regarding the Creeks were limited to acting as an adviser to Governor Wright and Lord Hillsborough.

Who can be blamed for the deterioration of trade, the abuse of rum, the purchasing of green skins, and the mutual cheating that occurred? The frequent rotation of secretaries of state and the subsequent shifts in Indian policy were one reason. The failure of the largest traders to manage their employees was another. The breakdown of the earlier domination of trade by a few large companies was a third. Perhaps the main reason was that the fear of the French was removed and British traders could cheat the Indians with comparative impunity. This last idea should be balanced with the caution that the Indians could and did kill traders who vexed them too much. Emistisiguo's enforcement of the regulations might have had good results, but the promising experiment was terminated too soon.

Despite the deplorable condition of the trade in the decade before the American Revolution, the Creek Nation was strong as ever. James Adair thought so when he wrote that the Creeks had increased in numbers and as a threat since 1763. "They are certainly the most powerful Indian nation we are acquainted with on this continent," he stated.[8]

Although traders played intermediary roles in the cessions of 1763 and 1773 and Cherokee debts to traders prompted the latter cession, traders were reluctant to take any additional land. They advised Governor Wright not to seek the Oconee strip in 1774, thereby earning the acute displeasure of the settlers. Thus the traders were not the dispossessors. The ever-encroaching frontier people were. The traders were themselves dispossessed as a result of the Revolution. Traders who remained loyal, like McGillivray, were forced to leave the country. Augusta lost the Indian trade to Mobile and Pensacola. Georgia politics was based on the expulsion of the Creeks from the Ogeechee-Oconee tract and the exploitation of lands to the west.

Even at the turn of the century, after Lachlan McGillivray's death, the fate of the Creeks was not sealed. Those who were responsible for Indian policy believed that Creek society could be transformed into a fascimile of Anglo-American society. It is true that Indians incurred debts to traders and were forced to sell land to pay these debts, but the expelling force continued to be the pressure caused by white intrusion. The Indians were dispossessed, not by those who did business with them but by those who had no intention of doing business with them.

As in the argument about the environment, however, assessing blame is probably an idle exercise.

Lachlan McGillivray did not cause the changes that occurred on the southern frontier; he was alert and opportunistic enough to take advantage of them. Whether his decision to remain loyal to the king at the outbreak of the Revolution was motivated by altruism or opportunism we do not know. He helped shape the frontier in the sense D. W. Meinig used the expression when he described "the continuous shaping of America." Meinig noted the influence of small groups of immigrants on the subsequent history of a region, referring to the groups as "nuclei."[9] The Darien Scots were one such nucleus. They played a role disproportionate to their numbers in their impact on the society of the Creek Indians as well as that of the colonial Georgians.

One wonders if Lachlan McGillivray pondered the lessons of his life as he sat before the fire in the great room of Dunmaglass. He had given much to the New World, and he had learned much. He had learned from his Indian friends that the continual accumulation of possessions did not bring contentment. Therefore, in his sixtieth year he turned over his estate to his cousin in return for a comfortable annuity. He learned also that it is good to die in a land inhabited by the shades of one's ancestors. And so he returned to the Highlands, where tales of fairy folk and water kelpies added a dimension to nature. He planted trees and drained bogs and improved the appearance of the valley of the Nairn. He rejoiced in the company of his grandson, his young cousins, and his kinsmen of the clan. And he died where he was born, among his ancestors at Dunmaglass not far from Inverness.

Abbreviations

AHQ	*Alabama Historical Quarterly*
AHR	*American Historical Review*
AO	Audit Office, PRO
CO	Colonial Office, PRO
CRG	*Colonial Records of Georgia*
EHR	*English Historical Review*
FHQ	*Florida Historical Quarterly*
GHQ	*Georgia Historical Quarterly*
GHS	Georgia Historical Society
HMC	Historical Manuscripts Commission
JAH	*Journal of American History*
JCHA	*Journal of Commons House of Assembly, Colonial Records of South Carolina*
LHQ	*Louisiana Historical Quarterly*
MVHR	*Mississippi Valley Historical Review*
NYHS	New-York Historical Society
PRO	British Public Record Office
PRO, SC	Records in the British Public Record Office Relating to South Carolina, South Carolina Archives Microcopy
RRG	*Revolutionary Records of Georgia*
SCCJ	South Carolina Council Journals, Library of Congress microfilm
SCHM	*South Carolina Historical Magazine*
T	Treasury Papers, PRO

WLCL   William L. Clements Library, Ann Arbor, Michigan
W&MQ   *William and Mary Quarterly*
WO   War Office, PRO

Notes

PROLOGUE

1. William P. Cumming, *The Southeast in Early Maps* (1958; rpt. Chapel Hill: University of North Carolina Press, 1962), 39.

2. James H. Merrell, " 'Our Bond of Peace': Patterns of Intercultural Exchange in the Carolina Piedmont, 1650–1750," in Peter H. Wood, Gregory A. Waselkov, and M. Thomas Hatley, *Powhatan's Mantle* (Lincoln: University of Nebraska Press, 1989), 202–3.

3. Ibid., 212.

4. Peter H. Wood, "The Changing Population of the Colonial South: An Overview by Race and Region, 1685–1790," in Wood, Waselkov, and Hatley, *Powhatan's Mantle*, 92. Wood's statistics graphically illustrate the changing demography of the southern frontier region. The number of Creek Indians grew from nine thousand in 1700 to fourteen thousand in 1775; by then, there were eighteen thousand whites and fifteen thousand blacks in Georgia and the Creek country (ibid., 38).

ONE. STRATHNAIRN IN INVERNESSHIRE

1. Albert James Pickett, *History of Alabama and Incidentally of Georgia and Mississippi, from the Earliest Period* (1851; rpt. Birmingham: Birmingham Book and Magazine Co., 1962), 342; William Mackenzie to I. K. Tift, February 1, 1844, William Mackenzie Papers, Georgia Historical Society, Savannah; J. P.

Maclean, *An Historical Account of the Settlement of Scotch Highlanders in America Prior to the Peace of 1783* (Cleveland: Hilman-Taylor, 1900), 150.

2. Robert McGillivray and George B. Macgillivray, *A History of the Clan MacGillivray* (Ontario: G. B. MacGillivray, 1973), 17–20, 227 (the authors listed sixty-four different spellings of McGillivray); Hugh Swinton McGillivray, "A Sketch of the McGillivrays of Charleston and Connections," McGillivray Family Papers, South Carolina Historical Society, Charleston. John McGillivray is mentioned in J. H. Easterby, *History of the St. Andrew's Society of Charleston, South Carolina, 1729–1929* (Charleston: Published by the society, 1929), 21, 26. For Forster's surrender and Sheriffmuir see Sir Charles Petrie, *The Jacobite Movement: The First Phase, 1688–1716* (London: Eyre and Spottiswoode, 1948), 186–89.

3. The expression is from Macaulay's essay "The Earl of Chatham," cited by Hugh Swinton McGillivray in "A Sketch of the McGillivrays."

4. Document dated February 9, 1714, recorded June 26, 1734, Fraser Mackintosh Collection, Scottish Record Office, Edinburgh.

5. McGillivray and Macgillivray, *Clan MacGillivray*, 63; McGillivray, "A Sketch of the McGillivrays"; Charles Fraser-Mackintosh, *An Account of the Confederation of Clan Chattan: Its Kith and Kin* (Glasgow: John Mackay, 1898), 1–4; A. M. Mackintosh, *The Mackintoshes and Clan Chattan* (Edinburgh: Printed for the author, 1903), 498–99.

6. McGillivray and Macgillivray, *Clan MacGillivray*, 63–64; William Mackay, ed., *The Letter-Book of Bailie John Steuart of Inverness, 1715–1752* (Edinburgh: T. and A. Constable, 1915), xli; T. C. Smout, *A History of the Scottish People* (New York: Charles Scribner's Sons, 1969), 42.

7. Henry Grey Graham, *The Social Life of Scotland in the Eighteenth Century*, 2 vols. (London: Adam and Charles Black, 1900), 1:33–35, 160, 169, 39.

8. Ibid., 8–11; quotation on p. 10.

9. Ibid., 192–93.

10. McGillivray and Macgillivray, *Clan MacGillivray*, 21–23.

11. William Mackenzie to William B. Hodgson, September 28, November 1, 1844, William Mackenzie Papers, GHS, also in *GHS Collections*, 18:134–242; Charles Fraser-Mackintosh, *Letters of Two Centuries Chiefly Connected with Inverness and the Highlands from 1616 to 1815* (Inverness: A. & W. Mackenzie, 1890), 386–87.

12. Oglethorpe to the Trustees, February 13, 1736, *GHS Collections*, 3:10–13.

13. John Mackintosh of Holme was a literate and courteous gentleman as is evidenced by a letter he wrote to a relative; he commented that one of his companions asked his father to send "servants and necessaries" (Fraser-Mackintosh, *Letters*, 203–4).

14. E. Merton Coulter and Albert B. Saye, *A List of the Early Settlers of Georgia* (Athens: University of Georgia Press, 1949), 83–84. The list of settlers is in the Phillips Collection, Special Collections, University of Georgia Libraries. There is evidence that Archibald was Lachlan's brother. Hugh Swinton McGillivray stated that Lachlan, Alexander, and Archibald were brothers, but nothing was otherwise known about Archibald ("A Sketch of the McGillivrays").

15. William Mackenzie to William B. Hodgson, September 28, 1844, William Mackenzie Papers, GHS.

16. The story of Lachlan's "running away" is part of the family legend. Hugh Swinton McGillivray mentioned it in his sketch of the Charleston McGillivrays, written around 1935. The clan historians McGillivray and Macgillivray follow Pickett's *History of Alabama*, 342–43. Benjamin W. Griffith, Jr., also uses Pickett's description of Lachlan's arrival in Charleston in 1738 with a shilling in his pocket in *McIntosh and Weatherford, Creek Indian Leaders* (Tuscaloosa: University of Alabama Press, 1988), 3. The first to record Lachlan's connection with the Darien contingent was Mary Ann Oglesby Neeley, "Lachlan McGillivray: A Scot on the Alabama Frontier," *AHQ* 36 (Spring 1974): 5–14.

17. Lines quoted in Maclean, *Historical Account*, 152.

TWO. FORMING A NEW COLONY

1. Maclean, *Historical Account*, 150–55; Oglethorpe to Trustees, February 13, 1736, *GHS Collections*, 3:10–13.

2. Oglethorpe to Trustees, February 27, 1736, *GHS Collections*, 3:14–16.

3. Oglethorpe to Trustees, February 13, 1736, ibid., 10–13.

4. Oglethorpe to Trustees, February 27, 1736, ibid., 14–16.

5. Oglethorpe to Egmont, February 1, 1736, in Mills Lane, ed., *General Oglethorpe's Georgia: Colonial Letters, 1733–37*, 2 vols. (Savannah: Beehive Press, 1975), 1:237–38. For John Wesley's description of the site, see Robert G. McPherson, ed., *The Journal of the Earl of Egmont: Abstract of the Trustees Pro-*

ceedings for Establishing the Colony of Georgia, 1732–1738 (Athens: University of Georgia Press, 1962), 293; Oglethorpe to Trustees, October 20, 1739, *GHS Collections*, 3:89–91.

6. McPherson, ed., *Egmont's Journal*, 217–18.

7. William McIntosh, oldest son of John Mohr Mackintosh, told his grandson Thomas Spalding of Sapelo that "the Indians were greatly attached to the Highlanders, not only as being the soldiers of their beloved man, General Oglethorpe, but because of their wild manners, of their manly sports, of their eastern costume, so much resembling their own." William stated that he had learned their language; it would have been equally possible for Lachlan to have done so (Thomas Spalding, "Sketch of the Life of General James Oglethorpe," *GHS Collections*, 1:271).

8. Oglethorpe to Verelst, December 21, 1738; Oglethorpe to Trustees, July 4, 1739, *GHS Collections*, 3:66–67, 75–76.

9. Oglethorpe to Trustees, June 9, 1733, *CRG*, 20:23–25.

10. Harold S. Maness, *Forgotten Outpost: Fort Moore and Savannah Town, 1685–1765* (Pickens, S.C.: BPB Publications, 1986), 65–110.

11. McPherson, ed., *Egmont's Journal*, 158; Oglethorpe to Noble Jones, June 14, 1736, Phillips Collection 14202:4, University of Georgia Libraries; Oglethorpe to Lacy, June 11, 1736, ibid., 14202:2. For the circumstances surrounding the founding of Augusta, see Edward J. Cashin, ed., *Colonial Augusta: "Key of the Indian Country"* (Macon, Ga.: Mercer University Press, 1986), 29–32, 59–62.

12. McPherson, ed., *Egmont's Journal*, 271–72. For Tanner's brash conduct, see Thomas John's Journal or Narrative on Oath, December 2, 1736, in J. H. Easterby, ed., *The Colonial Records of South Carolina: The Journal of the Commons House of Assembly*, 9 vols. (Columbia: Historical Commission of South Carolina and the South Carolina Archives Department, 1951–62), 1:138–40.

13. William C. Sturtevant, "Commentary," in *Eighteenth Century Florida and Its Borderlands*, ed. Samuel Proctor (Gainesville: University Presses of Florida, 1975), p. 44, cited in Kathryn E. Braund, "Mutual Convenience — Mutual Dependence: The Creeks, Augusta and the Deerskin Trade, 1733–1783" (Ph.D. dissertation, Florida State University, 1986), 221.

14. Patrick Mackay to [Thomas Causton], March 27, 1735, *CRG*, 20:290–91; Phinizy Spalding, "Georgia and South Carolina During the Oglethorpe Period, 1732–1743" (Ph.D. dissertation, University of North Carolina, 1963), 61–82; Trustees Minutes, April 18, 1743, *CRG*, 2:414.

15. Oglethorpe to Trustees, May 18, July 1, 1736, *GHS Collections*, 3:33–37.
16. McPherson, ed., *Egmont's Journal*, 192–95.
17. Minutes of President and Assistants, July 10, 1745, *CRG*, 6:137. This John McGillivray died February 24, 1748, leaving to his son Lachlan twelve head of cattle, six horses, and a slave named Glasco (Willard E. Wight, *Abstracts of Colonial Wills of the State of Georgia, 1733–1777* [Spartanburg, S.C.: Reprint Company, 1981], 83).
18. Charles Gayarre, *History of Louisiana*, 4 vols. (New Orleans: James A. Gresham, 1879), 1:481–82.
19. At an Audience of the Chickasaws at Savannah in Georgia, July 1736, William R. Coe Papers, South Carolina Historical Society, Charleston. The allusion to redness by the Indians and Oglethorpe is interesting in view of Alden Vaughan's thesis that the Indians were regarded as red-skinned only later in the century to imply the impossibility of assimilation ("From White Man to Redskin: Changing Anglo-American Perceptions of the American Indian," *AHR* 87 [October 1982]: 917–53).
20. Audience of the Chickasaws, Coe Papers, South Carolina Historical Society; also see Phillips Collection, 14202:46, University of Georgia Libraries.
21. Audience of the Chickasaws, Coe Papers, South Carolina Historical Society.
22. Oglethorpe to Trustees, July 26, 1736, *GHS Collections*, 3:40–42.
23. The best account of Oglethorpe's activities is Phinizy Spalding, *Oglethorpe in America* (1977; rpt. Athens: University of Georgia Press, 1984).
24. Oglethorpe to Trustees, July 26, 1736, *GHS Collections*, 3:40–42.
25. McPherson, ed., *Egmont's Journal*, 217–18, 344.
26. William Verelst to Thomas Causton, May 27, 1737, *CRG*, 29:194–97; John Mackintosh Moore [sic] to Verelst, November 15, 1737, *CRG*, 22, pt. 1:10–11.
27. Statement of Alexander Monroe, November 29, 1741, in Trevor Reese, ed., *The Clamorous Malcontents: Criticisms and Defenses of the Colony of Georgia, 1741–1743* (Savannah: Beehive Press, 1973), 301–4.
28. Ibid.; also Statement of John McLeod, November 12, 1741, ibid., 299–300.
29. Stephens Journal, December 4, 1738, *CRG*, 4:239.
30. Petition dated Savannah, December 9, 1738, in Reese, ed., *Clamorous Malcontents*, 75–80.

31. Harvey H. Jackson, "The Darien Antislavery Petition of 1739 and the Georgia Plan," *W&MQ* 3d ser., 34 (October 1977): 618–31.

32. Petition dated New Inverness, January 3, 1738/9, in Reese, ed., *Clamorous Malcontents*, 249–50.

33. Statement of Alexander Monroe, November 29, 1741, ibid., 301–4.

34. "A List of Complainants, who are stiled a few Clamorous Malecontents," October 27, 1741, ibid., 340–44.

35. Statement of Alexander Monroe, November 29, 1741, ibid., 301–4.

36. Statement of George Philp, February 16, 1740, ibid., 304–6.

37. John Mackintosh to Alexander Mackintosh, June 20, 1741, *CRG*, 35:340–43; John Mackintosh to Verelst, June 24, 1741, ibid., 344–46; Reese, ed., *Clamorous Malcontents*, 301–4. Lord Egmont contended that the Darien people forced Oglethorpe to let them go to Florida (Clarence L. VerSteeg, ed., *A True and Historical Narrative of the Colony of Georgia by Pat. Tailfer and Others with Comments by the Earl of Egmont* [Athens: University of Georgia Press, 1960], 128).

38. Bienville to Maurepas, February 28, 1737, in Dunbar Rowland, Albert Godfrey Sanders, and Patricia Ann Galloway, eds., *Mississippi Provincial Archives: French Dominion* (Jackson, Miss.: Press of the Mississippi Department of Archives and History, 1932–84), 3:693–98.

39. Thomas Jones to William Verelst, February 17, 1739, *CRG*, 22, pt. 2:79–80; Stephens' Journal, February 13, 1739, *CRG*, 4:279–80.

40. For the text of the treaty see *GHQ* 4 (March 1920): 5–8; Lachlan's sponsor, John Mackintosh of Holme was one of the witnesses (*CRG*, 26:485–90).

41. Oglethorpe to Trustees, March 8, 1739, *GHS Collections*, 3:68; also in *CRG*, 22, pt. 2:108.

42. Oglethorpe to Trustees, April 10, 1740, *GHS Collections*, 3:111–12; Oglethorpe to Trustees, October 19, 1739, *CRG*, 22, pt. 2:244–49.

43. Peter H. Wood, *Black Majority: Negroes in Colonial South Carolina from 1670 Through the Stono Rebellion* (New York: Knopf, 1975), 326; Larry E. Ivers, *British Drums on the Southern Frontier: The Military Colonization of Georgia, 1733–1749* (Chapel Hill: University of North Carolina Press, 1974), 88.

44. Stephens' Journal, December 19, 1739, *CRG*, 4:471.

45. Gayarre, *History of Louisiana*, 1:513.

46. Oglethorpe to Trustees, November 16, 1739, in Lane, ed., *General Oglethorpe's Georgia*, 2:420–22.

47. Ivers, *British Drums*, 92–95.

48. Thomas Eyre to Robert Eyre, December 4, 1740, in Lane, ed., *General Oglethorpe's Georgia*, 2:499–510; see also Edward J. Cashin, "Oglethorpe's Contest for the Backcountry," in Phinizy Spalding and Harvey H. Jackson, eds., *Oglethorpe in Perspective: Georgia's Founder After Two Hundred Years* (Tuscaloosa: University of Alabama Press, 1989), 108.

49. Ivers, *British Drums*, 102.

50. Ibid., 101.

51. Ibid., 108–12. Ivers defends Oglethorpe, stating that he did not deviate from his basic plan. For a different opinion, see Spalding, *Oglethorpe in Georgia*, 111, who contends that Oglethorpe "did not know what to do once his first plan" went awry.

52. Ivers, *British Drums*, 116–17.

53. Ibid., 120.

54. Ibid., 123.

55. John Mackintosh to Alexander Mackintosh, June 20, 1741, *CRG*, 35:340–43.

56. Ivers, *British Drums*, 139.

57. Andrew Grant and others to Trustees, August 10, 1740, in VerSteeg, ed., *True and Historical Narrative*, 126–27.

58. George Whitefield to Trustees, April 7, 1740, in Lane, ed., *General Oglethorpe's Georgia*, 2:440–41.

59. Thomas Eyre to Robert Eyre, December 4, 1740, ibid., 499–502.

60. Thomas Causton to Trustees, February 19, 1741, ibid., 546–70.

61. "Number of Inhabitants in Georgia by the latest information exclusive of the Regiment," Coe Papers, South Carolina Historical Society.

62. William Stephens, "A State of the Province of Georgia . . . ," *GHS Collections*, 2:72; "An Impartial Inquiry into the State and Utility of the Province of Georgia," ibid., 1:179; Tailfer et al., "A True and Historical Narrative . . . ," ibid., 2:260; Causton to Trustees, February 19, 1741, in Lane, ed., *General Oglethorpe's Georgia*, 2:567; Memorial of Captain Daniel Pepper, March 26, 1743, *JCHA*, 4:321–22.

63. Egmont's Journal, October 6, 1741, *CRG*, 5:558–59.

64. Stephens' Journal, June 3, 30, 1740, *CRG*, 4:585–86.

65. *South Carolina Gazette*, January 12, 1738, September 8, 1739, September 26, 1741.

66. Stephens' Journal, June 2, 1741, *CRG*, 4, supplement:156; Egmont's Journal, October 21, 1740, January 26, 1741, *CRG*, 5:402, 441.

67. Stephens' Journal, February 12, 1740, *CRG*, 4:511; Mackay, ed., *Letter-Book of Bailie John Steuart*, 424–25; Oglethorpe to Duncan Forbes, February 12, 1740, in Duncan Forbes, *Culloden Papers, Comprising An Extensive and Interesting Correspondence from the Year 1625 to 1748* . . . (London: T. Cadell and W. Davies, 1815), 155.

68. Mackay, ed., *Letter-Book of Bailie John Steuart*, 425.

69. Easterby, *History of the St. Andrew's Society*, 21, 26; David Moltke-Hansen, "The Empire of Scotsman Robert Wells, Loyalist, South Carolina Printer-Publisher" (M.A. thesis, University of South Carolina, 1984), 21.

70. *South Carolina Gazette*, November 20, December 25, 1740; McGillivray, "A Sketch of the McGillivrays."

71. *JCHA*, 1741–42, pp. 324–26, 441, 418.

72. Stephens' Journal, May 29, 1741, *CRG*, 4, supplement:154.

73. *South Carolina Gazette*, June 11, 1741.

74. Bienville to Maurepas, February 18, 1742, in Rowland, Sanders, and Galloway, eds., *Mississippi Provincial Archives*, 3:758–60.

75. David H. Corkran, *The Creek Frontier, 1540–1783* (Norman: University of Oklahoma Press, 1967), 107.

76. Stephens' Journal, June 6, 1741, *CRG*, 4, supplement:160, 162, 169, 178.

77. Oglethorpe to Trustees, July 20, 1741, *CRG*, 35:351.

78. Oglethorpe to Trustees, November 12, 1741, ibid., 379–80.

79. Thomas Jones to Trustees, October 23, 1741, *CRG*, 23:123–24.

THREE. THE CLAN CHATTAN CONNECTION

1. Pickett, *History of Alabama*, 342–43.

2. Thomas S. Woodward, *Woodward's Reminiscences of the Creek, or Muscogee Indians, Contained in Letters to Friends in Georgia and Alabama* (Montgomery: Barrett and Wimbish, 1859), 59. A Donald Macdonald and a Norman Macpherson came to Georgia on the same ship that carried Lachlan McGillivray (Coulter and Saye, *List of the Early Settlers*, 83, 87).

3. *South Carolina Gazette*, November 20, 1740.

4. Atkin to Lyttelton, November 30, 1759, Henry William Lyttelton Papers, WLCL. Archibald McGillivray announced that he intended to depart the province in November 1744 (*South Carolina Gazette*, August 20, 1744). Petition of Lachlan McGillivray, n.d., in William L. McDowell, Jr., ed., *Colonial Records*

of South Carolina: Documents Relating to Indian Affairs, May 21, 1750–August 7, 1754 (Columbia: South Carolina Archives Department, 1958), 518.

5. Walter B. Edgar, ed., *The Letterbook of Robert Pringle*, 2 vols. (Columbia: University of South Carolina Press, 1972), 2:807–9.

6. "Contract of Wadsett twixt the Laird of Mackintosh and Archibald Mackgillivray 1749," December 19, 1749, Mackintosh of Mackintosh Muniments, Scottish Record Office, Edinburgh.

7. I am indebted to Professor W. W. Wallace for sending me a copy of Lachlan McGillivray's will and to Professor William Coker for bringing it to my attention and putting me in touch with Professor Wallace. By coincidence, Professor Wallace is a direct descendant of Lachlan McGillivray through Sophia Durant.

8. Corkran, *Creek Frontier*, 112.

9. Daniel H. Thomas, "Fort Toulouse: The French Outpost at the Alibamos on the Coosa," *AHQ* 22 (Fall 1960):150.

10. Ibid., 143.

11. "Address to the Lords Commissioners for Trade and the Assembly's answers to their Lordship's Queries," January 29, 1719, Coe Papers, South Carolina Historical Society.

12. John Barnwell to Charles Lord Viscount Townshend, "The Present State of the French Settlements in Louisiana," 1720, ibid.

13. Larry E. Ivers, "The Soldiers of Fort Augusta," in Cashin, ed., *Colonial Augusta*, 79.

14. S.C. Council Minutes, December 10, 1743, March 21, 1744, SCCJ.

15. Ibid.

16. Ibid., December 15, 16, 1743.

17. B. R. Carroll, *Historical Collections of South Carolina*, 2 vols. (New York: Harper and Brothers, 1836), 1:358.

18. S.C. Council Minutes, April 20, 1744, SCCJ.

19. Patrick Brown announced his intention of establishing an indigo plantation, October 29, 1748 (*CRG*, 6:224–25). Alexander Wood applied for seventeen hundred acres stating that he had a family of sixty-four persons, thirty-four white and thirty black, November 21, 1746 (S.C. Council Minutes, PRO, CO 5/455).

20. Memorial of Captain Daniel Pepper, March 26, 1743, in *JCHA*, 4:321–22; Trustees Minutes, August 23, 1738, *CRG*, 1:331; John Pitts Corry, *Indian Affairs in Georgia, 1732–1756* (Philadelphia: George S. Ferguson, 1936), 51–66.

21. S.C. Council Minutes, March 1, 1744, SCCJ.

22. Martyn to Stephens, May 10, 1743, *CRG*, 30:277–86.

23. Vaudreuil and Salmon to Maurepas, July 21, 1743, in Rowland, Sanders, and Galloway, eds., *Mississippi Provincial Archives*, 4:207–10.

24. S.C. Council Minutes, December 10, 1743, SCCJ.

25. Vaudreuil to Maurepas, February 12, 1744, Rowland, Sanders, and Galloway, eds., *Mississippi Provincial Archives*, 4:214–24.

26. Extracts of paragraphs from Capt. Kent's Letter to General Oglethorpe dated 19 December 1742 at the Cowetas in the Creek Indian Nation, *CRG*, 36:180; *South Carolina Gazette*, September 13, 1741.

27. Samuel Cole Williams, ed., *Adair's History of the American Indians* (New York: Promontory Press, 1974), 257.

28. *South Carolina Gazette*, August 15, 1743. The *London Magazine* had a kinder assessment, saying Priber "was a short dapper man, with a pleasing, open countenance" (September 1760, pp. 443–45).

29. "Account of Christian Pryber's Proceedings," in Oglethorpe to Trustees, April 22, 1743, *CRG*, 36:129–31; *South Carolina Gazette*, August 15, 1743.

30. *South Carolina Gazette*, August 15, 1743.

31. Williams, *Adair's History*, 257; for a definitive account of Priber's career, see Knox Mellon, Jr., "Christian Priber's Cherokee 'Kingdom of Paradise,' " *GHQ* 57 (Spring 1973): 319–31.

32. Oglethorpe to Mary Mathews, July 20, 1742, *CRG*, 27:3–4. Larry E. Ivers has shown that the traditional account of the Battle of Bloody Marsh is spurious. Thomas Spalding of Sapelo was the source of the story that the Spaniards were sitting down to lunch when the Highlanders sprang their ambush (*GHS Collections*, 1:281–84). Margaret Cate Davis follows Spalding in "Fort Frederica; Battle of Bloody Marsh," *GHQ* 27 (June 1943): 148–50; see also Ivers, *British Drums*, 244–45, n. 16.

33. Amos Aschbach Ettinger, *Oglethorpe: A Brief Biography*, ed. Phinizy Spalding (Macon, Ga.: Mercer University Press, 1984), 75. It was erroneously reported that Oglethorpe had married a Miss Sambrooke.

34. Robert Chambers, *History of the Rebellion of 1745–6* (London: W. & R. Chambers, 1929), 176–92. The expression is from Macaulay's essay "The Earl of Chatham," cited by Hugh Swinton McGillivray in "A Sketch of the McGillivrays."

35. Proceedings of Oglethorpe's Court Martial, PRO, WO 71/19/195.

36. Dunbar and the Georgia Rangers are mentioned in the proceedings of Oglethorpe's court-martial, PRO, WO 71/19/195. Another familiar figure serving under Oglethorpe was Mary Bosomworth's husband, Thomas; see John Pitts Corry, "Some New Light on the Bosomworth Claims," *GHQ* 25 (September 1941): 199–200; Ettinger, *Oglethorpe*, 77.

37. Rodney M. Baine and Mary E. Williams, "Oglethorpe's Missing Years," *GHQ* 69 (Summer 1985): 193–210.

38. Chambers, *History of the Rebellion*, 230–39; Katherine Tomasson, *The Jacobite General* (Edinburgh and London: William Blackwood and Sons, 1958), 137–57.

39. Chambers, *History of the Rebellion*, 259–65.

40. The traditional version, given here, may contain more romance than truth; see McGillivray and Macgillivray, *Clan MacGillivray*, 29–30.

41. John Hossack, Baillie of Inverness, quoted in John Prebble, *Culloden* (London: Secker and Warburg, 1961), 97, see generally 93–100; Tomasson, *Jacobite General*, 230–38; Fraser-Mackintosh, *Clan Chattan*, 19; McGillivray and Macgillivray, *Clan MacGillivray*, 35.

42. Chambers, *History of the Rebellion*, 299.

43. Personal observation of Culloden battlefield, August 22, 1988. The stone markers were placed on the field by Duncan Forbes of Culloden in 1861 (McGillivray and Macgillivray, *Clan MacGillivray*, 39).

44. Fraser-Mackintosh, *Clan Chattan*, 19–20.

45. *South Carolina Gazette*, April 20, 1747.

FOUR. OUTPOST OF EMPIRE

1. John R. Swanton, *Early History of the Creek Indians and Their Neighbors* (Washington, D.C.: U.S. Government Printing Office, 1922), 241–54, 263–65, 274–82; Benjamin Hawkins, *A Sketch of the Creek Country in the Years 1798 and 1799* (1848; rpt. Spartanburg, S.C.: Reprint Company, 1974), 26–51.

2. Swanton, *Early History*, 242.

3. Petition of Lachlan McGillivray, n.d., in McDowell, ed., *Colonial Records of South Carolina: Indian Affairs*, 518.

4. The inscription on the stone reads, "McGillivray Plantation Known as Little Tallase and The Apple Grove 1740–1793. Here lived Lachlan McGillivray a Scotch Trader among the Indians. His wife Sehoy was the daughter

of the French Captain Marchand, and here was born their son, General Alexander McGillivray, who went in 1790 with Colo. Marinus Willett from this plantation to New York City to visit President George Washington. Here Leclerc Milfort, the Frenchman, was married to Alexander McGillivray's sister during the American Revolution. Lt. John Heth, USA, Treaty Commissioner and John Pope, traveler, were here." Longtime residents living nearby never heard of the marker, much less of the McGillivrays.

5. Corkran, *Creek Frontier*, 113.

6. Hawkins, *Sketch of the Creek Country*, 69–71.

7. "The Creek Nation, Debtor to John Forbes and Co., Successors to Panton, Leslie and Co., A Journal of John Innerarity, 1812," *FHQ* 9 (October 1980): 73.

8. The caffeine in the plant with the unfortunate name *Ilex Vomitoria* caused it to be mildly addictive. For a thorough discussion of the "black drink," see Charles H. Fairbanks, "The Function of Black Drink Among the Creeks," in Charles M. Hudson, ed., *Black Drink: A Native American Tea* (Athens: University of Georgia Press, 1979), 120–49.

9. Corkran, *Creek Frontier*, 8–9.

10. Williams, *Adair's History*, 433.

11. Calvin Martin initiated a lively debate among ethnohistorians by his explanation that the Indians began to slaughter game because they blamed the animals for spreading diseases (*Keepers of the Game: Indian-Animal Relationships and the Fur Trade* [Berkeley: University of California Press, 1978]). In a rebuttal, Charles M. Hudson, Jr., argued that the southeastern Indians were caught up in the European economic system; they had to trade deerskins in order to survive ("Why the Southeastern Indians Slaughtered Deer," in Shepard Krech III, *Indians, Animals, and the Fur Trade: A Critique of Keepers of the Game* [Athens: University of Georgia Press, 1981], 157–72). The wholesale killing of deer can be explained as an economic necessity, but the apparently wanton killing of buffalo and bear remains a puzzle.

12. Williams, *Adair's History*, 407.

13. Corkran, *Creek Frontier*, 24.

14. Angie Debo, *The Road to Disappearance* (Norman: University of Oklahoma Press, 1941), 15; Journal of Thomas Bosomworth, January 24, 1753, in McDowell, ed., *Colonial Records of South Carolina: Indian Affairs*, 315–16; Corkran, *Creek Frontier*, 26–27.

15. Williams, *Adair's History*, 151.

16. Ibid., 424. For Adair's description of a war party, see 409–20.

17. Daniel K. Richter, "War and Culture: The Iroquois Experience," *W&MQ* 3d ser., 40 (October 1983): 528–59; Theda Perdue, *Slavery and the Evolution of Cherokee Society, 1540–1866* (Knoxville: University of Tennessee Press, 1979), 8, 13.

18. Williams, *Adair's History*, 416; Corkran, *Creek Frontier*, 27–30.

19. Hawkins, *Sketch of the Creek Country*, 73.

20. Corkran, *Creek Frontier*, 30–34; Hawkins, *Sketch of the Creek Country*, 74.

21. *Letters of Benjamin Hawkins, 1796–1806*, GHS Collections, 9:83–84.

22. O'Neill to Miro, February 17, 1784, in John Walton Caughey, *McGillivray of the Creeks* (Norman: University of Oklahoma Press, 1938), 71–72. Alexander was fond of his uncle Red Shoes, who died in 1784. He praised him as a faithful and courageous leader and regretted that he could not cure him of an overfondness for strong drink (McGillivray to O'Neill, January 3, 1784, ibid., 66).

23. Pickett, *History of Alabama*, 229; Thomas, "Fort Toulouse," 160; Johnnie Andrews, Jr., *Fort Toulouse Colonials: A Compendium of the Colonial Families of Central Alabama, 1717–1823* (Prichard, Ala.: Bienville Historical Society, 1987), 13–16.

24. Pickett, *History of Alabama*, 343–44.

25. *Letters of Hawkins*, 40, 47.

26. Copy of Lachlan McGillivray's will, June 12, 1767, supplied by Professor W. W. Wallace; Samuel G. Drake, *Biography and History of the Indians of North America from Its First Discovery* (Boston: Benjamin B. Mussey, 1841), 382; Pickett, *History of Alabama*, 345. Milfort stated that Lachlan had two sons and three daughters and that he lost a son and two daughters at an early age (Louis LeClerc de Milfort, *Memoir, or A Cursory Glance at My Different Travels and My Sojourn in the Creek Nation*, trans. Geraldine deCourcy, ed. John Francis McDermott [Chicago: R. R. Donnelley & Sons, 1956]). Sophia and Jeannet (or Janet) survived, a fact which casts doubt on the accuracy of Milfort's memory.

27. Woodward, *Reminiscences*, 59–61; *Letters of Hawkins*, 45; Caughey, *McGillivray of the Creeks*, 11.

28. *Letters of Hawkins*, 44; Woodward, *Reminiscences*, 109–10; Caughey, *McGillivray of the Creeks*, 84, 100, 132, 356, 360–62. It is not likely that Lachlan's Sehoy was the mother of Sehoy McPherson because Sehoy McPherson had her last child by Charles Weatherford in 1804. Assuming that Lachlan married Sehoy in 1744, McPherson would have had to father a child by Sehoy before

that. She would have been beyond the childbearing age in 1804. I am indebted to Lynn Thompson for the information that Sehoy Taitt-Weatherford's last child was born in 1804; she has seen the tombstone. Thompson is working on a biography of William Weatherford. For a different opinion see Griffith, *McIntosh and Weatherford*, 3, which states that Lachlan's Sehoy married a Tabacha chieftain before she married Lachlan and Sehoy III was the daughter of that marriage.

29. Lachlan McGillivray's will, June 12, 1767.

30. Woodward, *Reminiscences*, 106–7.

31. Caroline T. Moore, ed., *Abstracts of the Wills of the State of South Carolina, 1740–1760* (Columbia: R. L. Bryan, 1964), 164.

32. Drake, *Indians of North America*, 382; George White, *Historical Collections of Georgia: Containing the Most Interesting Facts, Traditions, Biographical Sketches, Anecdotes, Etc. Relating to Its History and Antiquities, from Its First Settlement to the Present Time* (New York: Pudney and Russell, 1855), 154; *Georgia Gazette*, July 8, 1867, noted that the schooner *Nocturnal* left Savannah on July 2, 1767, for Charlestown, "from whence he [McGillivray] will go northward." I am indebted to Professor George Rogers of the University of South Carolina for the information that Sheed and Henderson were teachers at Charlestown's free school.

33. Caughey, *McGillivray of the Creeks*, 356.

34. John Pope, *A Tour Through the Southern and Western Territories of the United States of North America: The Spanish Dominions on the River Mississippi, and the Floridas: The Countries of the Creek Nation; and Many Uninhabited Parts* (1792; rpt. New York: Arno Press, 1971), 48.

35. Woodward to Pickett, June 21, 1858, in Woodward, *Reminiscences*, 58–66.

36. Pickett, *History of Alabama*, 419; *Letters of Hawkins*, 43, 48; Milford, *Memoir*, 225.

37. Milfort harbored different feelings than he displayed in his memoirs. In a letter to Baron de Carondelet he said, "McGilvrit and I feared each other. I feared him because I knew his spirit and the malice of his family, and he feared me because he knew how strong my influence was" (Milfort to Carondelet, May 26, 1793, in Caughey, *McGillivray of the Creeks*, 357–59).

38. *Letters of Hawkins*, 43; Pickett, *History of Alabama*, 418.

39. John Richard Alden, *John Stuart and the Southern Colonial Frontier: A Study of Indian Relations, War, Trade, and Land Problems in the Southern Wilder-*

ness, 1754–1755 (New York: Gordian Press, 1966), 297 n.

40. According to Woodward, who knew him personally, Davey Taitt was educated in Abernathy, Scotland (*Reminiscences*, 73). A reliable source reveals that the boy studied for a time under Mr. Robertson at Banf (John Innerarity to William Panton, September 24, 1798, *FHQ* 14 [1935]: 116–17).

41. Woodward, *Reminiscences*, 59; Claim of David Taitt, March 7, 1783; PRO, AO 13/37/181–85. I am indebted to Dr. Robert J. Morgan, University College of Cape Breton for the information that David Taitt went to Nova Scotia in 1784 as that colony's first provost marshall. He surveyed the site of the city of Sydney. He lived to an honored old age, dying at ninety-four. He is buried in St. Paul's Churchyard, Halifax, Nova Scotia.

42. Griffith, *McIntosh and Weatherford*, 5–6.

43. Pope, *Tour*, 51.

44. McGillivray and Macgillivray, *Clan MacGillivray*, 45.

45. Alden, *John Stuart*, 16–17, n. 38; Wright to Board of Trade, November 10, 1764, PRO, CO 323/20.

46. Michael Handford, *The Stroudwater Canal* (Gloucester: Alan Sutton, 1979), 35. I enjoyed a visit to Stroud in Gloucestershire in August 1988 and learned that Stroud cloth is still being manufactured. Among the users are the Buckingham Palace Guards and the Swiss Guards at the Vatican. Stroud cloth is exceptionally thickly woven wool; it does not fray when cut. Indians valued the cloth for blankets as well as clothing for the women.

47. Williams, *Adair's History*, 442.

48. Ibid., 394.

49. McGillivray to William Pinckney, December 18, 1751, in McDowell, ed., *Colonial Records of South Carolina: Indian Affairs*, 215–16.

50. McGillivray's Journal, January 1755, NYHS.

51. McGillivray to Glen, April 14, 1754, in McDowell, ed., *Colonial Records of South Carolina: Indian Affairs*, 501–2.

52. Petition of Lachlan McGillivray, n.d., ibid., 518.

FIVE. THE CHOCTAW REVOLT

1. S.C. Council Minutes, April 20, 1744, SCCJ.

2. S.C. Council Minutes, June 21, 1744, ibid.

3. S.C. Council Minutes, July 6, 28, September 8, 1744, ibid.

4. McGillivray to Glen, January 14, 1744/45, S.C. Council Minutes, January 25, 1745, ibid.

5. Ibid.

6. Vaudreuil to Maurepas, December 28, 1744, October 28, 1745; Louboey to Maurepas, November 6, 1745, in Rowland, Sanders, and Galloway, eds., *Mississippi Provincial Archives*, 4:231–33, 242–48, 253–58.

7. McGillivray to Glen, January 14, 1744/45, S.C. Council Minutes, January 25, 1745, SCCJ.

8. S.C. House Minutes, February 22, 1745, *JCHA*, 1744–45, p. 357.

9. John Fenwicke to Board of Trade, April 10, 1745, PRO, SC, 22:40–56.

10. Robert L. Meriwether, *The Expansion of South Carolina, 1729–1765* (Philadelphia: Porcupine Press, 1974), 26–27.

11. S.C. Council Minutes, May 2, 1745, SCCJ.

12. William Horton to Mary Bosomworth, March 30, 1746, *CRG*, 27:268.

13. Glen to Board of Trade, May 3, 1746, PRO, SC, 22:149.

14. Glen to Board of Trade, April 14, 1748, PRO, SC, 23.

15. Glen to Board of Trade, May 3, September 29, 1746, PRO, SC, 22:149–55, 199–204.

16. Glen to Board of Trade, September 29, 1746, PRO, SC, 22:199–204; S.C. Council Minutes, June 25, 1748, S.C. Council Journals, PRO, CO 5/456.

17. Meriwether, *Expansion of South Carolina*, 193.

18. The Council Minutes for November 1, 1746, indicate that four letters written by Lachlan McGillivray from various Creek villages were read; a letter from the king of the Savannahs to Glen, dated September 14, 1746, began, "I received your letter of Mr. McGillivray" (SCCJ).

19. S.C. Council Minutes, October 29, November 1, 3, 1746, SCCJ.

20. Ibid., November 1, 1746.

21. Ibid., June 6, 1747.

22. Glen to Board of Trade, October 10, 1848, PRO, SC, 23. Glen suspected McGillivray of trading with the French at Fort Toulouse; this was a favorite accusation of Edmond Atkin's.

23. Ibid. Croft resigned as Indian commissioner and was replaced by William Pinckney.

24. S.C. Council Minutes, November 1, 1746, SCCJ.

25. Ibid., November 3, 1746, June 6, 1747.

26. Ibid., June 6, 1747.

27. Ibid., November 1, 1746.

28. Ibid., June 6, 1747.

29. Ibid.

30. Ibid., February 17, 1746.

31. Ibid., April 15, 1747.

32. Ibid., April 15, May 16, 1747.

33. Malatchi's talk, December 7, 1747, *CRG*, 36:315–25.

34. Gentlemen and Landholders in the Parish of St. John in the Province of South Carolina to the Duke of Newcastle, March 7, 1748, PRO, SC, 23:81.

35. Vaudreuil to Maurepas, November 5, 1748, in Rowland, Sanders, and Galloway, eds., *Mississippi Provincial Archives*, 4:332–40.

36. Atkin's pamphlet, addressed to James West and dated January 20, 1753, is in the British Library, London.

37. *South Carolina Gazette*, February 26, 1750.

38. Williams, *Adair's History*, 345.

39. Ibid., 335; Edmond Atkin, *Historical Account of the Revolt of the Choctaw Indians in the Late War from the French to the British Alliance and of Their Return Since to That of the French* . . . (London, 1753); Testimony of John Campbell, S.C. Council Minutes, January 26, 1749, S.C. Council Journals, PRO, CO 5/457.

40. Testimony of John Campbell, ibid.

41. Ibid.; Memoir for the King on the Choctaws, September 6, 1748, in Rowland, Sanders, and Galloway, eds., *Mississippi Provincial Archives*, 4:324–25.

42. Williams, *Adair's History*, 352–53; Testimony of John Campbell, S.C. Council Minutes, January 26, 1749, S.C. Council Journal, PRO, CO 5/457.

43. Glen to Board of Trade, February 1751, PRO, SC, 24; *South Carolina Gazette*, April 20, 1747.

44. Atkin, *Historical Account*.

45. McNaire to Glen, October 6, 1747, PRO, CO 5/455.

46. Glen to Board of Trade, February 3, 1747, PRO, SC, 23:71; Atkin, *Historical Account*.

47. S.C. Council Minutes, December 14, 1747, S.C. Council Journal, PRO, CO 5/456.

48. Atkin, *Historical Account*; Williams, *Adair's History*, 351.

49. Atkin, *Historical Account*, S.C. Council Minutes, January 9, 1749, S.C. Council Journal, PRO, CO 5/457.

50. Glen to Board of Trade, October 10, 1748, PRO, SC, 23.

51. Deposition of John Vann, partner with Thomas Maxwell, Charles

McNaire, Arthur Harvey and others, in Glen to Board of Trade, December 1751, PRO, SC, 24. James Adair related virtually the same account (Williams, *Adair's History*, 346–47).

52. S.C. Council Minutes, January 26, 1749, S.C. Council Journal, PRO, CO 5/457.

53. Ibid., December 20, 1748; Williams, *Adair's History*, 353.

54. Williams, *Adair's History*, 355.

55. Vaudreuil to Rouille, March 3, 1749, January 12, 1751, in Rowland, Sanders, and Galloway, eds., *Mississippi Provincial Archives*, 5:15–25, 59–65.

56. Williams, *Adair's History*, 366.

57. *South Carolina Gazette*, October 9, 1750.

58. S.C. Council Minutes, April 3, May 7, 1750, S.C. Council Journals, PRO, CO 5/462.

59. Williams, *Adair's History*, 374.

60. Glen to Board of Trade, December 1751, PRO, SC, 24.

61. Glen to Board of Trade, October 2, 1750, PRO, SC, 24.

62. McNaire's petition in Holderness to Board of Trade, February 7, 1752; Minutes of McNaire interview before Lords Commissioners, February 26, 1752; Lords Commissioners to Holdernesse [sic], March 19, 1752, PRO, SC, 25.

63. Glen to Board of Trade, December 1751, PRO, SC, 24.

64. Atkin, *Historical Account*.

65. President and Assistants to Trustees, February 28, 1751, *CRG*, 26:168–72; Minutes of the President and Assistants, September 26, 1750, *CRG*, 6:332–33.

66. Brown, Rae and Company to Trustees, February 31, 1751, *CRG*, 26:152–55; Trustees' Minutes, May 24, 1751, *CRG*, 2:512; Habersham to Martyn, February 3, 1752, *CRG*, 26:334–40.

SIX. THE POWERFUL COMPANY AT AUGUSTA

1. Statement of Thomas Bosomworth, January 24, 1753, in McDowell, ed., *Colonial Records of South Carolina: Indian Affairs*, 329; Laurens to Devonsheir, Reeve and Lloyd, July 4, 1755, Philip M. Hamer, George R. Rogers, Jr., and David R. Chesnutt, eds., *The Papers of Henry Laurens*, 11 vols. (Columbia: University of South Carolina Press, 1966–88), 1:285; S.C. Council Minutes, September 7, 1749, S.C. Council Journals, PRO, CO 5/457.

2. Williams, *Adair's History*, 394–95.

3. Trustees Minutes, August 23, 1738, *CRG*, 1:331; for a history of the controversy see Corry, *Indian Affairs in Georgia*, 51–66.

4. Williams, *Adair's History*, 395.

5. Ga. Council Minutes, May 23, September 8, 1749, *CRG*, 6:248, 290. For a history of the garrison at Augusta see Larry E. Ivers, "The Soldiers of Fort Augusta," in Cashin, ed., *Colonial Augusta*, 76–93.

6. Ga. Council Minutes, March 3, 1750, *CRG*, 6:309.

7. Ibid., November 6, 1749, *CRG*, 6:294.

8. Credit for unraveling the confusion about the Mackey house belongs to Martha F. Norwood, in *A History of the White House Tract, Richmond County, Georgia, 1756–1975* (Atlanta: Georgia Department of Natural Resources, Historic Preservation Section, 1975).

9. The accepted tradition that the church was built within the curtain of the fort is based on a sketch entitled "The View Plan and Situation of the Church and Church Yard of Augusta in Georgia Executed on D. 1749 and Humbly Dedicated to the Venerable the Trustees for Establishing the Colony of Georgia in America by the Committee appointed for erecting thereof," DeRenne Collection, Special Collections, University of Georgia Libraries. For an account of the building of the fort and church, see Heard Robertson and Thomas H. Robertson, "The Town and Fort of Augusta," in Cashin, ed., *Colonial Augusta*, 59–74. A nagging doubt is caused by James Fraser's statement that the committee had decided not to build the church adjoining the fort (Ga. Council Minutes, July 26, 1749, *CRG*, 6:255). The fort may have been east of town. The church was to the west.

10. Copp to Martyn, September 30, 1751, *CRG*, 26:303–6.

11. Berry Fleming, *Autobiography of a Colony: The First Half-Century of Augusta, Georgia* (Athens: University of Georgia Press, 1957), 49–51.

12. Copp to Martyn, September 30, 1751, *CRG*, 26:303–7.

13. Ga. Council Minutes, October 4, 1750, *CRG*, 6:341–42.

14. John T. Juricek, ed., *Georgia Treaties, 1733–1763* (Frederick, Md.: University Publications of America, 1989), 171.

15. Galphin to Glen, April 23, 1748, S.C. Council Journals, PRO, CO 5/456.

16. Galphin to Glen, April 23, 1748, S.C. Council Minutes, May 3, 1748, ibid.

17. Bedford to Glen, June 9, 1748, Bosomworth to Glen, July 30, 1748, S.C.

Council Minutes, April 21, 1749, S.C. Council Journals, PRO, CO 5/457.

18. Parker to Glen, April 16, 1751, *CRG*, 26:192–95.

19. S.C. Council Minutes, May 27, June 1, 1749, S.C. Council Journals, PRO, CO 5/458; Joseph Piercy's deposition, September 27, 1751, *CRG*, 26:490–99. Piercy's desposition was sworn before John Mackintosh Mohr. The Darien Scots were sympathetic to the Bosomworths.

20. Ga. Council Minutes, July 24, 1749, *CRG*, 6:252–54.

21. Mary Bosomworth to Stephens, July 27, 1749, *CRG*, 6:256–57; Piercy's deposition, September 27, 1751, *CRG*, 26:490–99.

22. Ga. Council Minutes, August 7–9, 1749, *CRG*, 6:258–60; Piercy's deposition, September 27, 1751, *CRG*, 26:490–99.

23. Ga. Council Minutes, August 10, 1749, *CRG*, 6:259–60. For the custom of firing guns, see Affidavits of Augusta Indian Traders, December 20, 1755, *CRG*, 27:219.

24. Ga. Council Minutes, August 11, 1749, *CRG*, 6:263–68; Piercy's deposition, September 27, 1751, *CRG*, 26:490–99.

25. Ga. Council Minutes, August 12, 1749, *CRG*, 6:263–68. Thomas Bosomworth's answers to the accusation contained in the Council Minutes may be found in *CRG*, 27:155–93.

26. President and Assistants, Further Talks with Malatchi and Lower Creek Headmen, August 17, 1749, in Juricek, ed., *Georgia Treaties*, 184; document also in *CRG*, 6:269–80.

27. Ga. Council Minutes, August 22, 1749, *CRG*, 6:280–85.

28. Ibid.; Journal of Thomas Bosomworth, July 4–October 11, 1752, in McDowell, ed., *Colonial Records of South Carolina: Indian Affairs*, 305–6.

29. Ga. Council Minutes, August 31, November 16, 1749, *CRG*, 6:287, 295–97.

30. Ga. Council Minutes, October 4, 1750, *CRG*, 6:341–43; S.C. Council Minutes, September 5, 1750, S.C. Council Journals, PRO, CO 5/462.

31. Ga. Council Minutes, July 29, 1750, *CRG*, 6:329.

32. Ga. Council Minutes, September 15, 26, 1750, *CRG*, 6:331–34.

33. Deposition of Adam Bosomworth, October 2, 1750, *CRG*, 27:18–20.

34. Memorial and Representation of Coosaponakeesa, Princess of the Upper and Lower Creek Nations of Indians to the Board," August 2, 1750 (received November 26, 1754), *CRG*, 26:465–75.

35. Ga. Council Minutes, November 14, 1750, *CRG*, 6:354–57.

36. Ibid.

37. Glen to Board of Trade, August 12, 1749, PRO, SC, 23; S.C. Council Minutes, September 1, 1749, S.C. Council Journals, PRO, CO 5/459.

38. S.C. Council Minutes, September 5, 1749, S.C. Council Journals, PRO, CO 5/459.

39. Ga. Council Minutes, October 4, 1750, *CRG*, 6:341–43. Some thirty Charlestown merchants also complained about unclean skins (S.C. Council Minutes, September 5, 1749, S.C. Council Journals, PRO, CO 5/459).

40. Glen to Board of Trade, December 23, 1749, PRO, SC, 23; S.C. House Minutes, January 27, February 28, 1750, *JCHA*, 9:362, 417.

41. McGillivray to Glen, April 5, 1750, S.C. Council Minutes, May 7, 1750, S.C. Council Journals, PRO, CO 5/462.

42. S.C. Council Minutes, September 5, 1750, S.C. Council Journals, PRO, CO 5/462.

43. Glen to Board of Trade, October 2, 1750; Board of Trade to Glen, November 15, 1750; Crokatt to Henry Fox, January 31, 1749, enclosed in Board of Trade to Glen, November 19, 1750, in PRO, SC, 24.

44. President and Assistants to Martyn, February 28, 1751, *CRG*, 26:168–73.

45. Trustees Minutes, May 18, 1751, *CRG*, 1:561; Kenneth Coleman, *Colonial Georgia: A History* (New York: Charles Scribner's Sons, 1976), 105–6.

46. Brown, Rae and Company to Trustees, February 13, 1751, *CRG*, 26:152–55.

47. Extract from the Proceedings of the President and Assistants, June 21, 1751, *CRG*, 26:389–97.

48. Ibid.

49. Ibid., 397.

50. McGillivray to Pinckney, December 18, 1751, in McDowell, ed., *Colonial Records of South Carolina: Indian Affairs*, 215–16.

51. Vaudreuil to Rouille, April 28, 1751, in Rowland, Sanders, and Galloway, eds., *Mississippi Provincial Archives*, 5:67–73.

52. Michel de la Rouvilliere to Rouille, July 20, 1751, ibid., 97–104; Glen to Board of Trade, June 25, 1753, PRO, SC, 25; Journal of Thomas Bosomworth, July 4–October 11, 1752, in McDowell, ed., *Colonial Records of South Carolina: Indian Affairs*, 289; Journal of John Buckles, May 15, 1752, ibid., 382–85.

53. Glen to Board of Trade, December 16, 1752, PRO, SC, 25.

54. Journal of Thomas Bosomworth, July 4–October 11, 1752, in McDowell,

ed., *Colonial Records of South Carolina: Indian Affairs*, 269.

55. Ibid., 270–74.

56. Ibid., 274–75.

57. Ibid., 305–6.

58. Ibid., 316.

59. Glen to Board of Trade, December 16, 1752, PRO, SC, 25.

60. Williams, *Adair's History*, 299–300.

61. Ibid.

62. Ibid.

63. Glen to Board of Trade, June 25, 1753, PRO, SC, 25; Minutes of Conference, May 28, 31, June 2, 1753, in McDowell, ed., *Colonial Records of South Carolina: Indian Affairs*, 391–411.

64. Glen to Board of Trade, June 25, 1753, PRO, SC, 25; Minutes of Conference, May 31, June 2, 1753, in McDowell, ed., *Colonial Records of South Carolina: Indian Affairs*, 395, 404.

65. Minutes of Conference, May 31, June 2, 1753, in McDowell, ed., *Colonial Records of South Carolina: Indian Affairs*, 406–8.

66. Ibid., 408–13.

67. Glen to Board of Trade, June 25, 1753, PRO, SC, 25.

68. *South Carolina Gazette*, July 2, 1753.

69. Habersham to Martyn, July 7, 1752, *CRG*, 26:402–4.

70. Memorial and representation of the state and condition of the southern parts of Georgia from some freeholders, April 18, 1752, *CRG*, 27:47–51.

71. Thomas Bosomworth to the Lords of Treasury, February 24, 1755, *CRG*, 27:228–30.

72. *South Carolina Gazette*, November 7, 1754.

73. Reynolds to Board of Trade, December 5, 1754, *CRG*, 27:32–34; Ga. Council Minutes, November 4, 1754, *CRG*, 7:21.

74. Reynolds to Board of Trade, December 5, 1754, *CRG*, 27:32–34.

75. Reynolds to Board of Trade, September 25, 1756, *CRG*, 27:153–54.

76. McGillivray to Glen, February 17, 1756, in McDowell, ed., *Colonial Records of South Carolina: Indian Affairs*, 103–4, with enclosure, "State of money owed to Clark and McGillivray" dated February 12, 1756.

77. Corkran, *Creek Frontier*, 171.

78. Deposition of Lachlan McGillivray, December 22, 1755, *CRG*, 27:217–18.

79. Memorial of Alexander Kellet, July 7, 1756, *CRG*, 27:117–20.

80. Statement of Thomas Bosomworth, January 24, 1753, in McDowell, ed., *Colonial Records of South Carolina: Indian Affairs*, 329.

1. Ga. Council Minutes, January 13, 1755, *CRG*, 7:93–94.
2. McGillivray to Glen, February 1, 1755, in McDowell, ed., *South Carolina Colonial Records: Indian Affairs*, 38. Henry Laurens referred to Brown's death in his letter to Devonsheir, Reeve and Lloyd, July 4, 1755, in Hamer, Rogers, and Chesnutt, eds., *Laurens Papers*, 1:285. Atkin complained about McGillivray's giving Struthers a license, in a letter to Lyttelton, December 10, 1758, Lyttelton Papers, WLCL.
3. McGillivray's journal is in the New-York Historical Society. It also appears, with additions, in McDowell, ed., *Records of Colonial South Carolina: Indian Affairs*, 56–71. John Spencer testified that he had read McGillivray's journal and contributed to it; see S.C. House Minutes, September 15, 1755, in Terry W. Lipscomb, ed., *Colonial Records of South Carolina: The Journal of the Commons House of Assembly, November 12, 1754–September 23, 1755* (Columbia: University of South Carolina Press, 1986), 335–36; Kerlérec to d'Arnouville, September 15, 1754, in Rowland, Sanders, and Galloway, eds., *Mississippi Provincial Archives*, 5:142–50.
4. Reynolds to Lyttelton, September 8, 1756, Lyttelton Papers, WLCL.
5. McGillivray's Journal, NYHS.
6. Ibid.
7. Ibid.; Kerlérec to d'Arnouville, September 15, 1754, in Rowland, Sanders, and Galloway, eds., *Mississippi Provincial Archives*, 5:142–50.
8. Kerlérec to d'Arnouville, September 20, 1754, ibid.
9. Kerlérec to d'Arnouville, December 14, 1754, ibid., 154–59.
10. McGillivray to Glen, February 1, 1755, in McDowell, ed., *Colonial Records of South Carolina: Indian Affairs*, 38–40; Galphin to Glen, March 22, 1755, ibid., 55–56.
11. McGillivray to Glen, May 13, 1755, ibid., 72; McGillivray's Journal, NYHS.
12. McGillivray's Journal, NYHS.
13. Ibid.

14. McGillivray to Glen, October 15, 1755, in McDowell, ed., *Colonial Records of South Carolina: Indian Affairs*, 82.

15. Glen to Board of Trade, October 2, 1753, PRO, SC, 25; Glen to Board of Trade, August 26, 1754, Lyttelton to Robinson, September 7, 1755, PRO, SC, 26; Glen to Board of Trade, April 14, 1756, PRO, SC, 27.

16. Atkin to Lyttelton, May 20, 1756, Lyttelton Papers, WLCL.

17. S.C. House Minutes, September 17, 20, 1755, *JCHA*, November 12, 1754–September 23, 1755, pp. 317–29.

18. S.C. House Minutes, September 22, 1755, ibid., 332–35.

19. Ibid.

20. Ibid., 336–37.

21. Ga. Council Minutes, September 12, 1755, *CRG*, 7:251–54.

22. William Little's statement, September 22, 1755, *CRG*, 7:255–61; Ga. House Minutes, January 25, 1757, *CRG*, 13:127–31.

23. Ga. Council Minutes, January 7, 1755, *CRG*, 7:89–91; Ga. House Minutes, January 7, 9, 15, 1755, *CRG*, 13:7, 18, 23.

24. Ga. Council Minutes, January 20, 1755, *CRG*, 7:96–97; Ga. House Minutes, January 20, 1755, *CRG*, 13:33–34.

25. Ga. Council Minutes, January 17, 1755, *CRG*, 7:94–96.

26. Ga. Council Minutes, September 12, 1755, *CRG*, 7:251–61.

27. Ga. House Minutes, January 14, 1757, *CRG*, 13:110–12.

28. Memorial of Alexander Kellet to the Board of Trade, July 7, 1756, *CRG*, 27:117–20.

29. Glen to McGillivray, October 28, 1755, in McDowell, ed., *Colonial Records of South Carolina: Indian Affairs*, 83–84.

30. McGillivray to Glen, October 15, 1755, ibid., 82.

31. Gun Merchant's answer, October 30, 1755, ibid., 88.

32. McGillivray to Glen, February 17, 1756, ibid., 103–4. Malatchi's death and the French wooing of Togulki were considered important enough to be brought to the attention of the king (Commissioners Dunk Halifax, J. Oswald, Andrew Stone, and W.G. Hamilton to the King, December 12, 1756, PRO, SC, 27).

33. Glen to Board of Trade, April 14, 1756, ibid.

34. McGillivray to Glen, n.d., in McDowell, ed., *Colonial Records of South Carolina: Indian Affairs*, 89–90.

35. Glen to Lyttelton, August 10, 1756, Lyttelton Papers, WLCL.

36. Glen to Board of Trade, April 14, 1756, PRO, SC, 27.

37. Atkin to Lyttelton, May 20, 1756, Lyttelton Papers, WLCL.

38. Statement of money owed to Clark and McGillivray, October 14, 1755, in McGillivray to Glen, February 17, 1756, in McDowell, ed., *Colonial Records of South Carolina: Indian Affairs*, 103–4.

39. Ibid.

40. Headmen and Warriours of the Chickesaw Nation to the King of Carolina and his Beloved Men, April 6, 1756, in McDowell, ed., *Colonial Records of South Carolina: Indian Affairs*, 109–10.

41. Meriwether, *Expansion of South Carolina*, 211.

42. Germany to Rae and Barksdale, June 10, 1756, in Outerbridge to Lyttelton, July 17, 1756, Lyttelton Papers, WLCL.

43. Lyttelton to Board of Trade, June 19, 1756, PRO, SC, 27; *South Carolina Gazette*, June 3, 1756.

44. Lyttelton to Board of Trade, October 17, 1756, PRO, SC, 27.

45. Outerbridge to Lyttelton, August 14, 1756, Lyttelton Papers, WLCL.

46. Reynolds to Lyttelton, September 8, 1756, ibid.

47. Ga. Council Minutes, September 13, 1756, *CRG*, 7:390–91.

48. Petition signed by Gentlemen of Augusta, in Ga. Council Minutes, September 15, 1756, *CRG*, 7:392–400.

49. Douglass, Rae, and Campbell to Reynolds, September 12, 1756, *CRG*, 7:392–93; Lyttelton to Board of Trade, October 17, 1756, PRO, SC, 27; *South Carolina Gazette*, October 2, 1756; Outerbridge to Lyttelton, September 11, 1756, Lyttelton Papers, WLCL.

50. Talk of David Douglass, John Rae, and Martin Campbell in Outerbridge to Lyttelton, September 14, 1756, Lyttelton Papers, WLCL; Petition of the Inhabitants of Augusta in Georgia Council Minutes, September 15, 1756, *CRG*, 7:398–400.

51. Outerbridge to Lyttelton, September 14, 1756, Lyttelton Papers, WLCL.

52. Reynolds to Lyttelton, September 15, 1756, ibid.

53. Pepper to Lyttelton, September 22, 1756, ibid.

54. Ga. Council Minutes, November 16, 1756, *CRG*, 7:420–25.

55. Ibid.; Reynolds to Lyttelton, November 26, 1756, Lyttelton Papers, WLCL.

56. Reynolds to Lyttelton, December 11, 1756, Ellis to Lyttelton, February 18, 1757, ibid.; *South Carolina Gazette*, January 27, 1757.

EIGHT. THE FRENCH AND INDIAN WAR
ON THE SOUTHERN FRONTIER

1. Commissioners Halifax, Oswald, Stone, and Hamilton to the King, December 21, 1756, PRO, SC, 27; Pitt to Lyttelton, March 31, 1757, Lyttelton Papers, WLCL.

2. Ga. Council Minutes, March 29, 1757, *CRG*, 7:504–5.

3. Kerlérec to Peirene de Moras, August 12, 1758, in Rowland, Sanders, and Galloway, eds., *Mississippi Provincial Archives*, 5:190–92.

4. McGillivray to Lyttelton, July 14, 1758, Lyttelton Papers, WLCL; Kerlérec to Berryer, October 25, 1758, in Rowland, Sanders, and Galloway, eds., *Mississippi Provincial Archives*, 5:194–98.

5. McGillivray, "A Sketch of the McGillivrays."

6. I am indebted to Lynn Thompson of Stockton, Alabama, for a copy of John McGillivray's first will, made out in December 1767. In it he says that his brother Farquhar was then in Mobile. Presumably, this is the same Farquhar who was a carpenter in Charlestown and, according to family tradition, was a minister and tutor to Lachlan's son Alexander.

7. Moore, ed., *Abstracts of the Wills*, 228.

8. Ga. Council Minutes, July 5, 1757, November 1, 1757, *CRG*, 7:601–3, 653.

9. Ibid., December 6, 1757, *CRG*, 7:673–77.

10. Ibid., January 3, 1758, *CRG*, 7:699.

11. Ibid., February 1, March 29, 1757, *CRG*, 7:472, 504–5.

12. Outerbridge to Lyttelton, March 8, 1757, Lyttelton Papers, WLCL.

13. Outerbridge to Lyttelton, September 15, 1757, ibid.

14. William Wright Abbot, *The Royal Governors of Georgia, 1754–1775* (Chapel Hill: University of North Carolina Press, 1959), 57.

15. Ibid., 58–59.

16. Little to the Assembly, May 25, 1757, *CRG*, 28, pt. 1:34–37.

17. Ellis to Board of Trade, March 11, 1757, *CRG*, 28, pt. 1:2–14.

18. Ibid.

19. Ellis to Lyttelton, June 22, 1757, Lyttelton Papers, WLCL.

20. Lyttelton to Board of Trade, September 15, 1757, Mark Carr to Lyttelton, August 10, 1757, PRO, SC, 27; Ellis to Lyttelton, October 6, 1757, Lyttelton Papers, WLCL.

21. Ellis to Lyttelton, June 23, 1757, Lyttelton Papers, WLCL.

22. Ellis to Lyttelton, July 10, 1757, ibid.; Ellis to Board of Trade, September 20, 1757, *CRG*, 28, pt. 1:69.

23. Ellis to Lyttelton, August 25, 1757, ibid.

24. Daniel Pepper, "Some Remarks on the Creek Nation," n.d., ibid.

25. Daniel Pepper, "Head Men in the Lower Creeks," n.d., ibid. The title is misleading; the document deals more extensively with the Upper Creeks than the Lower.

26. Atkin to Lyttelton, October 13, 1756, ibid.; Atkin to Loudoun, March 8, 1756, Lord Loudoun Papers, Henry E. Huntington Library, San Marino, Calif.

27. Ellis to Lyttelton, July 21, 1757, Lyttelton Papers, WLCL; Ga. Council Minutes, July 30, 1757, *CRG*, 7:613–17.

28. Instructions for Joseph Wright, August 7, 1757, in Ellis to Lyttelton, August 25, 1757, Lyttelton Papers, WLCL.

29. Ellis to Board of Trade, November 25, 1757, *CRG*, 28, pt. 1:85–88.

30. Ellis to Board of Trade, January 1, 1758, *CRG*, 28, pt. 1:101–4.

31. Ga. Council Minutes, November 3, 1757, *CRG*, 7:657–64.

32. Ellis to Loudoun, February 28, 1757, Loudoun Papers, Huntington Library; Ellis to Board of Trade, November 25, 1757, *CRG*, 28, pt. 1:85–88.

33. Ellis to Board of Trade, February 18, 1758, *CRG*, 28, pt. 1:123–25.

34. Kerlérec to Berryer, December 1, 1758, in Rowland, Sanders, and Galloway, eds., *Mississippi Provincial Archives*, 5:199–202.

35. Ellis to Board of Trade, December 7, 1757, *CRG*, 28, pt. 1:89–91.

36. Agreement between Chiefs of Upper and Lower Creek Nations, April 22, 1758, *CRG*, 28, pt. 1:265–67.

37. Ellis to Board of Trade, June 28, 1758, July 26, 1759, March 15, 1760, *CRG*, 28, pt. 1:158–60, 210–14, 231–32.

38. Ellis to Lyttelton, February 4, 1760, Lyttelton Papers, WLCL.

39. Ellis to Loudoun, February 28, 1757, Loudoun Papers, Huntington Library.

40. Ellis to Loudoun, March 21, May 23, 1757; Ellis to Bouquet, June 26, 1757, Loudoun Papers, Huntington Library.

41. Ellis to Loudoun, August 10, 1757, ibid.

42. Ellis to Loudoun, September 20, 1757, ibid.

43. Abercromby to Ellis, August 15, October 20, 1758, General James Abercromby Papers, Henry E. Huntington Library, San Marino, Calif.

44. Glen to John Forbes, June 8, 1758, in Sir Henry Moore to Lyttelton, September 8, 1758, Lyttelton Papers, WLCL.

45. Pitt to Lyttelton, January 27, 1758, PRO, SC, 28; also in Lyttelton Papers, WLCL.

46. Pitt to Lyttelton, March 7, 1758, Lyttelton Papers, WLCL.

47. Glen to Lyttelton, January 23, 1758, ibid.

48. Meriwether, *Expansion of Carolina*, 216–17; Lyttelton to Board of Trade, August 7, 1758, PRO, SC, 28; Williams, *Adair's History*, 263.

49. Bull to Lyttelton, July 24, 1758, Lyttelton Papers, WLCL.

50. McGillivray to Lyttelton, July 14, 18, 1758, ibid. A transcript of the July 14 letter was sent to William Pitt and is in PRO, CO 5/18; the letter is copied verbatim but is identified only as a letter from two traders in Augusta.

51. McGillivray to Lyttelton, July 18, 1758, Lyttelton Papers, WLCL.

52. Lyttelton to Pitt, November 4, 1758, PRO, SC, 28; also in PRO, CO 5/18.

53. Ibid.

54. Boscawen to Lyttelton, July 5, August 28, 1758, Lyttelton Papers, WLCL.

55. Amherst to Lyttelton, March 21, 1759, ibid.

NINE. THE MISSION OF EDMOND ATKIN

1. Atkin's account of the Choctaw Revolt, *Historical Account*, is in the British Library; Wilbur R. Jacobs, *Indians of the Southern Colonial Frontier: The Edmond Atkin Report and Plan of 1755* (Columbia: University of South Carolina Press, 1954), xviii–xxx.

2. Edmond Atkin, "To the Right Honourable the Lords Commissioners for Trade and Plantations: (A Report on) the Regulation and Management of the Indian Trade and Commerce; An Account of the Situation, Characters and Disposition of the Several Indian Nations that have Intercourse or Connections with South Carolina: A Plan of a General Direction and Management of Indian Affairs throughout North America," May 30, 1755, Loudoun Papers, Huntington Library.

3. Ibid.

4. Atkin to Loudoun, May 14, March 8, 1756, Loudoun Papers, Huntington Library; Atkin to Lyttelton, October 13, 1756, Lyttelton Papers, WLCL.

5. Atkin to Lyttelton, November 16, 1756, Lyttelton Papers, WLCL.

6. Alden, *John Stuart*, 70–71.

7. Ibid., 72–73.

8. Atkin to Loudoun, March 25, 1758, Abercromby Papers, Huntington Library.

9. Atkin to Abercromby, May 20, 1758, Amherst Papers, PRO, WO 34/47.

10. Ellis to Lyttelton, March 29, 1758, Lyttelton Papers, WLCL; Ga. Council Minutes, October 10, 1758, *CRG*, 7:826.

11. Edmond Atkin, "Charges of carrying on the Indian service in the southern District from 6 October 1756 to 24 March 1760," Amherst Papers, PRO, WO 34/47.

12. Ellis to Board of Trade, October 25, 1758, *CRG*, 28, pt. 1:165–67; Ellis to Lyttelton, October 17, 1758, Lyttelton Papers, WLCL; Ga. Council Minutes, October 10, 1758, *CRG*, 7:826.

13. Ellis to Lyttelton, November 5, 1758, Lyttelton Papers, WLCL.

14. Atkin to Lyttelton, November 24, 1758, ibid.

15. Ibid.; Atkin to Lyttelton, December 10, 1758, ibid.

16. "A Private Conference with the King, next Head Warriour, and the two principal Old Headmen, and beloved Men of the Savano River Chicasaws, held by his Majesty's Agent in Augusta, 14 November, 1758, concerning their Leaving the Tract of Land (a few acres less than 20,000) laid apart for them in So. Carolina on that River above and joining Horse Creek, giving Leases, for a term of years upon it, and exchanging a large part thereof for other Land," in Lyttelton Papers, WLCL.

17. Ibid.

18. Atkin to Lyttelton, November 7, 1758, Lyttelton Papers, WLCL.

19. Ulrich Tobler to Atkin, October 31, 1758, ibid.

20. McGillivray to Lyttelton, August 14, 1758, ibid.; Bull to Lyttelton, June 25, 1758, in McDowell, ed., *Colonial Records of South Carolina: Indian Affairs*, 3:474–76.

21. Atkin to Lyttelton, December 10, 1758, Lyttelton Papers, WLCL.

22. Ibid.

23. McGillivray to Lyttelton, April 2, 1759, ibid.

24. Williams, *Adair's History*, 268.

25. Atkin to Lyttelton, December 10, 1758, Lyttelton Papers, WLCL.

26. McGillivray to Lyttelton, March 12, April 25, 1759, McGillivray to Ellis (extract), October 24, 1758, ibid.

27. Williams, *Adair's History*, 268.

28. Ellis to Lyttelton, February 12, March 13, 1759, Lyttelton Papers, WLCL.

29. Atkin to Lyttelton, June 17, 1759, Lyttelton Papers, WLCL; George Fuller Walker, comp., *Abstracts of Georgia Colonial Conveyance Book J, 1755–1762* (Atlanta: R.J. Taylor, Jr., Foundation, 1978), 176.

30. Williams, *Adair's History*, 269; Alden, *John Stuart*, 98; Jacobs, *Indians of the Southern Colonial Frontier*, xviii.

31. Williams, *Adair's History*, 269.

32. Atkin to Lyttelton, November 30, 1759, Lyttelton Papers, WLCL; Atkin's proclamation forbidding trade with the Alabama Indians, September 7, 1759, Amherst Papers, PRO, WO 34/47.

33. Atkin to Lyttelton, October 2, 1759; Deposition of John Reid, October 5, 1759, Lyttelton Papers, WLCL.

34. Atkin to Lyttelton, November 30, 1759, ibid.

35. Ellis to Lyttelton, August 27, 1759, ibid.

36. Ga. Council Minutes, October 10, 11, 1759, *CRG*, 8:160–70.

37. Ibid., November 9, 1759, January 31, 1760, *CRG*, 8:187–88, 226–27.

38. Ibid., June 5, 1760, *CRG*, 8:319–23.

39. Ellis to Board of Trade, January 6, 1760, *CRG*, 28, pt. 1:225–27.

40. Atkin to Amherst, November 20, 1760, Amherst Papers, PRO, WO 34/47; Atkin to Lyttelton, November 30, 1760, Lyttelton Papers, WLCL; Atkin to Pitt, March 27, 1760, PRO, CO 5/64.

41. Atkin to Lyttelton, November 30, 1760, Lyttelton Papers, WLCL.

42. Ibid.

43. There was a rumor current in 1760 that Atkin would be dismissed; for a carefully considered judgment of Atkin's place in history, see John Carl Parish, *The Persistence of the Westward Movement and Other Essays* (1943; rpt. Berkeley: University of California Press, 1968), 147–60. Parish states that Atkin's report to Halifax in 1755 was of major significance but that his career was a failure. A year after Atkin's report to Halifax, Thomas Pownall presented a "General Plan of Operations British service in North America" to the Duke of Cumberland in which he recommended a superintendent of Indian affairs who would be independent of the provincial governors and responsible to the commander in chief in America (Pownall, "A Memorial: Stating the Nature of the Service in North America . . . ," in Thomas Pownall, *The Administration of the Colonies* [1768; rpt. New York: DaCapo Press, 1971], 38).

TEN. THE CHEROKEE WAR

1. *South Carolina Gazette*, January 5, 1760. Upon his return from the Creek country, Atkin wrote a long, rambling letter to Governor Ellis in which he complained about Joseph Wright, his linguist, who wanted to be paid the standard South Carolina fee for his services, and he denounced John Spencer for spreading malicious stories about Atkin. A few days after Atkin's arrival in Augusta, Spencer got into a quarrel with Patrick Brown, who then threatened to show Atkin the critical letters Spencer had written about Atkin. Lachlan McGillivray prevailed upon Spencer to apologize (Edmond Atkin to Henry Ellis, January 25, 1760, in Albert Sidney Britt, Jr. and Anthony Roane Dees, eds., *Selected Eighteenth Century Manuscripts* [Savannah: Georgia Historical Society, 1980], 136–43).

2. "Extract of a letter from Mr. Lachlan McGillivray dated Augusta, 24 Oct. 1758," Lyttelton Papers, WLCL; Lyttelton to Board of Trade, September 1, 1760, PRO, SC, 28.

3. Tobler to Lyttelton, November 7, 1759, Lyttelton Papers, WLCL.

4. *South Carolina Gazette*, December 29, 1759; Ellis to Lyttelton, November 25, 1759, Lyttelton Papers, WLCL.

5. Ellis to Lyttelton, December 7, 1759, Lyttelton Papers, WLCL.

6. Outerbridge to Lyttelton, December 17, 1759; Ellis to Lyttelton, February 4, 1760, ibid.

7. Ellis to Lyttelton, February 16, 1760, ibid.; Ellis to Amherst, January 1760, PRO, WO 34/34.

8. Cochrane to Gage, November 17, 1764, January 4, 1765, General Thomas Gage Papers, WLCL.

9. Alden, *John Stuart*, 85–87.

10. John Rae to Outerbridge, December 3, 1759; Outerbridge to Lyttelton, December 19, 1759; John Williams to Outerbridge, December 11, 1759, Lyttelton Papers, WLCL.

11. Meriwether, *Expansion of South Carolina*, 222; Ellis to Lyttelton, February 4, 1760, Lyttelton Papers, WLCL.

12. Atkin to Lyttelton, February 5, 1760, Lyttelton Papers, WLCL.

13. Ellis to Lyttelton, February 5, 1760; Atkin to Lyttelton, January 9, 1760; Outerbridge to Lyttelton, February 6, 1760, ibid.

14. McGillivray, Williams, and Fitch to the Gentlemen of Augusta, February 6, 1760, ibid.

15. Outerbridge to Lyttelton, February 12, 1760, ibid.

16. Atkin to Lyttelton, February 13, 1760, ibid.

17. Document entitled "The Chickasaw Indians residing at New Savannah near Augusta, and the Inhabitants of Augusta, having mutually desired a meeting and conference with each other on occasion of the present disturbances with the Cherokees, the same was had on Monday, 11th February 1760, at Fort Augusta, when were present all the Gentlemen of Augusta, all the head men and Warriors of the Chickasaws with others of em about thirty men, the Young Lieutenant, a head warrior of the Cowetaw Town, another head warrior, Talhichico of the Cussitaw Town in the Lower Creeks. The following talk was given out by Lachlan McGillivray, Esq. in the name of and behalf of the white people," ibid.

18. Ibid.; Outerbridge to Lyttelton, February 12, 1760; Ellis to Lyttelton, February 5, 1760, ibid.

19. Outerbridge to Lyttelton, February 15, 1760, ibid.

20. Charles G. Cordle, ed., "The John Tobler Manuscripts: An Account of Swiss Immigrants in South Carolina in 1737," typescript, p. 8, Special Collections, Reese Library, Augusta College, Augusta, Ga.; Atkin to Lyttelton, February 16, 1760, Outerbridge to Lyttelton, February 16, 1760, Lyttelton Papers, WLCL; *South Carolina Gazette*, February 23, 1760.

21. Outerbridge to Lyttelton, February 16, 1760, Lyttelton Papers, WLCL.

22. Williams, *Adair's History*, 272; Atkin to Lyttelton, February 21, 1760, Lyttelton Papers, WLCL.

23. Shaw to Lyttelton, February 21, March 6, 1760, ibid.

24. Shaw to Lyttelton, March 6, 1760, ibid.

25. Ellis to Lyttelton, March 7, 1760, ibid.

26. Ga. Council Minutes, November 26, 1760, *CRG*, 16:524–25.

ELEVEN. THE WAR WINDS DOWN

1. Kerlérec to Berryer, June 8, 12, 1760, in Rowland, Sanders, and Galloway, eds., *Mississippi Provincial Archives*, 5:251–53, 271–73. Kerlérec's agent among the Creeks who was credited with influencing the Mortar was Lantagnac, who had left Fort Toulouse as a young cadet, lived for several years in Charlestown, and engaged in trade in the Cherokee country before returning to the French (Bull to Board of Trade, November 15, 1760, PRO, SC, 28).

2. Board of Trade to Lyttelton, November 14, 1759; Lyttelton to Board of Trade, February 22, 1760; Bull to Board of Trade, May 6, July 20, 1760, PRO, SC, 28.

3. Bull to Board of Trade, June 30, 1760, PRO, SC, 28.

4. Bull to Board of Trade, June 17, 30, July 20, 1760, PRO, SC, 28.

5. Bull to Board of Trade, August 15, 1760, PRO, SC, 28.

6. Alden, *John Stuart*, 117–19, 121–22; Bull to Board of Trade, August 15, September 9, 1760, PRO, SC, 28.

7. Bull to Board of Trade, January 29, 1761, PRO, SC, 28.

8. Bull to Board of Trade, February 17, April 30, May 16, 28, June 19, PRO, SC, 29.

9. Bull to Board of Trade, September 23, December 5, 1761, PRO, SC, 29.

10. Ellis to Lyttelton, February 27, 1760, Lyttelton Papers, WLCL; Ga. Council Minutes, April 14, 1760, May 2, 20, 1760, *CRG*, 8:284–85, 295–97, 308–13.

11. Ga. Council Minutes, May 26, 1760, *CRG*, 8:314–17.

12. Bull to Board of Trade, May 29, 1760, PRO, SC, 28; Alden, *John Stuart*, 109; Ga. Council Minutes, June 30, 1760, *CRG*, 8:325–34; Williams, *Adair's History*, 272–73.

13. Ga. Council Minutes, June 30, 1760, *CRG*, 8:325–34.

14. Wright to Board of Trade, October 23, 1760, *CRG*, 28, pt. 1:291; Ga. House Minutes, October 13, 16, *CRG*, 13:419–21, 428–30.

15. Williams, *Adair's History*, 393.

16. Atkin to Amherst, November 20, 1760, Lord Jeffrey Amherst Papers, PRO, WO 34/47.

17. Glen to Lyttelton, January 23, 1758, Lyttelton Papers, WLCL.

18. Alden, *John Stuart*, 135–36.

19. Knox to unknown, May 20, 1760, Historical Manuscripts Commission, *Report on Manuscripts in Various Collections* (Dublin, 1906), 6:84–85; William Knox, "Anecdotes and Characteristics, Lord Lansdowne," July 6, 1785, William Knox Papers, 10/35, WLCL.

20. Ga. Council Minutes, November 21, 1760, *CRG*, 8:427–33.

21. Ga. House Minutes, November 7, 11, 12, 1760, *CRG*, 8:441–42, 443–45.

22. Wright to Board of Trade, December 23, 1760, *CRG*, 28, pt. 1:292–99.

23. Ga. House Minutes, January 12, March 26, April 8, 21, 1761, *CRG*, 13:470–72, 477–84, 528–30. After a debate, Barnard's application for reimbursement was denied (ibid., 541–42).

24. Ga. Council Minutes, July 3, 1761, *CRG*, 8:522–24.

25. Ga. Council Minutes, July 6, 1762, *CRG*, 8:708.

26. Norwood, *History of the White House Tract*, 8; *Georgia Gazette*, March 1, 1764.

27. Ga. Council Minutes, September 4, 1759, January 5, 1762, *CRG*, 8:123, 624. Curiously, Lachlan referred to Alexander McGillivray as an "infant." Alexander was nine at the time. Later Lachlan used the term *infant* in reference to a seven-year-old boy, so the term meant child rather than baby.

28. Mrs. J. E. Hays, "Creek Indian Letters, Talks and Treaties, 1705–1793," typescript, Georgia Department of Archives and History, Atlanta.

29. *Georgia Gazette*, October 6, 13, 20, 1763, September 27, 1764.

30. Ga. Council Minutes, December 31, 1762, *CRG*, 8:777.

31. McGillivray and Macgillivray, *Clan MacGillivray*, 40–43.

32. Ibid.

33. McGillivray, "A Sketch of the McGillivrays."

34. McGillivray and Macgillivray, *Clan MacGillivray*, 45.

35. Laurens to Cowles and Harford, May 8, 1764, in Hamer, Rogers, and Chesnutt, eds., *Laurens Papers*, 4:119, 144.

36. For a history of the "conspiracy" see Dale Van Every, *Forth to the Wilderness: The First American Frontier, 1754–1774* (New York: William Morrow, 1961).

TWELVE. RESHAPING THE FRONTIER

1. Ellis to Knox, April 30, 1762, Knox Papers, WLCL.

2. Verner W. Crane noticed the importance of the document and printed it under the title "Hints Relative to the Division and Government of the Conquered and Newly Acquired Countries in America" in Notes and Documents, *MVHR* 8 (1922):367–73. In a footnote signed C.W.A. (Clarence W. Alvord) the document is attributed to Henry Ellis. A contemporary of Ellis, Francis Maseres, asserted that William Grant of London saw the initial draft of the Proclamation of 1763 and it was in Ellis's handwriting. Maseres later referred to Ellis as the one "who drew that unfortunate proclamation" (Francis Maseres to Fowler Walker, November 19, 1767, in W. Stewart Wallace, ed., *The Maseres Letters, 1766–1768* [Toronto: Oxford University Press, 1919], 62–63). For a thoughtful treatment of Ellis's post-Georgia career see John Shy, *A*

People Numerous and Armed (New York: Oxford University Press, 1976), 37–72. See also R. A. Humphreys, "Lord Shelburne and the Proclamation of 1763," *English Historical Review* 49 (April 1934): 246; Francis Paul Prucha, *American Indian Policy in the Formative Years: The Indian Trade and Intercourse Acts, 1790–1834* (Cambridge, Mass.: Harvard University Press, 1962), 15–16; Alden, *John Stuart*, 181; and Juricek, ed., *Georgia Treaties*, 295.

3. Humphreys, "Lord Shelburne," 246.

4. The proclamation is printed as an appendix to Humphreys, "Lord Shelburne," 258–64.

5. "On the method to prevent giving any alarms to the Indians by taking possession of Florida and Louisiana," attributed to Henry Ellis, Earl of Shelburne Papers, 60:131, WLCL. The attribution is correct. The original is Ellis to Egremont, December 15, 1762, in Egremont Papers, PRO 30/47/14. Other Ellis letters in the Egremont Papers illustrate Ellis's influence regarding the terms of the Treaty of Paris of 1763.

6. Egremont to Amherst, March 16, 1763, Amherst Papers, WLCL.

7. Stuart to Amherst, March 15, June 2, 1763, ibid.

8. Stuart to Amherst, March 15, 1763, ibid.

9. Amherst to Stuart, April 16, 1763; Stuart to Amherst, July 30, 1763, ibid.

10. Amherst to Stuart, August 17, 1763, ibid.; also in PRO, CO 5/63.

11. Amherst to Boone, August 17, 1763, Amherst Papers, WLCL; also PRO, CO 5/63.

12. Ga. Council Minutes, July 14, 1763, *CRG*, 9:70–77.

13. Stuart to Egremont, June 1, 1763, PRO, CO 5/65; Wright to Gentlemen, October 11, 1763, *Journal of the Congress of the Four Southern Governors and the Superintendent of That District, with the Five Nations of Indians at Augusta, 1763* (Charlestown: Peter Timothy, 1764); also in PRO, CO 5/65, pt. 3.

14. Boone, Dobbs, Fauquier, and Stuart to Wright, October 4, 1763; Wright to Gentlemen, October 8, 1763; Boone, Dobbs, and Fauquier to Wright, October 14, 1763; Wright to Gentlemen, October 11, 1763; Boone, Dobbs, and Fauquier to Wright, October 15, 1763, *Journal of the Congress*, PRO, CO 5/65, pt. 3; Wright to Egremont, June 10, 24, to Fauquier, June 22, 1763, *CRG*, 37, pt. 1:50–52, 57–60; Stuart to Boone, October 15, 1763, Lower Creeks' talk, September 16, 1763, *Journal of the Congress*, PRO, CO 5/65, pt. 3.

15. Boone, Dobbs, and Fauquier to Stuart, October 18, 1763, *Journal of the Congress*, PRO, CO 5/65, pt. 3.

16. Ga. Council Minutes, October 11, 1763, *CRG*, 9:97–99; *Georgia Gazette*, September 22, 1763; Stuart to Gentlemen, October 20, 23, 1763, *Journal of the Congress*, PRO, CO 5/65, pt. 3.

17. John Alden in his history of John Stuart's superintendency did not notice Emistisiguo's participation; David Corkran identified the Upper Creek chief whose name was recorded as "Mustisikah" as Emistisiguo (*Creek Frontier*, 240). Emistisiguo referred to his part in the Augusta Congress on several subsequent occasions. See talk given at Okchoys, May 1, 1771, in K. G. Davies, ed., *Documents of the American Revolution, 1770–1783*, 21 vols. (Shannon: Irish University Press, 1972–81), 3:118–21.

18. *Journal of the Congress*, PRO, CO 5/65, pt. 3; Stuart to Egremont, December 5, 1763, in Juricek, ed., *Georgia Treaties*, 359–61.

19. Talk by John Stuart, November 5, 1763, *Journal of the Congress*, PRO CO 5/65, pt. 3.

20. Talk by Tallachea, November 7, 1763, *Journal of the Congress*, PRO, CO 5/65, pt. 3. For an authoritative treatment of the 1763 boundary line, see Louis DeVorsey, Jr., *The Indian Boundary in the Southern Colonies, 1763–1775* (Chapel Hill: University of North Carolina Press, 1966), 149–57.

21. Talk given at Okchoys, May 1, 1771, in Davies, *Documents*, 3:118–21.

22. For the text of the treaty, see *Journal of the Congress*, PRO, CO 5/65, pt. 3.

23. Governors and Stuart to Egremont, November 10, 1763, PRO, CO 5/65, pt. 2; also in *Journal of the Congress*, PRO, CO 5/65, pt. 3. The governors had no way of knowing that Egremont had died of apoplexy the previous September.

24. Wright had to tell Egremont that the Indians already knew about the French and Spanish cessions long before they reached Augusta (Wright to Egremont, November 10, 1763, *CRG*, 37, pt. 1:62–65.

25. Stuart to Amherst, December 3, 1763, Amherst Papers, WLCL; Stuart to Egremont, December 5, 1763, PRO, CO 5/65, pt. 3.

26. C. L. Grant, ed., *Letters, Journals and Writings of Benjamin Hawkins*, 2 vols. (Savannah: Beehive Press, 1980), 1:40, 63, 92.

27. Martha Condray Searcy, "The Introduction of African Slavery into the Creek Indian Nation," *GHQ* 66 (Spring 1982): 21–32.

28. Stuart to Gage, December 28, 1763, Gage Papers, WLCL; Wright to Stuart, February 22, April 4, 1764, Ga. Council Minutes, January 16, 1764, *CRG*, 9:114–16.

29. Ga. Council Minutes, March 6, 1764, *CRG*, 9:148–50.

30. Gage to Stuart, January 27, May 1, 1764, Gage Papers, WLCL.

31. Emistisiguo's talk at Little Tallassee, April 10, 1764, in Stuart to Gage, May 20, 1764, ibid.

32. The Mortar's talk, August 13, 1764, in Wright to Gage, August 28, 1764, ibid.

33. D'Abbadie to Kerlérec, November 6, 1763, in Rowland, Sanders, and Galloway, eds., *Mississippi Provincial Archives*, 5:291–93.

34. Jean-Bernard Bossu, *New Travels in North America*, ed. Samuel Davis Dickinson (Natchitoches, La.: Northwestern State University Press, 1982), 54–55.

35. Cochrane to Gage, October 23, 1764, Gage to Cochrane, November 17, 1764, Gage Papers, WLCL.

36. Robert R. Rea, *Major Robert Farmar of Mobile* (Tuscaloosa, University of Alabama Press, 1990), 42–43.

37. Alden, *John Stuart*, 195, 199.

38. Ibid., 201–2; Stuart to Halifax, April 16, 1765, PRO, CO 5/66.

39. Stuart to John Pownall, August 24, 1765, CO 5/66.

40. Alden, *John Stuart*, 206.

41. Ibid., 212–13.

42. Johnstone to Montaut de Monberaut, June 26, 1765, PRO, CO 5/72.

43. Ga. Council Minutes, September 5, 1768, *CRG*, 10:571–82.

44. For a discussion of the genesis of the plan of 1764 see Clarence W. Alvord, *The Mississippi Valley in British Politics*, 2 vols. (New York: Russell and Russell, 1939), 1:221–24.

THIRTEEN. THE AFTERMATH OF 1763

1. The relevant part of the Proclamation of 1763 is cited in Alden, *John Stuart*, 207–8.

2. Ibid., 209.

3. Wright to Shelburne, November 29, 1766, *CRG*, 37, pt. 1:146–49.

4. William Knox, *Three Tracts Regarding the Conversion and Instruction of the Free Indians and Negroe Slaves in the Colonies* (London: J. Debrett, 1768), 4–10.

5. Wright to Shelburne, November 18, 1766, *CRG*, 37, pt. 1:141–44;

Newton D. Mereness, ed., *Travels in the American Colonies* (New York: Antiquarian Press, 1961), 396–97.

6. Ga. Council Minutes, March 6, 1764, August 6, 1765, *CRG*, 9:151, 381.

7. Ibid., January 1, 1765, *CRG*, 9:269–70. Bernard Bailyn cited McGillivray's project as an example of a speculative phenomenon that swept the colonies and threatened to drain Ireland and Scotland (*The Peopling of British North America* [New York: Vintage Books, 1988], 72–73).

8. Ga. House Minutes, March 6, 1766, *CRG*, 14:360.

9. E. R. R. Green, "Queensborough Township," *W&MQ* 3d ser., 17 (1960): 189–96.

10. Ga. Council Minutes, February 18, March 1, 9, 1768, *CRG*, 10:432, 435, 460.

11. Ga. Council Minutes, December 9, 1768, *CRG*, 10:671–72, 690. Robert Scott Davis, Jr., has set the record straight regarding Wrightsborough Quakers: they were in the minority at Wrightsborough, but, with few exceptions, only Quakers received grants before the Revolution (*Quaker Records in Georgia: Wrightsborough, 1772–1793, Friendsborough, 1776–1777* [Roswell, Ga.: W. H. Wolfe Associates, 1986], v, 10).

12. Wright to Shelburne, January 5, 1767, *CRG*, 37, pt. 1:157; Ga. Council Minutes, November 12, 1765, *CRG*, 9:436–37; Wright to the Mortar, Gun Merchant, Wolf, and Emistisiguo, December 27, 1765, *CRG*, 37, pt. 1:167–68; Wright to Lower Creek chiefs, January 3, 1767, *CRG*, 37, pt. 1:170–73.

13. Wright to Lower Creek chiefs, January 3, 1767, *CRG*, 37, pt. 1:170–73; Ga. Council Minutes, July 29, 1767, *CRG*, 10:246–47.

14. Ga. Council Minutes, August 4, 1767, *CRG*, 10:272–73.

15. Grant to Gage, August 29, 1767, Gage Papers, WLCL.

16. Gage to Stuart, November 14, 1767, ibid.; Shelburne to Wright, November 14, 1767, *CRG*, 37, pt. 1:253.

17. Ga. Council Minutes, September 1, 1767, *CRG*, 10:302–3.

18. Memorial from Merchants and Traders of the Province of Georgia Trading from Augusta to the Creek Nation, n.d.; Stuart to Gage, December 26, 1767, Gage Papers, WLCL.

19. Gage to Stuart, January 26, 1768; Fuser to Gage, May 10, 1768; Galphin to Stuart, June 2, 1768, ibid.

20. Williams, *Adair's History*, 295.

21. Stuart to Hillsborough, September 15, 1768, PRO, CO 5/227.

22. Ga. Council Minutes, September 3, 1768, *CRG*, 10:566–71.

23. Ibid.

24. Ibid., September 5, 1765, *CRG*, 10:571–82.

25. Wright to Hillsborough, September 17, 1768, *CRG*, 37, pt. 2:371.

26. Wright to Hillsborough, October 5, 1768; Hillsborough to Wright, December 10, 1768, *CRG*, 37, pt. 2:369, 374.

27. *Georgia Gazette*, December 14, 1768; McGillivray to Stuart, December 14, 1768, PRO, CO 5/70.

28. The map by Samuel Savery, dated March 13, 1769, is dedicated in bold letters "To Lachlan McGillivray, Esq., Deputy Superintendent" and bears the title "This Sketch of the Boundary Line between the Province of Georgia and the Creek Nation is address'd by His Most Obedient Serv't:," WLCL.

29. McGillivray to Stuart, December 14, 1768, PRO, CO 5/70; *Georgia Gazette*, December 14, 1768; Ga. House Minutes, December 23, 1768, *CRG*, 14:639.

30. Stuart's Journal of Congress at Augusta, November 12, 1768, PRO, CO 5/70.

31. Gage to Prevost, February 10, 1764, Gage Papers, WLCL.

32. Prevost to Gage, March 10, 20, 1764, ibid.

33. Wright to Gage, March 20, 1764; Gage to Prevost, May 1, 1764; Gage to Wright, May 2, 1764, ibid.

34. Gage to Wright, May 2, 1764; Cochrane to Gage, July 20, 1764, October 23, November 27, 1764, ibid.

35. Cochrane to Gage, November 27, 1764, ibid. I am indebted to Professor John Juricek of Emory University for the information that there is a similar description of Fort Augusta in letters from Cochrane to Dartmouth, June 10, 11, 1766, Dartmouth Papers, Staffordshire Public Record Office, Stafford, England. A visit to Stafford and a perusal of the Dartmouth Papers in August 1990 confirmed the information.

36. Cochrane to Gage, January 4, 1765; Cochrane to Wright, November 12, 1764, Gage Papers, WLCL.

37. Fuser to Gage, September 29, 1767, ibid.

38. Wright to Shelburne, April 6, 1767; Shelburne to Wright, June 18, 1767, *CRG*, 37, pt. 1:180, 213.

39. Wright to Shelburne, August 15, 1767, *CRG*, 37, pt. 1:240.

40. Gage to Wright, May 16, 1767; Wright to Fuser, August 6, 1767; Fuser to Gage, July 24, 1767, Gage Papers, WLCL.

41. Gage to Wright, February 27, 1767; Gage to Fuser, May 18, 1767, ibid.

42. Fuser to Gage, November 27, 1767; Wright to Gage, December 1, 1767, ibid.

43. House Resolution of October 28, 1767, enclosed in Wright to Gage, December 1, 1767; Wright reported that the tax bill was funded in his of April 22, 1767, to Gage; Fuser to Gage, June 9, 1768, ibid.

44. Gage to Wright, June 12, 1768, Gage to Fuser, June 25, 1768, ibid.; Gage to Hillsborough, August 18, 1768, in Clarence Edwin Carter, ed., *The Correspondence of General Thomas Gage with the Secretaries of State, 1763–1775*, 2 vols. (1931; rpt. New York: Archon, 1969), 1:186–88.

45. Stuart to Gage, August 13, 21, 1768; Gage to Lord Charles Montague, June 24, 1768; Bull to Gage, July 28, 1768, Gage Papers, WLCL.

46. Wright to Gage, August 25, 1768, ibid.

47. Wright to Board of Trade, February 1, 7, 1766, *CRG*, 28, pt. 2:135–37.

FOURTEEN. A SAVANNAH GENTLEMAN

1. Laurens to Smith and Baillies, January 15, 1768, in Hamer, Rogers, and Chesnutt, eds., *Laurens Papers*, 5:546. Laurens's business with Graham and Company concerned the sale of slaves.

2. Wood, *Black Majority*; see also Sylvia R. Frey, "In Search of Roots: The Colonial Antecedents of Slavery in the Plantation Colonies," *GHQ* 68 (Summer 1984): 246–47.

3. Vaughan, "From White Man to Redskin," 919.

4. Betty Wood, *Slavery in Colonial Georgia, 1730–1775* (Athens: University of Georgia Press, 1984); Alan Gallay, *The Formation of a Planter Elite: Jonathan Bryan and the Southern Colonial Frontier* (Athens: University of Georgia Press, 1989); Darold D. Wax, " 'New Negroes Are Always in Demand': The Slave Trade in Eighteenth-Century Georgia," *GHQ* 68 (Summer 1984): 193–220.

5. Harvey H. Jackson, "American Slavery, American Freedom, and the Revolution in the Lower South: The Case of Lachlan McIntosh," *Southern Studies* 19 (Spring 1980): 81–93.

6. William L. Withuhn, "Salzburgers and Slavery: A Problem of *Mentalité*," *GHQ* 68 (Summer 1984): 187.

7. Hugh Anderson and Others to the Trustees, December 2, 1740, in Lane, ed., *General Oglethorpe's Georgia*, 2:494.

8. Helen Callahan, "Colonial Life in Augusta," in Cashin, ed., *Colonial Augusta*, 101–2.

9. *Georgia Gazette*, March 8–May 31, 1769, cited in ibid., p. 106.

10. Marion Hemperley, ed., *English Crown Grants in St. Paul Parish in Georgia, 1755–1775* (Atlanta: State Printing Office, 1974).

11. Harold E. Davis, *The Fledgling Province: Social and Cultural Life in Colonial Georgia, 1733–1776* (Chapel Hill: University of North Carolina Press, 1976), 190.

12. E. Merton Coulter, *Georgia: A Short History* (Chapel Hill: University of North Carolina Press, 1960), 104–5; Davis, *Fledgling Province*, 156–58.

13. *Georgia Gazette*, February 23, September 27, 1764, February 24, 1768.

14. Wright to Hillsborough, May 28, 1770, CRG, 37, pt. 2:458.

15. Conveyances of July 22, 1761, CRG, Book J, 447; May 23, 1767, CRG, Book R, 141; March 12, 1764, CRG, Book O, 214; June 11, 1770, CRG, Book R, 374; May 28, 1767, CRG, Book R, 19.

16. Lachlan McGillivray's will, June 12, 1767, personal papers of Colonel and Commander of Clan George B. Macgillivray.

17. Conveyance of August 24, 1760, CRG, Book O, 157.

18. *Georgia Gazette*, April 4, 1765, June 3, 1767.

19. William H. Dumont, *Colonial Georgia Genealogical Data, 1748–1783* (Washington, D.C.: National Genealogical Society, 1971), 32.

20. Wax, "'New Negroes,'" 200.

21. House Minutes, November 10, 1766, 14:384. The tributary of the Savannah above Tybee Island is still known as Lazaretto Creek.

22. House Minutes, April 22, June 9, 1761, CRG, 13:531, 582, cited in Wax, "'New Negroes,'" 204.

23. Memorandum signed by James Wright, John Graham, Joseph Clay, Lachlan McGillivray, William McGillivray, William Struthers, and Stephen Deane, April 1775, Sir James Wright File, Box 29, Keith Read Collection, University of Georgia Libraries, Athens. Deane was captain of the transport vessel. See also *Georgia Gazette*, May 23, 1770; Wax, "'New Negroes,'" 212.

24. *Georgia Gazette*, May 23, 1770.

25. Wax, "'New Negroes,'" 212.

26. Gallay, *Formation of a Planter Elite*, 107; Memorial of Lachlan McGillivray, PRO, AO 13/36, pt. 2/560–61.

27. Roger A. Martin, "John Joachim Zubly," in Kenneth Coleman and

Charles Stephen Gurr, eds., *Dictionary of Georgia Biography*, 2 vols. (Athens: University of Georgia Press, 1983), 2:1107–8.

28. *Georgia Gazette*, June 3, 10, 17, 24, July 1, 1767, March 16, 1768.

29. *Georgia Gazette*, March 30, April 6, 1768.

30. *Georgia Gazette*, April 20, 1768.

31. Lowry Axley, *Holding Aloft the Torch: Savannah Independent Presbyterian Church* (Savannah: Savannah Independent Presbyterian Church, 1958), 5–6.

32. *Georgia Gazette*, May 10, 1769; William Harden, *A History of Savannah and South Georgia*, 2 vols. (Chicago: Lewis, 1913), 1:136–38; Davis, *Fledgling Province*, 202–3.

33. Wright to Messrs. Clark and Milligan, June 7, 1775, Loudoun Papers, Huntington Library; Laurens to Cowles and Harford, May 8, 1764, in Hamer, Rogers, and Chesnutt, eds., *Laurens Papers*, 4:270–71; *Georgia Gazette*, June 8, 1767.

34. *Georgia Gazette*, November 16, 1774. The *Inverness* was burned by Georgia Whigs on March 3, 1776, with a cargo worth £13,709. Fortunately for the McGillivrays, it was insured (Hamer, Rogers, and Chesnutt, eds., *Laurens Papers*, 11:140n). In a letter of August 4, 1775, Hannah Vincent of London informed Jacob Read of Savannah that she intended to write him "by Mac-Gillivray" but that he had sailed unexpectedly. She must have referred to Captain Daniel McGillivray (Britt and Dees, eds., *Selected Eighteenth Century Manuscripts*, 153–55).

35. *Georgia Gazette*, June 7, 1775.

36. Conveyance of May 23, 1767, *CRG*, Book R, 141.

37. Williams, *Adair's History*, 288–89.

38. Ibid., xxxiii.

39. Ibid., xxxiv.

40. Ibid., 393.

41. Ibid., 395–96.

42. Mark Van Doren, ed., *Travels of William Bartram* (New York: Dover, 1928), 347–48; Abstract of John McGillivray to Charles Stuart, May 10, 1766, PRO, CO 5/67.

43. Stuart to Board of Trade, July 10, 1766, PRO, CO 5/67.

44. Stuart to Board of Trade, November 16, December 2, 1766; Johnstone to Stuart, September 30, 1766, PRO, CO 5/67.

45. Shelburne to Wright, February 19, 1767, *CRG*, 37, pt. 1:152.

46. Shelburne to Stuart, December 11, 1766, February 19, 1767, PRO, CO 5/225. In 1767 Shelburne advanced a proposal to abolish the Indian departments so as to promote his notion of free trade. He was not averse to land speculation in the Northwest. He lost his post in January 1768 before he could carry out his plans. See Alvord, *Mississippi Valley*, 1:345–58.

47. Stuart to Hillsborough, April 14, 1769, PRO, CO 5/227.

48. Charles Stuart to John Stuart, June 17, 1770, in Stuart to Hillsborough, December 2, 1770, in Davies, ed., *Documents*, 2:108–10.

49. Gage to Hillsborough, July 7, 1770, ibid., 136–38.

50. Charles Stuart to John Stuart, June 12, 1770, ibid., 103.

51. Wright to Hillsborough, May 28, 1770, *CRG*, 37, pt. 1:458.

52. Hillsborough to Wright, July 31, 1770, PRO, CO 5/660.

53. Wright to Hillsborough, July 20, 1770, PRO, CO 5/660.

54. Hillsborough to Stuart, February 11, May 4, 1771, PRO, CO 5/72.

55. Gage to Hillsborough, January 6, 1770, in Davies, ed., *Documents*, 2:22–25; Stuart to Hillsborough, December 2, 1770, ibid., 280–83.

56. Charles Strachan to Peter Swanson, Kinnaber, October 15, 1770, Charles Strachan Letterbook, National Library of Scotland, Edinburgh. Strachan, a Mobile merchant, had inherited his uncle's estate near Montrose. Peter Swanson was John McGillivray's partner at Mobile. I am indebted to Russell Snapp for showing me his notes from the Strachan Letterbook.

57. Lachlan McGillivray to Jean Roy McGillivray, August 16, 1772, Fraser Mackintosh Collection, Scottish Record Office.

58. Lachlan McGillivray to Bailie John McIntosh, October 26, 1772, ibid., McGillivray and Macgillivray, *Clan MacGillivray*, 47.

59. Laurens to William Cowles, September 25, 1772, in Hamer, Rogers, and Chesnutt, eds., *Laurens Papers*, 8:477–78; Lachlan McGillivray to Bailie John McIntosh, October 26, 1772, Fraser Mackintosh Collection, Scottish Record Office; Memorial of Captain William McGillivray, received October 18, 1783, PRO, AO 13/36.

FIFTEEN. THE SECOND CONGRESS OF AUGUSTA, 1773

1. Statement of merchants, April 16, 1772, in Habersham to Hillsborough, April 24, 1772, *CRG*, 37, pt. 2:617–21; Cameron to Stuart, March 19, 1771;

Memorial of Traders to Creek and Cherokee Nations to Governor James Wright, in Wright to Hillsborough, December 12, 1771, in Davies, ed., *Documents*, 3:70–73, 125–27.

2. Stuart to Hillsborough, April 27, PRO, CO 5/72.

3. Hillsborough to Stuart, July 3, 1771, PRO, CO 5/72; Habersham to Hillsborough, April 24, 1772, *CRG*, 37, pt. 2:617–21.

4. Habersham to John Pownall, August 3, 1771, *CRG*, 37, pt. 2:547; Governor Wright's proposal laid before king by Dartmouth, Bamber Gascoyne, Greville, and Garlies, November 9, 1772, *CRG*, 38, pt. 1A:15–26. The petitioning merchants were William Thompson, William Greenwood, William Higginson, Charles Ogilvie, Basil Cowper, Alexander Watson, John Clark, James Graham, and John Nutt (Hamer, Rogers, and Chesnutt, eds., *Laurens Papers*, 9:103 n. 7).

5. Wright to Hillsborough, December 12, 1771; Habersham to Hillsborough, April 24, 1772, in Davies, ed., *Documents*, 3:269–75, 75–76.

6. Hillsborough to Stuart, January 11, 1772, PRO, CO 5/73.

7. Ga. Council Minutes, October 2, 1770, *CRG*, 11:155; Wright to Hillsborough, December 12, 1771, in Davies, ed., *Documents*, 3:269–75.

8. Hillsborough to Stuart, January 11, 1772, PRO, CO 5/73; Wright to Hillsborough, received December 12, 1771, *CRG*, 28, pt. 2B:789; also in *CRG*, 28, pt. 2:359–60.

9. Habersham to Hillsborough, August 12, 1772; Proclamation, August 4, 1772, *CRG*, 38, pt. 1A:4–8, 9–10; Stuart to Hillsborough, June 12, 1772, in Davies, ed., *Documents* 5:113–18.

10. Stuart to Hillsborough, June 12, 1772, in Davies, ed., *Documents*, 5:113–18.

11. Dartmouth to Wright, December 12, 1772, *CRG*, 38, pt. 1A:31–35.

12. Charles Stuart to John Stuart, June 17, 1770, in Davies, ed., *Documents*, 2:108–10.

13. Proceedings of Congress with Upper Creeks in John Stuart to Hillsborough, December 29, 1771, in Davies, ed., *Documents*, 3:212–28.

14. Talk given at Okchoys, May 1, 1771, transcribed by Philemon Kemp, June 6, 1771, in Davies, ed., *Documents*, 3:118–21.

15. Proceedings of a Congress with Upper Creeks, October 29 to November 2, 1771, in Stuart to Hillsborough, December 29, 1771, in Davies, ed., *Documents*, 3:212–28.

16. Ibid., 221.

17. Stuart to Hillsborough, June 13, 1772, PRO, CO 5/73.

18. Instructions to Mr. David Taitt, January 20, 1772, PRO, CO 5/73.

19. David Taitt, "A Journal to and Through the Lower Creek Nation," and "A Journal to and Through the Upper Creek Nation," July 19, 1772, PRO, CO 5/73.

20. Taitt to Stuart, March 16, 1772, PRO, CO 5/73.

21. Ibid.; Taitt's Journal, July 19, 1772, PRO, CO 5/73.

22. Taitt's Journal, July 19, 1772, PRO, CO 5/73. Taitt's Journal is also in Mereness, ed., *Travels in the American Colonies*, 497–565.

23. Ga. Council Minutes, October 23, 1772, *CRG*, 12:333–34.

24. Ibid., February 15, 1773, *CRG*, 17:687–89; for the equally effusive House address, see Ga. House Minutes, March 2, 1773, *CRG*, 15:393–94.

25. Wright to Dartmouth, March 24, April 8, 1773, *CRG*, 38, pt. 1A:43–45, 52–54.

26. Map enclosed in Wright to Dartmouth, August 10, 1773, *CRG*, 38, pt. 1A: following p. 88.

27. Alden, *John Stuart*, 305; Ga. House Minutes, June 28, 1773, *CRG*, 15:439.

28. Van Doren, ed., *Travels of William Bartram*, 53–54.

29. Wright to Dartmouth, August 10, 1773, *CRG*, 38, pt. 1A:80–83, also in Davies, ed., *Documents*, 6:201–2.

30. Wright to Dartmouth, June 17, 1773; Stuart to Dartmouth, June 21, 1773, in Davies, ed., *Documents*, 6:156–58, 158–59.

31. Van Doren, ed., *Travels of William Bartram*, 54–55. A copy of Philip Yonge's map is in PRO, MPG2.

32. Stuart to Dartmouth, August 5, 1773; Wright to Dartmouth, August 10, 1773, in Davies, ed., *Documents*, 6:200–201, 201–2.

33. Wright to Dartmouth, October 30, December 27, 1773, in Davies, ed., *Documents*, 6:237, 266–67.

34. Wright to Dartmouth, October 18, 1773, *CRG*, 38, pt. 1A:151–52; Wright to Dartmouth, December 27, 1773, in Davies, ed., *Documents*, 6:266–67.

35. Ga. House Minutes, June 28, 30, 1773, *CRG*, 15:439, 442. A recent historian of the period argued that the vote to recognize Galphin and McGillivray was meant as a slap at the governor by the dissident faction led by Jonathan Bryan (Gallay, *Formation of a Planter Elite*, 122–23). McGillivray is mistakenly identified as "Alexander."

36. *Georgia Gazette*, February 2, 1774.

37. Ibid., February 2, 16, 1774; Wright to Bull, *CRG*, 38:15–17.

38. Wright to Dartmouth, January 31, 1774, *CRG*, 38, pt. 1A:163–65.

39. Wright's address, January 28, 1774, *CRG*, 15:538–39, 539–41; Wright to Dartmouth, January 28, March 2, 12, 1774, *CRG*, 38, pt. 1A:176, 178–79, 182, 185–92.

40. *Georgia Gazette*, March 16, 23, 1774; Wright to Dartmouth, April 18, May 24, 1774, *CRG*, 38, pt. 1A:239, 244, 286.

41. *Georgia Gazette*, April 13, 1774.

42. Dartmouth to Wright, July 6, 1774; Wright to Dartmouth, September 6, 1774, *CRG*, 38, pt. 1A:273, 312.

43. Wright to Edward Barnard, n.d., "Instructions to Edw'd Barnard, Esquire, Captain of the Troop of Rangers to be raised to keep good order amongst and for the protection of the Inhabitants in the new Ceded Lands above Little River," in claim of Thomas Waters, PRO, AO 13/37; Ga. Council Minutes, August 30, 1774, *CRG*, 12:406–10.

44. *Georgia Gazette*, September 7, 28, October 12, 1774.

45. Stuart to Haldimand, February 3, 1774, in Davies, ed., *Documents*, 7:34–37.

46. Ga. Council Minutes, August 30, 1774, *CRG*, 12:406–10.

47. Wright to Dartmouth, September 23, 1774, *CRG*, 38, pt. 1B:326–27.

48. Ga. Council Minutes, August 30, 1774, *CRG*, 12:406–10.

49. *Georgia Gazette*, October 19, 1774.

50. "Petition of the Inhabitants of St. George and St. Paul, including the ceded lands in the Province of Georgia," July 31, 1776, *NYHS Collections*, 5:181.

51. *Georgia Gazette*, November 2, 1774.

52. Gallay, *Formation of a Planter Elite*, 152.

53. Alden, *John Stuart*, 310. David Corkran's characterization of the Mortar as a "nativist" is appropriate (*Creek Frontier*, 161).

54. Stuart to Gage, January 18, 1775, Gage Papers, WLCL.

55. Alden, *John Stuart*, 299–301, 301 n.

56. Brown to unknown, August 17, 1817, State Department Miscellaneous Collection, P. K. Yonge Library, University of Florida, Gainesville.

57. Wright to Dartmouth, December 12, 1774, *CRG*, 38, pt. 1B:359–60; Edward J. Cashin, *The King's Ranger: Thomas Brown and the American Revolution on the Southern Frontier* (Athens: University of Georgia Press, 1989), 16.

58. Address by Commons House of Assembly, January 20, 1775, *CRG*, 38, pt. 1B:387–88.

59. Wright to Dartmouth, June 20, 1775, *CRG*, 38, pt. 1B:475–77.

60. Later in the war Brown informed Lord North that he "had the honor to be considered a son of your lordship and an emissary of administration sent to poison the minds of the virtuous citizens" (Brown to North, June 4, 1783, PRO, CO 5/82).

61. *Georgia Gazette*, June 28, 1775.

62. Wright to Dartmouth, November 1, 1775, *CRG*, 38, pt. 2:13–16; *Georgia Gazette*, November 29, 1775.

63. For a description of Savannah's mercantile history, see Coleman, *Colonial Georgia*, 216–22.

64. "Redneck" was a name for religious dissenters in the north of England and "cracker" meant a low and vulgar braggart. See David Hackett Fisher, *Albion's Seed: Four British Folkways in America* (New York: Oxford University Press, 1989), 758. Fisher's thesis that four formative influences, originating in specific regions of Britain, swept across America in four parallel swaths is a brilliant interpretation, but it will not do when applied to the deep South. The Scots-Irish influence in the region west of the Savannah River was diluted by a heavy overlay of Virginia attitudes as Virginians moved into Georgia in great numbers after the American Revolution. The influence of Charlestown was at least as important as that of the Scots-Irish. Augusta and Savannah people copied Charlestown ways. Entrepreneurs from Augusta and Savannah migrated to Macon, Columbus, Rome, and Atlanta as the frontier receded. The Charlestown influence was urban, commercial, pragmatic, pleasure-loving, and social. Rural planters followed the Virginian agrarian tradition; urban planters imitated the absentee planters of Charlestown.

65. James Seymour to the Society for the Propagation of the Gospel, August 24, 1772, in Fleming, *Autobiography of a Colony*, 108.

66. "Unfinished memoirs of Robert Mackay," in Mackay-Stiles Papers, vol. 42, Southern Historical Collection, University of North Carolina, Chapel Hill. The author of these memoirs was Robert Mackay, Jr., who was born in Augusta in 1772. His father was Robert Mackay from Wick in the far north of Scotland, and his grandfather was the Rev. Robert Mackay from Inverness. Robert Mackay, the father, bought Lachlan McGillivray's White House just west of Augusta on the trading road. The house and its surroundings were the

scene of an important battle during the American Revolution. I am indebted to Clermont Lee of Savannah for information on the Mackay family.

67. Caughey, *McGillivray of the Creeks*, 16.

68. Galphin to Willie Jones, October 26, 1776, in Peter Force, ed., *American Archives*, 5th ser., 3 vols. (Washington, D.C.: M. St. Clair and Peter Force, 1848–53), 3:648–50.

69. Ga. House Minutes, June 8, 1780, *CRG*, 15:590–91.

70. "An Act for Preventing Improper or Disaffected Persons Emigrating from other Places," August 5, 1782, *CRG*, 19, pt. 2:162–66.

SIXTEEN. RETURN TO STRATHNAIRN

1. Edward J. Cashin and Heard Robertson, *Augusta and the American Revolution: Events in the Georgia Back Country, 1773–1783* (Darien, Ga.: Ashantilly Press, 1975), 23–29; Colin Campbell, ed., *Journal of an Expedition Against the Rebels of Georgia in North America Under the Orders of Archibald Campbell Esquire Lieut. Colol. of His Majesty's 71st Regimt. 1773* (Darien, Ga.: Ashantilly Press, 1981), 55–75.

2. Jacob Moniac to Stuart, April 16, 1779, PRO, CO 5/80.

3. Charles Shaw to Germain, June 19, 1780, Lord George Germain Papers, WLCL.

4. Lachlan McGillivray, account for provisions to Indians, June 1, 1780, in Historical Manuscripts Commission, *Report on American Manuscripts in the Royal Institution of Great Britain* (Dublin: John Falconer, 1906), 2:133.

5. Woodward, *Reminiscences*, 108. Woodward wrote that a faithful slave named Charles guided Sophia and Alexander away from Savannah.

6. Wright to Germain, November 5, 1779, *CRG*, 38, pt. 2:206–9.

7. "Plan of Attack and the Fortification of Savannah," 1779, De Renne Collection, University of Georgia Libraries. The information on the location of Springfield plantation was supplied by Farris Cadle, whose history of land surveying in Georgia is scheduled for publication by the University of Georgia Press in 1991.

8. Clinton to Newcastle, November 19, 1779, Duke of Newcastle Manuscripts, University of Nottingham, England; Alexander A. Lawrence, *Storm over Savannah: The Story of Count D'Estaing and the Siege of the Town in 1779* (Athens: University of Georgia Press, 1951), 91–103, 107; Richard C. Cole,

"The Siege of Savannah and the British Press, 1779–1780," *GHQ* 65 (Fall 1981): 189–202.

9. McGillivray's new business associate was a merchant named Hogg (*Royal Georgia Gazette*, November 15, 1781).

10. Memorial of Captain William McGillivray, read March 25, 1779, PRO, AO 13/36; William McGillivray to Farquhar McGillivray, September 9, April 28, 1779, Fraser Mackintosh Collection, Scottish Record Office.

11. Chester to Germain, March 25, May 7, 1778, in Davies, ed., *Documents*, 15:77–81, 116–19; Stuart to Germain, April 13, 1778, *CRG*, 15:94–97. John Caughey concluded that Willing was his own worst enemy. Not daring to risk capture by the British by ascending the Mississippi, he left New Orleans on an American sloop, which was taken by a British ship, and Willing was returned to New York as a prisoner ("Willing's Expedition down the Mississippi, 1778," *LHQ* 15 [January 1932]: 33–34). Ironically, a similar fate befell McGillivray.

12. Memorial of John McGillivray, March 17, 1784, PRO, AO 13/36.

13. For a detailed account of Brown's career, see Cashin, *King's Ranger*; for a condensed version see Edward J. Cashin, "'But Brothers, It Is Our Land We Are Talking About': Winners and Losers in the Georgia Backcountry," in Ronald Hoffman, Thad W. Tate, and Peter J. Albert, eds., *An Uncivil War: The Southern Backcountry During the American Revolution* (Charlottesville: University Press of Virginia, 1985), 240–75.

14. Corkran, *Creek Frontier*, 320–21.

15. Cashin, *King's Ranger*, 152; James H. O'Donnell, "Alexander McGillivray: Training for Leadership, 1777–1783," *GHQ* 49 (June 1965): 181.

16. Wright to Clinton, January 2, 1782; Leslie to Clinton, February 1, 1782, Headquarters Papers of the British Army in America (microfilm), 35:4005, 4096, Colonial Williamsburg Foundation, Williamsburg, Va.

17. Abstract of lands specified in the Memorial of Lieutenant Colonel John McGillivray . . . conveyed by Lachlan McGillivray to John McGillivray by deed, September 7, 1781; Lachlan McGillivray's memorial states that by indentures of September 10 and 11, 1781, he conveyed his properties to John, PRO, AO 13/36.

18. Affidavit of Lachlan McGillivray the younger, November 1, 1784, PRO, AO 13/36.

19. *Royal Georgia Gazette*, May 23, 1782; Historical Manuscripts Commission, *Report on American Manuscripts* (Hereford, Eng.: Anthony Brothers, 1909), 4:19.

20. Act of Confiscation, May 4, 1782, *RRG*, 1:373–97; Memorial of Lachlan, John and William McGillivray and supporting schedules, PRO, AO 13/36. Robert G. Mitchell, "The Losses and Compensation of Georgia Loyalists," *GHQ* 68 (Summer 1984): 240.

21. McGillivray and Macgillivray, *Clan MacGillivray*, 45; John McGillivray to Farquhar McGillivray, July 28, 1783, Fraser Mackintosh Collection, Scottish Record Office.

22. McGillivray and Macgillivray, *Clan MacGillivray*, 45, 63.

23. John McGillivray to Farquhar McGillivray, November 30, 1736, Fraser Mackintosh Collection, Scottish Record Office; Fraser-Mackintosh, *Clan Chattan*, 20–24; Lachlan McGillivray (the younger) to Charles Graham, March 5, 1788; Ralph Fisher to Graham, February 10, 1788; Desposition and assignation of Torridens Bond, March 9, 1804 (gives disposition of John McGillivray's will), Fraser Mackintosh Collection, Scottish Record Office.

24. Lachlan McGillivray (the younger) to Graham, March 1, 1788, Fraser Mackintosh Collection, Scottish Record Office.

25. Account of money paid by Charles Graham to Lachlan McGillivray on account of Mr. John McGillivray, July 27, 1786, PRO, AO 13/36.

26. Lachlan McGillivray to Campbell McIntosh, November 18, 1790; to Mr. Alex Fraser, September 7, 1790; to Messrs. William Ingles and Campbell McIntosh, November 14, 1790; to Campbell McIntosh, November 3, 23, 1790, October 3, 1791, Fraser Mackintosh Collection, Scottish Record Office.

27. Lachlan McGillivray to Campbell McIntosh, November 3, 1790, ibid.

28. Lachlan McGillivray to Campbell McIntosh, November 18, 1790, November 11, 1791, ibid.

29. Rev. Mr. Alexander Gordon, "United Parishes of Daviot and Dunlichity," in Sir John Sinclair, ed., *The Statistical Account of Scotland, 1791–1799*, 20 vols. (East Ardsley, Wakefield, Engl.: E. P. Publishing, 1981), 17:54–64. Sir John Sinclair sent queries to parish ministers for this monumental survey.

30. Lachlan McGillivray to Campbell McIntosh, August 16, 1791, September 8, 1791, Fraser Mackintosh Collection, Scottish Record Office.

31. Pope, *Tour*, 51.

32. O'Donnell, "Alexander McGillivray," 182.

33. Caughey, *McGillivray of the Creeks*, 23–25.

34. Alexander McGillivray to O'Neill, February 10, 1786, in Caughey, *McGillivray of the Creeks*, 102–3.

35. Edward J. Cashin, "Georgia, Searching for Security," in Michael Allen Gillespie and Michael Lienesch, eds., *Ratifying the Constitution* (Lawrence: University Press of Kansas, 1989), 93–116.

36. Caughey, *McGillivray of the Creeks*, 40–46; Pope, *Tour*, 51.

37. Abigail Adams to Mary Cranch, August 8, 1790, quoted in J. Leitch Wright, Jr., *Creeks and Seminoles: The Destruction and Regeneration of the Muscogulge People* (Lincoln: University of Nebraska Press, 1986), 61; Drake, *Indians of North America*, 386.

38. Pope, *Tour*, 46–51. A large quartz boulder marks the site of Lachlan McGillivray's plantation at Little Tallassee. When I visited the place in 1988, the marker was difficult to locate because the locals, some of whom lived within a mile of the site, did not know of its existence.

39. Pope, *Tour*, 51; Benjamin Hawkins to William Eustis, August 27, 1809, in Grant, ed., *Writings of Hawkins*, 2:556.

40. Pope, *Tour*, 51–52.

41. Ibid.

42. Caughey, *McGillivray of the Creeks*, 57.

43. Obituary notice in the *Gentleman's Magazine*, August 1793, ibid., 362.

44. Panton to Lachlan McGillivray, April 10, 1794, obituary notice, ibid., 362–63.

45. Panton to Lachlan McGillivray, April 10, 1794, ibid., 362–63; Marie Taylor Greenslade, "William Panton, c. 1745–1801," *FHQ* 14 (1935): 116.

46. Benjamin Hawkins to William Eustis, August 27, 1809 in Grant, ed., *Writings of Hawkins*, 2:556.

47. John Innerarity to William Panton, September 24, 1798, in Greenslade, "William Panton," 116–17.

48. Innerarity to Panton, 1798, ibid., 118.

49. Benjamin Hawkins to William Eustis, August 27, 1809 in Grant, ed., *Writings of Hawkins*, 2:556.

50. Marjorie Wilkins Campbell, *McGillivray, Lord of the Northwest* (Toronto: Clarke-Irwin, 1962), 10–20, 31–52, 55–99, 75–76.

51. Ibid., 84–85, 139, 144–45, 157; see also Alan B. Lawson, "The North West Company of Canada: The Highland Connection," *An Inverness Miscellancy* 2 (1987): 30–40.

52. *Inverness Courier*, August 23, 1988.

53. Lachlan McGillivray to Campbell McIntosh, August 28, 1795, Fraser

Mackintosh Collection, Scottish Record Office. A brief notice in the *Georgia Gazette*, August 21, 1800, said simply, "Died on the 16th of November last, at Inverness, in Scotland, Lachlan McGillivray, Esq., formerly of this state."

54. John Leslie to John Forbes, July 15, 1802, in Greenslade, "William Panton," 118–19.

55. McGillivray and Macgillivray, *Clan MacGillivray*, 49–51.

EPILOGUE

1. Braund, "Mutual Convenience—Mutual Dependence," 228.

2. Daniel H. Usner, Jr., "American Indians on the Cotton Frontier: Changing Economic Relations with Citizens and Slaves in the Mississippi Territory," *JAH* 72 (September 1985): 297–317.

3. Knox, *Three Tracts*.

4. Benjamin Hawkins to James Madison, July 11, 1803, in Grant, ed., *Writings of Hawkins*, 2:458–59.

5. Herman J. Viola, *Thomas L. McKenney: Architect of America's Early Indian Policy, 1816–1830* (Chicago: Swallow Press, 1974), 24.

6. "Journal of Occurrences in the Creek Agency from January to the Conclusion of the Conference and Treaty at Fort Wilkinson by the Agent for Indian Affairs," 1802, in Grant, ed., *Writings of Hawkins*, 2:419.

7. Timothy Silver, *A New Face on the Countryside: Indians, Colonists, and Slaves in South Atlantic Forests, 1500–1800* (Cambridge: Cambridge University Press, 1990), 103.

8. Williams, *Adair's History*, 275.

9. D. W. Meinig, "The Continuous Shaping of America: A Prospectus for Geographers and Historians," *AHR* 83 (December 1978): 1186–1205.

Bibliography

Primary Sources

MANUSCRIPT COLLECTIONS
British Museum, London
  Landsdowne Papers
British Public Record Office, Chancery Lane
  Egremont Papers
British Public Record Office, Kew
  Audit Office
  Colonial Office
  Treasury Office
  War Office
Colonial Williamsburg Foundation, Williamsburg, Virginia
  Headquarters Papers of the British Army in America (microfilm)
Farraline Park Library, Inverness, Scotland
  Local histories, maps, and newspapers
Fort Toulouse Library, Wetumpka, Alabama
  Collection of maps, pamphlets, and articles pertaining to Fort Toulouse
Georgia Department of Archives and History, Atlanta
  Colonial Conveyances, Creek Letters, Talks, and Treaties, 1705–93, typescript
Georgia Historical Society, Savannah
  William Mackenzie Papers
  Antonio Waring Papers

Hagley Hall, Stourbridge, England
  Lyttelton Papers
Henry E. Huntington Library, San Marino, California
  General James Abercromby Papers
  Lord Loudoun Papers
Macgillivray, Colonel and Commander of the Clan George Brown, personal
  papers
    The first wills of Lachlan and John McGillivray belonged to this collection.
    Copies in possession of Colonel W. W. Wallace were obtained courtesy of
    Professor William S. Coker and Lynn Thompson
National Library of Scotland, Edinburgh
  Charles Strachan Letterbook
  Clan histories
New-York Historical Society
  Journal of Lachlan McGillivray
Reese Library, Augusta College, Augusta, Georgia
  Charles T. Cordle, "The John Tobler Manuscript: An Account of Swiss
    Immigrants in South Carolina in 1737," typescript
Scottish Record Office, Edinburgh
  Dalhousie Muniments (including James Glen correspondence)
  Fraser Mackintosh Collection
  Mackintosh of Mackintosh Muniments
South Caroliniana Library, Columbia, South Carolina
  Yates Snowden Collection
South Carolina Department of Archives and History, Columbia
  County of Charleston, Office of Register and Mesne, Conveyances
  Records in the British Public Record Office Relating to South Carolina
  Records of the Secretary of State, Office of Surveyor General, Colonial Plats
  Records of the States of the United States of America, South Carolina
  Council Journals, Library of Congress microfilm
  South Carolina Sessional Papers, Journal of Assembly (microfilm)
South Carolina Historical Society, Charleston
  McGillivray Family Papers
  Phillip M. Hamer Papers
  William R. Coe Papers
Staffordshire Record Office, Stafford, England
  Dartmouth Papers

Stroud Industrial Museum, Stroud, England
  Exhibition of cloth manufacture
Stroud Public Library, Stroud, England
  Histories of woolen industry
University of Edinburgh, Edinburgh
  William Robertson Papers
University of Florida, Gainesville
  State Department Miscellaneous Collection, P. K. Yonge Library
University of Georgia Libraries, Athens
  Phillips Collection
  Keith Read Collection
  Telemon Cuyler Collection
  DeRenne Collection
University of North Carolina, Southern Historical Collection, Chapel Hill
  Mackay-Stiles Papers
University of Nottingham, England
  Duke of Newcastle Manuscripts
William L. Clements Library, Ann Arbor, Michigan
  Lord Jeffrey Amherst Papers
  Sir Henry Clinton Papers
  General Thomas Gage Papers
  Lord George Germain Papers
  William Knox Papers
  William Henry Lyttelton Papers
  Earl of Shelburne Papers

NEWSPAPERS

Gentleman's Magazine, Georgia Gazette, Inverness Courier, London Magazine, Royal Georgia Gazette, South Carolina Gazette

PUBLISHED COLLECTIONS AND CONTEMPORARY SOURCES

Atkin, Edmond. *Historical Account of the Revolt of the Choctaw Indians in the Late War from the French to the British Alliance and of Their Return Since to That of the French.* . . . London, 1753.

Barron, William, ed. *The Vaudreuil Papers.* New Orleans: Polyanthos, 1975.

Beckemeyer, Frances Howell, comp. *Abstracts of Georgia Colonial Conveyence Book C-1, 1750–1761.* Atlanta: R.J. Taylor, Jr., Foundation, 1975.

Bossu, Jean-Bernard. *New Travels in North America*. Edited by Samuel Davis Dickinson. Natchitoches, La.: Northwestern State University Press, 1982.

Britt, Albert Sidney, Jr., and Anthony Roane Dees, eds. *Selected Eighteenth Century Manuscripts*. Savannah: Georgia Historical Society, 1980.

Campbell, Colin, ed. *Journal of an Expedition Against the Rebels of Georgia in North Carolina Under the Orders of Archibald Campbell Esquire Lieut. Colol. of His Majesty's 71st Regimt. 1778*. Darien, Ga.: Ashantilly Press, 1981.

Candler, Allan D., Lucian L. Knight, Kenneth Coleman, and Milton Ready, eds. *The Colonial Records of the State of Georgia*. 30 vols. Atlanta: Various printers 1904–16, 1979–82; vols. 29–39 are in typescript at the Georgia Department of Archives and History, Atlanta.

Carter, Clarence Edwin, ed. *The Correspondence of General Thomas Gage with the Secretaries of State, 1763–1775*. 2 vols. 1931. Reprint. New York: Archon, 1969.

Clark, Murtie June. *Loyalists in the Southern Campaign of the Revolutionary War*. 3 vols. Baltimore: Genealogical Publishing Co., 1981.

Crane, Verner W. "Hints Relative to the Division and Government of the Conquered and Newly Acquired Countries in America." *MVHR* 8 (1922): 367–73.

Davies, K. G., ed. *Calendar of State Papers Colonial Series, America and West Indies, 1737*. London: Her Majesty's Stationery Office, 1963.

———. *Documents of the American Revolution, 1770–1783*. 21 vols. Shannon: Irish University Press, 1972–81.

Davis, Robert Scott, Jr. *Quaker Records in Georgia: Wrightsborough, 1772–1793, Friendsborough, 1776–1777*. Roswell, Ga.: W. H. Wolfe Associates, 1986.

Easterby, J. H., ed. *The Colonial Records of South Carolina: The Journal of the Commons House of Assembly*. 9 vols. (1736–50). Columbia: Historical Commission of South Carolina and the South Carolina Archives Department, 1951–62.

Edgar, Walter B. *The Letterbook of Robert Pringle*. 2 vols. Columbia: University of South Carolina Press, 1972.

Forbes, Duncan. *Culloden Papers: Comprising an Extensive and Interesting Correspondence from the Year 1625 to 1748; Including Numerous Letters from the Unfortunate Lord Lovat, and Other Distinguished Persons of the Time; with Occasional State Papers of Much Historical Importance*. London: T. Cadwell and W. Davies, 1815.

Force, Peter, ed. *American Archives*. 5th ser. 3 vols. Washington, D.C.: M. St. Clair and Peter Force, 1848–53.

Forsyth, Alice Daly. *Louisiana Marriage Contracts: A Compilation of Abstracts from Records of the Superior Council of Louisiana During the French Regime, 1725–1758.* New Orleans: Polyanthos, 1890.

Fraser-Mackintosh, Charles. *Letters of Two Centuries Chiefly Connected with Inverness and the Highlands from 1616 to 1815.* Inverness: A. & W. Mackenzie, 1890.

Georgia Historical Society Collections. 20 vols. Savannah: Published by the Society, 1840–1980. Vol. 3 contains letters from General Oglethorpe and letters from Sir James Wright.

Gordon, Rev. Mr. Alexander. "The United Parishes of Daviot and Dunlichty." In Sir John Sinclair, ed., *The Statistical Account of Scotland*, 17:54–64. 20 vols. East Ardsley, Wakefield, Eng.: E. P. Publishing, 1981.

Grant, C. L., ed. *Letters, Journals and Writings of Benjamin Hawkins.* 2 vols. Savannah: Beehive Press, 1980.

Hamer, Philip M., George C. Rogers, Jr., and David R. Chesnutt, eds. *The Papers of Henry Laurens.* 11 vols. Columbia: University of South Carolina Press, 1968–88.

Hawes, Lilla Mills. *The Journal of the Reverend John Joachim Zubly A.M., D.D., March 5, 1770, Through June 22, 1781.* Savannah: Georgia Historical Society, 1989.

Hawkins, Benjamin. *A Sketch of the Creek Country in the Years 1798 and 1799.* 1848. Reprint. Spartanburg, S.C.: Reprint Company, 1974. Reprinted in combination with *Letters of Benjamin Hawkins, 1796–1806.*

Hemperley, Marion, ed. *England Crown Grants in St. Paul Parish in Georgia, 1755–1775.* Atlanta: State Printing Office, 1974.

Historical Manuscripts Commission. *Report on American Manuscripts in the Royal Institution of Great Britain.* 4 vols. London: Various printers, 1904–9.
———. *Report on Manuscripts in Various Collections.* Vol. 6. Dublin, 1906.

Journal of the Congress of the Four Southern Governors and the Superintendent of That District, with the Five Nations of Indians, at Augusta, 1763. Charlestown: Peter Timothy, 1764.

Juricek, John T., ed. *Georgia Treaties, 1733–1763.* Frederick, Md.: University Publications of America, 1989. Vol. 11 in Alden T. Vaughan, ed., *Early American Indian Documents: Treaties and Laws, 1607–1789.*

Knox, William. *Three Tracts Respecting the Conversion and Instruction of the Free Indians and Negroe Slaves in the Colonies.* London: J. Debrett, 1768.

Labaree, Leonard Woods. *Royal Instructions to British Colonial Governors, 1670–1776.* 2 vols. New York: Octagon Books, 1967.

Lane, Mills, ed. *General Oglethorpe's Georgia: Colonial Letters, 1733–43.* 2 vols. Savannah: Beehive Press, 1975.

Lipscomb, Terry W., ed. *Colonial Records of South Carolina: The Journal of the Commons House of Assembly, November 21, 1752–September 6, 1754.* Columbia: University of South Carolina Press, 1983.

———. *Colonial Records of South Carolina: The Journal of the Commons House of Assembly, November 12, 1754–September 23, 1755.* Columbia: University of South Carolina Press, 1986.

Lipscomb, Terry W., and R. Nicholas Olsberg, eds. *Colonial Records of South Carolina, the Journal of the Commons House of Assembly, Nov. 14, 1751–Oct. 7, 1752.* Columbia: University of South Carolina Press, 1977.

McDowell, William L., Jr., ed. *Colonial Records of South Carolina: Documents Relating to Indian Affairs, May 21, 1750–August 7, 1754.* Columbia: South Carolina Archives Department, 1958.

Mackay, William, ed. *The Letter-Book of Bailie John Steuart of Inverness, 1715–1752.* Edinburgh: T. and A. Constable, 1915.

McPherson, Robert G., ed. *The Journal of the Earl of Egmont: Abstract of the Trustees Proceedings for Establishing the Colony of Georgia, 1732–1738.* Athens: University of Georgia Press, 1962.

Milfort, Louis LeClerc de. *Memoir, or A Cursory Glance at My Different Travels and My Sojourn in the Creek Nation.* Translated by Geraldine deCourcy. Edited by John Francis McDermott. Chicago: R. R. Donnelley & Sons, 1956.

Moore, Caroline T., ed. *Abstracts of the Wills of the State of South Carolina, 1740–1760.* Columbia: R. L. Bryan, 1964.

———. *Abstracts of the Wills of the State of South Carolina, 1760–1783.* Columbia: R. L. Bryan, 1969.

Moore, Caroline T., and Agatha Aimar Simmons. *Abstracts of the Wills of the State of South Carolina, 1670–1740.* Columbia: R. L. Bryan, 1960.

Paton, Henry. *The Mackintosh Muniments, 1442–1820.* Preserved in the Charter-room at Moy Hall, Invernesshire. Edinburgh: Privately printed, 1903.

———, ed. *The Lyon in Mourning, or A Collection of Speeches, Letters, Journals, Etc. Relative to the Affairs of Prince Charles Edward Stuart by the Rev. Robert Forbes, A.M., 1746–1775.* 3 vols. Edinburgh: Scottish Academic Press, 1975.

Pope, John. *A Tour Through the Southern and Western Territories of the United*

States of North America: The Spanish Dominions on the River Mississippi, and the Floridas: The Countries of the Creek Nations; and Many Uninhabited Parts. 1792. Reprint. New York: Arno Press, 1971.

Pownall, Thomas. *The Administration of the Colonies.* 1768. Reprint. New York: DaCapo Press, 1971.

Rowland, Dunbar, Albert Godfrey Sanders, and Patricia Ann Galloway, eds. *Mississippi Provincial Archives: French Dominion.* 5 vols. Jackson and Baton Rouge: Mississippi Department of Archives and History and Louisiana State University Press, 1932–84.

Sinclair, Sir John, ed. *Statistical Account of Scotland.* 20 vols. 1791–99. Reprint. East Ardsley, Wakefield, Eng.: E. P. Publishing, 1981.

Van Doren, Mark, ed. *Travels of William Bartram.* New York: Dover, 1928.

VerSteeg, Clarence L., ed. *A True and Historical Narrative of the Colony of Georgia by Pat, Tailfer and Others with Comments by the Earl of Egmont.* Athens: University of Georgia Press, 1960.

Walker, George Fuller, comp. *Abstracts of Georgia Colonial Book J, 1755–1762.* Atlanta: R.J. Taylor, Jr., Foundation, 1978.

Wallace, W. Stewart, ed. *The Maseres Letters, 1766–1768.* Toronto: Oxford University Press, 1919.

Wight, Willard E. *Abstracts of Colonial Wills of the State of Georgia, 1733–1777.* Spartanburg, S.C.: Reprint Company, 1981.

Williams, Samuel Cole, ed. *Adair's History of the American Indians.* 1930. Reprint. New York: Promontory Press, 1974.

Woodward, Thomas S. *Woodward's Reminiscences of the Creek, or Muscogee Indians, Contained in Letters to Friends in Georgia and Alabama.* Montgomery: Barrett and Wimbish, 1859.

Secondary Works

BOOKS

Abbot, William Wright. *The Royal Governors of Georgia, 1754–1775.* Chapel Hill: University of North Carolina Press, 1959.

Alden, John Richard. *John Stuart and the Southern Colonial Frontier: A Study of Indian Relations, War, Trade, and Land Problems in the Southern Wilderness, 1754–1775.* New York: Gordian Press, 1966.

Alvord, Clarence W. *The Mississippi Valley in British Politics.* 2 vols. New York: Russell and Russell, 1939.

Andrews, Johnnie, Jr. *Fort Toulouse Colonials: A Compendium of the Colonial Families of Central Alabama, 1717–1823.* Prichard, Ala.: Bienville Historical Society, 1987.

Axley, Lowry. *Holding Aloft the Torch: Savannah Independent Presbyterian Church.* Savannah: Savannah Independent Presbyterian Church, 1958.

Bailyn, Bernard. *The Peopling of British North America.* New York: Vintage Books, 1988.

Brannon, Peter A. *The Southern Indian Trade.* Montgomery: Paragon Press, 1935.

Butterfield, L. H., Wilcomb E. Washburn, and William N. Fenton, eds. *American Indian and White Relations to 1830: Needs and Opportunities for Study.* Chapel Hill: University of North Carolina Press, 1957.

Campbell, Marjorie Wilkins. *McGillivray, Lord of the Northwest.* Toronto: Clarke, Irwin, 1962.

Carroll, B. R. *Historical Collections of South Carolina.* 2 vols. New York: Harper and Brothers, 1836.

Cashin, Edward J. *The King's Ranger: Thomas Brown and the American Revolution on the Southern Frontier.* Athens: University of Georgia Press, 1989.

——. "Georgia: Search for Security." In Michael Allen Gillespie and Michael Lienisch, eds. *Ratifying the Constitution.* Lawrence: University Press of Kansas, 1989.

——, ed. *Colonial Augusta: "Key of the Indian Countrey."* Macon, Ga.: Mercer University Press, 1986.

Cashin, Edward J., and Heard Robertson. *Augusta and the American Revolution: Events in the Georgia Back Country, 1773–1783.* Darien, Ga.: Ashantilly Press, 1975.

Caughey, John Walton. *McGillivray of the Creeks.* Norman: University of Oklahoma Press, 1938.

Chambers, Robert. *History of the Rebellion of 1745–6.* London: W. & R. Chambers, 1929.

Coker, William, and Robert Rea, eds. *Anglo-Spanish Confrontation on the Gulf Coast During the American Revolution.* Pensacola: Gulf Coast History and Humanities Conference, 1982.

Coker, William S., and Thomas D. Walton. *Indian Traders of the Southeastern*

Spanish Borderlands: Panton, Leslie and Company and John Forbes and Company, 1783–1847. Pensacola: University of West Florida Press, 1986.

Coleman, Kenneth. *Colonial Georgia: A History*. New York: Charles Scribner's Sons, 1976.

Coleman, Kenneth, and Charles Stephen Gurr, eds. *Dictionary of Georgia Biography*. 2 vols. Athens: University of Georgia Press, 1983.

Corkran, David H. *The Creek Frontier, 1540–1783*. Norman: University of Oklahoma Press, 1967.

Corry, John Pitts. *Indian Affairs in Georgia, 1732–1756*. Philadelphia: George S. Ferguson, 1936.

Cotterill, Robert Spencer. *The Southern Indians: The Story of the Civilized Tribes Before Removal*. Norman: University of Oklahoma Press, 1954.

Coulter, E. Merton. *Georgia: A Short History*. Chapel Hill: University of North Carolina Press, 1960.

Coulter, E. Merton, and Albert B. Saye. *A List of the Early Settlers of Georgia*. Athens: University of Georgia Press, 1949.

Crane, Verner W. *The Southern Frontier, 1670–1732*. Ann Arbor: University of Michigan Press, 1929.

Cronon, William. *Changes in the Land: Indians, Colonists, and the Ecology of New England*. New York: Hill and Wang, 1983.

Cumming, William P. *The Southeast in Early Maps*. 1958. Reprint. Chapel Hill: University of North Carolina Press, 1962.

Davis, Harold E. *The Fledgling Province: Social and Cultural Life in Colonial Georgia, 1733–1776*. Chapel Hill: University of North Carolina Press, 1976.

Davis, Robert Scott, Jr. *A Guide to Native American (Indian) Research Sources at the Georgia Department of Archives and History*. Jasper, Ga.: Published by the author, 1985.

Debo, Angie. *The Road to Disappearance*. Norman: University of Oklahoma Press, 1941.

DeVorsey, Louis, Jr. *The Indian Boundary in the Southern Colonies, 1763–1775*. Chapel Hill: University of North Carolina Press, 1966.

Doster, James Fletcher. *The Creek Indians and Their Florida Lands, 1740–1823*. 2 vols. New York: Garland, 1974.

Drake, Samuel G. *Biography and History of the Indians of North America from Its First Discovery*. Boston: Benjamin B. Mussey, 1841.

Dumont, William H. *Colonial Georgia Genealogical Data, 1748–1783*. Washington, D.C.: National Genealogical Society, 1971.

Easterby, J. H. *History of the St. Andrew's Society of Charleston, South Carolina, 1729–1929.* Charleston: Published by the Society, 1929.

Ettinger, Amos Aschbach. *James Edward Oglethorpe: Imperial Idealist.* Oxford: Clarendon Press, 1936.

——. *Oglethorpe: A Brief Biography.* Edited by Phinizy Spalding. Macon, Ga.: Mercer University Press, 1984.

Eyre-Todd, George. *The Highland Clans of Scotland: Their History and Traditions.* 1923. Reprint. 2 vols. in 1. Charleston: Garnier, 1969.

Fisher, David Hackett. *Albion's Seed: Four British Folkways in America.* New York: Oxford University Press, 1989.

Fleming, Berry. *Autobiography of a Colony: The First Half-Century of Augusta, Georgia.* Athens: University of Georgia Press, 1957.

Fraser-Mackintosh, Charles. *An Account of the Confederation of Clan Chattan: Its Kith and Kin.* Glasgow: John Mackay, 1898.

——. *Antiquarian Notes: A Series of Papers Regarding Families and Places in the Highlands.* Sterling, Scotland: Eneas Mackay, 1913.

Gallay, Alan. *The Formation of a Planter Elite: Jonathan Bryan and the Southern Colonial Frontier.* Athens: University of Georgia Press, 1989.

Garrison, Webb. *Oglethorpe's Folly: The Birth of Georgia.* Lakemont, Ga.: Copple House Books, 1982.

Gayarré, Charles. *History of Louisiana.* 4 vols. New Orleans: James A. Gresham, 1879.

Graham, Henry Grey. *The Social Life of Scotland in the Eighteenth Century.* 2 vols. London: Adam and Charles Black, 1900.

Graham, Ian Charles Cargill. *Colonists from Scotland: Emigration to North America, 1707–1783.* Ithaca, N.Y.: Cornell University Press, 1956.

Granger, Mary, ed. *Savannah River Plantations.* Savannah: Georgia Historical Society, 1947.

Green, Michael D. *The Creeks: A Critical Bibliography.* Bloomington: Indiana University Press, 1979.

Greene, Jack P. *The Quest for Power: The Lower Houses of Assembly in the Southern Royal Colonies, 1689–1776.* Chapel Hill: University of North Carolina Press, 1963.

Griffith, Benjamin W., Jr. *McIntosh and Weatherford, Creek Indian Leaders.* Tuscaloosa: University of Alabama Press, 1988.

Handford, Michael. *The Stroudwater Canal.* Gloucester, Eng.: Alan Sutton, 1979.

Harden, William. *A History of Savannah and South Georgia.* 2 vols. Chicago: Lewis, 1913.

Harris, Walter A. *Here the Creeks Sat Down.* Macon, Ga.: J. W. Burke, 1958.

Hoffman, Ronald, Thad W. Tate, and Peter J. Albert, eds. *An Uncivil War: The Southern Backcountry During the American Revolution.* Charlottesville: University Press of Virginia, 1985.

Hollingsworth, Dixon. *Indians on the Savannah River.* Sylvania, Ga.: Partridge Pond Press, 1976.

Hudson, Charles M., ed. *Black Drink: A Native American Tea.* Athens: University of Georgia Press, 1979.

———. *The Southeastern Indians.* Knoxville: University of Tennessee Press, 1976.

Innes, Sir Thomas of Learney. *The Tartans of the Clans and Families of Scotland.* Edinburgh and London: W. and A. K. Johnston, 1952.

Ivers, Larry E. *British Drums on the Southern Frontier: The Military Colonization of Georgia, 1733–1749.* Chapel Hill: University of North Carolina Press, 1974.

Jackson, Harvey H. *Lachlan McIntosh and the Politics of Revolutionary Georgia.* Athens: University of Georgia Press, 1979.

Jackson, Harvey H., and Phinizy Spalding. *Forty Years of Diversity: Essays on Colonial Georgia.* Athens: University of Georgia Press, 1984.

Jacobs, Wilbur R. *Indians of the Southern Colonial Frontier: The Edmond Atkin Report and Plan of 1755.* Columbia: University of South Carolina Press, 1954.

Jenkins, D. T., and K. G. Ponting. *The British Wool Textile Industry, 1770–1914.* London: Heinemann Educational Books, 1982.

Jones, Dorothy, comp. *Wrightsborough, 1768, Wrightsboro, 1799, McDuffie County, Georgia, 1870.* Thomson, Ga.: Wrightsboro Quaker Community Foundation, 1982.

Krech, Shepard, III, ed. *Indians, Animals, and the Fur Trade: A Critique of Keepers of the Game.* Athens: University of Georgia Press, 1981.

Lawrence, Alexander A. *Storm over Savannah: The Story of Count D'Estaing and the Siege of the Town in 1779.* Athens: University of Georgia Press, 1951.

Lyson, E. *The History of the Woollen and Worsted Industries.* London: A and C Black, 1921.

McGillivray, Robert, and George B. Macgillivray. *A History of the Clan MacGillivray.* Ontario: G. B. Macgillivray, 1973.

Mackintosh, A. M. *The Mackintoshes and Clan Chattan.* Edinburgh: Printed for the author, 1903.

Maclean, J. P. *An Historical Account of the Settlements of Scotch Highlanders in America Prior to the Peace of 1783*. Cleveland: Hilman-Taylor, 1900.

Maness, Harold S. *Forgotten Outpost: Fort Moore and Savannah Town, 1685–1765*. Pickens, S.C.: BPB Publications, 1986.

Mann, J. de L. *The Cloth Industry in the West of England from 1640 to 1880*. Oxford: Clarendon Press, 1971.

Martin, Calvin. *Keepers of the Game: Indian-Animal Relationships and the Fur Trade*. Berkeley: University of California Press, 1978.

Mereness, Newton D., ed. *Travels in the American Colonies*. 1916. Reprint. New York: Antiquarian Press, 1961.

Meriwether, Robert L. *The Expansion of South Carolina, 1729–1765*. 1940. Reprint. Philadelphia: Porcupine Press, 1974.

Merrell, James H. *The Indians' New World: Catawbas and Their Neighbors from European Contact Through the Era of Removal*. Chapel Hill: University of North Carolina Press, 1989.

Meyer, Duane. *The Highland Scots of North Carolina, 1732–1776*. 1957. Reprint. Raleigh: North Carolina University Press, 1966.

Norwood, Martha F. *A History of the White House Tract, Richmond County, Georgia, 1756–1975*. Atlanta: Georgia Department of Natural Resources, Historic Preservation Section, 1975.

Parish, John Carl. *The Persistence of the Westward Movement and Other Essays*. 1943. Reprint. Berkeley: University of California Press, 1968.

Perdue, Theda. *Slavery and the Evolution of Cherokee Society, 1540–1866*. Knoxville: University of Tennessee Press, 1979.

Petrie, Sir Charles. *The Jacobite Movement: The First Phase, 1688–1716*. London: Eyre and Spottiswoode, 1948.

Pickett, Albert James. *History of Alabama and Incidentally of Georgia and Mississippi from the Earliest Period*. 1851. Reprint. Birmingham: Birmingham Book and Magazine Co., 1962.

Prebble, John. *Culloden*. London: Secker and Warburg, 1961.

Prucha, Francis Paul. *American Indian Policy in the Formative Years: The Indian Trade and Intercourse Acts, 1790–1834*. Cambridge, Mass.: Harvard University Press, 1962.

Rea, Robert R. *Major Robert Farmar of Mobile*. Tuscaloosa: University of Alabama Press, 1990.

Reese, Trevor Richard. *Colonial Georgia: A Study in British Imperial Policy in the Eighteenth Century*. Athens: University of Georgia Press, 1963.

384

——, ed. *The Clamorous Malcontents: Criticisms and Defenses of the Colony of Georgia, 1741–1743.* Savannah: Beehive Press, 1973.

Royce, Charles, comp. *Indian Land Cessions in the United States.* 1900. Reprint. New York: Arno Press, 1961.

Sheehan, Bernard W. *Seeds of Extinction: Jeffersonian Philanthropy and the American Indian.* Chapel Hill: University of North Carolina Press, 1973.

Shy, John. *A People Numerous and Armed.* New York: Oxford University Press, 1976.

Silver, Timothy. *A New Face on the Countryside: Indians, Colonists, and Slaves in South Atlantic Forests, 1500–1800.* Cambridge: Cambridge University Press, 1990.

Sirmans, M. Eugene. *Colonial South Carolina.* Chapel Hill: University of North Carolina Press, 1966.

Smout, T. C. *A History of the Scottish People.* New York: Charles Scribner's Sons, 1969.

Spalding, Phinizy. *Oglethorpe in America.* 1977. Reprint. Athens: University of Georgia Press, 1984.

Spalding, Phinizy, and Harvey H. Jackson, eds. *Oglethorpe in Perspective: Georgia's Founder After Two Hundred Years.* Tuscaloosa: University of Alabama Press, 1989.

Swanton, John R. *Early History of the Creek Indians and Their Neighbors.* Washington, D.C.: U.S. Government Printing Office, 1922.

Taylor, Alistair, and Henrietta Taylor. *1745 and After.* Edinburgh: Thomas Nelson and Sons, 1938.

Tomasson, Katherine. *The Jacobite General.* Edinburgh and London: William Blackwood and Sons, 1958.

Van Every, Dale. *Forth to the Wilderness: The First American Frontier, 1754–1774.* New York: William Morrow, 1961.

Viola, Herman J. *Thomas L. McKenney: Architect of America's Early Indian Policy, 1816–1830.* Chicago: Swallow Press, 1974.

Weir, Robert M. *Colonial South Carolina: A History.* Millwood, N.Y.: KTO Press, 1983.

White, George. *Historical Collections of Georgia: Containing the Most Interesting Facts, Traditions, Biographical Sketches, Anecdotes, Etc. Relating to Its History and Antiquities, from Its First Settlement to the Present Time.* New York: Pudney and Russell, 1855.

Wood, Betty. *Slavery in Colonial Georgia, 1730–1775*. Athens: University of Georgia Press, 1984.

Wood, Peter H. *Black Majority: Negroes in Colonial South Carolina from 1670 Through the Stono Rebellion*. New York: Knopf, 1975.

Wood, Peter H., Gregory A. Waselkov, and M. Thomas Hatley. *Powhatan's Mantle*. Lincoln: University of Nebraska Press, 1989.

Wright, J. Leitch, Jr. *Creeks and Seminoles: The Destruction and Regeneration of the Muscogulge People*. Lincoln: University of Nebraska Press, 1986.

Wyman, Walker D., and Clifton B. Kroeber, eds. *The Frontier in Perspective*. Madison: University of Wisconsin Press, 1965.

ARTICLES

Baine, Rodney M., and Mary E. Williams. "Oglethorpe's Missing Years." *GHQ* 69 (Summer 1985): 193–210.

Bast, Homer. "Creek Indian Affairs, 1775–1778." *GHQ* 33 (March 1949): 1–25.

Brannon, Peter A. "Pensacola Indian Trade." *FHQ* 31 (1952): 1–15.

Calmer, Alan. "The Lyttelton Expedition of 1759: Military Failures and Financial Successes." *SCHM* 77 (January 1976): 10–33.

Caughey, John. "Willing's Expedition down the Mississippi, 1778." *LHQ* 15 (January 1932): 5–36.

Cole, Richard C. "The Siege of Savannah and the British Press, 1779–1780." *GHQ* 65 (Fall 1981): 189–202.

Corry, John Pitts. "Some New Light on the Bosomworth Claims." *GHQ* 25 (September 1941): 195–224.

Crane, Verner W. "Hints Relative to the Division and Government of the Conquered and Newly Acquired Countries in America." *MVHR* 8 (1922): 367–73.

Davis, Margaret Cate. "Fort Frederica: Battle of Bloody Marsh." *GHQ* 27 (June 1943): 111–74.

DeVorsey, Louis, Jr. "Indian Boundaries in Colonial Georgia." *GHQ* 54 (Spring 1970): 63–78.

Downes, Randolph C. "Creek-American Relations, 1782–1790." *GHQ* 21 (June 1937): 142–84.

Fant, H. B. "The Indian Trade Policy of the Trustees for Establishing the Colony of Georgia in America." *GHQ* 15 (September 1931): 207–22.

Ferguson, Worshipful Chancellor. "The Retreat of the Highlanders Through Westmorland in 1745." *Transactions of the Cumberland and Westmorland Anti-*

quarian and Archeological Society (1889): 186–228.

Frey, Sylvia R. "In Search of Roots: The Colonial Antecedents of Slavery in the Plantation Colonies." *GHQ* 68 (Summer 1984): 244–59.

Gallay, Alan. "The Search for an Alternate Source of Trade: The Creek Indians and Jonathan Bryan." *GHQ* 73 (Summer 1989): 209–30.

Gordon, G. Arthur. "The Arrival of the Scotch Highlanders at Darien." *GHQ* 30 (September 1936): 199–209.

Green, Edward R. R. "Queensborough Township." *W&MQ* 3d ser., 17 (April 1960): 183–99.

Greenslade, Marie Taylor. "William Panton, c. 1745–1801." *FHQ* 14 (1935): 107–29.

Haan, Richard L. "'The Trade Do's Not Flourish as Formerly': The Ecological Origins of the Yamassee War of 1715." *Ethnohistory* 28 (Fall 1981): 347–51.

Humphreys, R. A. "Lord Shelburne and the Proclamation of 1763." *English Historical Review* 49 (April 1934): 241–64.

Jackson, Harvey H. "American Slavery, American Freedom, and the Revolution in the Lower South: The Case of Lachlan McIntosh." *Southern Studies* 19 (Spring 1980): 81–93.

——. "The Carolina Connection: Jonathan Bryan, His Brothers, and the Founding of Georgia, 1733–1752." *GHQ* 68 (Summer 1984): 147–72.

——. "The Darien Antislavery Petition of 1739 and the Georgia Plan." *W&MQ* 3d ser., 34 (October 1977): 618–31.

Lawson, Alan B. "The North West Company of Canada: The Highland Connection." *An Inverness Miscellany* 2 (1987): 30–40.

Lewis, Bessie Mary. "Darien: A Symbol of Defiance and Achievement." *GHQ* 30 (September 1936): 185–98.

MacDonnell, Alexander R. "The Settlement of the Scotch Highlanders at Darien." *GHQ* 30 (September 1936): 250–62.

Meinig, D. W. "The Continuous Shaping of America: A Prospectus for Geographers and Historians." *AHR* 83 (December 1978): 1186–1205.

Mellon, Knox, Jr. "Christian Priber's Cherokee 'Kingdom of Paradise.'" *GHQ* 57 (Spring 1973): 319–31.

Meroney, Geraldine. "The London Entrepot Merchants and the Georgia Colony." *W&MQ* 3d ser., 25 (April 1968): 230–44.

Mitchell, Robert G. "The Losses and Compensation of Georgia Loyalists." *GHQ* 68 (Summer 1984): 233–43.

Moore, Warner Oland, Jr. "The Largest Exporters of Deerskins from Charles Town, 1735–1775." *SCHM* 74 (July 1973): 144–50.

Neeley, Mary Ann Oglesby. "Lachlan McGillivray: A Scot on the Alabama Frontier." *AHQ* 36 (Spring 1974): 5–14.

O'Donnell, James H. "Alexander McGillivray: Training for Leadership, 1777–1783." *GHQ* 49 (June 1965): 172–86.

"Oglethorpe's Treaty with the Lower Creek Indians." *GHQ* 4 (March 1920): 3–16.

Richter, Daniel K. "War and Culture: The Iroquois Experience." *W&MQ* 3d ser. 40 (Oct. 1983): 528–59.

Ritchie, Carson I. A. "The Blue Cockade." *The Dalesman, A Monthly Magazine of Yorkshire and Its People*, May 1986, pp. 125–28.

Romine, Dannye. "Alexander McGillivray: Shrewd Scot, Cunning Indian." *Southern Humanities Review* 9 (Fall 1975): 409–21.

Searcy, Martha Condray. "The Introduction of African Slavery into the Creek Indian Nation." *GHQ* 66 (Spring 1982): 21–32.

Sirmans, M. Eugene. "The South Carolina Royal Council, 1720–1763." *W&MQ* 3d ser., 18 (July 1961): 375–92.

Spalding, Thomas. "Sketch of the Life of General James Oglethorpe." *GHS Collections* 1 (1840): 240–95.

Stumpf, Stuart O. "Implications of King George's War for the Charleston Mercantile Community." *SCHM* 77 (July 1976): 161–81.

——. "South Carolina Importers of General Merchandise, 1735–1765." *SCHM* 84 (January 1983): 1–10.

Thomas, Daniel H. "Fort Toulouse, the French Outpost at the Alibamos on the Coosa." *AHQ* 22 (Fall 1960): 141–230.

Usner, Daniel H., Jr. "American Indians on the Cotton Frontier: Changing Economic Relations with Citizens and Slaves in the Mississippi Territory." *JAH* 72 (September 1985): 297–317.

Vaughan, Alden T. "From White Man to Redskin: Changing Anglo-American Perceptions of the American Indian." *AHR* 87 (October 1982): 917–53.

Wax, Darold D. " 'New Negroes Are Always in Demand': The Slave Trade in Eighteenth-Century Georgia," *GHQ* 68 (Summer 1984): 193–220.

Withuhn, William L. "Salzburgers and Slavery: A Problem of *Mentalité*." *GHQ* 68 (Summer 1984): 173–92.

Wood, Brian M. "Fort Okfuskee: A British Challenge to Fort Toulouse aux

Alibamos." *Fort Toulouse Studies*. Auburn University Archeological Monograph, 1984.

Wright, J. Leitch, Jr. "Creek-American Treaty of 1790: Alexander McGillivray and the Diplomacy of the Old Southwest." *GHQ* 51 (December 1967): 379–400.

DISSERTATIONS AND THESES

Braund, Kathryn E. "Mutual Convenience—Mutual Dependence: The Creeks, Augusta and the Deerskin Trade, 1733–1782." Ph.D. dissertation, Florida State University, 1986.

Clowes, Converse D. "Charles Town Export Trade, 1717–1737." Ph.D. dissertation, Northwestern University, 1963.

Harley, Mary Parker. "Georgia Indian Trade: The Trustee Period, 1733–1752." M.A. thesis, University of Georgia, 1935.

Moltke-Hansen, David. "The Empire of Scotsman Robert Wells, Loyalist, South Carolina Printer-Publisher." M.A. thesis, University of South Carolina, 1984.

Rabac, Donna Marie. "Economy and Society in Early Georgia: A Functional Analysis of the Colony's Origins and Evolution." Ph.D. dissertation, University of Michigan, 1978.

Smith, W. Calvin. "Georgia Gentlemen: The Habershams of Eighteenth-Century Savannah." Ph.D. dissertation, University of North Carolina, 1971.

Snapp, James Russell. "Exploitation and Control: The Southern Frontier in Anglo-American Politics in the Era of the American Revolution." Ph.D. dissertation, Harvard University, 1988.

Sonderegger, Richard Paul. "The Southern Frontier from the Founding of Georgia to the End of King George's War." Ph.D. dissertation, University of Michigan, 1964.

Spalding, B. Phinizy. "Georgia and South Carolina During the Oglethorpe Period, 1732–1743." Ph.D. dissertation, University of North Carolina, 1963.

Wright, Homer E. "Diplomacy of Trade on the Southern Frontier: A Case Study of the Influence of William Panton and John Forbes, 1784–1817." Ph.D. dissertation, University of Georgia, 1971.

Index

CPSIA information can be obtained at www.ICGtesting.com
Printed in the USA
LVOW090559280712

291902LV00003B/1/P